Thinking Small:
Global Perspectives on
Microlithization

东北亚与欧亚草原考古学译丛

小工具 大思考

全球细石器化的研究

(美)罗伯特·G·埃尔斯顿 史蒂文·L·库恩 主编
陈胜前 译 杨建华 校

上海古籍出版社

本丛书为

国家社科基金重大项目（2012&ZD152）成果

吉林大学考古学院"双一流"学科建设经费资助出版

《东北亚与欧亚草原考古学译丛》
总　　序

　　21世纪的中国考古学进入了新的发展阶段,随着国际交流的深入和考古学自身发展的需要,2012年国家社会科学基金重大项目首次设立了国外著名考古学著作的翻译项目。我们在申报中,原本提出考古学理论与周边邻国考古学两个角度的翻译课题,后经过国家社科基金评审组的建议,把译著内容集中到周邻国家考古著作,即现在的《东北亚与欧亚草原考古学译丛》。

　　在东北亚考古学方面,我们选译了日本学者高仓洋彰的《金印国家群的时代——东亚世界与弥生社会》和韩国学者崔梦龙等的《汉江流域史》。日本考古著作是从东亚的视野下研究弥生时代的国际化过程。所谓"金印国家群"是这些被纳入以汉字和汉语为沟通手段的中国统治秩序中的民族的总称。作者从东亚的宏观角度着眼,从九州北部地区的细微研究入手的研究方法,对中国的考古学研究很有借鉴意义。韩国考古著作构建了朝鲜半岛先史时代的时空框架和文化发展序列。新石器时代朝鲜半岛的圜底筒形罐和"之"字纹装饰为中国东北地区新石器时代陶器研究提供了重要的对比材料。朝鲜半岛青铜时代的标志性器物——琵琶形铜剑,是从中国辽东半岛经鸭绿江下游地区传入的。这些来自中国东北地区的文化影响,可以追溯到大连地区年代相当于商代末期的于家村下层文化,年代相当于中国历史文献中记载的商周之际。

　　在欧亚大陆旧石器研究方面我们翻译了《欧洲旧石器时代社会》(Clive Gamble)和《小工具的大思考:全球细石器化的研究》考古论文集(Robert G. Elston主编)。前者侧重欧亚草原的欧洲部分,在旧石器研究中具有年代标尺的作用。作者还运用了一种新的方法,把来自石器、狩猎与营地遗址的考古证据汇聚起来,用以探讨社会交往以及社会生活的形式。后者涉及了欧亚草原的亚洲部分,包括细石叶工艺以及相关技术的起源、制作技术和人类对环境的适应等诸多重要的问题。本书的全球视野、运用的石器分析理论与方法、研究的思路与观点,对于中国细石器考古学研究来说非常具有启发性。

在欧亚草原考古方面,我们分别选译了宏观著作《俄罗斯、中亚和蒙古史——内欧亚大陆的史前时代到蒙古帝国》(David Christian)和微观研究的《印度—伊朗人的起源》(Kuzmina, E.),以及一本蒙古考古专著。第一本宏观著作将欧亚大陆分为处于内陆和靠北的内欧亚大陆(Inner Eurasia)与靠海的外欧亚大陆(Outer Eurasia)两部分,前者是游牧和渔猎民族活动的舞台,后者是文化发达的农业文明分布区。该书以宏观的视角系统阐述了内欧亚大陆的历史,认为两地的互动是历史发展的重要动因,并从社会交往的角度研究农业与游牧业的互动。作者提出农牧交错地带为内欧亚大陆发展提供了重要的推动力,因为这里不仅有农牧社会的军事接触,还有技术、思想、贸易和人群的接触。从这个意义上,我们就不难理解中国北方地区在东部草原中的重要作用了。第二本微观研究的著作是作者用 50 年时间对安德罗诺沃文化联盟的详尽研究,使我们了解到俄罗斯学者是如何研究一个考古学文化,以及如何结合文化的发展演变与民族学和历史语言学来研究考古学文化族属的。同时我们也可以发现国外学者对中国考古资料的了解十分有限,中国学者有责任把自己的发现与研究介绍给世界的学者。蒙古是游牧文明的一个中心,是中国北方与欧亚草原接壤的重要国家。《蒙古考古》是目前唯一的关于蒙古的考古发现和研究的综合性专著,该译著能够使中国学者了解蒙古各时期考古遗存的概况以及蒙古学者的考古研究现状与方法,为从事蒙古考古研究提供最系统的基础性材料。

这套考古学译著有两个特点,一是在资料占有方面重点选择了本土学者的著作,二是我们的翻译团队多是从事东北亚和欧亚草原考古研究的学者,是我们以边疆考古为依托的外国考古学研究的实践。译丛的出版将开启关注邻国考古、注重本土学者和有计划有针对性的系列考古学著作的翻译与出版,打破英文译著"一统天下"的局面。这套丛书还将有助于把中国考古学放在东亚与欧亚视野下考察,提升我国边疆考古在东北亚与欧亚大陆考古研究中的影响力。在完成项目的这五年期间,中国社会科学院成立了外国考古学研究中心,有相当数量的考古团队开始赴国外开展田野考古工作。在这里我们非常感谢国家社科基金评审组非常有预见性地设立译丛课题,这些译著为了解中国周边国家的历史以及与中国的文化交往提供了大量的物质材料证据,并为中国考古学走出国门提供了必要的知识准备。

杨建华

2017 年 6 月

目　　录

《东北亚与欧亚草原考古学译丛》总序 ································ 1

导言：小工具大思考的全球视角
　　·························· 史蒂文·L·库恩　罗伯特·G·埃尔斯顿　1
千里的鹅毛：撒哈拉以南非洲早期细石器工业的起源
　　·· 斯坦丽·H·阿姆布鲁斯　11
琢背细小石叶是舶来品 ······················· 安吉拉·E·卡洛斯　52
走向细石器：从利凡特地区看细石器技术的起源 ········· 迈克 P. 尼勒　75
为什么是细石器？利凡特地区的细石器化
　　······················ 安娜·贝尔福—科恩　尼基尔·格林—莫里斯　90
选择小工具：有关西欧旧石器时代晚期至中石器时代细石器的思考
　　··································· 劳伦斯·G·施特劳斯　107
细石器化的开拓者：南欧"原奥瑞纳工业" ············ 史蒂夫 L. 库恩　128
便宜、规范、可靠：日本晚更新世细石器技术设计差异的意义
　　··· 彼得·布雷德　144
北亚的细石器技术：旧石器时代晚期与早全新世的风险最小化策略
　　························ 罗伯特·G·埃尔斯顿　P·杰夫·班廷汉姆　155
"细石叶适应"与晚更新世晚段西伯利亚的重新殖民
　　··· 泰德·戈贝尔　179

细石叶与迁徙：移民美洲的族群与经济模型

.... 戴维·R·耶斯纳　乔治·皮尔森　203

全新世澳大利亚琢背石器激增的方式与背景............ 皮特·西斯科克　242

小工具　大思考...................................... 罗宾·托伦斯　268

译名对照表..284
译后记..293

缩小比例我们正好看到美丽

缩小尺度人生也许趋向完美

      ——本·约翰逊,1640 年

导言：小工具大思考的全球视角

史蒂文·L·库恩　　　　罗伯特·G·埃尔斯顿
（亚利桑那大学　图森市）　　（银城　内华达州）

随着考古学知识领域的扩展，人类史前史中明显具有统一性的认识在减少。人类文化发展所遵循的历史路径千奇百怪，区分文化演化的一般发展阶段的尝试常常是徒劳无功的。例如，即便是格拉汉姆·克拉克[1]将旧石器时代技术简单分为"五个模式"这样宽泛与包容的分类体系，也仅仅适用于西半球而已。

有关人类演化趋势的归纳可能脱离现实，但是某些趋势的存在还是引人注目的。就旧石器时代的技术而言，地理分布范围最广的一个趋势可能是细石器化。晚更新世细石器的器物与组合最早出现于欧洲、非洲与亚洲。末次盛冰期时，大约距今 18 000 到 20 000 年间，大部分旧石器时代晚期与后旧石器时代组合都含有相当比例的细石器成分。东亚地区晚更新世较晚阶段出现细石叶技术是一件具有分水岭意义的事件，至少从表面上来看是如此的，当地漫长而连续的技术传统发生了突然的变化。全新世中期，北美与澳大利亚也发现了一种或是另一种形式的细石器技术。显然，如此广大区域的细石器技术变化范围巨大，但是基本事实未变，万年前各大洲上的采食群体都在制作与使用大量的细小石器工具。

晚更新世的细石器化趋势对当前考古学思维模式提出了严重的挑战。这个领域基本放弃了理论探讨，与之相关的文化进化论、新进化论对其都无能为力。这些理论视人类文化按照一定的发展阶段不断进步，某些内因驱动文化自我提升。单线进化论的观点无疑在许多层面上都存在不足，但是它们至少可以有效解释普遍存在的文化现象。大多数现代考古学理论，无论其立足的因果关联是生态的、进化论的、社会的还是意识形态的，都是特定与偶然的：它都是根据当地的历史与物质环境来解释的。如今已经很少有考古学家从全球的角度来解释一个事件。

更新世之末,全球石器技术的发展趋向为细石器化,这样的论断并不需要我们回归到单线进化论。准确地说,它并不是同时发生的：在晚更新世这个宏观的时间框架内来看,世界不同区域细石器技术出现的时间早晚差异显著。与此同时,所谓的细石器技术也不都是一回事。要想了解其广泛存在的意义,如果真有这么回事的话,还是必须理解当地的情况。然而,用这样一种技术把上万年左右世界不同地区的工具统合起来,就不能简单地视其为仅仅是一个历史事件而已。晚更新世的人类社会、经济与环境条件都需要考虑到,它们使得细石器技术在各种各样的情况下成为特别有吸引力的技术选择。

本书诸文从不同的视角来讨论全球细石器化的问题。文章涉及欧洲、非洲、西亚与东亚、澳大利亚以及美洲的考古研究,其研究范围宏大时可以包括整个次大陆,细微时限于某个遗址。与此同时,若干重要的议题将之联系在一起。

1. 什么是细石器技术？

2. 细石器技术生产石器的优点与缺点是什么？镶嵌了细石器的复合工具有什么优缺点？

3. 细石器技术在世界特定地区出现与发展（有时是消失的）的年代序列如何？

4. 地区的特殊发展跟全球细石器化的普遍现象有何关联？

一、什么是细石器技术？

细石器的定义非常模糊。广义上说,细石器就是指非常细小的石器——这不是一个令人满意的定义。中国[2]、叙利亚[3]、东南欧[4]旧石器时代早中期也有所谓的细石器,仅仅是因为它相对于同时代其他地区的石器更小一点。也就是说,大小其实是相对的：在一个地方看起来细小的石器换个地方可能会显得很大。例如,贝尔福—科恩和格林—莫里斯,以及卡洛斯都追随提克斯耶（Tixier）*,将9毫米宽作为区分修理石叶与细石叶的标准。这个定义当然不那么适用于东北亚地区,这里的细石叶更细小；也不很适用于欧洲部分地区,这里的琢背细石叶其实比较大。本书的许多作者大都是根据特定的地区或是考古材

---

* Tixier,旧石器考古石器分类专家,他的分类体系与博尔德（Bordes）的分类体系并称,主要用于北非地区。——译注

料来确定自己的细石器定义的。

更新世较晚阶段的细石器化趋势并不只是根据细小石器的生产来确定的。四个特征把晚更新世细石器组合结合在一起。首先是细小石叶(bladelet)与细石叶(microblade)技术的提高,用以生产精致、细长的小石片。其次,人们修理加工这些毛坯时,通常的修理方式是再加工(琢背),使刃缘更钝、更结实,而非使之更锋利。这两条特征出现的频率存在大范围的区别。一般来说,东亚的细石器技术以细石叶技术为特征,通过精细的石核技术来生产细石叶。它们明显就是这么使用的,直到中石器时代以后才开始有进一步修理的证据。与之相对的是,欧洲、西亚与非洲晚更新世的石器组合中琢背与一般修理更发达。并非所有的修理细石器都由细小石叶制作而成,但大多数时候都如此。

石核技术与修理结合起来构成第三个普遍的特征:石器成品大小或形状比较标准,或是同时都具备。有不少方法可以达到这个目的。某些细小石叶与细石叶工具很少或没有明显的修理痕迹,有些则有意折断成一定大小的片段。几何形细石器比较特殊,数条边缘会被修理以形成固定的形制。但是一般的印象是其形制与数量非常引人注目。当然并非所有包含细小石器的组合都可以成为细石器。

晚更新世细石器技术的第四项特征是其数量特征,仅就数量来说,细石器在石器组合中占有相当的份额,虽然它们常常与大石器共出。

以上所有特征都指向晚更新世石器技术的第五个特征:一般都认为这些细小、规整、标准化的石制品是用作复合工具的,镶嵌在有弹性的有机物柄上,用在各种复合工具上作为刃缘、倒刺、钩子或是尖齿。有不少情况下镶嵌用的柄部或是支架保存下来,所以当我们遇到不论采用什么其他方式都无法使用的石制品时,就可以推断柄部的存在。而卡洛斯指出,西南亚与北非的考古材料几乎没有证据支持细石器是镶嵌使用的。某些单件标本上保存有乳香或是其他黏接剂的痕迹,微痕研究也显示出有装柄的痕迹(参见本书卡洛斯所著文章),但是这样的证据毕竟不多。另一方面,东北亚地区随同柄部一同发现的细石叶柄并不罕见(参见本书埃尔斯顿和班廷汉姆所著文章)。无论如何,很难在讨论细石器技术时不提及镶嵌装柄与用作复合工具,原因很简单,因为很多研究者都认为两者是一体的。

二、如何解释细石器化?

本书讨论了一系列共同的主题。不少作者采用进化的视角,关注镶嵌了细石器的复合工具所带来的投射能量与适应策略上的优势。细石器技术在食物获取，尤其是狩猎大中型猎物时具有某些优势，成为研究的重心。长期以来考古学家相信细小的琢背修理细石器大多是投掷武器的组件，数位作者明确地采纳这种观点。但是托伦斯与卡洛斯注意到，这种观点并没有得到充分的经验材料的证明：事实上，微痕分析的证据仅部分支持它[5]。

与进化视角一致的是，所有的作者在某种程度上都关注细石器技术的起源与消失。一项令人惊奇的共同发现是，细石器早在繁荣之前就已经在许多地区出现了（西斯科克、库恩、施特劳斯的文章）。其主要原因可能是，早期的发掘没有做细致筛选，以至于许多年来考古学家都认为旧石器晚期较早阶段石器工业如奥瑞纳与格拉韦丁文化中没有细石器。更细致的发掘工作证明细石器大小的石制品见于绝大多数旧石器晚期的石器组合中。即便与更新世之末的细石器数量相比，它们也说不上是贫乏，当然最重要的是它们的确存在。东亚的情况有所不同，细石叶组合在更早的石器工业中似乎没有明显的先驱[6]：这里的问题是，细石叶技术的出现是否是来自思想传播（或重新发明），或是由于新的人群到来所致。更新世之末细石器技术也没有消失。细石器因素，从细石叶到几何形细石器，在全新世晚期复杂的采食者甚至农耕者群体的打制石器工具组合中有时依旧占有重要地位[7]。

旧石器时代晚期早段细石器技术出现，全新世继续存留，了解这一点对于讨论它的宏观分布极为重要，因为这使得我们能够把细石器技术的普遍分布与更新世之末特定的历史因素区分开来。正如数位研究者指出的，细石器技术在某些地区很早就出现了，但是它只是在更新世之末才迅速扩散开来。也就是说很多情况下细石器技术的优点并不那么突出或者只是昙花一现。我们在解释细石器技术的全球化时需要考虑晚更新世最后阶段的经济、人口与社会条件，因为正是这些条件使得细石器技术的优势在许多地方突显出来。

沿着这样的历史主题，不少研究者也注意到，镶嵌细石器的复合工具只是一种有效的工具设计，其他设计也同样有效。西斯科克研究了全新世中期澳大利亚不同地区琢背修理石器与两面修理尖状器的使用状况。此项研究生动说明了石器技术大范围形态变化的历史偶然性。更新世之末，欧亚与非洲大陆以细石器为中心的技术策略广泛流行，非常引人注目，进化的视角解释了这种一致性，但在考虑经济与适应策略因素之外，也需要考虑历史因素的作用。欧亚西部与非洲地区棱形石叶的生产比细石器化要早数万年，这种技术可能是细石器技术的基础，基于大小与形制标准化的石器生产技术更容易在棱形石叶技术基础上发展起来,可能还不止发明过一次。间接打击技术生产石叶是旧石器晚期的独有技术,不见于更早的时期[8],这种技术有助于更好地控制石器毛坯的形状,是生产细小、规整细小石叶必不可少的技术。东亚地区的面貌有所不同,这里精致的两面器技术与石片压制技术似乎汇集于楔形细石核技术中。

尽管文集作者的一般理论立场相似,但是他们对细石器化的解释并不完全一致。不同研究者强调的细石器技术优势有所不同,有的强调它适合频繁的居址流动(戈贝尔、纳利),有的特别注意它有助于减少在陌生区域采食或是与狩猎相关的生计风险(西斯科克、埃尔斯顿与班廷汉姆),还有的注意它有利于工具组合与生计组织的多样化(戈贝尔、西斯科克与库恩)。施特劳斯在评估了西南欧的材料之后,提出细石器材料形制与关联背景的多样性可能与许多不同的因素相关,唯有如此,才能有效解释旧石器时代晚期文化序列中细石器作用的变化。

尽管存在多样性,有关细石器技术的各种经济、适应策略与历史解释都有一个共同的基础。从许多方面来说,所谓流动性、生计多样化,甚至是更普遍的风险最小化的观点都不过是同一现象的不同方面而已。面对风险的技术反应分析倾向于最直接的反应,也就是减小器物失败的概率(运用时的风险),或是降低生产与维护的成本[9]。当然,古人的流动形态与生计多样化本身也是控制经济风险的策略。如果当地的优质资源短缺,一个解决办法就是搬到有这种资源的地方去。类似之,如果找到最佳食物资源的机会并不确定(有风险),还有一个方法就是转向数量丰富,但是成本高昂或是营养价值较低的食物。流动性与资源选择无疑会很大程度上影响石器技术体系的组织。风险与技术之间的关系可能不那么直接,但结果还是很明显的。

所有这些都指向一个明显需要回答的问题,为什么欧亚地区更新世之末(澳大利亚地区是全新世中期)人类生活的风险更高。有几个解释是不言而喻的,其中一个由来已久的解释是人口。许多研究者都认为欧亚地区更新世的最后一万年间人口增长比从前的时代更迅速,人口规模也更庞大[10]。稠密的人口会限制人群的流动性:更多的人口意味着当环境质量下降的时候,人们迁往丰饶地带的机会必然减少。随之而来的现象是,人类向新的区域扩张。更新世之末,从未有人类居住的美洲大陆迅速为人类所殖民,还包括重新占领末次冰期时无法居住的广大区域[11]。人类迁往从未有人生活或是不熟悉的区域似乎并不是什么特别冒险的事。从另一方面来看,早期人类就已经有过扩张——第一次走出非洲与中更新世的人类入侵，当时所用的技术更简单，尽管早期人类扩散的速度可能相当缓慢。最后，晚更新世人类还遭遇了剧烈的气候变化：短时间内气候条件大幅波动[12]。即便某一群体并不迁移，新的环境条件也会在短短的几代人的时间里找上门来。

当然，除了解释晚更新世细石器技术的普遍存在之外，还有其他东西需要讨论。正如施特劳斯、贝尔福—科恩与格林—莫里斯所言，考古材料组合中细石器的形制和数量可能在相对较小的区域内与很短的时间范围内变化明显。数位研究者（布雷德、卡洛斯、戈贝尔、贝尔福—科恩、格林—莫里斯、纳利、耶斯纳与皮尔森）都注意到细石器组合内与组合之间的差异。意料之中的是，其间的一致程度不高。戈贝尔认为规整的工具与多用途的细石核跟高流动性的适应方式相关，纳利与卡洛斯则认为细石器工具的形制与数量变化存在遗址之间的差异，这似乎激活了一个长期存在的争论，即细石器形制变化的意义[13]。基于古人生活的流动形态与居址使用上的变化，纳利提出一种观点，用以解释约旦近乎同时的遗址之间的差异。卡洛斯具有丰富的北非地区工作经验，她引用了众多的例子，来说明许多遗址功能与石器原材料不同，但细石器形制仍有较高的一致性。她的结论是，细石器的形态特征可以指示当时社会群体的边界。在这一方面，她认为细石器可能是最有效的。我们应当期望，而且确实应该鼓励丰富多彩的具体材料与地区历史的研究。当地的条件总是比全球层面上的更具有偶然性，而且自然也更加多样。解决风格与功能之间长期存在的争论，回答潜移默化的风格（isochrestic）*相对于表现的（expressive）风格的差异，或是弄清狩猎采集者的技术对流动性的影响，这些都不足以让我们感到荣耀。真正的挑战在于，分析每一种可能影响遗存组合形式的因素如何真正影响一个特定的石器组合、遗址或是区域。

书中有三篇文章采用非传统的方法来分析细石器技术，其研究的重点不是细小工具的形制与数量，而是产生成品的过程。贝尔福—科恩与格林—莫里斯研究近东地区旧石器时代晚期与后旧石器时代石器工业材料，把石核全面拼合的证据跟修理方式的证据结合起来，用以揭示生产细小标准化器物的不同策略之间的变迁。早在旧石器时代晚期，许多器物的最后形制在毛坯生产阶段就已经确定了。石核的预制越精细，最终的成品细石叶或细小石叶就更可能合乎要

---

* Isochrestic，石器风格的一种，指那种通过长期文化熏陶，但通常是意识不到的，具有社会群体边界意义的风格。——译注

求,所需要的修理也更少。随着时间的推移,石核的加工越来越不规范,毛坯的形制也越来越不固定,琢背修理的运用也逐渐增加,以得到最后的成品工具。虽然有时存在这样的认识,认为这反映了技术的衰落,但作者认为并非如此,它反映的是工具生产过程中的不同阶段,人们重新调整了着力点与关注点。后旧石器时代之末标准化几何形细石器的生产可能反映的是多样与弹性的工具与边刃形制需求。布雷德运用事件树分析法(event tree analysis)*解析三个日本晚更新世遗址细石叶生产的方式。不同加工环节的风险区分得到一系列新的认识,可以回答土地使用、原材料等方面的问题,尤其有意思的是,三个遗址的居民因不同技术特长所造成的影响。埃尔斯顿与班廷汉姆比较石质投掷枪头与镶嵌细石叶的骨角象牙质复合枪头的相对成本与收益。他们的分析表明后一种技术的成本更高,当然它在严寒的冬季捕获大型动物的可靠性也更高。末次盛冰期时这些工具出现在东北亚地区,保证捕猎到大型动物对于度过严冬至关重要,提高工具的可靠性也就是一项重要的减小风险的适应策略。通过运用风险敏感性的Z-score模型分析,埃尔斯顿与班廷汉姆进一步指出东北亚细石叶生产技术的变化可能与降低风险的特殊条件相关。例如,利用两面器毛坯的精致楔形细石核可能用于高风险的条件下,像捕猎大动物,以获取冬季所需的储备。此时生产的可靠性非常重要,简单的船形石核技术可靠性稍逊,可能用于风险较低的条件下。

三、结论

书中的不同文章的内容显示细石器所能解决的问题是高度多样的,跟具体的条件密切相关,并不存在单独一个解释就能回答细石器的技术发明与接受。当然,这些研究也有某些共同的基础。细石器产品从来就没有囊括整个石器工业,而是跟用石核、石叶或是石片制作的较大型的工具一起使用的。实际上不同地区细石器技术的产生与消失时间差异明显,通常跟变化相对缓慢的大石器混合在一起。本书中的大多数研究都支持细石器工具的使用有助于提高工作效率

---

* 事件树分析(Event Tree Analysis,简称ETA)起源于决策树分析(简称DTA),它是一种按事故发展的时间顺序由初始事件开始推论可能的后果,从而进行危险源辨识的方法。事件树分析法是一种时序逻辑的事故分析方法,它以一初始事件为起点,按照事故的发展顺序,分成阶段,一步一步地进行分析,每一事件可能的后续事件只能取完全对立的两种状态(成功或失败,正常或故障,安全或危险等)之一的原则,逐步向结果方面发展,直到导致系统故障或事故为止。所分析的情况用树枝状图表示,故叫事件树。它既可以定性地了解整个事件的动态变化过程,又可以定量计算出各阶段的概率,最终了解事故发展过程中各种状态的发生概率。——译注

与工具的可靠性。或是如卡洛斯在通信中所认为的,细石器并非唯一的解决问题的方法,它们通常更有利于解决需要重复与有风险的任务,工具的边刃需要不断维护。镰刀刃、狩猎工具的镶嵌刃、穿珠孔的钻子都可能从事其他活动,不过,每种工具每次几乎做同样的事情。晚更新世与全新世细石器技术的日益流行表明当时存在对工具效率与可靠性的需求,随着人口前所未有的增长,人们扩张到新的生活领地,加之气候与环境的迅速改变,需求也就随之产生了。与此同时,人类的食谱也在扩展,新的技术与组织策略应运而生,包括改变流动方式、出现投掷工具以及发展食物储备等。晚更新世依赖细石器技术的流行很可能反映了更加复杂的策略,以减小生计不确定性,从而更好地保障关键生计资源的安全或是维护社会协作关系。

注释:

[1] Clark, G. *World Prehistory: A New Outline*. Cambridge: Cambridge University Press, 1971.

[2] Gao, X. Explanations of Typological Variability in Paleolithic Remains from Zhoukoudian Locality 15 (China). Ph. D. dissertation, Department of Anthropology, University of Arizona, Tucson, 2000.

Miller-Antonio, S. Lithic Variability and the Cultural Elaboration of Upper Pleistocene North China. Ph. D. dissertation, Department of Anthropology, University of Arizona, Tucson, 1992.

[3] Rust, A. *Die Hohlenfunde von Jabrud (Syrien)*. Neumunster, Germany: Karl Wachholtz Vedag, 1950.

[4] Papaconstantinou, E. Micromousterien: les idees et les pierres. These de Doctorat, Universite de Paris X, 1989.

[5] Finlayson, B., and S. Mithen. The Microwear and Morphology of Microliths from Gleann Mor. In *Projectile Technology*. H. Knecht, ed. Pp. 107-129. New York: Plenum, 1997.

Rigaud, J.-P. L'Aurignacien dans le Sud-Ouest de la France. In *Aurignacien en Europe et au Proche Orient*. L. Banesz and J. Kozlowski, eds. Pp. 181-185. Actes du XII Congres International des Sciences Prehistoriques et Protohistoriques, vol. 2. Bratislava, 1993.

[6] Lu, L. D. The Microblade Tradition in China: Regional Chronologies and Significance in the Transition to Neolithic. *Asian Perspectives* 37: 85-112, 1998, p. 106.

Madsen, D. L., J. Li, P. J. Brantingham, X. Gao, R. G. Elston, and R. L. Bettinger. Dating Shuidonggou and the Upper Paleolithic Blade Industry in North China. *Antiquity* 75: 706-716, 2001.

[7] Johnson, J. Cahokia Core Technology in Mississippi: A View from the South. In *The Organization of Core Technology*. J. Johnson and C. Morrow, eds. Pp. 187 – 207. Boulder: Westview, 1987.

Lu, L. D. The Microblade Tradition in China: Regional Chronologies and Significance in the Transition to Neolithic. *Asian Perspectives* 37: 85 – 112, 1998, p. 106.

McNerney, M. Crab Orchard Core Technology at the Consol Site, Jackson County, Illinois. In *The Organization of Core Technology*. J. Johnson and C. Morrow, eds. Pp. 63 – 87. Boulder: Westview, 1987.

Odell, G. H. The Role of Stone Bladelets in Middle Woodland Society. *American Antiquity* 59: 102 – 120, 1994.

Rosen, S. *Lithics after the Stone Age: A Handbook of Stone Tools from the Levant*. Walnut Creek, Calif.: Altamira, 1997.

[8] Bar-Yosef, O., and S. L. Kuhn. The Big Deal about Blades: Laminar Technologies and Human Evolution. *American Anthropologist* 101: 322 – 338, 1999.

Meignen L. Les premices du Paleolithique superieur au proche orient. In *The Last Neandertals, the First Anatomically Modern Humans*. E. Carbonell and M. Vaquero, eds. Pp. 107 – 127. Tarragona, Spain: Fundacio Catalana per la Recerca, 1996.

[9] Bamforth, D. B., and P. Bleed. Technology, Flaked Stone Technology, and Risk. In *Rediscovering Darwin: Evolutionary Theory and Archeological Explanation*. CM. Barton and G. A. Clark, eds. Pp. 109 – 139. Archeological Papers of the American Anthropological Association, 7. Arlington, Va.: American Anthropological Association, 1997.

[10] Gamble, C. *The Paleolithic Settlement of Europe*. Cambridge: Cambridge University Press, 1986.

Klein, R. *The Human Career*. Chicago: University of Chicago Press, 1989.

Seong, C. Microblade Technology in Korea and Adjacent Northeast Asia. *Asian Perspectives* 37: 245 – 278, 1998.

Stiner, M., N. Munro, T. Surovell, E. Tchernov, and O. Bar-Yosef. Paleolithic Population Growth Pulses Evidenced by Small Animal Exploitation. *Science* 283: 190 – 194, 1999.

[11] Gamble, C. *The Paleolithic Settlement of Europe*. Cambridge: Cambridge University Press, 1986.

Jochim, M., C. Herhahn, and H. Starr. The Magdalenian Colonization of Southern Germany. *American Anthropologist* 101: 129 – 142, 1999.

[12] vonGrafenstein, U., H. Erlenkeuser, A. Brauer, J. Jouzel, and S. J. Johnson. A Mid-European Decadal Isotope-Climate Record from 15 500 to 5 000 Years B. P. *Science* 284(4 June): 1654 – 1657, 1999.

[13] Barton, C. M., and M. Neeley. Phantom Cultures of the Levantine Epipaleolithic. *Antiquity* 70: 139–147, 1996.

Neeley, M., and C. M. Barton. New Approach to Interpreting Late Pleistocene Microlith Industries in Southwest Asia. *Antiquity* 68: 275–288, 1994.

千里的鹅毛：撒哈拉以南非洲早期细石器工业的起源

斯坦丽·H·阿姆布鲁斯

（伊利诺伊大学　厄巴纳）

摘　要：以小石片与石叶为毛坯琢背修理的细石器是撒哈拉以南非洲石器时代晚期（Later Stone Age，简称LSA）[*]石器工业的标志。当然，某些较早阶段的LSA细石器工业缺少琢背修理的工具，还有些石器工业中有较大的琢背工具。此外，某些石器时代中期（Middle Stone Age，简称MSA）[**]的石器工业中有很多石叶和较大的琢背"细石器"。因此，撒哈拉以南非洲，石叶、琢背细石器与细石器化的起源是独立的现象。鉴于情况如此多样与复杂，"一刀切"的方案既不能准确地把握，也不能有效地解释以石叶为中心的技术、MSA阶段较大的琢背工具，以及LSA阶段细石器工业的起源。本文首先将简要归纳琢背工具与细石器工业的早期证据，然后评估几种细石器化与琢背工具起源的假说，其中包括带柄复合工具的发明、间接打片生产石叶技术、封闭栖居地里运用弓箭狩猎、投枪头上使用毒物的起源、精细原料的增加、流动性的提高、稀有原料的收集、使用精细外来原料制作的琢背细石器的礼品馈赠，以及当信息分享足以保证可靠的任务预测之后更高效的专业化工具的生产。如果细石器与琢背石叶工业起源于非洲，那么了解

---

[*] Later Stone Age 非洲史前史的最后阶段，其开始时间约相当于欧洲旧石器时代晚期，一直持续到历史时期，包括其他地区的中石器与新石器时代。——译注

[**] Middle Stone Age 非洲史前史的年代阶段，一般认为始于距今28万年，结束于5万至2.5万年前。这个阶段相当于现代人（晚期智人）与早期智人阶段。——译注

其起源过程将有助于研究现代人行为的演化、现代人与现代人的技术从非洲的扩散。

欧亚与北非旧石器时代中期（MP）与撒哈拉以南地区 MSA 石器工业传统上以预制石核（勒瓦娄哇与放射状打片的石核）生产石片与石叶。许多 MP 与 MSA 阶段的石器工业都是以石叶为中心的，但通常都不视作细石器[1]。石叶、琢背工具与细石器技术是许多非洲与欧亚地区旧石器时代晚期（UP）与石器时代晚期（LSA）石器工业的共同特征。然而，早在 5 万年前非洲就有一些 MSA 阶段石器工业，以及技术上类似 MP 阶段的石器工业以石叶为中心，并伴有琢背修理的细石器，远在其普遍分布于其他地区之前。尽管欧亚地区行为"古老"的人类制作石叶与琢背工具，但是石叶与琢背修理通常被视作非洲地区 MSA 阶段行为上"现代"的人类的重要技术特征[2]。遗传学的、考古学的以及古生物学的证据表明，现代人类与现代行为都起源于非洲，并在距今 5 至 6 万年后传播到非洲以外的旧大陆地区[3]。如果这一假说是正确的，现代技术行为在人口扩充与最后冰期时现代人从非洲扩散的过程中发挥了重要作用[4]。那么，探索非洲细石器技术与琢背石叶技术的起源，以及 MSA/LSA 之间的过渡，将有助于深入了解现代人与其行为的起源与扩散过程。

本文简要回顾撒哈拉以南非洲地区琢背石叶与细石器技术的起源与发展的证据，然后评估几种起源假说。这里讨论的假说包括复合工具技术的发明、封闭栖居地环境中运用弓箭狩猎、轻型投枪头用毒的发明、精细原料的增加、流动性的提高、精细原料的储备、用外来精细原料制作的礼物的交换，以及在系统化的信息传递更方便、任务预测更可靠、资源更容易获取后更高效专业化工具的生产。某些假说强调环境变化、流动性与原料使用之间的关系。非本地产精细原料的使用可能有利于细石器技术的形成。MSA 之末强化利用外来原材料也许反映了高风险冰期环境中的社会适应策略，人们通过优质外来石器原料的礼物交换来创造一种互惠合作关系，从而降低风险[5]。这种通过建立远距离社会同盟的方式降低社会风险的策略使得远距离行动成为可能，有助于发展更专业化的工具。降低风险的社会策略与更有效的细石器技术相结合，也有利于距今 5 至 6 万年现代人类扩散出非洲，以及取代更古老的人类[6]。

一、石叶、琢背修理与细石器技术

在评价细石器起源的不同假说之前，有必要先澄清以石叶为中心的石器工业、细石器工业以及琢背细石器的定义。习惯上讲，石叶就是那种长度大于宽度两倍的石片，细小石叶一定要比石叶小，但是两者之间的区分本来就很模糊且主观，因为石叶与细小石叶的长度范围重叠，不同研究所设定的石叶与细小石叶的数量定义差异显著[7]。设定一个石叶与细小石叶区分的普遍标准也是不可能的，因为不同地区在石器原料大小、力学属性、丰富程度、绑柄的类型、风格以及其他方面变化多样。器物长度的量化描述与长宽比能够使主观性降到最低，但并不能完全消除。尽管某些LSA的石器工业明显可以称为以石叶为中心的，而另外的石器工业以细小石叶为中心，但是把一个连续分布、缺乏两极分化的组合人为地分为石叶与细小石叶是不合适的。同样，在撒哈拉以南非洲地区发现石叶就认为其是细石器工业也是不合适的，因为数个早期细石器工业并不是以石叶或是细小石叶为中心的，而在其他石器工业中石叶并不总是石片的唯一形态。

非洲LSA石器工业中，石叶与石叶断片通常会受到陡向修理（通常采用砸击法），使与锐利刃缘平行的边缘钝化（琢背），或是修理截断处的断口。琢背修理的几何形细石器或断片包括新月形、三角形、梯形、深弯月形、长梯形与长方形等形制；非几何形的形制包括弯曲琢背、直形琢背、对角线的、倾斜的以及按长轴截断的等形制。琢背细石器可能非常大，平均长度接近50毫米（最大长度近10厘米），比如厄巴兰石器工业的较早阶段；也可能非常小，平均长度不超过17毫米，某些全新世LSA与新石器时代工业中可以见到[8]（表1.1）。琢背工具的大小分布常常是单峰的，几何形琢背石器比非几何形的平均尺寸要稍稍小一些[9]。只是在埃尔孟特坦石器工业中才观察到大小分布明显的双峰形态（表1.1）[10]。开阔地环境沉积物浅薄地区的琢背工具通常尺寸更小。因为常被踩踏，这些本来就脆弱、轻薄的器物断裂成更小的碎片[11]。

含有细石器工业特征的晚第四纪石器组合惊人地多样，某些LSA较早阶段的石器工业几乎没有非洲LSA或是旧石器时代晚期的典型特征。例如，最早LSA工业（早于3万年前），喀麦隆的舒姆拉卡[12]、扎伊尔的马图皮洞[13]、南非的边界洞[14]和肯尼亚的纳图卡河3号遗址[15]等都含有非常小的石片，而非石叶或是细小石叶，实际上也没有琢背或是其他形制规范的工具。仅就大小而言确实是细石器而已。4万年前，甚至更早，肯尼亚与坦桑尼亚地区某些LSA以及MSA/LSA过渡阶段的遗址含有相当数量的较大的琢背细石器[16]。其他工业具有许多LSA阶段的特征，但通常又认为是MSA的。例如，南非MSA的霍韦森斯港[17]，坦桑尼亚姆巴洞的姆巴工业[18]，都有很多较大的几何形琢背细石器。那

表 1.1 南非、肯尼亚与坦桑尼亚部分晚更新世与全新世石器工业（A）琢背细石器与（B）完整石片与石核的年代、平均值与标准差

遗址（工业）	年代 ka	长度（毫米） 均值	长度 标准差	长度 最小	长度 最大	宽度（毫米） 均值	宽度 标准差	宽度 最小	宽度 最大	厚度（毫米） 均值	厚度 标准差	厚度 最小	厚度 最大	宽/长 均值	标准差	样本数
A																
卡拉西斯河（霍维茨斯港）	~70	36.0	9.6			15.8				4.8				0.44		519
威尔顿（威森斯港）	>8	15.4	3.9													54
奈苏苏 1969（勒穆塔）	>42	27.6	10.4	14.6	51.3	10.8	4.1	18.5	5.1	3.7	1.1	2.1	7.3	0.40	0.14	15
奈苏苏 1931（勒穆塔）	>42	28.8	8.0	11.4	46.0	10.0	2.4	14.8	6.2	4.0	1.2	3.1	5.4	0.38	0.15	25
恩卡彭亚莫托（恩丁基）	>50	27.3	0.9	26.6	28.4	9.5	0.4	10.0	9.3					0.35	0.01	3
恩卡彭亚莫托（纳萨姆珀来）	>40	32.7	10.4	17.9	77.6	12.2	4.0	25.6	5.8	3.8	1.3	1.7	8.5	0.38	0.10	89
恩卡彭亚莫托（萨库特克）	>35	24.1	7.9	13.8	31.0	11.6	3.7	21.1	6.4	3.7	0.8	2.6	5.6	0.50	0.15	32

续 表

遗址（工业）	年代 ka	长度（毫米）均值	长度 标准差	长度 最小	长度 最大	宽度（毫米）均值	宽度 标准差	宽度 最小	宽度 最大	厚度（毫米）均值	厚度 标准差	厚度 最小	厚度 最大	宽/长 均值	宽/长 标准差	样本数
纳德里特滩（埃布尔1期）	12	49.3	18.5	23.2	91.5	14.0	3.5	21.7	7.6	4.4	1.8	2.7	8.2	0.30		13
马赛峡谷 RS（埃布尔2期）	~10	37.4	16.0	16.1	94.0	11.2	4.7	26.0	5.5	3.6	0.9	2.3	4.9	0.30		33
玛如拉岩夏（埃布尔3期）	8	33.5	14.3	9.7	107.2	9.3	3.6	35.4	2.8	3.6	1.4	1.2	10.8	0.29		465
甘博洞（埃布尔3期）	9	34.4	11.2	16.0	81.0	11.3	4.3	32.6	5.4	4.0	1.4	1.8	8.4	0.33		92
甘博洞（埃布尔4期）	<7	26.8	7.9	9.5	48.6	7.7	2.8	19.9	3.6	3.0	0.9	1.0	6.2	0.29		129
恩卡彭亚莫托 RBL2.3（Eb4）	<6	26.3	7.9	15.0	48.2	7.4	1.6	12.0	4.9	3.0	0.9	1.2	6.6	0.29		49
马赛峡谷 RS（埃布尔5期）	<3	26.5	11.0	11.5	58.3	8.3	3.1	18.5	4.5	2.9	0.9	1.5	4.5	0.33	0.06	29
马赛峡谷 RS（埃尔孟特坦 G）	2	16.1	2.4	9.0	21.3	6.6	0.9	8.7	4.8	2.7	0.8	1.6	5.0	0.32		74

续 表

遗址(工业)	年代 ka	长度(毫米) 均值	长度(毫米) 标准差	长度(毫米) 最小	长度(毫米) 最大	宽度(毫米) 均值	宽度(毫米) 标准差	宽度(毫米) 最小	宽度(毫米) 最大	厚度(毫米) 均值	厚度(毫米) 标准差	厚度(毫米) 最小	厚度(毫米) 最大	宽/长 均值	标准差	样本数
马赛峡谷 RS(埃尔孟特坦 NG)	2	51.3	11.7	31.6	74.5	17.3	4.4	24.0	9.0	5.8	2.2	2.5	9.9	0.34		12
恩尔彭亚莫托 ELM(ELM G)	2	19.0	3.3	12.5	30.5	7.1	1.2	9.8	4.9	2.8	0.7	1.3	4.4	0.38	0.08	61
恩尔彭亚莫托 ELM(ELM NG)	2	43.8	18.9	18.2	68.2	13.9	3.5	19.0	9.7	4.3	1.3	2.8	7.0	0.36	0.10	9
B																
纳图卡河 3(8N 层石片)	30	13.4	4.1	5.7	24.6	7.3	2.4	14.0	4.2	2.7	1.3	1.0	8.6	0.37	0.13	67
纳图卡河 3(8N 层石核)	30	15.2	4.4	6.8	23.9	10.6	4.0	20.5	5.0	9.7	3.8	3.6	19.6	0.73	0.29	57

卡纳西河与威尔顿的材料来自伍尔茨[19];其他材料来自阿姆布鲁斯[20]所做的测量。1969年发掘的勒穆柱工业的材料与1931年奥杜威柱威峡谷东苏遗址地表采集的材料分开统计。埃尔孟特坦(ELM)新石器工业的琢背细石器的大小具有双峰分布形态,细小的几何形石器(G)平均长度大约16~17毫米,较大的琢背石叶及其他非几何形石器(NG)平均长度大于40毫米。

种把窄长石叶折断制作琢背细石器的微雕刻器技术在非洲某些地区全新世 LSA 石器工业中很常见[21],但在 LSA 的较早阶段以及中期带琢背工具的石器工业中鲜有存在。

二、非洲细石器与琢背细石器工业的年代与特征

（一）最早的石叶技术

阿舍利的最后阶段在大约距今 30 万年前。石叶技术最早出现在非洲与利凡特地区。最早的材料包括南非的法勒史密斯[22]、肯尼亚巴林戈的卡普苏林组[23]和利凡特地区的马格哈兰工业[24]。厚且大的石叶从棱柱状石核上打制下来,可能是通过硬锤直接打击剥片的。这些工业中还不见琢背石叶与几何形细石器。南非 MSA 石叶工业很常见[25],欧亚大陆西部的旧石器时代中期工业中也是如此[26]。肯尼亚与埃塞俄比亚地区的黑曜石比较丰富,这里很少或是完全缺乏以石叶为中心的 MSA 工业。

（二）南非的 MSA 与 LSA

南非 MSA 较早阶段的石器工业,按照当前的分类框架称为 MSA1 与 MSA2[27],都有许多相对较厚的大石叶,主要采用当地的原料制作,但缺乏琢背细石器。MSA1、2 阶段遗址的年代可以早到末次间冰期(氧同位素阶段 6,距今 19 至 12.8 万年,阶段 5,距今 12.8 万年至 7.4 万年),还有的遗址早到倒数第二个间冰期阶段(氧同位素阶段 7,距今 24.9 至 19 万年),甚至还可能更早[28]。静湾石器工业,发现于南非近十个遗址中,一般认为是连接 MSA2 阶段的,年代较为明确,距今 7 至 8 万年[29]。值得注意的是,这里两面修理的尖状器比较丰富,采用的是细腻硅质岩与其他罕见的、可能是外来的原料。另外,这里的赤铁矿石极其丰富[30]。霍韦森斯港石器工业最早出现于末次盛冰期的开端之时(氧同位素阶段 4,距今 7 至 6 万年),距今约 7 万年。这种"早熟的"石器工业含有较大的琢背细石器,采用硅质岩、石英以及其他细腻的非本地产原料生产的窄石叶来制作。霍韦森斯港石器工业为 MSA3/4 阶段石叶工业所取代。这些石器工业与氧同位素阶段 3(大约距今 6 至 2.4 万年)的 MSA2 石器工业类似。MSA3/4 阶段石器组合中细腻原料的比例只是稍稍高于 MSA2 阶段。MSA3、4 阶段的考古材料非常罕见:主要分布于洞穴与岩厦中,沉积物少,居住堆积稀薄[31]。因为 MSA 的较晚阶段琢背细石器消失,所以通常不认为霍韦森斯港石器工业是走向

LSA的过渡阶段。

南非MSA/LSA过渡的标志包括更多的精细原料、砸击石核、石核修理石片（outils ecailles）、不规则的小石片、琢背细石器以及极少的放射状打片的石核、修理台面的石片、尖状器、锯齿刮削器等[32]。石叶与细小石叶在石器组合中只占少部分，大部分石核都是砸击石核。按照古德温和罗维[33]所定义的MSA，这些石器组合中很少有称得上属于MSA阶段的技术与类型学特征，应该将之归为LSA的较早阶段（ELSA）。如果将过渡型的石器工业定义为LSA的工具类型不断增加，中期的工具类型日益减少，那么南非石器时代MSA/LSA"过渡"根本就不存在。这些LSA较早阶段的石器工业晚到距今3万年，某些遗址晚到距今2.2万年，还保留着典型的MSA的面貌[34]。边界洞可能是个例外，因为这里有一支LSA较早阶段的石器工业，属于非细石叶类似的细石器，较为确切的年代不晚于距今3.8万年[35]。测年证据表明南非地区向细石器工业过渡的过程相当复杂，时代断断续续，或是说逐渐过渡，年代也比较晚（晚于距今2.5万年）。

南非LSA的罗伯格工业距今约2.2万年到1.2万年之间，具有典型的细石叶与小石片，绝大部分（将近85%）都是用非当地产的精细原料所制[36]。尽管这种工业毫无疑问是细石器的，但是琢背断片工具与其他形制较规范的工具非常少[37]。南非更新世至全新世之交代表性的工业是一系列地区的LSA工业变体，称为阿尔巴尼、罗克希克、珀莫各万、史密斯菲尔德A[38]，其石制品基本都是采用当地原料所制，原料的质量通常很差。形制规范的工具主要是凸刃的大刮削器，琢背细石器极其少见。罗伯格与阿尔巴尼石器工业组合都属于LSA阶段，但是两类石器工业中都缺乏琢背细石器与凸刃小端刮器（拇指盖刮削器）等习惯上代表LSA的工具类型[39]。

南非全新世早、中、晚阶段（距今约8千至3千年）的遗址多含有威尔顿工业的地方变体。其标志性特征是非常细小的琢背几何形细石器、拇指盖刮削器，多用精细的石料制作[40]。"典型的威尔顿"期所处的年代正值中更新世最干旱的阶段，形制规范的细石器工具与精细石料的比例最高[41]。博茨瓦纳的MSA/LSA过渡更像东非，而非南非。白画岩厦遗址的MSA/LSA过渡阶段早到距今3.4万年[42]，代表性器物包括丰富的石叶、细小石叶、琢背工具以及尖状器。东部到中部非洲地区林地与森林地带MSA/LSA过渡通常晚于距今3万年[43]。

（三）东非MSA与LSA

东非MSA与LSA早期的年代及其相关研究已为不少学者所关注，如克拉克[44]、布鲁克斯和罗伯特肖[45]、麦克布里提[46]、安布罗斯[47]等。这个部分将集中讨论近年来肯尼亚和坦桑尼亚的晚第四纪研究。MSA 晚段与 LSA 早期的测年工作问题比较大,因为此时已经超过放射性碳测年极限,而且很少有遗址采用了其他断代技术进行较为准确的测年[48]。

石叶与琢背细石器在大多数 MSA 东非石器工业中都是无足轻重的成分[49]。MSA 早期(大约早于距今 7 万年)工业的主要特征为修理台面的石片,是从放射状打片的石核或勒瓦娄哇石核上打制下来的。早于距今 7 万年的遗址所用石器原料基本都产自当地[50]。姆巴洞岩厦位于坦桑尼亚厄亚斯湖附近,其中少量出土的黑曜石来自北方 320 公里外的肯尼亚中部大裂谷地区[51]。就南非而言,琢背工具最早出现于 MSA 晚段,距今约 6.5 万年[52]。当然,东非地区石器组合可以认为是向 LSA 过渡的,因为琢背工具在 LSA 之前并没有消失,大约距今 4 至 5 万年。

姆巴工业中琢背大工具的比例很高,尖状器与放射状打片石核的比例较低。骨骼铀系断代与氨基酸消旋断代的年代距今 3.5 至 6.5 万年[53]。这样的断代技术与材料本来就不是很可靠。姆巴洞上层的纳色拉工业中非标准化加工的小尖状器比例较高,更小的琢背细石器比例较低。骨磷灰石、鸵鸟蛋壳、腹足软体动物贝壳的铀系断代与放射性碳断代法测定的年代是距今 1.8 至 3.7 万年。位于坦桑尼亚塞伦盖提平原的纳色拉岩厦遗址中,MSA/LSA 的纳色拉工业为 LSA 早段的勒莫塔工业所叠压,测定年代为距今 1.8 至 2.2 万年[54]。勒莫塔工业也见于奥杜威峡谷的奈苏苏遗址,最初用放射性碳测年技术对骨"胶原"断代[55],年代为距今 1.7 万年,然而骨胶原是很难保持如此之长的时间的[56]。奈苏苏遗址重新用氨基酸消旋断代法与氩 40/氩 39 单晶激光融合法对鸵鸟蛋壳断代[57],年代为距今 4.2 万年。这些测年数据表明 MSA/LSA 过渡阶段的姆巴与纳色拉工业年代都应该早于距今 4.2 万年,它们都在勒莫塔工业之下。勒莫塔工业中石英、燧石与黑曜石制作的琢背大工具的比例较高(表 1.1),而凸刃端刮器的比例较低;雕刻器完全缺失,较大的砸击石核很常见[58],主要是石英岩质的。燧石与石英在奥杜威峡谷地区都有出产,但黑曜石则要来自 250 公里开外的肯尼亚中部大裂谷地区[59]。

肯尼亚大裂谷地区的遗址材料同样表明 MSA/LSA 过渡早于距今 5 万年。肯尼亚普罗斯帕克特农场遗址 MSA 的最晚阶段(普罗斯帕克特工业 4 期)运用黑曜石水合断代法测定年代为距今 4.6 至 5.3 万年[60]。黑曜石水合断代法测定的是最晚的年代,因为 1.2 万年前的气温更低[61],这会降低水合的速率。这一地区最晚的 MSA 证据来自普罗龙德滩附近(GrJil 1),文化层位于一层古土壤层下 1.4 米处,上覆一层火山灰,年代约距今 3.5 万年[62]。出土物中绝大部分(95%)的燧石来自遗址以南 50 公里远的地方,虽然遗址附近有更近的出露地点[63]。

恩卡彭亚莫托岩厦(GtJi 12)遗址 MSA/LSA 过渡阶段(恩丁基工业)最晚的放射性碳测年年代早于距今 4.1 万年[64]。出土物中发现从放射状打片石核上打制的预制台面石片、琢背几何形细石器、边刮器、石核修理石片、尖状器、雕刻器等,但石叶与石叶石核罕见。琢背新月形刮削器、雕刻器、石核修理石片的存在表明,它是一种过渡类型的石器工业。其 5.6 米深处的文化序列中非当地原料的比例最高[65]。恩卡彭亚莫托最早的 LSA 工业(纳萨姆珀莱工业)早于距今 4 万年,接近距今 5 万年,可能是世界最早的 LSA 或旧石器时代晚期石器技术。这种特殊的石器工业几乎完全由琢背大工具构成,雕刻器、石核修理石片与刮削器较少。恩卡彭亚莫托的第二种 LSA 工业(萨库特克工业)运用放射性碳测年法测定木炭与鸵鸟蛋壳所得年代为距今 3.5 至 4 万年[66]。最丰富的工具类型是凸刃端刮器(拇指盖刮削器)与石核修理石片。加工粗糙的琢背细石器(表1.1)、部分两面修理的石刀或尖状器、小而薄的盘状与放射状打片石核所占比例甚小[67]。尽管从大小上来说它们明显都是细石器,但这种工业并不是以石叶为中心的。它含有 MSA/LSA 过渡阶段石器工业的特征,但是它叠压在以石叶为中心的纳萨姆珀莱工业之上,后者没有过渡特征。

奥尔特佩斯岩厦遗址(GsJi53)存在一种特殊的细石叶工业(克特科工业),测定年代距今 1.4 万年。纳德里特滩遗址(GsJi2)的石器工业类似之,测定年代距今 1.3 至 1.4 万年[68]。其中细石叶很丰富,细石核、雕刻器形石核、石核形雕刻器,以及其他类型的雕刻器构成超过 40% 的形制规范的工具。琢背细石器基本不存在。由于奥尔特佩斯遗址位于东非地区许多广泛利用的黑曜石原料产地 10 公里范围内,所以其细石叶的小尺寸不应该归因于原料的节约使用。

纳图穆特遗址(纳图卡河 3 号,GvJhl 1)是一处旷野遗址,位于南段大裂谷的西部边缘地带,距离最近的黑曜石原料产地 60 至 90 公里。其 9 米深的文化层是早期细石器工业与细石器化的重要证据。尽管发掘与分析研究还在进行中,这里还是可以做一些初步的归纳的。15 与 16 层含有 MSA/LSA 过渡阶段石器组合,包括放射状打片石核,还包括生产石叶的石核、两面修理的小尖状器以及琢背细石器。15 与 16 层有 2.7 米厚,上覆一层火山灰(14 层),距离放射性碳测年年代 3 万年的层位 5 米,15、16 层 MSA/LSA 过渡阶段的工业估计年代早于距今 5 万年。15 层黑曜石石制品的比例最高(64%)(图 1.1)。

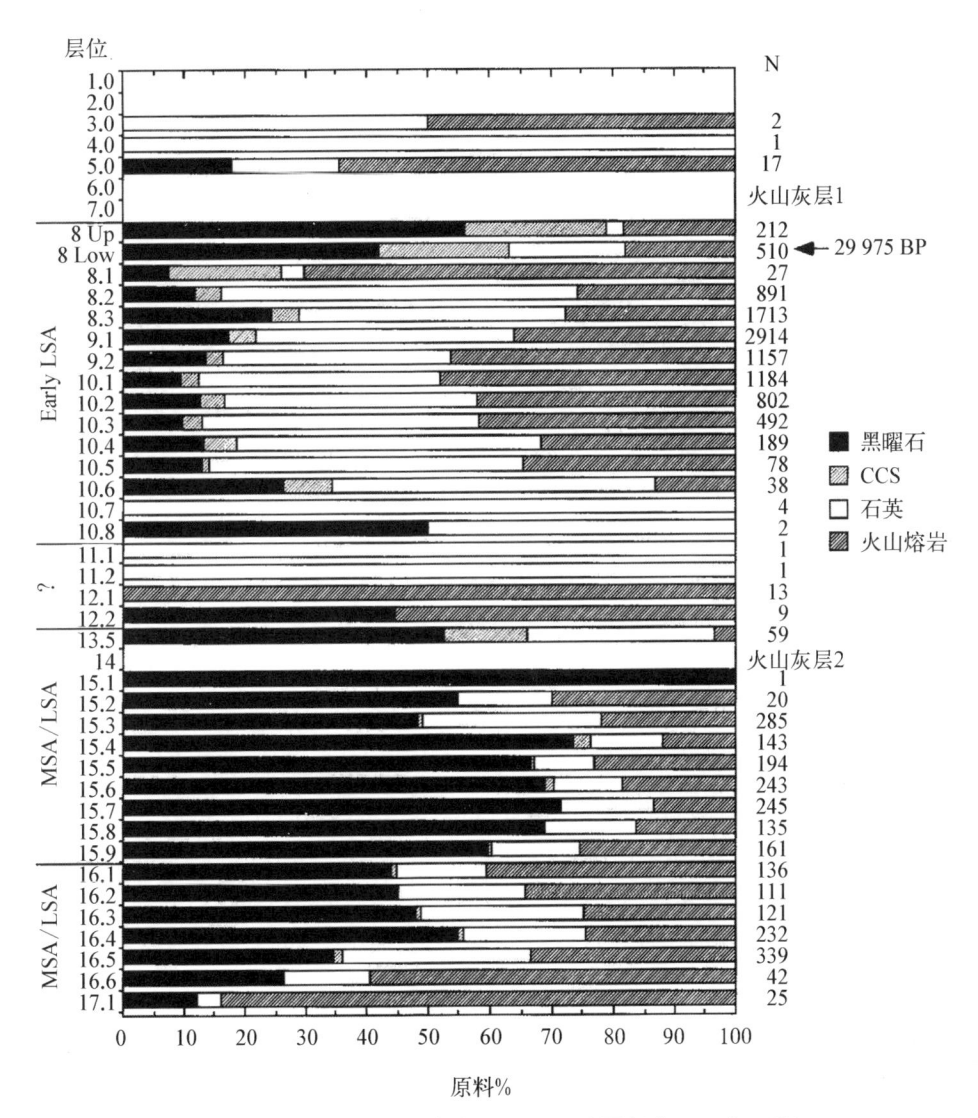

图 1.1 肯尼亚南部纳图穆特(GvJh11)晚更新世 LSA 与 MSA 阶段考古遗址中黑曜石、燧石与石英打片的比例

[注意 8N 层高频率的黑曜石可能主要来自循环使用了 MSA 阶段较大的黑曜石石制品,这些器物可能就来自遗址附近。15 与 16 层黑曜石(MSA/LSA 过渡)非循环使用,更可能反映了长距离的搬运与交换,而非直接采集。CCS:隐晶质硅质岩]

最早的 LSA 工业（8 层下部、9 层、10 层）大约位于 15、16 层 MSA/LSA 过渡阶段工业之上 2.5 至 4.5 米。尽管是细石器的大小，但是它主要包含的是小石片与砸击石核，而非石叶与细小石叶。琢背工具缺乏，其他形制规范的工具同样罕见。黑曜石原料在石器组合中占 16%。LSA 最晚阶段的石器工业位于第 8 层，是两个独立的薄层（2~4 厘米），在一层薄火山灰层（7 层）之下 30 至 60 厘米，下文化层的加速质谱仪测年年代为距今 29 975 年，还有一个温度校正的氨基酸消旋测年年代，距今 3.2 万年，两者基本一致。第 8 层上部的石器工业包含有细小的细石叶与细石核（表 1.1，B）。雕刻器、石核修理石片为最常见的工具类型，琢背工具完全缺乏。许多石核为雕刻器形（占 24.5%），但少数为砸击石核（占 8.2%）。大部分燧石与黑曜石石核的基本形制是大石片。部分燧石与黑曜石石叶侧面石片背疤有风化的迹象，也见于许多细石核的边缘。这表明石核可能是循环使用了 MSA 的燧石与黑曜石石制品，很可能来自遗址附近。因此，尽管黑曜石占到石器原料的 46%，其原料来源主要是当地的。

纳图穆特细石叶性质的 LSA 工业与奥尔特佩斯的克特科工业相似，都缺少琢背细石器，强调雕刻器形的细石叶小石核，可以归为核型雕刻器。纳图卡河 3 号遗址距今 1.5 万年，比奥尔特佩斯更早，因此不清楚两者是否属于同一石器工业。它们与南非同时代的罗伯格细石叶工业的相似性引人注目，但是目前还没有证据表明存在共同的起源。此外，卢肯亚山以及东非其他地区距今 1.5 至 3 万年之间的 LSA 遗存并不像这些细石叶工业[69]。纳图穆特遗址 8 至 10 层细石器工业似乎更像是南部与中部非洲不标准的 LSA 早段的石器工业。

诺里库辛遗址（纳图卡河 4 号、GvJhl 2）也含有 MSA/LSA 过渡阶段石器组合，但还含有一些非常大的琢背石叶、新月形刮削器、修理台面的石叶、石片尖状器以及放射状打片石核与石叶石核[70]。与姆巴遗址最早的 MSA/LSA 过渡阶段的石器工业相似，因此年代可能早于距今 6 万年。撒哈拉以南非洲 MSA 与 LSA 年代序列回顾显示早在 7 万年前后，南非 MSA 的霍韦森斯港工业就短暂出现使用非本地产精细原料琢背大工具的现象，当时正值寒冷、干燥的氧同位素阶段 4，但是传统的 MSA 工业主要利用本地产较为粗糙的原料制作石器。这样的工业在更温暖湿润的氧同位素第 3 阶段重新出现。细石器性质的 LSA 工业距今 2 至 4 万年流行于南部非洲，但琢背细石器在大部分 LSA 较早阶段的石器工业中不占重要地位。东非地区的琢背细石器最早出现于 MSA 的较晚阶段，可能早到距今 6.5 万年，在某些距今 4 至 5 万年的较早的 LSA 工业中相当常见，但在其他距今 3 至 1.3 万年的工业中又极为罕见。东非地区 MSA/LSA 的过渡显然比旧大陆其他地区更早,过渡阶段以及 LSA 早段的石器技术的多样性相当可观。

东非地区 MSA 最后阶段以及 LSA 的早段出现装饰品,当地与非当地的石器原料的比例也发生了改变,这样的变化是下文所提假说的重要基础。MSA 的最晚阶段(普罗龙德滩)与 MSA/LSA 过渡阶段的石器工业(恩卡彭亚莫托与纳图卡河3号)非常值得关注,因为它们拥有较高比例的非当地原料,比当地 LSA 的石器工业还要高[71]。类似的情形也见于博茨瓦纳的白画岩厦遗址,这里 MSA 的最后阶段石器工业中燧石占到55%,相反 LSA 早期只占到35%[72]。南非、坦桑尼亚、肯尼亚的 MSA 晚段与 LSA 早段都发现鸵鸟蛋壳所制的珠子,波姆普拉斯遗址放射性碳测年年代为距今4.2万年[73],边界洞遗址测定年代距今3.8万年[74],克塞斯遗址距今3.3万年[75],恩卡彭亚莫托遗址距今4万年[76],姆巴遗址则距今5.2万年(氨基酸消旋断代)[77]。非洲地区装饰品的生产整体上要比世界其他地区早。精细原料的交换、装饰品的生产与细石器工业之间的关系将在下文讨论。

三、细石叶工业的起源

(一)复合工具技术

细石器化是复合工具技术发展的结果吗?微痕分析[78]、黏接物与赤铁矿的痕迹[79]、器物大小与形制的标准化[80]以及阿特林与卢佩姆班工业石器上的梃[81],都表明 MSA 阶段出现把石片、石叶捆绑成复合工具的技术。尽管大部分捆绑的直接证据来自 MSA 或旧石器时代中期晚段,但是类似大小与形制的工具在早段就已经开始生产了。如果复合工具的生产起源于 MSA 与旧石器时代中期的开始阶段,也就是距今约30万年[82],那么距今7万年前后开始的细石器化可能与复合工具的发明没有直接的联系。

(二)弓箭与有毒的尖部

细石器化是否与弓箭以及有毒的箭头的发明相关呢?毒箭仅仅需要刺破动物的表皮就能杀死猎物,因此箭头可以很小、很轻。没有毒的话,要杀死大型动物就需要大且重的箭头或是标枪。单个琢背修理片段横着安装在箭头上,或是两片倾斜、背对背地安装,就可以在射中猎物后形成有效的血槽[83]。比较古埃及的箭、威尔顿型 LSA 工业以及现代布须曼人的毒箭之后,克拉克[84]指出 LSA 琢背细石器应该用作箭头。这些民族学与考古学的例子都使用较为细小的镶嵌石刃,比霍韦森斯港、姆巴、勒莫塔、纳萨姆珀莱的 MSA/LSA 过渡阶段以及 LSA 早段的石器工业的琢背石器更小(表 1.1)。迪肯[85]因此认为霍韦森斯港的琢背大石器是标枪的枪头而非箭头。姆巴与纳色拉(纳色拉工业)、恩卡彭亚莫托(恩丁基工业)、纳图卡河 3 号(15、16 层)所出土 MSA/LSA 过渡阶段的石器工业含有更细小的琢背细石器,可能用作箭头。其实,石片并不必在琢背修理之后才能捆绑安装用作箭头,而是直接就可以使用[86]。肯尼亚、扎伊尔、南非距今 4 万年与更早的细石器工业中缺乏琢背工具,但其石制品足够小,完全可以用作箭头、弓箭、用毒与细石器技术起源之间存在联系,检验这一假说需要做残留物的化学分析以确认黏接剂与毒物的成分,复原捆绑技术以及容易腐烂的复合工具组件。

(三)特定环境的狩猎策略

琢背细石器可能镶嵌用作箭头,基于这样的前提,菲利普森[87]提出细石器起源的环境假说,认为"琢背细石器技术的采用跟新的狩猎技术紧密相连,这种狩猎技术本身是对茂密植被的适应"。在这种假说提出的时候,LSA 早段细石器技术的年代序列、分布、环境背景还不清晰。现在我们知道最早的细石器工业出现年代相对较早,当时正值末次冰期(阶段 3)的干旱气候,开阔地环境可能占主导地位。最早的细石器遗址中动物遗存一般都非常罕见,而细石器存在的地方往往都是开阔地环境[88]。

(四)间接打击生产石叶技术

间接打击生产石叶技术的发明是否是细石器技术起源的影响因素之一呢?迪肯与伍尔茨[89]通过台面属性进行了定性描述,发现霍韦森斯港的长、薄的石叶是由间接打击技术生产的。"台面小、平,角度大,垂直于石叶的主轴"。伍尔茨[90]就台面类型、台面宽与厚进行了统计。基于唇形台面这样的属性,[91]指出霍韦森斯港石叶可能由软锤打击技术生产。博尔德与卡拉布垂[92]的间接打击生产石叶的实验表明,这种技术的台面相对于直接打击所需要的台面更小。相对的台面大小可以通过计算台面厚与石片厚之比(PT/FT)以及台面宽与石片宽之比(PW/FW)来衡量。如果比率比较低,台面就小,属于间接打片的形态;如果比率高,台面就大,更可能像直接打击实验所显示的形态。图 1.2 显示的是肯尼亚大裂谷中段厄布鲁火山熔岩烟管洞(GsJj55)遗址新石器时代厄巴兰工业 5a 期与埃尔孟特坦工业的测量数据。所有石制品都系黑曜石所制。厄巴兰的台面平均大小相对更大(宽且厚),通常呈现多个小平面。它们更像是直接打制实验的台面类型。

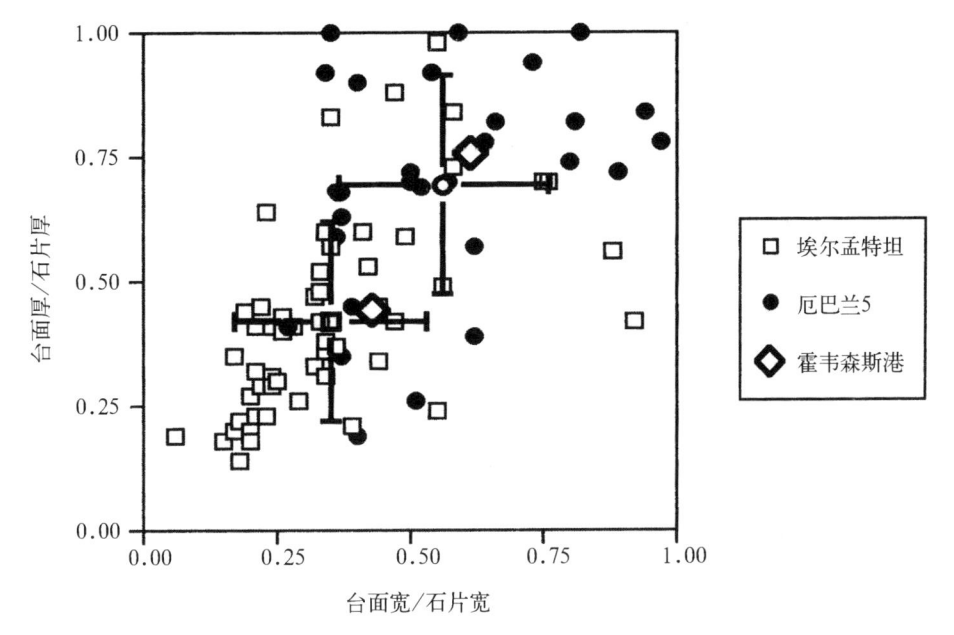

图1.2 台面宽与石片宽比例(台面宽/石片宽)、台面厚与石片厚比例(台面厚/石片厚)双变量统计图

[图中显示了厄巴兰5与埃尔孟特坦新石器组合的标准差,材料来自厄布鲁火山熔岩烟管洞遗址。低比例多见于间接打击法,而高比例多见于直接打击。霍韦森斯港的台面近似于间接打击技术所致,伍尔茨[93]的材料统计支持这一点。不过,伍尔茨[94]的材料(表54与56)提供的平均比例更接近厄巴兰工业的直接打击石片。]

厄巴兰的石叶相对窄而厚,反映石核的剥片面相对窄而凸起。埃尔孟特坦石制品的台面小,没有剥片,通常磨圆或是有擦痕。石叶相对宽而薄,反映石核的剥片面宽且平。通过摩擦来准备台面通常会在石核台面边缘(背面近端也是如此)留下一系列的小石片疤,这也许可以解释为什么台面如此之小。

伍尔茨[95]测量了霍韦森斯港石叶台面的平均宽与厚,但是台面与石叶样本所得到的尺寸不同。运用伍尔茨1997年的数据估计台面宽与石片宽之比为0.43,台面厚与石片厚之比为0.44,这接近埃尔孟特坦间接打击生产石叶、石核的平均尺寸(图1.2)。然而,运用伍尔茨2000年表54与表56中的数据上述比例分别为0.62与0.76,更接近厄巴兰采用直接打击技术的石核数据。由于还没有霍韦森斯港石叶与台面准确的测量数据,还无法判断究竟采用的是间接打击技术还是软锤技术。我们还需要更多的实验数据以检验间接打击技术、软锤与硬锤打击技术之间的区别。

（五）精细原料的力学属性

MSA 琢背工具工业的出现是否与精细原料的增加有关呢？这样的原料更有利于生产薄而锋利的石叶。研究东非 MSA/LSA 过渡阶段原料使用方式与非石器技术的发明，支持多个假说，或是说可以解释细石器技术的起源。卡纳西斯河的霍韦森斯港含有 12% 至 59% 的非当地产精细原料（非石英岩）[96]（参考文献的表 16），相反下面的 MSA1 段与 2 段，以及更晚的 3 段与 4 段所含非本地原料的比例分别为 0.4%、1.2%、4.0%、0.7%[97]。MSA2 段层位较晚的时期，在向霍韦森斯港过渡之前，非本地原料的石器开始增加，至霍韦森斯港工业之末与 MSA3 段之初又逐渐下降[98]。在技术改变之前的原料的变化方式表明小石叶与琢背细石器技术的起源跟精细原料的属性密不可分，原料特性是细石器技术的基础条件。当精细原料不容易得到时，石器技术可能发生重组以适应本地较为粗糙的石料特性[99]。

（六）精细原料与社会区域组织策略

如上所述，精细原料的供给可能促进了细石器化。石器原料的长距离搬运，也就是说超过 40 公里[100]，东非地区的 MSA 后段以及 MSA/LSA 过渡阶段达到最高比例[101]。这些形态既见于黑曜石普遍分布的肯尼亚中部大裂谷地区，也见于大裂谷地区之外。普罗斯帕克特农场遗址中下部文化层中 60% 到 90% 的石制品都来自以遗址为中心的 15 公里范围内[102]，文化层年代可能早到最后间冰期时（氧同位素阶段 5）[103]。最晚的 MSA 层位可能是在末次冰期中（氧同位素第 3 或第 4 阶段），超过 60% 的原料来自 30 公里开外，不过只有 2% 来自 40 公里以及更远的地区。普罗龙德滩遗址是梅里克等研究的最晚的 MSA 遗址[104]，其中 45% 的原料来自 40 公里范围内，50% 来自 50 公里开外，即便有不少黑曜石产地就分布在距遗址 30 公里的范围内。几乎所有黑曜石都来自狩猎采集者利用区域内最远的地方，或是超越这个范围。恩卡彭亚莫托遗址 MSA/LSA 过渡阶段之末含有较高比例的燧石与石英，比所有 LSA 遗址都要高[105]；最近的石英产地都在 75 公里远的地方，位于中部大裂谷外变质岩露头区域。肯尼亚南部裂谷的纳图穆特遗址 15 层（GvJh1 1，纳图卡河 3 号）MSA/LSA 过渡阶段含有更多来自中部裂谷地区的黑曜石，比任何 LSA 遗址都要多（图 1.1）。这表明 MSA 之末人类的流动性与交换都有实质性的提高[106]。

普罗斯帕克特农场遗址当时很可能就位于厄布鲁山的森林—草原生态交错地带附近,可能是一个较为稳定的聚落体系的中心区,此时正值间冰期,气候温暖湿润[107]。相反,普罗龙德滩遗址则是一处 MSA 之末的临时狩猎营地[108],处在氧同位素阶段 4 或阶段 3 之初,气候干冷。它几乎没有来自最近原料产地的黑曜石,这些产地同样靠近普罗斯帕克特农场遗址,当时为该遗址所利用,所以普罗龙德滩遗址不是这个生态交错带聚落体系的部分。如果普罗龙德滩遗址处在干冷的氧同位素第 3、第 4 阶段之间,生态交错带当时可能已经解体,资源变得稀少且不稳定,这促成一种流动不定、机会捕捉式的聚落体系,其中领域范围、信息与石料交换都是开放的[109]。这种新的居住与原料使用方式可能反映了 MSA 之内所发生的某种变化,类似于利凡特地区旧石器时代中期的"放射状"与旧石器时代晚期的"环状"聚落体系[110]。如果这种高度流动的策略不利于规律地到访石料露头区域,或是说,如果在频繁的流动中携带更轻的负荷更有优势[111]。那么,就像利凡特地区所显示的,这种新的聚落体系可能是促成细石器技术起源的重要因素之一,它有利于节约使用原料。

坦桑尼亚 MSA 材料中黑曜石的比例较高,比更新世范围内的 LSA 材料更高[112]。MSA 阶段人们更短的居留时间或可以解释这种差异[113],更短的时间必然积累更少的本地原料。当然,中部大裂谷的黑曜石产地距离这些遗址 225 至 325 公里远,所以这里的黑曜石很可能是通过交换获得的,而非就地采集。类似的形态见于博茨瓦纳的白画岩厦遗址,这里 MSA 之末材料中有 55% 的燧石,相反 LSA 之初的层位只有不到 35%[114]。南非 MSA 之末则不见这样的形态:尽管霍韦森斯港有较多的可能属于外地的原料(达到 35%),比其他 MSA 遗址都要多,但还是远低于更新世范围内的 LSA 工业的比例(罗伯格工业中高达 85%),并且相对于霍韦森斯港工业,较晚的 MSA 工业外来原料更少[115]。

南非的霍韦森斯港、肯尼亚的 MSA 之末以及 MSA/LSA 过渡阶段,精细原料的长距离搬运的频率提高,究竟是什么因素导致如此呢?非本地原料比例实质性提高首先出现于末次盛冰期之初。是否与当时的环境条件相关呢?末次盛冰期之初(氧同位素阶段 4)资源的密度与可预见性降低,群体的活动范围扩大,相邻群体间的往来、合作与信息交流的机会增加,从而应对当时的环境变化。这种假说强调:(1)冰期时群体活动范围扩大,可以在群体领域范围内采集到精细的原料[116];(2)跨越社会领域的边界,信息与资源交换日益普遍[117]。

(七)精细原料与高风险环境的互助机制

琢背细石器是否如同"千里的鹅毛",象征着群体之间相互依赖、相互帮助的关系纽带？换句话说,修理成型的琢背细石器作为延后互惠习俗体系中的礼物,是否就像卡拉哈里沙漠的桑人那样呢？威斯勒[118]描述过卡拉哈里沙漠桑人的哈克萨罗(hxaro)——礼物赠予合作体系,它可以减少在贫瘠多变环境中的生存风险。迪肯提出这一假说用以解释 MSA 的情形。假说强调外来的精细原料具有象征与社会功能[119]。迪肯与伍尔茨认为利用琢背修理的片段制作复合工具,然后进行延后互惠交换,在细石器技术的起源过程中起着重要的作用。他们得出结论,桑人的"哈克萨罗"体系起源于霍韦森斯港,而且认为这是一条主要的证据线索,可以解释 MSA 较晚阶段南部非洲远古狩猎采集者形成了完全现代的人类行为。

就地采集外加普遍交换的假说相对于"哈克萨罗"延后的互惠假说相互竞争,如何才能进行检验呢？采集与交换非本地产精细原料会涉及石核的搬运,而非成型工具。如果确实如此,那么成型工具相对于废片的比例应该与利用本地产原料的比例相似,因为成型工具还留在了原地。当然,如果成型的琢背工具进行了交换,那么工具对废片的比例应该比利用本地所有原料的比例低得多。伍尔茨[120]提供的卡纳西斯河材料表明当时的确偏好使用精细原料制作琢背工具,但是这些原料中废片对成型工具的比例似乎与利用本地原料的比例相似。

东非 MSA 之末石器原料长距离搬运的加强是否意味着社会关联与礼物赠予实质性的提高呢？如果"哈克萨罗"体系的确是一种重要的生存策略,那么外来原料应该随着时间的推移而不断增加。然而,LSA 之初的恩卡彭亚莫托、纳图卡河 3 号、姆巴、纳色拉遗址中看到的是长距离石料搬运的下降。上文已提及,非洲东部与南部地区若干遗址中鸵鸟蛋壳所制的珠子早到距今 4 万年,甚至更古老[121]。这种东西也正是现代桑人"哈克萨罗"延后互惠体系中不可或缺的组成部分,串好的珠饰品几乎就是"哈克萨罗"礼物的代名词,珠饰品也被认为是各种场合都适用的礼物[122]。这表明交换礼物的"哈克萨罗"体系中使用珠饰非常古老。是否鸵鸟蛋壳珠以及其他非石器物品作为外来精细原料石制品的补充,构成"哈克萨罗"体系的礼物,并且导致 LSA 之初非本地原料石制品比例的下降呢？

霍韦森斯港 MSA 利用外来原料制作的琢背工具可能用作"哈克萨罗"礼物交换[123],这个假说得到普遍存在的非实用性物品的支持,如使用鸵鸟蛋皮珠[124]。MSA 后段,外来精细原料与成型石器工具可能获得的象征的价值,但它们仍然具有实用功能。生产、维护、修理与使用最终导致外来原料的废弃与损耗。非实用器物如珠子通常用作个人穿戴的装饰品,循环使用成为新的礼物。

由于具有纯粹的象征价值,这样的器物可能是一种更有效的途径,表示与强化"哈克萨罗"合作者之间相互依存的纽带。我们不妨比较一下结婚周年纪念品中一件家庭日用品与一颗钻石的象征意义,日用品意味着"我注重你的劳作";钻石的含义是"我爱你"。个人装饰品这样的礼物可能在促进社会团结与生存方面起着更普遍的作用,它促进愿意成为互惠者的成员之间的认同感[125],尤其是在末次冰期高风险的环境中。

装饰品是象征相互依赖更有效的符号,随着它的发明,是否精细石器原料的减少会促进细石器化呢? MSA 晚段以及 MSA/LSA 过渡阶段,石叶与琢背细石器生产的起源可能与精细石器原料的增加有关。当时人类重组石器技术以充分利用精细石料的力学属性[126]。如果精细原料的供给最终下降,那么就会有利于节约使用原料的策略形成。东非 LSA 早段小石片与细石叶工业以及砸击石核技术可能都反映了节约使用原料技术的革新。末次冰期的早段,东非琢背石器工业的连续性表明在东部非洲细石器化可能早到 MSA/LSA 过渡阶段已经出现了,其时间是距今 5 至 6 万年。为什么南部非洲霍韦森斯港之后的 MSA 工业中没有出现这样的技术革新呢? 这依旧是一个谜,下面将进行一些推测。

(八) 社交网络、信息交流、策略规划与技术组织

颇有一些有关工具设计与技术组织理论的评论[127]强调工具本身的属性,诸如可靠性、灵活性、适应性、可维护性以及采用技术途径与发明的微观经济学等等。流动的狩猎采集者在每天外出采食的过程中只能随身携带有限的工具与其他个人物品,同时居住地的经常变换也限制了人们财产的数量[128],所以他们需要仔细考虑携带最合适的东西,以利用资源,保障生存。

宾福德[129]、罗布鲁克斯等[130]、库恩[131]、特林考斯[132]、科林[133]以及其他研究者都曾指出 MSA 或旧石器时代中期与 LSA 或旧石器时代晚期在规划的时间长度与组织能力上存在着重大区别。旧石器时代中期的人类似乎只能就遇到的机会与环境做出行动反应,而不能有预见、有计划地利用环境。MSA 或是旧石器时代中期的较早阶段是否存在计划、组织与合作能力尚难以确定[134]。不过,末次冰期开始之时有明显的证据表明存在长距离的精细原料的搬运[135],LSA 早段出现系统的季节性资源利用[136]。如果合作与信息交流有助于居住流动性与资源利用的计划安排,那么这可能会影响技术发明。

如果 MSA 或是旧石器中期的人类在其生活区域内高度流动,而且就其遇到的环境或资源了解甚少,那么含有耐用、可靠或可维护工具的通用工具组合就将

十分必要。与之相应,工具组合的多样性程度较低[137]。相对于许多(尽管不是所有的)LSA或旧石器时代晚期石器组合,MSA或旧石器时代中期石器组合类型多样性的确比较低,类似静湾遗址[138]的两面器工具相对耐用、灵活、可维护性好[139]。

如果外来石制品长距离搬运的出现能反映信息交流社交网络的发明,如果信息交流能够满足预计远距离外特定任务的所需的工具,那么专业化工具组合就可能形成。细石器工业中如琢背细石器与细石叶是相对细小、轻薄、脆弱但刃缘锋利的工具,它们是更专业化与更有效的复合工具的组成部分,这些工具更加复杂多样。其可替换性、可修复性以及轻小石叶部件的低携带成本可以补偿这些脆弱工具降低的可靠性。距今7万年前后末次冰期开始,环境恶化,风险提高,资源可预测性低,琢背细石器与细小石叶最早出现于霍韦森斯港以及东非与南非同时代的石器工业中。不过南部非洲末次冰期中段,MSA阶段3或4时,外来石制品的比例下降,表明南部非洲地区信息交流网络衰落。相反,东非MSA晚段外来原料的交换,以及可能的信息交流加强了[140]。整个MSA晚段琢背细石器持续存在,距今5万年真正的细石器技术取代了MSA/LSA工业。

四、讨论与结论

上文评述的几种细石器工业起源的假说,部分相互补充,极少数相互矛盾。环境的、社会的、技术的因素可能都影响了细石器工业的起源。琢背细石器至少在距今7万年出现于南部与东部非洲MSA石器工业中。这些遗址兼有MSA(尖状器、放射状打片石核、修理台面)与LSA(琢背细石器、小石叶、砸击打片技术)的技术特征。真正具有细石器性质的LSA工业在距今4至5万年前出现于热带非洲,东部非洲可能是最早的。非本地产精细原料比例的增加正好与这些技术发明同时,或者说开启了这些技术发明。精细原料的获取一方面通过扩大区域的搜寻,末次冰期时,地表生产力降低,人群的生活区域扩大;另一方面通过贸易与互惠交换体系,就像卡拉哈里沙漠中的桑人狩猎采集者中所见到的。某些工业的细石器化(如霍韦森斯港MSA)可能是一种针对石器原料力学属性的反应,这些原料便于生产薄石叶。在相互依赖与基于延后互惠的社会体系中,它也有利于生产具有象征含义的工具[141]。距今5万年,细石器技术的进一步发展可能受到外来精细原料减少的刺激:细石器技术可以节约外来的精细原料,同时礼物交换同盟中非实用的装饰品部分取得了石制品的地位。

与MSA或旧石器时代中期的前身相比,细石器技术相对多样、专业化,也更脆弱。末次冰期早期,人类计划与预测事务的能力提高,地区合作与信息分享的社会体系形成,这进一步促进了发展专业化工具组合的能力。细石器技术的发明可能反映一种技术需求的转换,从 MSA 或旧石器时代中期的"样样通"(但无一精)式的工具发展到 LSA 或旧石器时代晚期专精的工具。

晚更新世细石器与石叶技术的起源与现代人的行为起源密切相关[142]。欧洲旧石器时代中期晚段非本地产石器原料的比例跟早段相比微不足道[143],欧亚大陆西部地区琢背细石器与细石器工业的出现不早于距今 4.7 万年[144],可能是欧洲莫斯特工业的最后阶段(阿舍利传统 B 类型的莫斯特)[145]。因此,非洲末次冰期遗址中所看到的石料资源利用形式与石器技术不可能来自旧大陆其他地区,而是本地起源的。本文及其他文章讨论的证据都表明行为上现代的技术与社会信息分享体系都起源于赤道非洲地区[146]。

石料来源距离的证据表明,MSA 早段以及晚期尼安德特人群体之间超出每年活动范围之外的关系并不密切。宏观区域水平上地区采食群体之间稀少的相互关联意味着社会地域组织与群体间关系更接近于灵长类的群体,而非人类的群体。末次冰期开始,环境条件恶化,这形成特别强大的选择压力,促进地区人类群体间社交网络的形成。互惠式的社会安全体系的形成与动物群体向人类群体关系的过渡是现代人类行为演化的重要发明。它们可能有利于现代人类扩散,走出非洲,在欧亚大陆地区末次冰期时取代当代古老的人种。

线粒体与核 DNA 研究显示,距今约 4 万至 7.5 万年现代人不断扩张,走出非洲[147]。撒哈拉以南非洲地区现代人技术的发明是人口扩张的主要动力之一[148]。所有不见于非洲的线粒体与核 DNA 联系都是在距今约 5 万至 7.5 万年分化形成的[149]。遗传学的证据表明最早迁出非洲的人口存在两个地理瓶颈,形成于距今约 7.5 万年后:一个是西奈半岛到西亚与欧洲的瓶颈;另一个是红海南端到澳亚地区亚丁湾海峡的瓶颈[150]。氧同位素第 3 阶段非洲之外人口的增长可能就来自人口扩散,走出非洲的人类进入欧亚大陆的新栖居地。

社会与技术上的创新提高了人类的适应水平,同时也提高了非洲 MSA 晚段与 LSA 高风险的冰期环境的相对人口承载力,可能也促进了非洲地区人口的增长[151]。东非地区早在距今 5 万年前,LSA 与 MSA/LSA 过渡阶段工业的起源支持非洲末次冰期之初技术发明促进人口扩张假说[152]。赤道非洲可能是这次人口辐射的源头地区,因为它可能是末次冰期严酷气候中的避难所[153]。

延后互惠社会体系的出现与精细原料的交流相关,有助于琢背细石器与细石器技术的发展。社会风险缓冲体系加强,与社会团结与高效的石器技术发展相辅相成,进而促进了非洲的人口增长、现代人走出非洲以及现代人替代欧亚大陆的古老人类群体。

注释：

[1] Bar-Yosef, O., and S. L. Kuhn. The Big Deal about Blades: Laminar Technologies and Human Evolution. *American Anthropologist* 101: 322 – 338, 1999.

Conard, N. Laminar Lithic Assemblages from the Last Interglacial Complex in Northwestern Europe. *Journal of Anthropological Research* 46: 243 – 262, 1990.

[2] McBrearty, S., and A. S. Brooks. The Revolution That Wasn't: A New Interpretation of the Origin of Modern Human Behavior. *Journal of Human Evolution* 39: 453 – 563, 2000.

[3] Ambrose, S. H. Chronology of the Later Stone Age and Food Production in East Africa. *Journal of Archaeological Science* 25: 377 – 392, 1998a. Late Pleistocene Human Population Bottlenecks, Volcanic Winter, and the Differentiation of Modern Humans. *Journal of Human Evolution* 34: 623 – 651, 1998b.

Lahr, M., and R. Foley. Multiple Dispersals and Modern Human Origins. *Evolutionary Anthropology* 3: 48 – 60, 1994.

Stringer, C., and P. Andrews Volman, T. Genetic and Fossil Evidence for the Origin of Modern Humans. *Science* 239: 1263 – 1268, 1988.

[4] Ambrose, S. H. Chronology of the Later Stone Age and Food Production in East Africa. *Journal of Archaeological Science* 25: 377 – 392, 1998a. Late Pleistocene Human Population Bottlenecks, Volcanic Winter, and the Differentiation of Modern Humans. *Journal of Human Evolution* 34: 623 – 651, 1998b.

Harpending, H. C., S. T. Sherry, A. L. Rogers, and M. Stoneking. The Genetic Structure of Ancient Human Populations. *Current Anthropology* 34: 483 – 496, 1993.

Klein, R. G. Anatomy, Behavior, and Modern Human Origins. *Journal of World Prehistory* 9: 167 – 198, 1995.

Klein, R. G. Milo, K. M. Stewart, W. S. Downey, and N. J. Steven. Archaeology, Paleoenvironment, and Chronology of the Tsodilo Hills White Paintings Rock Shelter, Northwest Kalahari Desert, Botswana. *Journal of Archaeological Science* 27: 1085 – 1113, 2000.

Sherry, S., A. R. Rogers, H. Harpending, H. Soodyall, T. Jenkins, and M. Stoneking. Mismatch Distributions of mtDNA Reveal Recent Human Population Expansions. *Human Biology* 66: 761 – 775, 1994.

[5] Ambrose, S. H., and K. G. Lorenz. Social and Ecological Models for the Middle Stone Age in

Southern Africa. In *The Emergence of Modern Humans*. P. A. Mellars, ed. Pp. 3 – 33. Edinburgh: Edinburgh University Press, 1990.

Deacon, H. J. Southern Africa and Modern Human Origins. *Philosophical Transactions of the Royal Society*, London B337: 177 – 183, 1992.

Deacon, H. J., and S, J. D. Wurz. Klasies River Main Site, Cave 2: A Howiesons Poort Occurrence. In *Aspects of African Archaeology*. G. Pwiti and R. Soper, eds. Pp. 213 – 218. Harare: University of Zimbabwe Publications, 1996.

[6] Ambrose, S. H. Chronology of the Later Stone Age and Food Production in East Africa. *Journal of Archaeological Science* 25: 377 – 392, 1998a.

[7] Kaufman, D. A Proposed Method for Distinguishing between Blades and Bladelets. *Lithic Technology* 15: 34 – 40, 1986.

Wurz, S. The Howiesons Poort at Klasies River: From Artifacts to Cognition. M. A. thesis, Department of Anthropology, University of Stellenbosch, Stellenbosch, South Africa, 1997.

[8] Ambrose, S. H. Holocene Environments and Human Adaptations in the Central Rift Valley, Kenya. Ph. D. dissertation, Department of Anthropology, University of California, Berkeley, 1984a. The Introduction of Pastoral Adaptations to the Central Highlands of East Africa. In *From Hunters to Farmers: Considerations of the Causes and Consequences of Food Production in Africa*. J. D. Clark and S. A. Brandt, eds. Pp. 212 – 239. Berkeley: University of California Press, 1984b.

Ambrose, S. H., F. Hivernel, and C. M. Nelson. The Taxonomic Status of the Kenya Capsian. In *Proceedings of the Eighth Pan-African Congress of Prehistory and Quaternary Studies*. B. A. Ogot and R. E. Leakey, eds. Pp. 248 – 252. Nairobi: International Louis Leakey Memorial Institute for Prehistory and Paleontology, 1980.

[9] Ambrose, S. H. Holocene Environments and Human Adaptations in the Central Rift Valley, Kenya. Ph. D. dissertation, Pp. 277 – 278. Department of Anthropology, University of California, Berkeley, 1984a.

[10] Ambrose, S. The Introduction of Pastoral Adaptations to the Central Highlands of East Africa. In *From Hunters to Farmers: Considerations of the Causes and Consequences of Food Production in Africa*. J. D. Clark and S. A. Brandt, eds. Pp. 212 – 239. Berkeley: University of California Press, 1984b. Excavations at Masai Gorge Rock Shelter, Naivasha. *Azania* 20: 29 – 67, 1985.

[11] Ambrose, S. H. Holocene Environments and Human Adaptations in the Central Rift Valley, Kenya. Ph. D. dissertation, Department of Anthropology, University of California, Berkeley. 1984a.

[12] Cornelissen, E. Shum Laka (Cameroon): Late Pleistocene and Early Holocene Deposits. In

Aspects of African Archaeology. G. Pwiti and R. Soper, eds. Pp. 257 – 263. Harare: University of Zimbabwe Publications, 1996.

de Maret, P., B. Clist, and W. van Neer. Resultats des premiers fouilles dans les abris de Shum Laka et d'Abeke. L'Anthropologie 91: 559 – 584, 1997.

[13] Van Noten, F. Excavations at Munyama Cave. Antiquity 45: 56 – 58, 1971.

[14] Beaumont, P. B., H. de Villiers, and J. C. Vogel. Modern Man in Sub-Saharan Africa prior to 49 000 years B. P.: A Review and Evaluation with Particular Reference to Border Cave. South African Journal of Science 74: 409 – 419, 1978.

[15] Kyule, M. D., S. H. Ambrose, M. P. Noll, and J. L. Atkinson. Pliocene and Pleistocene Sites in Southern Narok District, Southwest Kenya. Journal of Human Evolution 32(4): A9 – 10, 1997.

[16] Ambrose, S. H. Chronology of the Later Stone Age and Food Production in East Africa. Journal of Archaeological Science 25: 377 – 392, 1998a.

Leakey, M. D., R. L. Hay, R. Thurber, R. Protsch, and R. Berger. Stratigraphy, Archaeology, and Age of the Ndutu and Naisiusiu Beds, Olduvai Gorge, Tanzania. World Archaeology 3: 328 – 341, 1972.

Mehlman, M. J. Late Quaternary Archaeological Sequences in Northern Tanzania. Ph. D. dissertation, Department of Anthropology, University of Illinois, Urbana, 1989.

Context for the Emergence of Modern Man in Eastern Africa: Some New Tanzanian Evidence. In *Cultural Beginnings*. J. D. Clark, ed. Pp. 177 – 196. Bonn: Dr. Rudolf Habelt GMBH, 1991.

[17] Singer, R., and J. Wymer. *The Middle Stone Age at Klasies River Mouth in South Africa*. Chicago: University of Chicago Press, 1982.

Wurz, S. The Howiesons Poort at Klasies River: From Artifacts to Cognition. M. A. thesis, Department of Anthropology, University of Stellenbosch, Stellenbosch, South Africa, 1997.

[18] Mehlman, M. J. Late Quaternary Archaeological Sequences in Northern Tanzania. Ph. D. dissertation, Department of Anthropology, University of Illinois, Urbana, 1989.

[19] Wurz, S. The Howiesons Poort at Klasies River: From Artifacts to Cognition. M. A. thesis, Department of Anthropology, University of Stellenbosch, Stellenbosch, South Africa, 1997.

[20] Ambrose, S. H. Holocene Environments and Human Adaptations in the Central Rift Valley, Kenya. Ph. D. dissertation, Department of Anthropology, University of California, Berkeley, 1984a. The Introduction of Pastoral Adaptations to the Central Highlands of East Africa. In *From Hunters to Farmers: Considerations of the Causes and Consequences of Food Production in Africa*. J. D. Clark and S. A. Brandt, eds. Pp. 212 – 239. Berkeley: University of California Press, 1984b. Excavations at Masai Gorge Rock Shelter, Naivasha. Azania 20:

29 - 67, 1985.

[21] Inizan, M.-L., M. Reduron-Ballinger, H. Roche, and J. Tixier. *Technology and Terminology of Knapped Stone*. Prehistoire de la Pierre Taillee, Tome 5. Nanterre: CREP, 1999.

[22] Volman, T. Early Prehistory and Paleoenvironments in South-ern Africa. In *Paleoenvironments*. R. G. Klein, ed. Pp. 169 - 220. Rotterdam: Balkema, 1984.

[23] Deino, A., and S. McBrearty. 40Ar/39Ar Chronology for the Kapthurin Formation, Baringo, Kenya. *Journal of Human Evolution* 42: 1 - 10, 2002.

McBrearty, S. The Archaeology of the Kapthurin Formation. In *Late Cenozoic Environments and Hominid Evolution: A Tribute to Bill Bishop*. P. Andrews and P. Banham, eds. Pp. 143 - 156. London: The Geological Society. 1999.

McBrearty, S., and A. S. Brooks. The Revolution That Wasn't: A New Interpretation of the Origin of Modern Human Behavior. *Journal of Human Evolution* 39: 453 - 563. 2000.

[24] Jelinek, A. J. The Amudian in the Context of the Mugharan Tradition at the Tabun Cave (Mount Carmel), Israel. In *The Emergence of Modern Humans*. P. A. Mellars, ed. Pp. 81 - 90. Edinburgh: Edinburgh University Press, 1990.

Mercier, N., H. Valladas, G. Valladas, J.-L. Reyss, A. Jelinek, L. Meignen, and J.-L. Joron. TL Dates of Burnt Flints from Jelinek's Excavations at Tabun and Their Implications. *Journal of Archaeological Science* 22: 495 - 509, 1995.

Weinstein-Evron, M., A. Tsatskin, N. Porat, and J. Kronfeld. A 230 Th / 234U Date for the Acheulo-Yabrudian Layer in the Jamal Cave, Mt. Carmel, Israel. *South African Journal of Science* 95: 186 - 188, 1999.

[25] Volman, T. Early Prehistory and Paleoenvironments in South-ern Africa. In *Paleoenvironments*. R. G. Klein, ed. Pp. 169 - 220. Rotterdam: Balkema, 1984.

[26] Bar-Yosef, O., and S. L. Kuhn. The Big Deal about Blades: Laminar Technologies and Human Evolution. *American Anthropologist* 101: 322 - 338, 1999.

[27] Singer, R., and J. Wymer. *The Middle Stone Age at Klasies River Mouth in South Africa*. Chicago: University of Chicago Press, 1982.

Volman, T. Early Prehistory and Paleoenvironments in South-ern Africa. In *Paleoenvironments*. R. G. Klein, ed. Pp. 169 - 220. Rotterdam: Balkema, 1984.

[28] Griin, R., J. S. Brink, N. A. Spooner, L. Taylor, C. B. Stringer, R. G. Franciscus, and A. S. Murray. Direct Dating of Florisbad Hominid. *Nature* 382: 500 - 501, 1996.

[29] Henshilwood, C. S., F. d'Errico, R. Yates, Z. Jacobs, C. Tribolo, G. A. T. Duller, N. Mercier, J. C. Sealy, H. Valladas, I. Watts, and A. G. Wintle. Emergence of Modern Human Behavior: Middle Stone Age Engravings from South Africa. *Science* 295: 1278 - 1280, 2002.

[30] Evans, U. Hollow Rock Shelter: A Middle Stone Age Site in the Cedarberg. *Southern African*

Field Archaeology 3: 63 – 72, 1994.

Henshilwood, C. S., J. C. Sealy, R. Yates, K. Cruz-Uribe, P. Goldberg, F. E. Grine, R. G. Klein, C. Poggenpoel, K. van Neikerk, and I. Watts. Blombos Cave, Southern Cape, South Africa: Preliminary Report on the 1992 – 1999 Excavation of the Middle Stone Age Levels. *Journal of Archaeological Science* 28: 421 – 448, 2001.

Emergence of Modern Human Behavior: Middle Stone Age Engravings from South Africa. *Science* 295: 1278 – 1280, 2002.

Watts, I. The Origin of Symbolic Culture. In *The Evolution of Culture*. R. Dunbar, C. Night, and C. Power, eds. Pp. 113 – 146. Edinburgh: Edinburgh University Press, 1999.

[31] Deacon, H. J. Two Late Pleistocene-Holocene Archaeological Depositories from the Southern Cape, South Africa. *South African Archaeological Bulletin* 50: 121 – 131. Deacon, H. J., and J. Deacon, 1995.

Singer, R., and J. Wymer. *The Middle Stone Age at Klasies River Mouth in South Africa*. Chicago: University of Chicago Press, 1982.

Thackeray, A. I. The Middle Stone Age South of the Limpopo River. *Journal of World Prehistory* 6: 385 – 440, 1992.

Middle Stone Age Artifacts from the 1993 and 1995 Excavations of Die Kelders Cave 1, South Africa. *Journal of Human Evolution* 38: 147 – 168, 2000.

Volman, T. Early Prehistory and Paleoenvironments in South-ern Africa. In *Paleoenvironments*. R. G. Klein, ed. Pp. 169 – 220. Rotterdam: Balkema, 1984.

[32] Clark, A. M. B. The Final Middle Stone Age at Rose Cottage Cave: A Distinct Industry in the Basutolian Ecozone. *South African Journal of Science* 93: 449 – 458, 1997.

Late Pleistocene Technology at Rose Cottage Cave: A Search for Modern Behavior in an MSA Context. *African Archaeological Review* 16: 93 – 119, 1999.

[33] Goodwin, A. J. H. An Introduction to the Middle Stone Age of South Africa. *South African Journal of Science* 25: 410 – 418, 1928.

Goodwin, A. J. H., and C. Van Riet Lowe. The Stone Age Cultures of South Africa. *Annals of the South African Museum* 27: 1 – 289, 1929.

[34] Clark, A. M. B. The Final Middle Stone Age at Rose Cottage Cave: A Distinct Industry in the Basutolian Ecozone. *South African Journal of Science* 93: 449 – 458, 1997.

[35] Beaumont, P. B., H. de Villiers, and J. C. Vogel. Modern Man in Sub-Saharan Africa prior to 49 000 years B. P.: A Review and Evaluation with Particular Reference to Border Cave. *South African Journal of Science* 74: 409 – 419, 1978.

Miller, G. H., P. B. Beaumont, A. J. T. Jull, and B. Johnson. Pleistocene Geochronology and Paleothermometry from Protein Diagenesis of Ostrich Eggshells: Implications for the

Evolution of Modern Humans. *Philosophical Transactions of the Royal Society*, London B337: 149 – 157, 1992. Miller, G. H., P. B. Beaumont, H. J. Deacon, A. S. Brooks, P. E. Hare, and A. J. T. Jull. Earliest Modern Humans in Southern Africa Dated by lsoleucine Epimerization in Ostrich Eggshell. *Quaternary Science Reviews* 18: 1537 – 1548, 1999.

[36] Ambrose, S. H., and K. G. Lorenz. Social and Ecological Models for the Middle Stone Age in Southern Africa. In *The Emergence of Modern Humans*. P. A. Mellars, ed. Pp. 3 – 33. Edinburgh: Edinburgh University Press, 1990.

Deacon, J. Later Stone Age Peoples and Their Descendants in Southern Africa. In *Southern African Prehistory and Paleoenvironments*. R. G. Klein, ed. Pp. 221 – 328. Rotterdam: Balkema, 1984.

[37] Deacon, J. Later Stone Age Peoples and Their Descendants in Southern Africa. In *Southern African Prehistory and Paleoenvironments*. R. G. Klein, ed. Pp. 221 – 328. Rotterdam: Balkema, 1984.

[38] Deacon, J. Later Stone Age Peoples and Their Descendants in Southern Africa. In *Southern African Prehistory and Paleoenvironments*. R. G. Klein, ed. Pp. 221 – 328. Rotterdam: Balkema, 1984.

Sampson, C. G. *The Stone Age Archaeology of Southern Africa*. New York: Academic Press, 1974.

[39] Goodwin, A. J. H., and C. Van Riet Lowe. The Stone Age Cultures of South Africa. *Annals of the South African Museum* 27: 1 – 289, 1929.

[40] Deacon, J. Later Stone Age Peoples and Their Descendants in Southern Africa. In *Southern African Prehistory and Paleoenvironments*. R. G. Klein, ed. Pp. 221 – 328. Rotterdam: Balkema, 1984.

Deacon, H. J., and J. Deacon. *Human Beginnings in South Africa*. Cape Town: David Philip, 1999.

Sampson, C. G. *The Stone Age Archaeology of Southern Africa*. New York: Academic Press, 1974.

[41] Deacon, J. Later Stone Age Peoples and Their Descendants in Southern Africa. In *Southern African Prehistory and Paleoenvironments*. R. G. Klein, ed. Pp. 221 – 328. Rotterdam: Balkema, 1984.

Humphreys, A. B. J. Comments on Aspects of Raw Material Usage in the Later Stone Age of the Orange River Area. *South African Archaeological Society*, *Goodwin Series* 1: 46 – 53, 1972.

[42] Robbins, L. H., M. L. Murphy, G. A. Brook, A. H. Ivester, A. C. Campbell, R. G. Klein, R. G. Milo, K. M. Stewart, W. S. Downey, and N. J. Steven. Archaeology,

Paleoenvironment, and Chronology of the Tsodilo Hills White Paintings Rock Shelter, Northwest Kalahari Desert, Botswana. *Journal of Archaeological Science* 27: 1085 – 1113, 2000.

[43] Brooks, A. S., and P. T. Robertshaw. The Glacial Maximum in Tropical Africa: 22 000 to 12 000 BP. In *The World at 18 000 BP*, Vol. 2: *Low Latitudes*. C. Gamble and O. Soffer, eds. Pp. 121 – 169. London: Unwin Hyman, 1990.

[44] Clark, J. D. The Middle Stone Age in East Africa and the Beginnings of Regional Identity. *Journal of World Prehistory* 2: 235 – 305, 1988.

[45] Brooks, A. S., and P. T. Robertshaw. The Glacial Maximum in Tropical Africa: 22 000 to 12 000 BP. In *The World at 18 000 BP*, Vol. 2: *Low Latitudes*. C. Gamble and O. Soffer, eds. Pp. 121 – 169. London: Unwin Hyman, 1990.

[46] McBrearty, S., and A. S. Brooks. The Revolution That Wasn't: A New Interpretation of the Origin of Modern Human Behavior. *Journal of Human Evolution* 39: 453 – 563. 2000.

[47] Ambrose, S. H. Chronology of the Later Stone Age and Food Production in East Africa. *Journal of Archaeological Science* 25: 377 – 392, 1998a.

[48] Ambrose, S. H. Chronology of the Later Stone Age and Food Production in East Africa. *Journal of Archaeological Science* 25: 377 – 392, 1998a.

[49] Clark, J. D. The Middle Stone Age in East Africa and the Beginnings of Regional Identity. *Journal of World Prehistory* 2: 235 – 305, 1988.

[50] Ambrose, S. H., A. Deino, M. D. Kyule, 1. Steele, and M. A. J. Williams. The Emergence of Modern Human Behavior during the Late Middle Stone Age in the Kenya Rift Valley. *Journal of Human Evolution* 42(3): A3 – 4, 2002.

Merrick, H. V., and F. H. Brown. Obsidian Sources and Patterns of Source Utilization in Kenya and Northern Tanzania: Some Initial Findings. *African Archaeological Review* 2: 129 – 152, 1984.

Merrick, H. V., F. H. Brown, and W. P. Nash. Use and Movement of Obsidian in the Early and Middle Stone Ages of Kenya and Northern Tanzania. In *Society, Culture, and Technology in Africa*. S. T. Childs, ed. MASCA 11(supplement): 29 – 44, 1994.

[51] Mehlman, M. J. Late Quaternary Archaeological Sequences in Northern Tanzania. Ph. D. dissertation, Department of Anthropology, University of Illinois, Urbana, 1989.

Merrick, H. V., and F. H. Brown. Obsidian Sources and Patterns of Source Utilization in Kenya and Northern Tanzania: Some Initial Findings. *African Archaeological Review* 2: 129 – 152, 1984.

[52] Mehlman, M. J. Late Quaternary Archaeological Sequences in Northern Tanzania. Ph. D. dissertation, Department of Anthropology, University of Illinois, Urbana, 1989.

Context for the Emergence of Modern Man in Eastern Africa: Some New Tanzanian Evidence. In *Cultural Beginnings*. J. D. Clark, ed. Pp. 177 – 196. Bonn: Dr. Rudolf Habelt GMBH, 1991.

[53] McBrearty, S., and A. S. Brooks. The Revolution That Wasn't: A New Interpretation of the Origin of Modern Human Behavior. *Journal of Human Evolution* 39: 453 – 563, 2000.

Mehlman, M. J. Late. Context for the Emergence of Modern Man in Eastern Africa: Some New Tanzanian Evidence. In *Cultural Beginnings*. J. D. Clark, ed. Pp. 177 – 196. Bonn: Dr. Rudolf Habelt GMBH, 1991.

[54] Mehlman, M. J. Late Quaternary Archaeological Sequences in Northern Tanzania. Ph. D. dissertation, Department of Anthropology, University of Illinois, Urbana, 1989.

Context for the Emergence of Modern Man in Eastern Africa: Some New Tanzanian Evidence. In *Cultural Beginnings*. J. D. Clark, ed. Pp. 177 – 196. Bonn: Dr. Rudolf Habelt GMBH, 1991.

[55] Leakey, M. D., R. L. Hay, R. Thurber, R. Protsch, and R. Berger. Stratigraphy, Archaeology, and Age of the Ndutu and Naisiusiu Beds, Olduvai Gorge, Tanzania. *World Archaeology* 3: 328 – 341, 1972.

[56] Ambrose, S. H. Preparation and Characterization of Bone and Tooth Collagen for Isotopic Analysis. *Journal of Archaeological Science* 17: 431 – 451, 1990.

[57] Manega, P. C. Geochronology, Geochemistry, and Isotopic Study of the Plio-Pleistocene Hominid Sites and the Ngorongoro Volcanic Highland in Northern Tanzania. Ph. D. dissertation, Department of Anthropology, University of Colorado, Boulder, 1993.

[58] Leakey, M. D., R. L. Hay, R. Thurber, R. Protsch, and R. Berger. Stratigraphy, Archaeology, and Age of the Ndutu and Naisiusiu Beds, Olduvai Gorge, Tanzania. *World Archaeology* 3: 328 – 341, 1972.

Merrick, H. V. Change in Later Pleistocene Lithic Industries in Eastern Africa. Ph. D. dissertation, Department of Anthropology, University of California, Berkeley, 1975.

[59] Merrick, H. V., and F. H. Brown. Obsidian Sources and Patterns of Source Utilization in Kenya and Northern Tanzania: Some Initial Findings. *African Archaeological Review* 2: 129 – 152, 1984.

[60] Michels, J. W., I. Tsong, and L. M. Nelson. Obsidian Dating and East African Archaeology. *Science* 219: 361 – 366, 1983.

[61] Bonnefille, R., J. J. Roeland, and J. Guiot. Temperature and Rainfall Estimates for the Past 40 000 Years in Equatorial Africa. *Nature* 346: 347 – 349, 1990.

Schroeder, R. A., and J. L. Bada. Glacial-Postglacial Temperature Differences Deduced from Aspartic Acid Racemization in Fossil Bones. *Science* 182: 479 – 482, 1973.

[62] Merrick, H. V. Change in Later Pleistocene Lithic Industries in Eastern Africa. Ph. D. dissertation, Department of Anthropology, University of California, Berkeley, 1975.

[63] Merrick, H. V., F. H. Brown, and W. P. Nash. Use and Movement of Obsidian in the Early and Middle Stone Ages of Kenya and Northern Tanzania. In *Society, Culture, and Technology in Africa*. S. T. Childs, ed. MASCA 11(supplement): 29 – 44, 1994.

[64] Ambrose, S. H. Chronology of the Later Stone Age and Food Production in East Africa. *Journal of Archaeological Science* 25: 377 – 392, 1998a.

[65] Ambrose, S. H. Middle and Later Stone Age Settlement Patterns in the Central Rift Valley, Kenya: Comparisons and Contrasts. In *Settlement Dynamics of the Middle Paleolithic and Middle Stone Age*. N. Conard, ed. Pp. 21 – 43. Tubingen: Kerns Verlag, 2001a.

[66] Ambrose, S. H. Chronology of the Later Stone Age and Food Production in East Africa. *Journal of Archaeological Science* 25: 377 – 392, 1998a.

[67] Ambrose, S. H. Chronology of the Later Stone Age and Food Production in East Africa. *Journal of Archaeological Science* 25: 377 – 392, 1998a.

[68] Bovwer, J. R. F., C. M. Nelson, A. F. Waibel, and S. Wandibba. The University of Massachusetts' Later Stone Age/Pastoral Neolithic Comparative Study in Central Kenya: An Overview. *Azania* 12: 119 – 146, 1977.

Merrick, H. V. Change in Later Pleistocene Lithic Industries in Eastern Africa. Ph. D. dissertation, Department of Anthropology, University of California, Berkeley, 1975.

[69] Ambrose, S. H. Holocene Environments and Human Adaptations in the Central Rift Valley, Kenya. Ph. D. dissertation, Department of Anthropology, University of California, Berkeley, 1984a.

Chronology of the Later Stone Age and Food Production in East Africa. *Journal of Archaeological Science* 25: 377 – 392, 1998a.

Gramly, R. M. Upper Pleistocene Archaeological Occurrences at Site GvJm/22, Lukenya Hill, Kenya. *Man* 11: 319 – 344, 1976.

Merrick, H. V. Change in Later Pleistocene Lithic Industries in Eastern Africa. Ph. D. dissertation, Department of Anthropology, University of California, Berkeley, 1975.

Miller, S. F. Lukenya Hill, GvJm46, Excavation Report. *Nyame Akuma* 14: 31 – 34, 1979.

Van Noten, F. Excavations at Munyama Cave. *Antiquity* 45: 56 – 58, 1971.

[70] Ambrose, S. H., A. Deino, M. D. Kyule, 1. Steele, and M. A. J. Williams. The Emergence of Modern Human Behavior during the Late Middle Stone Age in the Kenya Rift Valley. *Journal of Human Evolution* 42(3): A3 – 4, 2002.

[71] Ambrose, S. H. Middle and Later Stone Age Settlement Patterns in the Central Rift Valley, Kenya: Comparisons and Contrasts. In *Settlement Dynamics of the Middle Paleolithic and*

Middle Stone Age. N. Conard, ed. Pp. 21 - 43. Tubingen: Kerns Verlag, 2001a.

[72] Robbins, L. H., M. L. Murphy, G. A. Brook, A. H. Ivester, A. C. Campbell, R. G. Klein, R. G. Milo, K. M. Stewart, W. S. Downey, and N. J. Steven. Archaeology, Paleoenvironment, and Chronology of the Tsodilo Hills White Paintings Rock Shelter, Northwest Kalahari Desert, Botswana. *Journal of Archaeological Science* 27: 1085 - 1113, 2000.

[73] Deacon, H. J. Two Late Pleistocene-Holocene Archaeological Depositories from the Southern Cape, South Africa. *South African Archaeological Bulletin* 50: 121 - 131. Deacon, H. J., and J. Deacon, 1995.

[74] Beaumont, P. B., H. de Villiers, and J. C. Vogel. Modern Man in Sub-Saharan Africa prior to 49 000 years B. P.: A Review and Evaluation with Particular Reference to Border Cave. *South African Journal of Science* 74: 409 - 419, 1978.

Miller, G. H., P. B. Beaumont, A. J. T. Jull, and B. Johnson. Pleistocene Geochronology and Paleothermometry from Protein Diagenesis of Ostrich Eggshells: Implications for the Evolution of Modern Humans. *Philosophical Transactions of the Royal Society*, London B337: 149 - 157, 1992.

[75] Deacon, J. An Annotated List of Radiocarbon Dates for Sub-Saharan Africa. *Annals of the Cape Provincial Museum* 5: 5 - 84, 1966.

Inskeep, R. The Age of the Kondoa Rock Paintings in Light of Recent Excavations at Kisese II Rock Shelter. In *Actes du IVe Congres Panafricain de Prehistoire et de l'Etude du Quaternaire*. G. Mortelmans and J. Nenquin, eds. Pp. 249 - 256. Tervuren: Musee Royal de L'Afrique Central, Belgique, 1962.

[76] Ambrose, S. Chronology of the Later Stone Age and Food Production in East Africa. *Journal of Archaeological Science* 25: 377 - 392, 1998a.

[77] McBrearty, S., and A. S. Brooks. The Revolution That Wasn't: A New Interpretation of the Origin of Modern Human Behavior. *Journal of Human Evolution* 39: 453 - 563, 2000.

Mehlman, M. J. Late Quaternary Archaeological Sequences in Northern Tanzania. Ph. D. dissertation, Department of Anthropology, University of Illinois, Urbana, 1989.

[78] Anderson-Gerfaud, P. Aspects of Behavior in the Middle Paleolithic: Functional Analysis of Stone Tools from Southwest France. In *The Emergence of Modern Humans*. P. A. Mellars, ed. Pp. 389 - 418. Edinburgh: Edinburgh University Press, 1990.

Beyries, S. Quelques examples de stigmates d'emmanchements observez sur des outils du Paleolithique Moyen. In *La main et l'outil: manches et emmanchements prehistoriques*. D. Stordeur, ed. Pp. 57 - 62. Travaux de la Maison de l'Orient No. 15, Lyon, 1987.

Variability de l'industrie lithique au Mouste'rien: approche functionelle sur quelques gisements

[79] Ambrose, S. Chronology of the Later Stone Age and Food Production in East Africa. *Journal of Archaeological Science* 25: 377 – 392, 1998a.

Boeda, E., J. Connan, D. Dessort, S. Muhesen, N. Mercier, H. Valladas, and N. Tisnerat. Bitumen as a Hafting Material on Middle Paleolithic Artifacts. *Nature* 380: 336 – 338, 1996.

[80] McBrearty, S., and A. S. Brooks. The Revolution That Wasn't: A New Interpretation of the Origin of Modern Human Behavior. *Journal of Human Evolution* 39: 453 – 563, 2000.

[81] Clark, J. D. The Origins and Spread of Modern Humans: A Broad Perspective on the African Evidence. In *The Human Revolution: Behavioral and Biological Perspectives on the Origin of Modern Humans*. P. Mellars and C. Stringer, eds. Pp. 565 – 588. Edinburgh: Edinburgh University Press, 1989.

African and Asian Perspectives on the Origins of Modern Humans. *Philosophical Transactions of the Royal Society*, London B337: 201 – 215, 1992.

[82] Ambrose, S. H. Paleolithic Technology and Human Evolution. *Science* 291: 1748 – 1753, 2001b.

Wurz, S. The Middle Stone Age at Klasies River Mouth. Ph. D. dissertation, Department of Anthropology, University of Stellenbosch, Stellenbosch, South Africa, 2000.

[83] Clark, J. D. Interpretations of Prehistoric Technology from Ancient Egyptian and Other Sources. Part II: Prehistoric Arrow Forms in Africa as Shown by Surviving Examples of Traditional Arrows of the San Bushmen. *Paleorient* 3: 127 – 150, 1977.

[84] Clark, J. D. Interpretations of Prehistoric Technology from Ancient Egyptian and Other Sources. Part II: Prehistoric Arrow Forms in Africa as Shown by Surviving Examples of Traditional Arrows of the San Bushmen. *Paleorient* 3: 127 – 150, 1977.

Clark, J. D., J. L. Phillips, and P. S. Staley. Interpretations of Prehistoric Technology from Ancient Egyptian and Other Sources. Part 1: Ancient Egyptian Bows and Arrows and Their Relevance for African Prehistory. *Paleorient* 2: 323 – 388, 1974.

[85] Deacon, H. J. Southern Africa and Modern Human Origins. *Philosophical Transactions of the Royal Society*, London B337: 177 – 183, 1992.

[86] Clark, J. D. Interpretations of Prehistoric Technology from Ancient Egyptian and Other Sources. Part II: Prehistoric Arrow Forms in Africa as Shown by Surviving Examples of Traditional Arrows of the San Bushmen. *Paleorient* 3: 127 – 150, 1977.

[87] Phillipson, D. W. Some Speculations on the Beginning of Backed-Microlith Manufacture. In *Proceedings of the Eighth Pan-African Congress of Prehistory and Quaternary Studies*. B. A. Ogot and R. E. Leakey, eds. Pp. 229 – 230. Nairobi: The International Louis Leakey Memorial Institute for Prehistory and Paleontology, 1980.

[88] Klein, R. G. Environmental and Ecological Implications of Large Mammals from Upper Pleistocene and Holocene Sites in Southern Africa. *Annals of the South African Museum* 81: 223-283, 1980.

Leakey, M. D., R. L. Hay, R. Thurber, R. Protsch, and R. Berger. Stratigraphy, Archaeology, and Age of the Ndutu and Naisiusiu Beds, Olduvai Gorge, Tanzania. *World Archaeology* 3: 328-341, 1972.

Marean, C. W. Implications of Late Quaternary Mammalian Fauna from Lukenya Hill (South-Central Kenya) for Paleoenvironmental Change and Faunal Extinction. *Quaternary Research* 37: 239-255, 1992.

Mehlman, M. J. Late Quaternary Archaeological Sequences in Northern Tanzania. Ph. D. dissertation, Department of Anthropology, University of Illinois, Urbana, 1989.

[89] Deacon, H. J., and S, J. D. Wurz. Klasies River Main Site, Cave 2: A Howiesons Poort Occurrence. In *Aspects of African Archaeology*. G. Pwiti and R. Soper, eds. Pp. 216. Harare: University of Zimbabwe Publications, 1996.

[90] Wurz, S. The Howiesons Poort at Klasies River: From Artifacts to Cognition. M. A. thesis, Department of Anthropology, University of Stellenbosch, Stellenbosch, South Africa, 1997.
The Middle Stone Age at Klasies River Mouth. Ph. D. dissertation, Department of Anthropology, University of Stellenbosch, Stellenbosch, South Africa, 2000.

[91] Wurz, S. The Middle Stone Age at Klasies River Mouth. Ph. D. dissertation, Department of Anthropology, University of Stellenbosch, Stellenbosch, South Africa, 2000.

[92] Bordes, F., and D. Crabtree. The Corbiac Blade Technique and Other Experiments. *Tebiwa* 12: 1-21, 1969.

[93] Wurz, S. The Howiesons Poort at Klasies River: From Artifacts to Cognition. M. A. thesis, Department of Anthropology, University of Stellenbosch, Stellenbosch, South Africa, 1997.

[94] Wurz, S. The Middle Stone Age at Klasies River Mouth. Ph. D. dissertation, Department of Anthropology, University of Stellenbosch, Stellenbosch, South Africa, 2000.

[95] Wurz, S. The Howiesons Poort at Klasies River: From Artifacts to Cognition. M. A. thesis, Department of Anthropology, University of Stellenbosch, Stellenbosch, South Africa, 1997.
The Middle Stone Age at Klasies River Mouth. Ph. D. dissertation, Department of Anthropology, University of Stellenbosch, Stellenbosch, South Africa, 2000.

[96] Wurz, S. The Middle Stone Age at Klasies River Mouth. Ph. D. dissertation, Department of Anthropology, University of Stellenbosch, Stellenbosch, South Africa, 2000.

[97] Wurz, S. The Howiesons Poort at Klasies River: From Artifacts to Cognition. M. A. thesis, Department of Anthropology, University of Stellenbosch, Stellenbosch, South Africa, 1997.

[98] Singer, R., and J. Wymer. *The Middle Stone Age at Klasies River Mouth in South Africa.*

Chicago: University of Chicago Press, 1982.

Wurz, S. The Middle Stone Age at Klasies River Mouth. Ph. D. dissertation, Department of Anthropology, University of Stellenbosch, Stellenbosch, South Africa, 2000.

[99] Ambrose, S. H., and K. G. Lorenz. Social and Ecological Models for the Middle Stone Age in Southern Africa. In *The Emergence of Modern Humans*. P. A. Mellars, ed. Pp. 3 – 33. Edinburgh: Edinburgh University Press, 1990.

[100] Gamble, C. Exchange and Local Hominid Networks. In *Trade and Exchange in Prehistoric Europe*. C. Scarre and F. Healy, eds. Pp. 35 – 44. Oxbow Monographs 33. Oxford: Oxbow Books, 1993.

Gould, R. A., and S. Saggers. Lithic Procurement in Central Australia: A Closer Look at Binford's Idea of Embeddedness in Archaeology. *American Antiquity* 50: 117 – 136, 1985.

[101] Ambrose, S. H. Middle and Later Stone Age Settlement Patterns in the Central Rift Valley, Kenya: Comparisons and Contrasts. In *Settlement Dynamics of the Middle Paleolithic and Middle Stone Age*. N. Conard, ed. Pp. 21 – 43. Tubingen: Kerns Verlag, 2001a.

Ambrose, S. H., A. Deino, M. D. Kyule, 1. Steele, and M. A. J. Williams. The Emergence of Modern Human Behavior during the Late Middle Stone Age in the Kenya Rift Valley. *Journal of Human Evolution* 42(3): A3 – 4, 2002.

[102] Merrick, H. V., F. H. Brown, and W. P. Nash. Use and Movement of Obsidian in the Early and Middle Stone Ages of Kenya and Northern Tanzania. In *Society, Culture, and Technology in Africa*. S. T. Childs, ed. MASCA 11(supplement): 29 – 44, 1994.

[103] Michels, J. W., I. Tsong, and L. M. Nelson. Obsidian Dating and East African Archaeology. *Science* 219: 361 – 366, 1983.

[104] Merrick, H. V., F. H. Brown, and W. P. Nash. Use and Movement of Obsidian in the Early and Middle Stone Ages of Kenya and Northern Tanzania. In *Society, Culture, and Technology in Africa*. S. T. Childs, ed. MASCA 11(supplement): 29 – 44, 1994.

[105] Ambrose, S. H. Middle and Later Stone Age Settlement Patterns in the Central Rift Valley, Kenya: Comparisons and Contrasts. In *Settlement Dynamics of the Middle Paleolithic and Middle Stone Age*. N. Conard, ed. Pp. 21 – 43. Tubingen: Kerns Verlag, 2001a.

[106] Ambrose, S. H. Middle and Later Stone Age Settlement Patterns in the Central Rift Valley, Kenya: Comparisons and Contrasts. In *Settlement Dynamics of the Middle Paleolithic and Middle Stone Age*. N. Conard, ed. Pp. 21 – 43. Tubingen: Kerns Verlag, 2001a.

[107] Ambrose, S. H. Middle and Later Stone Age Settlement Patterns in the Central Rift Valley, Kenya: Comparisons and Contrasts. In *Settlement Dynamics of the Middle Paleolithic and Middle Stone Age*. N. Conard, ed. Pp. 21 – 43. Tubingen: Kerns Verlag, 2001a.

[108] Merrick, H. V. Change in Later Pleistocene Lithic Industries in Eastern Africa. Ph. D.

dissertation, Department of Anthropology, University of California, Berkeley, 1975.

Merrick, H. V., F. H. Brown, and W. P. Nash. Use and Movement of Obsidian in the Early and Middle Stone Ages of Kenya and Northern Tanzania. In *Society, Culture, and Technology in Africa*. S. T. Childs, ed. MASCA 11(supplement): 29–44, 1994.

[109] Ambrose, S. H. Middle and Later Stone Age Settlement Patterns in the Central Rift Valley, Kenya: Comparisons and Contrasts. In *Settlement Dynamics of the Middle Paleolithic and Middle Stone Age*. N. Conard, ed. Pp. 21–43. Tubingen: Kerns Verlag, 2001a.

[110] Marks, A. E. The Middle to Upper Paleolithic Transition in the Southern Levant: Technological Change as an Adaptation to Increasing Mobility. In *L hommede Neandertal, Vol. 8: La mutation*. J. K. Kozlowski, ed. Pp. 109–123. Etudes et Recherches Archeologiques de l'Universite de Liege, No. 35. Liege, 1988.

Marks, A. E., and D. A. Friedel. Prehistoric Settlement Patterns in the Avdat/Aqev Area. In *Prehistory and Paleoenvironments in the CentralNegev, Israel*, Vol. 2. A. E. Marks, ed. Pp. 35–60. Dallas: Southern Methodist University Press, 1977.

[111] Kuhn, S. L. A Formal Approach to the Design and Assembly of Mobile Toolkits. *American Antiquity* 59(3): 426–442, 1994.

[112] Barut, S. Middle and Later Stone Age Lithic Technology and Land Use in East African Savannas. *African Archaeological Review* 12: 43–72, 1994.

Mehlman, M. J. Late Quaternary Archaeological Sequences in Northern Tanzania. Ph. D. dissertation, Department of Anthropology, University of Illinois, Urbana, 1989.

[113] Barut, S. Middle and Later Stone Age Lithic Technology and Land Use in East African Savannas. *African Archaeological Review* 12: 43–72, 1994.

[114] Robbins, L. H., M. L. Murphy, G. A. Brook, A. H. Ivester, A. C. Campbell, R. G. Klein, R. G. Milo, K. M. Stewart, W. S. Downey, and N. J. Steven. Archaeology, Paleoenvironment, and Chronology of the Tsodilo Hills White Paintings Rock Shelter, Northwest Kalahari Desert, Botswana. *Journal of Archaeological Science* 27: 1085–1113, 2000.

[115] Ambrose, S. H., and K. G. Lorenz. Social and Ecological Models for the Middle Stone Age in Southern Africa. In *The Emergence of Modern Humans*. P. A. Mellars, ed. Pp. 3–33. Edinburgh: Edinburgh University Press, 1990.

Deacon, J. Later Stone Age Peoples and Their Descendants in Southern Africa. In *Southern African Prehistory and Paleoenvironments*. R. G. Klein, ed. Pp. 221–328. Rotterdam: Balkema, 1984.

Singer, R., and J. Wymer. *The Middle Stone Age at Klasies River Mouth in South Africa*. Chicago: University of Chicago Press, 1982.

Thackeray, A. I. Middle Stone Age Artifacts from the 1993 and 1995 Excavations of Die Kelders Cave 1, South Africa. *Journal of Human Evolution* 38: 147 – 168, 2000.

Wurz, S. The Middle Stone Age at Klasies River Mouth. Ph. D. dissertation, Department of Anthropology, University of Stellenbosch, Stellenbosch, South Africa, 2000.

[116] Binford, L. R. Organization and Formation Processes: Looking at Curated Technologies. *Journal of Anthropological Research* 35: 255 – 273, 1979.

Gould, R. A., and S. Saggers. Lithic Procurement in Central Australia: A Closer Look at Binford's Idea of Embeddedness in Archaeology. *American Antiquity* 50: 117 – 136, 1985.

[117] Ambrose, S. H., and K. G. Lorenz. Social and Ecological Models for the Middle Stone Age in Southern Africa. In *The Emergence of Modern Humans*. P. A. Mellars, ed. Pp. 3 – 33. Edinburgh: Edinburgh University Press, 1990.

Dyson-Hudson, R., and E. A. Smith. Human Territoriality: An Ecological Reassessment. *American Anthropologist* 80: 21 – 41, 1978.

[118] Wiessner, P. Risk, Reciprocity and Social Influences on ! Kung San Economics. In *Politics and History in Band Societies*. E. Leacock and R. Lee, eds. Pp. 61 – 84. Cambridge and Paris: Cambridge University Press and Editions de la Maison des Sciences de Thomme, 1982.

Style and Social Information in Kalahari San Projectile Points. *American Antiquity* 48: 253 – 276, 1983.

! Kung San Networks in a Generational Perspective. In *The Past and Future of. 'Kung San Ethnography*. M. Biesele, R. Gordon, and R. Lee, eds. Pp. 103 – 136. Quellen zur Khoisan-Forschung, Band 4. Hamburg: Helmut Buske Verlag, 1986.

[119] Deacon, H. J. Southern Africa and Modern Human Origins. *Philosophical Transactions of the Royal Society*, London B337: 177 – 183, 1992.

Two Late Pleistocene-Holocene Archaeological Depositories from the Southern Cape, South Africa. *South African Archaeological Bulletin* 50: 121 – 131, 1995.

Deacon, H. J., and S, J. D. Wurz. Klasies River Main Site, Cave 2: A Howiesons Poort Occurrence. In *Aspects of African Archaeology*. G. Pwiti and R. Soper, eds. Pp. 213 – 218. Harare: University of Zimbabwe Publications, 1996.

Wurz, S. The Howiesons Poort at Klasies River: From Artifacts to Cognition. M. A. thesis, Department of Anthropology, University of Stellenbosch, Stellenbosch, South Africa, 1997.

The Howiesons Poort Backed Artefacts from Klasies River: An Argument for Symbolic Behaviour. *South African Archaeological Bulletin* 169: 38 – 50, 1999.

The Middle Stone Age at Klasies River Mouth. Ph. D. dissertation, Department of Anthropology, University of Stellenbosch, Stellenbosch, South Africa, 2000.

[120] Wurz, S. The Howiesons Poort at Klasies River: From Artifacts to Cognition. M. A. thesis, Department of Anthropology, University of Stellenbosch, Stellenbosch, South Africa, 1997.

[121] Ambrose, S. H. Chronology of the Later Stone Age and Food Production in East Africa. *Journal of Archaeological Science* 25: 377 – 392, 1998a.

[122] Wiessner, P. ! Kung San Networks in a Generational Perspective. In *The Past and Future of. 'Kung San Ethnography*. M. Biesele, R. Gordon, and R. Lee, eds. Pp. 103 – 136. Quellen zur Khoisan-Forschung, Band 4. Hamburg: Helmut Buske Verlag, 1986.

[123] Deacon, H. J. Southern Africa and Modern Human Origins. *Philosophical Transactions of the Royal Society*, London B337: 177 – 183, 1992.

Two Late Pleistocene-Holocene Archaeological Depositories from the Southern Cape, South Africa. *South African Archaeological Bulletin* 50: 121 – 131, 1995.

Deacon, H. J., and S, J. D. Wurz. Klasies River Main Site, Cave 2: A Howiesons Poort Occurrence. In *Aspects of African Archaeology*. G. Pwiti and R. Soper, eds. Pp. 213 – 218. Harare: University of Zimbabwe Publications, 1996.

[124] Ambrose, S. H. Chronology of the Later Stone Age and Food Production in East Africa. *Journal of Archaeological Science* 25: 377 – 392, 1998a.

Barut, S. Middle and Later Stone Age Lithic Technology and Land Use in East African Savannas. *African Archaeological Review* 12: 43 – 72, 1994.

Mitchell, P. J. Prehistoric Exchange and Interaction in Southeastern Southern Africa: Marine Shell and Ostrich Eggshell. *African Archaeological Review* 13: 35 – 76, 1996.

[125] Riolo, R. L., M. D. Cohen, and R. Axelrod. Evolution of Cooperation without Reciprocity. *Nature* 414: 441 – 443, 2001.

[126] Ambrose, S. H., and K. G. Lorenz. Social and Ecological Models for the Middle Stone Age in Southern Africa. In *The Emergence of Modern Humans*. P. A. Mellars, ed. Pp. 3 – 33. Edinburgh: Edinburgh University Press, 1990.

[127] Bousman, B. Hunter-Gatherer Adaptations, Economic Risk and Tool Design. *Lithic Technology* 18: 59 – 86, 1993.

Fitzhugh, B. Risk and Invention in Technological Evolution. *Journal of Anthropological Archaeology* 20: 125 – 167, 2001.

Kuhn, S. L. A Formal Approach to the Design and Assembly of Mobile Toolkits. *American Antiquity* 59(3): 426 – 442, 1994.

Nelson, M. C. The Study of Technological Organization. *Archaeological Method and Theory* 3: 57 – 100, 1991.

Shott, M. Technological Organization and Settlement Mobility: An Ethnographic Example. *Journal of Anthropological Research* 42: 15 – 51, 1986.

Torrence, R. Time Budgeting and Hunter-Gatherer Technology. In *Hunter-Gatherer Economy in Prehistory*. G. Bailey, ed. Pp. 11-22. Cambridge: Cambridge University Press, 1983.

[128] Kuhn, S. L. A Formal Approach to the Design and Assembly of Mobile Toolkits. *American Antiquity* 59(3): 426-442, 1994.

[129] Binford, L. R. *Faunal Remains from Klasies River Mouth*. New York: Academic Press, 1984.

Isolating the Transition to Cultural Adaptations: An Organizational Approach. In *The Emergence of Modern Humans: Biocultural Adaptations in the Later Pleistocene*. E. Trinkaus, ed. Pp. 18-41. Cambridge: Cambridge University Press, 1989.

[130] Roebrooks, W., J. Kolen, and E. Rensink. Planning Depth, Anticipation and the Organization of Middle Palaeolithic Technology: The "Archaic" Natives Meet Eve's Descendants. *Helinium* 28: 17-34, 1988.

[131] Kuhn, S. L. A Formal Approach to the Design and Assembly of Mobile Toolkits. *American Antiquity* 59(3): 426-442, 1994.

[132] Trinkaus, E. Neanderthal Mortality Patterns. *Journal of Archaeological Science* 22: 121-142, 1995.

[133] Klein, R. G. Biological and Behavioral Perspectives on Modern Human Origins in Southern Africa. In *The Human Revolution: Behavioral and Biological Perspectives on the Origin of Modern Humans*. P. Mellars and C. Stringer, eds. Pp. 529-546. Edinburgh: Edinburgh University Press, 1989.

Archaeology and the Evolution of Human Behavior. *Evolutionary Anthropology* 9: 17-36, 2000.

[134] Ambrose, S. H., and K. G. Lorenz. Social and Ecological Models for the Middle Stone Age in Southern Africa. In The Emergence of Modern Humans. P. A. Mellars, ed. Pp. 3-33. Edinburgh: Edinburgh University Press, 1990.

[135] Ambrose, S. H. Middle and Later Stone Age Settlement Patterns in the Central Rift Valley, Kenya: Comparisons and Contrasts. In *Settlement Dynamics of the Middle Paleolithic and Middle Stone Age*. N. Conard, ed. Pp. 21-43. Tubingen: Kerns Verlag, 2001a.

Ambrose, S. H., and K. G. Lorenz. Social and Ecological Models for the Middle Stone Age in Southern Africa. In The Emergence of Modern Humans. P. A. Mellars, ed. Pp. 3-33. Edinburgh: Edinburgh University Press, 1990.

[136] Klein, R. G. Biological and Behavioral Perspectives on Modern Human Origins in Southern Africa. In *The Human Revolution: Behavioral and Biological Perspectives on the Origin of Modern Humans*. P. Mellars and C. Stringer, eds. Pp. 529-546. Edinburgh: Edinburgh University Press, 1989.

[137] Torrence, R. Time Budgeting and Hunter-Gatherer Technology. In *Hunter-Gatherer Economy in Prehistory*. G. Bailey, ed. Pp. 11 – 22. Cambridge: Cambridge University Press, 1983.

[138] Henshilwood, C. S., J. C. Sealy, R. Yates, K. Cruz-Uribe, P. Goldberg, F. E. Grine, R. G. Klein, C. Poggenpoel, K. van Neikerk, and I. Watts. Blombos Cave, Southern Cape, South Africa: Preliminary Report on the 1992 – 1999 Excavation of the Middle Stone Age Levels. *Journal of Archaeological Science* 28: 421 – 448, 2001.

[139] Bousman, B. Hunter-Gatherer Adaptations, Economic Risk and Tool Design. *Lithic Technology* 18: 59 – 86, 1993.

[140] Ambrose, S. H. Middle and Later Stone Age Settlement Patterns in the Central Rift Valley, Kenya: Comparisons and Contrasts. In *Settlement Dynamics of the Middle Paleolithic and Middle Stone Age*. N. Conard, ed. Pp. 21 – 43. Tubingen: Kerns Verlag, 2001a.

[141] Wurz, S. The Howiesons Poort Backed Artefacts from Klasies River: An Argument for Symbolic Behaviour. *South African Archaeological Bulletin* 169: 38 – 50, 1999.

[142] Klein, R. G. Anatomy, Behavior, and Modern Human Origins. *Journal of World Prehistory* 9: 167 – 198, 1995.

Archaeology and the Evolution of Human Behavior. *Evolutionary Anthropology* 9: 17 – 36, 2000.

[143] Feblot-Augustins, J. Raw Material Transport Patterns and Settlement Systems in the European Lower and Middle Paleolithic: Continuity, Change and Variability. In *The Middle Paleolithic Occupation of Europe*. W. Roebroeks and C. Gamble, eds. Pp. 193 – 214. Leiden: University of Leiden Press, 1999.

[144] Bar-Yosef, O., and S. L. Kuhn. The Big Deal about Blades: Laminar Technologies and Human Evolution. *American Anthropologist* 101: 322 – 338, 1999.

[145] Bordes, F. *A Tale of Two Caves*. Pp. 54. New York: Harper and Row, 1972.

[146] Ambrose, S. H. Chronology of the Later Stone Age and Food Production in East Africa. *Journal of Archaeological Science* 25: 377 – 392, 1998a.

McBrearty, S., and A. S. Brooks. The Revolution That Wasn't: A New Interpretation of the Origin of Modern Human Behavior. *Journal of Human Evolution* 39: 453 – 563, 2000.

[147] Harpending, H. C, S. T. Sherry, A. L. Rogers, and M. Stoneking. The Genetic Structure of Ancient Human Populations. *Current Anthropology* 34: 483 – 496, 1993.

Mountain, J. L., and L. L. Cavalli-Sforza. Multilocus Genotypes, a Tree of Individuals, and Human Evolutionary History. *American Journal of Human Genetics* 61: 701 – 718, 1997.

Sherry, S., A. R. Rogers, H. Harpending, H. Soodyall, T. Jenkins, and M. Stoneking. Mismatch Distributions of mtDNA Reveal Recent Human Population Expansions. *Human Biology* 66: 761 – 775, 1994.

Watson, E., P. Forster, M. Richards, and H.-J. Bandelt. Mitochondria 1 Footprints of Human Expansions in Africa. *American Journal of Human Genetics* 61: 691-704, 1997.

[148] Harpending, H. C, S. T. Sherry, A. L. Rogers, and M. Stoneking. The Genetic Structure of Ancient Human Populations. *Current Anthropology* 34: 483-496, 1993.

Sherry, S., A. R. Rogers, H. Harpending, H. Soodyall, T. Jenkins, and M. Stoneking. Mismatch Distributions of mtDNA Reveal Recent Human Population Expansions. *Human Biology* 66: 761-775, 1994.

[149] Ingman, M., H. Kaessmann, S. Paabo, and U. Gyllensten. Mitochondrial Genome Variation and the Origin of Modern Humans. *Nature* 408: 708-713, 2000.

Pritchard, J. K.. M. T. Seielstadt, A. Perez-Lezaun, and M. W. Feldman. Population Growth of Human Y Chromosomes: A Study of Y Chromosome Satellites. *Molecular Biology and Evolution* 16: 1791-1798, 1999.

Underhill, P. A., P. Shen, A. A. Lin, G. Passarino, W. H. Yang, E. Kauffman, B. Bonne-Tamir, J. Bertranpetit, P. Francalacci, M. Ibrahim, T. Jenkins, K. R. Kidd, Q. Mehdi, M. T. Seielstad, R. S. Wells, A. Piazza, R. W. Davis, M. W. Feldman, L. L. Cavalli-Sforza, and P. Oefner. Y Chromosome Sequence Variation and the History of Human Populations. *Nature Genetics* 26: 358-361, 2000.

[150] Jin, L., P. A. Underhill, V. Doctor, R. W. Davis, P. Shen, L. L. Cavalli-Sforza, and P. J. Oefner. Distribution of Haplotypes from a Chromosome 21 Region Distinguishes Multiple Prehistoric Migrations. *Proceedings of the National Academy of Science*, USA 96: 3796-3800, 1999.

Lahr, M., and R. Foley. Multiple Dispersals and Modern Human Origins. *Evolutionary Anthropology* 3: 48-60, 1994. Toward a Theory of Modern Human Origins: Geography, Demography, and Diversity in Recent Human Evolution. *Yearbook of Physical Anthropology* 41: 137-176, 1998.

Pritchard, J. K.. M. T. Seielstadt, A. Perez-Lezaun, and M. W. Feldman. Population Growth of Human Y Chromosomes: A Study of Y Chromosome Satellites. *Molecular Biology and Evolution* 16: 1791-1798, 1999.

Qamar, R., Q. Ayub, S. Khaliq, A. Mansoor, T. Karafet, S. Mehdi, and M. F. Hammer. African and Levantine Origin of Pakistani YAP+Y Chromosomes. *Human Biology* 71: 745-755, 1999.

Quintana-Murci, L., O. Semino, H.-J. Bandelt, G. Passarino, K. McElreavey, and A. S. Santachiara-Benerecetti. Genetic Evidence of an Early Exit of Homo Sapiens from Africa through Eastern Africa. *Nature* Thackeray, A. I. *Genetics* 23: 437-441, 1999.

Tishkoff, S. A., E. Dietzsch, W. Speed, A. J. Pakstis, J. R. Kidd, K. Cheung, B. Bonne-

Tamir, A. S. Santachiara-Benerecetti, P. Moral, M. Krings, S. Paabo, E. Watson, N. Risch, T. Jenkins, and K. K. Kidd. Global Patterns of Linkage Disequilibrium at the CD4 Locus and Modern Human Origins. *Science* 271: 1380 – 1387, 1996.

Tishkoff, S., A. J. Pakstis, M. Stoneking, J. R. Kidd, G. Destro-Bisol, A. Sanjantila, R.-B. Lu, A. S. Deindard, S. Sirugo, T. Jenkins, K. K. Kidd, and A. G. Clark. Short Tandem Repeat Polymorphism/Alu Haplotype Variation at the PLAT Locus: Implications for Modern Human Origins. *American Journal of Human Genetics* 67: 901 – 923, 2000.

[151] Chronology of the Later Stone Age and Food Production in East Africa. *Journal of Archaeological Science* 25: 377 – 392, 1998a.

Late Pleistocene Human Population Bottlenecks, Volcanic Winter, and the Differentiation of Modern Humans. *Journal of Human Evolution* 34: 623 – 651, 1998b.

Harpending, H. C, S. T. Sherry, A. L. Rogers, and M. Stoneking. The Genetic Structure of Ancient Human Populations. *Current Anthropology* 34: 483 – 496, 1993.

Klein, R. G. The Human Career. 2nd ed. Chicago: University of Chicago Press, 2000. Archaeology and the Evolution of Human Behavior. *Evolutionary Anthropology* 9: 17 – 36, 1999.

McBrearty, S., and A. S. Brooks. The Revolution That Wasn't: A New Interpretation of the Origin of Modern Human Behavior. *Journal of Human Evolution* 39: 453 – 563, 2000.

[152] Harpending, H. C, S. T. Sherry, A. L. Rogers, and M. Stoneking. The Genetic Structure of Ancient Human Populations. *Current Anthropology* 34: 483 – 496, 1993.

Sherry, S., A. R. Rogers, H. Harpending, H. Soodyall, T. Jenkins, and M. Stoneking. Mismatch Distributions of mtDNA Reveal Recent Human Population Expansions. *Human Biology* 66: 761 – 775, 1994.

[153] Ambrose, S. H. Late Pleistocene Human Population Bottlenecks, Volcanic Winter, and the Differentiation of Modern Humans. *Journal of Human Evolution* 34: 623 – 651, 1998b.

琢背细小石叶是舶来品

安吉拉·E·卡洛斯
(华盛顿大学　西雅图)

摘　要：数万年来,细石器工业的琢背细小石叶主宰着北非的石器工业,有时几乎是唯一的器物类型。器物的制作与使用都是在非常小的、关系紧密的社会群体中进行的,因此它们可能在规范与协调社会身份认同的过程中发挥了重要作用。这可以从其形制(如大小与形状)的高度一致性中得到绝佳的体现。虽然文化背景条件千差万别,但是横贯半个非洲大陆,琢背细小石叶的变化微不足道。导致我们不得不追问除了社会关系协调这个影响因素之外,是否还有其他决定因素起作用。似乎可以这么说,就像所有事物一样,凡事都可能有例外,非社会关系因素是可能存在的,但寻找它犹如大海捞针。

北非地区跟旧大陆其他地区一样,虽然更新世之末、全新世之初的石器工业变化多样,但基本面貌还是以细石器为主。本文中我将研究范围限定于琢背细小石叶,年代范围(绝大部分内容中)限于"琢背细小石叶工业"的较早阶段,此时琢背细小石叶是石器工具中的主要组成成分,有时是唯一有加工与使用痕迹的工具(Retouched tools)*。根据收集的、散布于北非地区的遗址材料(图2.1),我将就这一极端依赖某一类工具类型的现象以及确定其生产过程的物理属性

---

*　Retouched tools,字面含义是"修理工具",实际对应中文中的意思是"有修理或使用痕迹的工具"。——译注

(形制与大小)的意义进行广泛讨论。不过首要的问题还是要回答什么是"琢背细小石叶"。

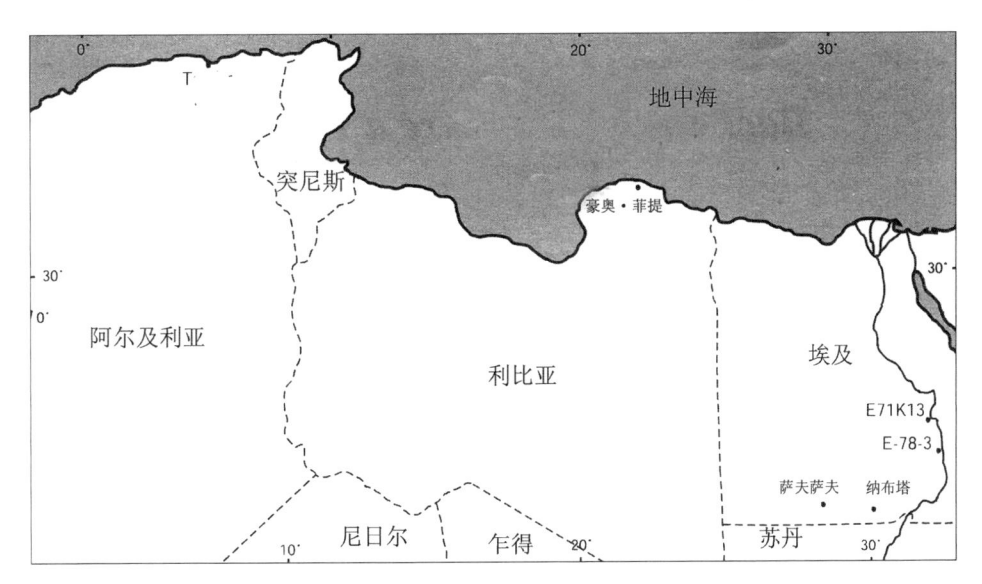

图 2.1　本研究讨论的北非主要遗址

就琢背细小石叶而言,北非西部恰好有明确且广泛使用的定义:琢背细小石叶(也就是石片的长度至少是宽度的两倍)是宽不超过 9 毫米的石叶[1],采用陡向或半陡向的琢背修理,或采用奥恰塔塔修理*。定义所依据的石器类型学[2]是基于马格里布的后旧石器时代而特别设计的,是独一无二的。当然,它也成功用于旧石器时代晚期与后旧石器时代的其他地区,东至西奈半岛(例如[3]),南至苏丹北部[4]与利比亚南部[5],还远及毛里塔尼亚西部撒哈拉地区[6]至埃及南部[7]诸新石器时代遗存。实际运用中,琢背细小石叶的定义并不像定义所设定的那样严格。北非的石叶工业(广义上的)或是明显偏向较大石叶(严格地说),或是偏向较小的细小石叶。就后者而言,宽于 9 毫米的琢背石叶可以视为细小石叶的延伸,它与细小石叶并没有严格的界限,而不应该视为单独一类"石叶"[8]。类似之,长宽比的分布基本上总是单峰状态的,因此长宽比小于2∶1的石制品最好视为细小石叶序列的延伸,只是"不那么修长",而非另类的"石片"。极端情况中,石器原料的尺寸就很小[9],石叶的长度也就被限定了,长宽比的实际峰值也就是 2.0,就像努比亚 443 号遗址

---

*　Ouchtata retouch,这种修理方法跟普通的琢背修理的区别在于,其修理痕迹不规则。——译注

所见到的[10]。

一、北非琢背细小石叶工业的起源

大约距今 2 万年前琢背细小石叶开始流行于北非部分地区，并持续到距今 8 千到 1 万年前（未校正的年代）。就在这 1 万到 1.2 万年的时间范围内，除了琢背细小石叶工业，北非的考古材料中罕有其他的工业类型。仅有的例外也就是尼罗河谷的少数石器工业，强调非细石器或其他类型的工具，如伊斯南、马卡哈德马 4 号与阿芬工业相关联的遗址[11]，但不包括托马斯阿弗拉村的阿芬工业遗址[12]、色比连工业以及埃杜方工业。埃杜方并不是一个定义清晰的石器工业[13]，色比连工业甚至可能属于旧石器时代中期[14]，也有相反的观点[15]。

琢背细小石叶工业似乎不知来自何处。马格里布地区最早与最重要的琢背细小石叶工业称为伊比诺毛露西亚。它见于摩洛哥东部的塔佛拉尔特，距今 2.2 万年前[16]，以及阿尔及利亚东部的塔马尔哈特，距今 2 万年前[17]。马格里布地区没有更早的旧石器时代晚期遗存，伊比诺毛露西亚之前是阿特林工业，它属于旧石器时代中期，跟琢背细小石叶工业毫无相似之处。有不少观点认为阿特林工业可能比较晚，但是所有晚于距今 3 万[18]或 3.5 万年前[19]的年代都不可信，其余观点认为阿特林的年代已经超越了放射性碳测年的范围[20]，其他有关阿特林遗址以及马格里布东部与南部气候重建的年代估计都表明，阿特林基本不可能晚于距今 4 万年前，很可能不晚于距今 6 至 7 万年前[21]。因此没有理由认为马格里布残存有较晚的旧石器时代中期工业。相反，考古材料中有至少 1 万年的空白，很可能更长。

利比亚东部的昔兰尼加的情况可能差不多（图 2.1）。豪奥菲提是一处经典的旧石器时代晚期洞穴遗址，有多个文化层，地层深厚，是典型的石叶与雕刻器工业，又称达班工业（最早发现于典型遗址哈格菲特德达巴）[22]，其上就是麦克贝尼所谓的"东奥兰尼"工业，是伊比诺毛露西亚工业的地方变体。东奥兰尼工业中琢背细小石叶占到所有工具的 82% 到 94%。它与下面的达班工业无论技术还是类型都完全不同[23]。差异是如此之大，变化是如此之突然，以至于麦克贝尼[24]认为发生了人口的变迁。

麦克贝尼认为距今 1.4 万年前达班工业为琢背细小石叶所取代，他之所以这么认为是因为在他写论文的时候，北非地区还没有发现早于距今 1.2 万年前的琢背细小石器（塔福拉尔特）[25]。不过，他按主观水平层发掘豪奥遗址，随后重建了遗址地层。从达班与伊比诺毛露西亚工业交界面上得到两个放射性碳测年样本,分别是距今 1.6 万年前与距今 1.86 万年前。麦克贝尼将之归为达班工业,主要原因是这两个年代都在已知的伊比诺毛露西亚工业年代范围之外。而从现在马格里布与尼罗河流域(见下文)所有的伊比诺毛露西亚年代来看,这两个年代更可能指的是琢背细小石叶工业。因此豪奥遗址达班工业的年代不晚于距今 2.85 万年前,这个年代是 1952 年获得的,值得怀疑[26]。距今大约 1.8 至 1.9 万年前沉积的速率与沉积物的性质存在明显变化[27],表明此前可能并没有连续、未中断的居住利用。就该遗址而言,可能存在另一个时间间隔,间隔至少超过万年。

数十万年来撒哈拉大沙漠一直无人居住,直到全新世之初才有所改变。旧石器时代中期与末期或新石器时代之间存在的时间空白可以通过气候来解释。

尼罗河流域的情况没有那么极端。那则勒特卡哈特有一些旧石器晚期的燧石采石场(图 2.1),年代距今 3 万至 3.5 万年前。由于是采石场,遗址中工具非常罕见,但石器技术还是为了生产石叶的,而非细小石叶[28]。旧石器时代晚期典型的石叶与雕刻器组合见于更靠南的舒维卡哈天工业的遗址中。这一工业距今约 2.5 至 2.2 万年前,缺乏琢背细小石叶[29]。苏丹努比亚地区有一处哈尔范工业遗址,编号为 6B32,含有琢背细小石叶以及奥恰塔塔技术细小石叶,距今接近 2.8 万年[30]。不过,由于哈尔范工业的其他遗址都处在距今 1.95 万年至 1.75 万年间,这个年代可能偏老了[31],相反的意见可参见维尔美思奇的研究[32]。

最早的真正琢背细小石叶工业是法克胡连以及类似于法克胡连的石器工业,距今 2.1 万年前见于上埃及[33]。其中细小石叶占绝对优势,基本上缺乏严格意义上的大石叶,大石叶是细小石叶的前身。同样可以肯定的是,后续的库班尼亚与哈尔范工业中琢背细小石叶有时占到所有修理工具的 90%[34]。实际上,尼罗河下游直到全新世琢背细小石叶在史前石器材料中都占主导地位,绝少例外[35]。

总而言之,琢背细小石叶工业起源之前的数万年间,北非大部分地区根本就没有考古材料的发现。有考古材料的地方,如在尼罗河流域,所用的石器跟琢背细小石叶又毫无相似之处。大约距今 2.1 至 2.2 万年前,琢背细小石叶工业突然出现,不知来自哪里。遍及北非地区,从埃及到摩洛哥,都没有其渊源的踪迹。两类考古材料可能有助于解释北非琢背细小石叶工业的起源:与之相关的人骨遗存,以及器物的风格分析。

不仅埃及[36],而且马格里布[37]都有与最早的琢背细小石叶工业相关的人骨遗存。他们属于一种非常独特的、粗壮的现代人,又称梅其塔—阿发娄类型或"梅其塔人"。实际上,北非琢背细小石叶工业时期所有的人骨遗存都属于梅其塔人[38],他们彼此十分相似,而与更早期的人类遗存差异明显,只有一例除外[39]。这个例外就是发现于那则勒特卡哈特(参见上文)燧石采石场遗址的人骨遗存[40]。如果这种联系不错的话,那么这具称为"梅其塔人"[41]的人类骨骼要比琢背细小石叶早数万年。

琢背细小石叶工业的分布横贯整个北非,并存在了至少一万年。因此,其中存在相当大的时空差异也就不足为奇了,与之相关的众多命名就是标志。苏丹、埃及、利比亚、阿尔及利亚石器组合的风格分析显示,每个地区都有引人注目的风格连续性,尤其是在漫长、多层的文化序列中[42]。有种解释认为,这反映了社会群体自我意识的连续性[43],某些遗址中这种连续性存在了数千年[44],不免让人感到奇怪。正如我们所知,洲际范围或是千年尺度的社会结构是很难保持的,所以也许最好将之理解为某种性质尚不明确的"地区连续性"。风格分析还表明阿尔及利亚最早的琢背细小石叶与埃及最早的琢背细小石叶之间关系紧密[45],它们的相似程度要大于各自与该地区晚期工业组合的相似程度。

这也就是说,北非地区经过长期的人类居住空白时期之后,一种独特类型的现代人突然占领了这一幅员广阔的地区,也就是使用琢背细小石叶工业的梅其塔人。开始阶段器物风格非常相似,随着时间推移,地区之间与地区之内开始出现分化。这非常像一次殖民事件的考古学表达!北非地区(尼罗河流域可能例外)很可能是氧同位素阶段4开始时在环境恶化下人类居住失败的主要地区之一[46]。

二、技术联系中的琢背细小石叶

这里我重点讨论琢背细小石叶工业的早期发现,其中大部分的加工工具都是琢背细小石叶,有时超过90%的加工工具都是琢背细小石叶。

当某一类加工工具占绝对主导地位时,这类工具就可能垄断整个石器技术流程[47]。也就是说,加工工具不止包括90%的琢背细小石叶,外加少量的大端刮器与雕刻器。总之,所有的东西基本都很小。如果端刮器与雕刻器这样的工具类型确实存在,那么它们就是用石片制作的,这些石片是生产细小石叶的副产品：如初级石片、预修理石片、细小石叶石核更新石片。因此，除了下面所说唯一例外，这些工业中所有的产品都很小，因为所有产品的目的都是为了生产细小石叶，随后对其中一些细小石叶进行琢背修理。

几乎所有研究北非不同时期琢背细小石叶的研究者都需要采用提克斯耶的后旧石器时代类型学来描述石制品。这种石器类型学无疑是以石器形态为中心的[48]，如今广泛应用于北非地区，因为如果所有考古学家都采用统一的类型学体系，那么交流起来就容易得多。从这方面来说，其类型学是"合理的"（某种意义上）[49]。提克斯耶所定义的琢背细小石叶类型见于考古材料中。因此，琢背细小石叶类型确实"存在"，即使其定义与分类可能并不能告诉我们太多有关伊比诺毛露西亚工业制作者的信息，跟四十年前杰克斯·提克斯耶所认为的相比，甚至更少。但是只要我们能进行描述，这也就无足轻重。解释自然比描述更有趣，相应也更困难。

三、社会联系中的琢背细小石叶

我们倾向认为简单打制的石器工具如琢背细小石叶在经济生活领域可能发挥某些作用，不能排除它们还可能在其他领域发挥作用。生产、使用以及废弃，严格而论，在时间上是分开的，尽管对于那些权宜性的工具*来说，其时间间隔可能很短暂。因此生产、使用、废弃的情境并不相同，不同情况下石器工具的基本功能很可能也不一样。比如说，生产一件细小石叶的时候，其意义主要是"社会技术的"（某种意义上说，如宾福德的说法[50]），而在使用的时候，其意义则是"技术经济的"。

石器的功能可能随情形而改变，就北非旧石器时代晚期而言（事实上，不同时期许多地方都是如此），特别值得注意的是，当时的社会与技术背景的联系跟我们现代社会，尤其是工业化社会相比，差异显著。古人与其技术的关系不同于我们与现代技术之间的关系[51]。古今共同之处在于我们都运用物质文化来协调与维护社会关系。不过，工业化社会中，实现的途径主要是通过物质文化的"消费"，而非生产：通过我们选择使用什么以及如何选择去使用物质文化。于是，一个西方的青少年可能因为穿"错"了运动鞋而受到羞辱，社会意义仅仅来自展示。无论是穿"对"还是穿"错"了，西方的青少年都不会生产自己的运动鞋

---

* expedient tools 权宜性的工具，就是那些用完后就扔掉的工具，通常形制简单或是难以维护。——译注

(那些生产鞋的人可能根本就不在乎对错)。生活在工业社会的我们很少生产我们使用的东西,生产可能很大程度上脱离了人,已经机械化了,所以大部分复杂人工制品甚至带有如何使用的说明书[52]。

相对于同时依赖物质文化制作与使用的社会,依赖物质文化使用的社会更有效率,人与人的关系也不那么亲密。许许多多的人参与社会交往过程,非常快捷,但是人与人的交往并不深入。也许正因为如此,我们会不自觉地忽略一个小活动空间的许多陌生人,与此同时,可能会跟从未见过的人交往,并且以后再不来往。

尽管我们会与许多人不期而遇,但是我们现代人的社会关系网络中每个个体所能处理的不超过150人("认知群体的规模"[53])。无论我们是城里人还是狩猎采集者都是如此,对于旧石器时代晚期的现代人来说也可能是这一数字。这不是指同时住在一块的人数,而是一个个体能够"掌控与自己相关社会信息"的人数[54]。天天生活在一起的群体的实际规模无疑要小得多。许多考古遗址的面积都很有限,就是那些大遗址,无论是旷野遗址如埃及南部的 E-78-3 遗址[55],还是利比亚昔兰尼加的豪奥菲提大洞遗址[56],都不过是单独且小规模堆积事件的叠加,它们之间没有什么明显的联系[57]。

因此,我们认为小群体的人们,白天中的部分时间(或晚上)都是在非常有限的范围内活动,与邻居之间没有明显的界线来区分。这不是工业化社会的社会背景联系。其技术背景联系也非如此,这样的社会中物质文化的生产不是脱离个人与机械化的。即使有些人工制品的生产需要非同寻常的知识与技巧(北非旧石器时代晚期显然没有这样的器物),生产仍然是在非常公开的小空间中进行的。

在这样一种社会与技术背景的联系中,人与人之间的关系非常亲近,彼此之间很清楚对方在做什么,社会身份的产生与维系应该是稳定持续的,即可以通过物质的行动(包括生产与使用东西),也可以通过非物质的(包括语言及其他形式)行动来体现。两类行为可能都参与到社会过程中,就像我们现在一样,我们无需去猜测究竟哪一种途径更有效。

这种社会与当代工业化社会的主要区别在于我们广泛使用物品,但很少制造物品。把我们当代工业化社会的生活跟旧石器时代晚期的技术活动相比,最贴近的类比可能是给我的亲友准备饭食。这涉及获取原材料、使用工具、或多或少地运用技巧——一系列相关的知识[58],从而得到期望的最终产品。由于期望的最终产品是全家人的食物消费,因此关键的决定因素是避免饥饿,至少是不要营养不良。情况显然并非如此。我不认为,因为约翰看起来有点憔悴,就会有人额外给他一个橙子。实际情况是,吃什么,如何吃,何时何地吃主要由社会群体的组成来决定,社会认同通过它们来维系与改变。

旧石器时代晚期技术运用的规模决定了它所影响的社会结构的规模;它所涉及的是关系紧密的小群体,而不是"我们和他们"这样的群体区分。它也不涉及通过器物非功能性的方面来传递已确立的社会信息——有些学者称之为"风格"[59]。正相反,它所传递的信息是即时的,来自对技术动作的观察,这些信息导致社会结构的生成,而不只是表达社会结构。

由于所涉及的人工制品相当简单,无须有意识或有目的。就另一个不同的旧石器时代晚期背景联系,辛卡莱尔[60]提出"梭鲁特石器"存在"过度生产"的特征,显示"坚强、勇敢与灵活"[61]以及类似的男性猎人特征,他所说的梭鲁特石器指的是桂叶形两面器与有肩尖状器。相反,他将"非梭鲁特石器"(所有其他工具)视为完全是由功能与技术流程(计划的形制)决定的[62]。他称之为"非梭鲁特石器"是因为这些工具简单,且缺乏梭鲁特石器的典型特征,许多时候在一些地方的石器组合中可能会"被遗忘"。北非旧石器时代晚期的琢背细小石叶同样如此。因此,其生产并不是一种自我表现或是表达"伊比诺毛露西亚"认同的行为。相反,如同多布里斯[63]有点让人心寒的说法:"器物生产的方式与时间细节……允许有细小的改变,比如熟练的男女制作者跟那些老年制作者相比,老年人已经难以成功制作所期望的工具了。"

四、经济背景联系中的琢背细小石叶

器物与技术行为当然在社会进程中发挥了某种作用,这并不必定是其唯一的作用(上文提及辛卡莱尔所认为的梭鲁特尖状器异乎寻常的精美,这可能是个例外)。沃布斯特[64]将器物视为"介入社会领域的物质",但是器物同时(沃布斯特当然不会否认)也在物质领域发挥作用,我们也许认为介入物质领域的要求可能会限制器物的形制。

(一)形制与功能

有人可能会说每个琢背细小石叶占绝对主导地位的石器组合不仅反映了制作者的社会关系网络,也反映了细小石叶本身在更加物质的领域所发挥的(有意制作的)功能。不过,我们也知道,通过形制推定石器功能的研究大多是在北非之外的地区进行的[65],不能通过石器类型来推定功能,尽管石器的实际用途可能跟计划的用途并不很一致。就北非而言，有关琢背细小石叶的使用痕迹研究并不多。有些已做过的研究并没有发现使用痕迹[66]。这当然支持一种看法，琢背细小石叶的制作完全是为了满足发展社会认同的目的。北非地区琢背细小石叶上发现有使用痕迹的地方，主要是在埃及，那里也跟其他地区一样，琢背细小石叶用于众多的彼此并无关联的活动中，或者说完全跟石器的类型没有任何关系[67]。

尽管这些研究都表明琢背细小石叶的制作者并不认同现代石器分类学的精髓，但是它们也显示，偶尔琢背细小石叶也用于实际工作中。这可能是人们为什么制作它的真实原因。令人惊奇的地方是制作者把形制与功能分离的程度：分离程度有时是如此彻底，使得功能与形制的关联看起来相当反常。

例如，尼罗河流域有两个遗址，都属于库班尼亚工业，一个是 E-78-3 遗址[68]，位于瓦迪库班尼亚，靠近阿斯旺地区，另一个是 E71K13[69]，位于伊斯纳以北 150 公里处（图 2.1）。它们在技术与类型上几乎完全一致。只有一个类型例外，两个石器组合都以琢背细小石叶为中心，几乎所有的加工工具都是端部钝加工的细小石叶，采用的是非常轻的琢背修理（奥克塔塔修理技术），一般从细小石叶左侧边的近端开始，然后在尾端逐渐消失。唯一值得注意的例外，就是少量精致修理的雕刻器，通常用勒瓦娄哇石片为毛坯，这是唯一没有利用细小石叶技术的器物。

不过，就生计活动而言，两个遗址差异明显。E-78-3 遗址表现出非常宽的经济基础，利用相当多的植物性食物，尤其是湿地植物，使用厚重的磨石来处理它们；还有大量的鱼骨（占可鉴定标本的 98%）；少量的鸟骨；非常少的大型哺乳动物骨骼[70]。而 E71K13 遗址的发掘面积要小得多，保存状况也差，没有出土磨石、鱼骨、鸟骨，仅有的动植物遗存就是少量的大型哺乳动物，特别是大羚羊（hartebeest）[71]。

迄今为止，我们可以说，两个遗址的生计基础迥然不同。然而打制石器的技术与类型却相同，燧石原料产地近伊斯纳，被古人搬运到瓦迪库班尼亚，燧石在这里是珍贵的原料[72]。两个遗址的居民关系自然很密切，我甚至怀疑两个遗址是同一群体的人们所留下的（尽管我们试图拼合两个遗址间雕刻器与其石碴*的努力不出意料地失败了）。显然，两地的古人制作相同的器物，不管是要去做

---

* spall，制作雕刻器时，通常需要打下一条石片，从而形成雕刻器刃口，这条石片通常称为雕刻器的 spall。——译注

什么,形制完全独立于功能之外。

(二) 琢背细小石叶大小的限制因素

1. 原料的供给

琢背细小石叶的大小并不必然受到距离原料产地远近的影响。研究撒哈拉东部纳布塔地区三个关系紧密的新石器时代早期遗址(图2.1),发现琢背细小石叶的大小基本一致,甚至未修理的细小石叶大小也接近。其中一个遗址距离原料产地不到10公里,另外两个遗址距离原料产地大约40公里[73]。琢背细小石叶作为最重要的修理工具类型,显然必须具有一定的大小与形状,细小石叶毛坯的大小范围因此也相当狭窄,即便石核可以生产较大的毛坯。类似之,那些不再能够生产理想尺寸细小石叶的石核还是会被放弃,即使石器原料产地遥远,石核还可以生产更小的石制品。

2. 原料的差异

细小石叶的大小也可以不受原料巨大差异的影响。撒哈拉东部有一处靠近萨夫萨夫的早全新世遗址(图2.1),燧石原料来自100公里外,人们用它来制作久已习惯的细小石叶(图2.2b)。萨夫萨夫地区当地(15公里范围内)仅有的石料是石英质砂岩,人们也用它来制作细小石叶,跟燧石一样[74],有些产品还进一步修理成几何形的细石器(图2.2a)。文化约束对细小石叶的大小与形状的影响非常明显,人们除了不用微雕刻器技术加工砂岩外,燧石与石英质砂岩产品之间看不出任何差异。

3. 装柄

细小石叶严格的大小范围可以通过装柄的条件限制来解释,这样的观点广为流传,未经批判地被接受,并视为不言而喻。人们通常认为生产柄比生产琢背细小石叶更费事,所以要让细小石叶来适合柄,而不是相反。这可能是对的,但条件是细小石叶必须直接镶进硬材料所制的柄中,如骨头或木头。如果装柄确实是重要的影响因素,那么细小石叶的长度可能就是最不需要考虑的东西了,细小石叶可以一端伸出来,或是镶成一排,或是修理成合适的大小[75]。宽度相对更重要,不过通过琢背修理很容易控制。厚度应该是捆绑细小石叶的最关键的变量。

塔马尔哈特是阿尔及利亚一处伊比诺毛露西亚工业的遗址,其所有琢背细小石叶长度的数据表明,某些变化还是存在的,尽管大部分细小石叶的长度位于16至35毫米之间(图2.3)。绝大部分(超过70%)塔马尔哈特琢背细小石叶的

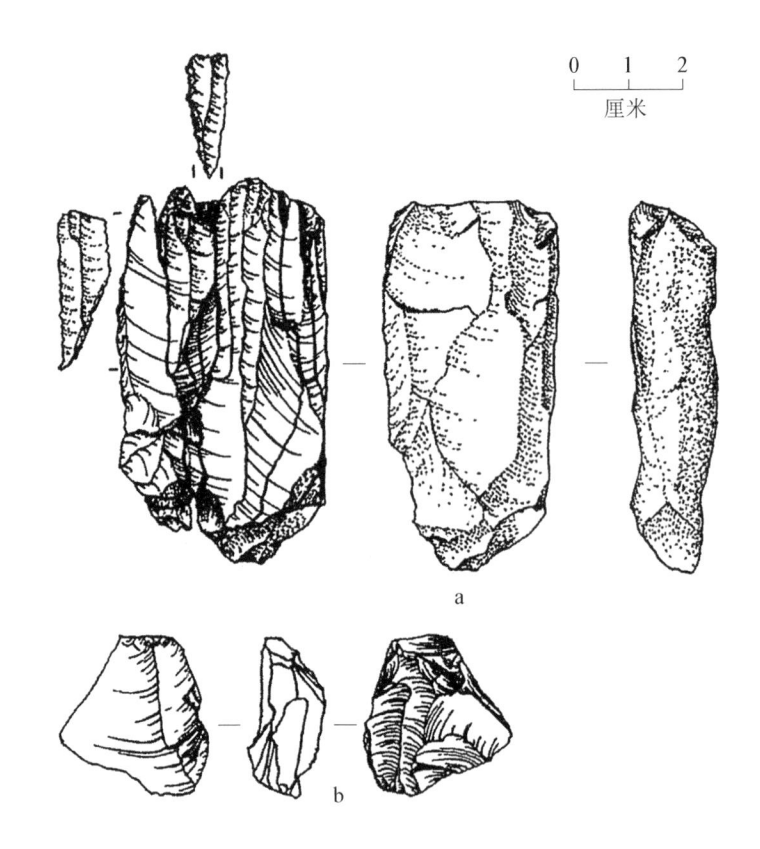

图 2.2 萨夫萨夫 60 号遗址出土器物

[a. 石英岩—砂岩石核(从不到 15 公里远的地方获得的)与拼合的细小石叶(包括修理的细小石叶);b. 耗尽的燧石细小石叶石核(来自超过 100 公里外的地方)]

宽度在 5 至 8 毫米之间(图 2.4),并且几乎所有(超过 80%)的细小石叶厚 2 至 3 毫米(图 2.5)。当然,如果考虑相对而非绝对的变化,那么这种变化范围就不是运用硬质柄所能解释的。细小石叶的宽与厚之间几乎没有区别,其变异系数*分别为 0.344 和 0.315。相反,理论上说,长度可能变化范围更大,其变异系数仅有 0.274。这样的差别可能与细小石叶装柄使用相关。

硬质柄本身尚不见于北非地区(克鲁姆纳塔[76]发现的新石器时代骨质"镰刀"以及法尤姆[77]新石器时代的木质镰刀算是例外)。当然,如果都是木质的,我们就不能指望它们都能保存下来。(另一方面,大部分纳吐夫文化的镰刀柄

---

* 变异系数的计算公式为:变异系数 C·V =(标准偏差 SD÷平均值 MN)×100%。——译注

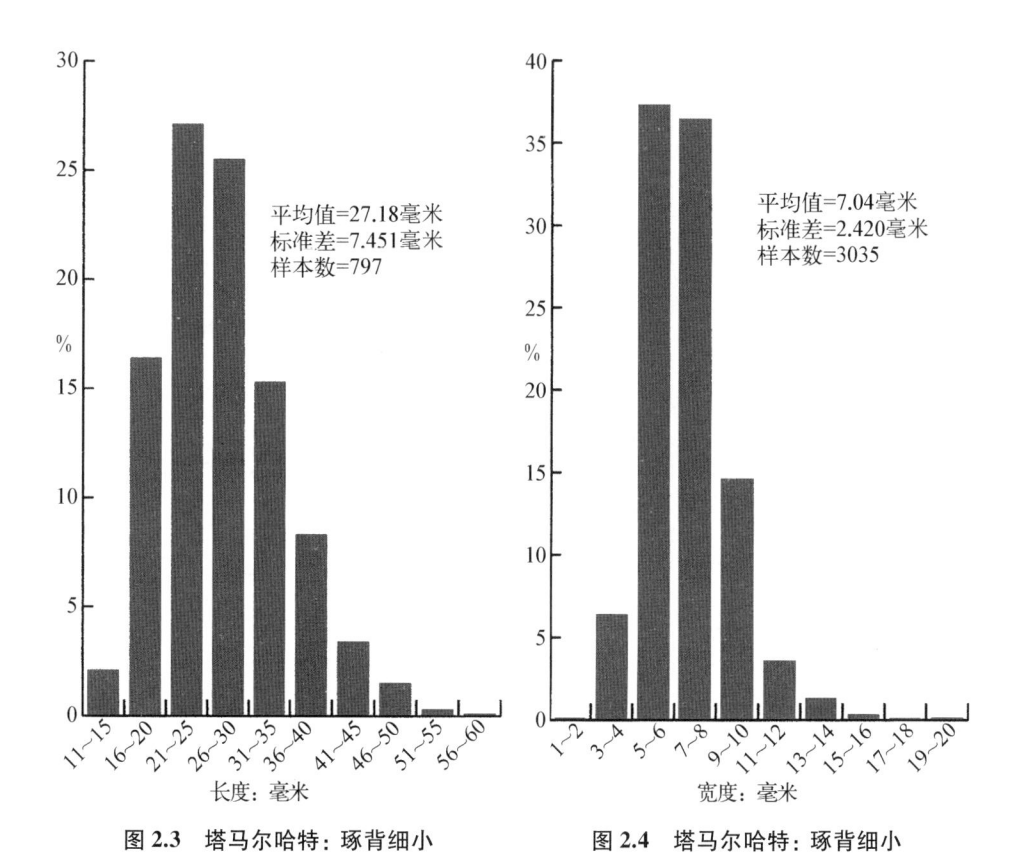

图 2.3 塔马尔哈特：琢背细小石叶的长度分布

图 2.4 塔马尔哈特：琢背细小石叶的宽度分布

都是骨制的[78]，保存条件也很恶劣，甚至比木质的保存条件更差）。不过，装柄的假说并没有使用痕迹研究的支持。

除去一个例外，目前没有研究表明琢背细小石叶上有装柄的痕迹。实际上，连使用痕迹都很少发现，虽然有研究显示，琢背细小石叶用于切割、刮削以及其他不合乎其形制的活动，但没有装柄的痕迹发现。在研究唯一例外的过程中，研究者号称在超过60%的"使用器物"上发现了装柄的痕迹[79]。然而，这项研究的方法有问题，没有迹象表明研究者采用了实验控制，把观察的破损（但没有描述）与装柄行为联系起来是缺乏证据的。将痕迹认定为由装柄所致失之简单，装柄痕迹以如此高的频率出现是其他地方未曾见到的。

装柄的判断实际是使用痕迹研究中最困难的领域之一[80]。就像是其他考古背景联系中的"礼仪"因素一样，"装柄"常常是痕迹学家遭遇困惑时的避难所，他们认为装柄在工具上很少会留下痕迹[81]。克里[82]在一项研究维基里的马格德林文化的评论说道:"琢背石叶的使用无疑是装柄的,但是很少会留下装柄的痕迹。"很不幸,他继续将之视为装柄的[83],尽管并没有得到真正的确认。

实际上,大多数视为装柄留下的痕迹都可能是其他原因所致[84],其存在并不能证明就是装柄所致。例如,器物表面而非边缘的突起上明亮的光斑与磨圆指示装柄,但是我们知道这样的痕迹可能来自制作过程中的摩擦[85],也可能来自运输[86]以及沉积后的改造过程[87]。即便是长期使用的装柄器物也不必定会留下捆绑痕迹[88]。

装柄的痕迹在克鲁维斯及其他尖状器上已经得到证实,它与尖状器在柄部前端的侧向运动相关[89]。不过,更有效的装柄技术,尤其是运用黏接剂或松脂,可能根本就不会留下任何微痕[90]。实际上,已知北非最早用作箭头的细石器(前王朝与早期法老时代的标本,箭头还保留在箭杆上)采用的就是这种装柄方式,器物只跟黏接剂接触,而不与箭杆前端摩擦[91],所以箭头的大小根本就不必受制于它所插入的箭杆的大小。

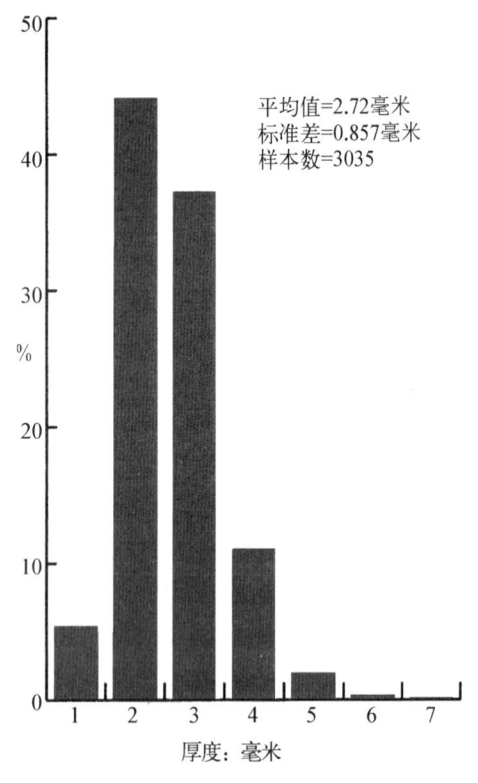

图 2.5 塔马尔哈特:琢背细小石叶的厚度分布

平均值=2.72毫米
标准差=0.857毫米
样本数=3035

五、结论

迄今所知,大约距今2万至1万年前,琢背细小石叶广泛流行于北非地区。制造与使用它们的是真正意义上的现代人,人们在面对面的小群体的社会条件中运用这种技术。我们也许可以这样假定,至少优先考虑这种可能,细小石叶在形成与发展社会认同的过程中发挥了重要作用,这在不同环境条件中所发现细小石叶形制上的高度一致性(大小与形状)上可以看出来。不同条件下琢背细小石叶的高度一致——通常用"单调"一词来形容,人们也许想知道还有什么因素比协调社会关系更重要。通过考察北非细小石叶的时空分布,尽管范围有限,我们还是可以说上述认识还是可能的,至于其他因素,目前还难以发现。"形状"(类型学)并不能指示功能,无论是在一般意义上(生计行为),还是在特殊意义上(使用痕迹研究)。细小石叶的大小与形状跟原料的供给或质量关系并不大。没有证据表明细小石叶镶嵌在"硬"柄(骨头或木头)上,理论上这样的镶嵌会制约细石器的大小,然而较晚的证据(古埃及时期的)表明采用"软的"(黏接剂)装柄方式,这不会限制细石器的大小。琢背细小石叶"必须"采用某个范围的大小与形状,不同的文化背景条件的要求有所变化。因此,至少存在某些因素在限定细小石叶变化范围,这些因素无疑有社会的。我认为这些社会因素可能是影响细小石叶形制的最重要因素。

注释:

[1] Tixier, J. *Typologie de l'Epipaleolithique du Maghreb*. Memoires du Centre de Recherches Anthropologiques, Prehistoriques et Ethnographiques 2. Paris: Arts et Metiers Graphiques. 1963: 39, 48, 94 – 96.

[2] Tixier, J. *Typologie de l'Epipaleolithique du Maghreb*. Memoires du Centre de Recherches Anthropologiques, Prehistoriques et Ethnographiques 2. Paris: Arts et Metiers Graphiques, 1963.

[3] Bar-Yosef, O., and J. L. Phillips. *Prehistoric Investigations in Gebel Maghara, Northern Sinai*. Qedem 7. Jerusalem: Monographs of the Institute of Archaeology of the Hebrew University, 1977.

Phillips, J. L. The Upper Paleolithic of Wadi Feiran, Southern Sinai. *Paleorient*. 14: 183 – 200, 1988.

[4] Schild, R., M. Chmielewska, and H. Wieckowska. The Arkinian and Shamarkian Industries. In *The Prehistory of Nubia*. F. Wendorf, ed. Pp. 651 – 767. Dallas: Fort Burgwin Research Center and Southern Methodist University Press, 1968.

[5] Garcea, E. A. A. Aterian and "Early" and "Late Acacus" from the Uan Tabu Rockshelter, Tadrart Acacus (Libyan Sahara). In *Wadi Teshuinat — Palaeoenvironment and Prehistory in South-Western Fezzan (Libyan Sahara)*. M. Cremaschi and S. Di Lernia, eds. Pp. 155 – 181. C. N. R. Quaderni di Geodinamica Alpina e Quaternaria 7. Milan: Edizioni All'lnsegna del Giglio, 1999.

[6] Bathily, M. S., M. o/ Khattar, R. Vernet, C. Cluzel, J. M. Ott, S. Beckouche, R. Caruha, M. F. Delaroziere, and J. Evin. *Les sites neolithiques de Khatt Lemaiteg (Amatlich) en Mauretanie occidentale*. Nouakchott, Mauretania: Departement d'Histoire de TUniversite de

Nouakchott, 1998.

[7] Close, A. E. Report on Site E-80-1. In *Cattle-Keepers of the Eastern Sahara: The Neolithic of Bir Kiseiba*. F. Wendorf and R. Schild, assemblers, A. E. Close, ed. Pp. 251-297. Dallas: Department of Anthropology, Southern Methodist University, 1984b.

[8] Close, A. E. Report on Site E-78-3: A Deeply Stratified Sequence of Early Kubbaniyan Occupations. In *The Prehistory of Wadi Kubbaniya, vol. 3: Late Paleolithic Archaeology*. F. Wendorf and R. Schild, assemblers, A. E. Close, ed. Pp. 375-469. Dallas: Southern Methodist University Press, 1989b.

[9] Marks, A. E. The Halfan Industry. In *The Prehistory of Nubia*. F. Wendorf, ed. Pp. 392-460. Dallas: Fort Burgwin Research Center and Southern Methodist University Press, 1968.

[10] Close, A. E. *The Identification of Style in Lithic Artefacts from Northeast Africa*. Memoires de l'Institut d'Egypte 61. Cairo: Institut d'Egypte, 1977.

[11] Vermeersch, P. M., E. Paulissen, and W. Van Neer. The Late Palaeolithic Makhadma Sites (Egypt): Environment and Subsistence. In *Late Prehistory of the Nile Basin and the Sahara*. L. Krzyzaniak and M. Kobusiewicz, eds. Pp. 87-114. Poznan, Poland: Poznan Archaeological Museum, 1989.
Vermeersch, P. M., E. Paulissen, and D. Huyge. Makhadma 4, a Late Palaeolithic Fishing Site. In *Palaeolithic Living Sites in Upper and Middle Egypt*. P. M. Vermeersch, ed. Pp. 227-270. Leuven, Belgium: Leuven University Press, 2000.

[12] Close, A. E., F. Wendorf, and R. Schild. *The Afian: A Study of Stylistic Variation in Nilotic Industry*. Dallas: Department of Anthropology and Institute for the Study of Earth and Man, Southern Methodist University, 1979.

[13] Vermeersch, P. M. The Upper and Late Palaeolithic of Northern and Eastern Africa. In *New Light on the Northeast African Past*. F. Klees and R. Kuper, eds. Pp. 99-153. Kflln: Heinrich-Barth-lnstitut, 1992.

[14] Paulissen, E., and P. M. Vermeersch. Earth, Man and Climate in the Egyptian Nile Valley during the Pleistocene. In *Prehistory of Arid North Africa: Essays in Honor of Fred Wendorf*. A. E. Close, ed. Pp. 29-67. Dallas. Southern Methodist University Press, 1987.

[15] Wendorf, F., and R. Schild. Summary and Synthesis. In The Prehistory of Wadi Kubbaniya, vol. 3: Late Paleolithic Archaeology. F. Wendorf and R. Schild, assemblers, and A. E. Close, ed. Pp. 768-824. Dallas: Southern Methodist University Press, 1989.

[16] Roche, J. Cadre chronologique de l'Epipaleolithique marocain. Colloque II, IXe Congres U. I. S. P. P., Nice, Pp. 153-167, 1976.

[17] Saxon, E. C, A. E. Close, C. Cluzel, V. Morse, and N. J. Shackleton. Results of Recent Investigations at Tamar Hat. *Libyca* 22: 49-91, 1974.

[18] Close, A. E. Current Research and Recent Radiocarbon Dates from Northern Africa. *Journal of African History* 21: 145 – 167, 1980.

Close, A. E. Current Research and Recent Radiocarbon Dates from Northern Africa, II. *Journal of African History* 25: 1 – 24, 1984a.

[19] Debenath, A., J.-P. Raynal, J. Roche, J.-P. Texier, and D. Ferembach. Position, habitat, typologie et devenir de l'aterien marocain: donnees recentes. *L'Anthropologie* 90: 233 – 246, 1986.

[20] Cremaschi, M., S. Di Lernia, and E. A. A. Garcea. Some Insights on the Aterian in the Libyan Sahara: Chronology, Environment and Archaeology. *African Archaeological Review* 15: 261 – 286. *Backed Blade lets Are a Foreign Country 41, 1998*: Table 1.

Wendorf, F., and R. Schild. The Middle Paleolithic of North Africa: A Status Report. In *New Light on the Northeast African Past*. F. Klees and R. Kuper, eds. Pp. 39 – 78. Koln: Heinrich-Barth-lnstitut, 1992.

[21] Cremaschi, M., S. Di Lernia, and E. A. A. Garcea. Some Insights on the Aterian in the Libyan Sahara: Chronology, Environment and Archaeology. *African Archaeological Review* 15: 261 – 286. *Backed Blade lets Are a Foreign Country*, 1998.

Fontes, J.-C, and F. Gasse. PALHYDAF (Palaeohydrology in Africa) Program: Objectives, Methods, Major Results. *Palaeogeography, Palaeoclimatology, Palaeoecology* 84: 191 – 215. 1991.

Kleindienst, M. R., H. P. Schwarcz, K. Nicoll, C. S. Churcher, J. Frizano, R. W. Giegengack, and M. F. Wiseman. Pleistocene Geochronology and Paleoclimates at Dakhleh Oasis and Kharga Oasis. Western Desert, Egypt, Based upon Uranium-Thorium Determinations from Water-Laid Tufas. *Nyame Akuma* 46: 96, 1996.

Wendorf, F., and R. Schild. The Middle Paleolithic of North Africa: A Status Report. In *New Light on the Northeast African Past*. F. Klees and R. Kuper, eds. Pp. 39 – 78. Koln: Heinrich-Barth-lnstitut, 1992.

Wendorf, F., R. Schild, A. E. Close, and Associates. *Egypt during the Last Interglacial: The Middle Paleolithic of Bir Tarfawi and Bir Sahara East*. New York: Plenum. 1993.

[22] McBurney, C. B. M., and R. W. Hey. *Prehistory and Pleistocene Geology in Cyrenaican Libya*. Cambridge: Cambridge University Press. 1955.

[23] Close, A. E. The Place of the Haua Fteah in the Late Palaeolithic of North Africa. In *Stone Age Prehistory: Studies in Memory of Charles McBurney*. G. N. Bailey and P. Callow, eds. Pp. 169 – 180. Cambridge: Cambridge University Press, 1986: Table 10. 1 and 10. 2.

[24] McBurney, C. B. M. *The Haua Fteah (Cyrenaica) and the Stone Age of the South-East Mediterranean*. Cambridge: Cambridge University Press, 1967.

[25] McBurney, C. B. M. *The Haua Fteah (Cyrenaica) and the Stone Age of the South-East Mediterranean.* Cambridge: Cambridge University Press, 1967: 215.

[26] McBurney, C. B. M. *The Haua Fteah (Cyrenaica) and the Stone Age of the South-East Mediterranean.* Cambridge: Cambridge University Press, 1967: Table III. I.

[27] McBurney, C. B. M. *The Haua Fteah (Cyrenaica) and the Stone Age of the South-East Mediterranean.* Cambridge: Cambridge University Press, 1967: 48 – 50.

[28] Vermeersch, P. M., E. Paulissen, and P. Van Peer. Palaeolithic Chert Exploitation in the Limestone Stretch of the Egyptian Nile Valley. *African Archaeological Review* 8: 77 – 102, 1990.

[29] Paulissen, E., P. M. Vermeersch, and W. Van Neer. Progress Report on the Late Paleolithic Shuwikhat Sites (Qena, Upper Egypt). *Nyame Akuma* 26: 7 – 14, 1985.
Vermeersch, P. M., and E. Paulissen. Conclusions. In *Palaeolithic Living Sites in Upper and Middle Egypt.* P. M. Vermeersch, ed. Pp. 321 – 326. Leuven, Belgium: Leuven University Press, 2000: 323 – 324.
Wendorf, F., and R. Schild. *Prehistory of the Nile Valley.* New York: Academic, 1976: 82 – 86.

[30] Irwin, H. T., J. B. Wheat, and L. G. Irwin. *University of Colorado Investigations of Paleolithic and Epipaleolithic Sites in Sudan, Africa.* University of Utah Papers in Anthropology 90. Salt Lake City: University of Utah Press, 1968.

[31] Wendorf, F., and R. Schild. Summary and Synthesis. In *The Prehistory of Wadi Kubbaniya*, vol. 3: *Late Paleolithic Archaeology.* F. Wendorf and R. Schild, assemblers, and A. E. Close, ed. Pp. 768 – 824. Dallas: Southern Methodist University Press, 1989.

[32] Vermeersch, P. M. The Upper and Late Palaeolithic of Northern and Eastern Africa. In *New Light on the Northeast African Past.* F. Klees and R. Kuper, eds. Pp. 99 – 153. Kflln: Heinrich-Barth-lnstitut, 1992: 122.

[33] Lubell, D. *The Fakhurian: A Late Paleolithic Industry from Upper Egypt.* Papers of the Geological Survey of Egypt 58. Cairo: Geological Survey of Egypt, 1974.
Wendorf, F., and R. Schild. Summary and Synthesis. In *The Prehistory of Wadi Kubbaniya*, vol. 3: *Late Paleolithic Archaeology.* F. Wendorf and R. Schild, assemblers, and A. E. Close, ed. Pp. 768 – 824. Dallas: Southern Methodist University Press, 1989.
Wendorf, F., R. Schild, P. Baker, A. Gautier, L. Longo, and A. Mohamed. *A Late Paleolithic Kill-Butchery-Camp in Upper Egypt.* Dallas and Warsaw: Department of Anthropology (Institute for the Study of Earth and Man, *44 Angela E. Close* Southern Methodist University) and Institute of Archaeology and Ethnology, Polish Academy of Sciences, 1997.

[34] Close, A. E. *The Identification of Style in Lithic Artefacts from Northeast Africa.* Memoires de l'Institut d'Egypte 61. Cairo: Institut d'Egypte, 1977. Report on Site E – 78 – 3: A Deeply Stratified Sequence of Early Kubbaniyan Occupations. In *The Prehistory of Wadi Kubbaniya, vol. 3: Late Paleolithic Archaeology.* F. Wendorf and R. Schild, assemblers, A. E. Close, ed. Pp. 375 – 469. Dallas: Southern Methodist University Press, 1989b.

Marks, A. E. The Halfan Industry. In *The Prehistory of Nubia.* F. Wendorf, ed. Pp. 392 – 460. Dallas: Fort Burgwin Research Center and Southern Methodist University Press, 1968.

Phillips, J. L. *Two Final Paleolithic Sites in the Nile Valley and Their External Relations.* Papers of the Geological Survey of Egypt 57. Cairo: Geological Survey of Egypt, 1973.

[35] Vermeersch, P. M. *Elkab II. L'Elkabien, epipaleolithique de la vallee du Nil egyptien.* Leuven and Brussels: Universitaire Pers Leuven and Fondation Egyptologique Reine Elisabeth, 1978.

[36] Wendorf, F., and R. Schild, assemblers, and A. E. Close, ed. *The Prehistory of Wadi Kubbaniya, vol. 1: The Wadi Kubbaniya Skeleton: A Late Paleolithic Burial from Southern Egypt.* Dallas: Southern Methodist University Press, 1986.

[37] Arambourg, C, M. Boule, H. Vallois, and R. Verneau. *Les grottes paleolithiques des Beni-Segoual (Algerie).* Archives de l'Institut de Paleontologie Humaine 13. Paris: Masson, 1934.

Ferembach, D. Les restes humains epipaleolithiques de la grotte de Taforalt (Maroc oriental). *Comptes-rendus Hebdomadaires des Seances de l'Academie des Sciences* 248: 3405 – 3467, 1959.

Ferembach, D., J. Dastugue, and M.-J. Poitrat-Targowla. *La necropole e'pipaleolithique de Taforalt (Maroc oriental). Etude des squelettes humains.* Paris: Centre National de la Recherche Scientifique, 1962.

[38] Wendorf, F., and R. Schild, assemblers, and A. E. Close, ed. The Prehistory of Wadi Kubbaniya, vol. 1: The Wadi Kubbaniya Skeleton: A Late Paleolithic Burial from Southern Egypt. Dallas: Southern Methodist University Press, 1986: 73.

[39] Vermeersch, P. M., E. Paulissen, S. Stokes, C. Charlier, P. Van Peer, C. Stringer, and W. Lindsay. A Middle Palaeolithic Burial of a Modern Human at Taramsa Hill, Egypt. *Antiquity* 1998: 481.

[40] Vermeersch, P. M., E. Paulissen, G. Gijselings, M. Otte, A. Thoma, P. Van Peer, and R. Lauwers. 33 000-Yr Old Mining Site and Related Homo in the Egyptian Nile Valley. *Nature* 309: 342 – 344, 1984.

[41] Vermeersch, P. M. The Upper and Late Palaeolithic of Northern and Eastern Africa. In *New Light on the Northeast African Past.* F. Klees and R. Kuper, eds. Pp. 99 – 153. Kflln: Heinrich-Barth-lnstitut, 1992: 122.

[42] Close, A. E. *The Identification of Style in Lithic Artefacts from Northeast Africa.* Memoires de

l'Institut d'Egypte 61. Cairo: Institut d'Egypte, 1977. Identifying Style in Stone Artefacts: A Case Study from the Nile Valley. In *Alternative Approaches to Lithic Analysis*. D. O. Henry and G. H. Odell, eds. Pp. 3 – 26. Archaeological Papers of the American Anthropological Association, 1. Washington D. C.: American Anthropological Association, 1989a.

[43] Close, A. E. Identifying Style in Stone Artefacts: A Case Study from the Nile Valley. In *Alternative Approaches to Lithic Analysis*. D. O. Henry and G. H. Odell, eds. Pp. 3 – 26. Archaeological Papers of the American Anthropological Association, 1. Washington D. C.: American Anthropological Association, 1989a: 4 – 7.

[44] Close, A. E. *The Identification of Style in Lithic Artefacts from Northeast Africa*. Memoires de l'Institut d'Egypte 61. Cairo: Institut d'Egypte, 1977: 252 – 253.

[45] Close, A. E. *The Identification of Style in Lithic Artefacts from Northeast Africa*. Memoires de l'Institut d'Egypte 61. Cairo: Institut d'Egypte, 1977: figs.8. 1 – 8. 4.

[46] Rampino, M. R., and S. H. Ambrose. Volcanic Winter in the Garden of Eden: The Toba Supereruption and the Late Pleistocene Human Populations Crash. In *Volcanic Hazards and Disasters in Human Antiquity*. F. W. McCoy and G. Heiken, eds. Pp. 71 – 82. Special Paper 345. Boulder: Geological Society of America, 2000.

[47] Pelegrin, J. *Technologie lithique: Le Chdtelperronien de Rocde-Combe (Lot) et de La Cote (Dordogne)*. Cahiers du Quaternaire 20. Paris: Centre National de la Recherche Scientifique, 1995: 253.

Perles, C. In Search of Lithic Strategies: A Cognitive Approach to Prehistoric Chipped Stone Assemblages. In *Representations in Archaeology*. J. C. Gardin and C. S. Peebles, eds. Pp. 223 – 247. Bloomington: Indiana University Press, 1992: 234 – 235.

[48] Tixier, J. *Typologie de l'Epipaleolithique du Maghreb*. Memoires du Centre de Recherches Anthropologiques, Prehistoriques et Ethnographiques 2. Paris: Arts et Metiers Graphiques, 1963.

[49] Adams, W. Y., and E. W. Adams. *A rchaeological Typology and Practical Reality: A Dialectical Approach to Artifact Classificationand Sorting*. Cambridge: Cambridge University Press, 1991: 8.

[50] Binford, L. R. Archaeology as Anthropology. *American Antiquity* 28: 217 – 225. 1962.

[51] Dobres, M.-A. *Technology and Social Agency: Outlining a Practice Framework for Archaeology*. Oxford: Blackwell, 2000: 227.

[52] Sinclair, A. Constellation of Knowledge: Human Agency and Material Affordance in Lithic Technology. In *Agency in Archaeology*. M.-A. Dobres and J. E. Robb, eds. Pp. 196 – 212. London: Routledge, 2000: 200.

[53] Dunbar, R. I. M. The Social Brain Hypothesis. *Evolutionary Anthropology*, 1998: 186 – 188.

Roebroeks, W. Hominid Behaviour and the Earliest Occupation of Europe: An Exploration. *Journal of Human Evolution*, 2001: 451-452.

[54] Dunbar, R. I. M. The Social Brain Hypothesis. *Evolutionary Anthropology*, 1998: 185.

[55] Close, A. E. Report on Site E-78-3: A Deeply Stratified Sequence of Early Kubbaniyan Occupations. In *The Prehistory of Wadi Kubbaniya, vol. 3: Late Paleolithic Archaeology*. F. Wendorf and R. Schild, assemblers, A. E. Close, ed. Pp. 375-469. Dallas: Southern Methodist University Press, 1989b.

[56] McBurney, C. B. M. *The Haua Fteah (Cyrenaica) and the Stone Age of the South-East Mediterranean*. Cambridge: Cambridge University Press, 1967.

[57] Roebroeks, W. Hominid Behaviour and the Earliest Occupation of Europe: An Exploration. *Journal of Human Evolution*, 2001: 451.

[58] Dougherty, J., and C. M. Keller. Taskonomy: A Practical Approach to Knowledge Structures. *American Ethnologist* 5: 763-774, 1982.
Sinclair, A. Constellation of Knowledge: Human Agency and Material Affordance in Lithic Technology. In *Agency in Archaeology*. M.-A. Dobres and J. E. Robb, eds. Pp. 196-212. London: Routledge, 2000.

[59] Close, A. E. *The Identification of Style in Lithic Artefacts from Northeast Africa*. Memoires de l'Institut d'Egypte 61. Cairo: Institut d'Egypte, 1977. Identifying Style in Stone Artefacts: A Case Study from the Nile Valley. In *Alternative Approaches to Lithic Analysis*. D. O. Henry and G. H. Odell, eds. Pp. 3-26. Archaeological Papers of the American Anthropological Association, 1. Washington D. C.: American Anthropological Association, 1989a.
Sackett, J. R. The Meaning of Style in Archaeology: A General Model. *American Antiquity* 42: 369-380, 1977. Approaches to Style in Lithic Archaeology. *Journal of Anthropological Archaeology* 1: 59-12, 1982.

[60] Sinclair, A. Constellation of Knowledge: Human Agency and Material Affordance in Lithic Technology. In *Agency in Archaeology*. M.-A. Dobres and J. E. Robb, eds. Pp. 196-212. London: Routledge, 2000.

[61] Sinclair, A. Constellation of Knowledge: Human Agency and Material Affordance in Lithic Technology. In *Agency in Archaeology*. M.-A. Dobres and J. E. Robb, eds. Pp. 196-212. London: Routledge, 2000: 207.

[62] Sinclair, A. Constellation of Knowledge: Human Agency and Material Affordance in Lithic Technology. In *Agency in Archaeology*. M.-A. Dobres and J. E. Robb, eds. Pp. 196-212. London: Routledg, 2000: 202-203.

[63] Dobres, M.-A. *Technology and Social Agency: Outlining a Practice Framework for Archaeology*. Oxford: Blackwell, 2000: 209.

[64] Wobst, H. M. Agency in (Spite of) Material Culture. In *Agency in Archaeology*. M.-A. Dobres and J. E. Robb, eds. Pp. 40–50. London: Routledge, 2000: 47.

[65] Andrefsky, W., Jr. Thoughts on Stone Tool Shape and Inferred Function. *Journal of Middle Atlantic Archaeology* 13: 125–143, 1997.

Finlayson, B., and S. Mithen. The Microwear and Morphology of Microliths from Gleann Mor. In *Projectile Technology*. H. Knecht, ed. Pp. 107–129. New York: Plenum, 1997.

Juel Jensen, H. Functional Analysis of Prehistoric Flint Tools by High-Power Microscopy: A Review of West European Research. *Journal of World Prehistory* 2: 53–88, 1988.

Levi Sala, I. *A Study of Microscopic Polish on Flint Implements*. British Archaeological Reports International Series 629. Oxford: Tempus Repararum, 1996: 25–26.

Odell, G. H. The Morphological Express at Function Junction: Searching for Meaning in Lithic Tool-Types. *Journal of Anthropological Research* 37: 319–342, 1981.

[66] Close A. E. Report on Site E–78–3: A Deeply Stratified Sequence of Early Kubbaniyan Occupations. In *The Prehistory of Wadi Kubbaniya, vol. 3: Late Paleolithic Archaeology*. F. Wendorf and R. Schild, assemblers, A. E. Close, ed. Pp. 375–469. Dallas: Southern Methodist University Press, 1989b: 452–453.

Kobusiewicz, M. Report on Site E–80–4: The Archaeology of El Ghorab Playa. In *Cattle-Keepers of the Eastern Sahara: The Neolithic of Bir Kiseiba*. F. Wendorf and R. Schild, assemblers, A. E. Close, ed. Pp. 135–164. Dallas: Department of Anthropology, Southern Methodist University, 1984: 158.

[67] Becker, M., and F. Wendorf. A Microwear Study of a Late Pleistocene Qadan Assemblage from Southern Egypt. *Journal of Field Archaeology* 20: 389–398, 1993.

Juel Jensen, H., R. Schild, F. Wendorf, and A. E. Close. Understanding the Late Palaeolithic Tools with Lustrous Edges from the Lower Nile Valley. *Antiquity* 65: 122–128, 1991.

Longo, L. Functional Analysis. In *A Late Paleolithic Kill-Butchery-Camp in Upper Egypt*. F. Wendorf, R. Schild, P. Baker, A. Gautier, L. Longo, and A. Mohamed, co-authors. Pp. 33–41. Dallas and Warsaw: Department of Anthropology (Institute for the Study of Earth and Man, Southern Methodist University) and Institute of Archaeology and Ethnology, Polish Academy of Sciences, 1997.

[68] Close A. E. Report on Site E–78–3: A Deeply Stratified Sequence of Early Kubbaniyan Occupations. In The Prehistory of Wadi Kubbaniya, vol. 3: Late Paleolithic Archaeology. F. Wendorf and R. Schild, assemblers, A. E. Close, ed. Pp. 375–469. Dallas: Southern Methodist University Press, 1989b.

[69] Phillips, J. L. *Two Final Paleolithic Sites in the Nile Valley and Their External Relations.*

Papers of the Geological Survey of Egypt 57. Cairo: Geological Survey of Egypt, 1973.

[70] Close A. E. Report on Site E - 78 - 3: A Deeply Stratified Sequence of Early Kubbaniyan Occupations. In The Prehistory of Wadi Kubbaniya, vol. 3: Late Paleolithic Archaeology. F. Wendorf and R. Schild, assemblers, A. E. Close, ed. Pp. 375 - 469. Dallas: Southern Methodist University Press, 1989b: 458 - 461.

[71] Phillips, J. L. *Two Final Paleolithic Sites in the Nile Valley and Their External Relations*. Papers of the Geological Survey of Egypt 57. Cairo: Geological Survey of Egypt, 1973: 52.

[72] Close, A. E. Identifying Style in Stone Artefacts: A Case Study from the Nile Valley. In *Alternative Approaches to Lithic Analysis*. D. O. Henry and G. H. Odell, eds. Pp. 3 - 26. Archaeological Papers of the American Anthropological Association, 1. Washington D. C.: American Anthropological Association, 1989a.

[73] Close, A. E. Distance and Decay: An Uneasy Relationship. *Antiquity* 73: 24 - 32, 1999.

[74] Close, A. E. Lithic Economy in the Absence of Stone. *Journal of Middle Atlantic Archaeology*, 1997: 50.

[75] Close, A. E., and C. G. Sampson. Recent Backed Microlith Production in Central South Africa. *Lithic Technology*, 1998.

[76] Tixier, J. Examen en laboratoire de la "faucille n° T" de Columnata. *Libyca*, 1960.

[77] Caton Thompson, G., and E. W. Gardner. *The Desert Fayum*. London: Royal Anthropological Institute, 1934.

[78] Stordeur, D. Le Natoufien et son evolution a travers les artefacts en os. In *The Natufian Culture in the Levant*. O. Bar-Yosef and F. R. Valla, eds. Pp. 467 - 482. Ann Arbor: International Monographs in Prehistory, 1991.

[79] Longo, L. Functional Analysis. In *A Late Paleolithic Kill-Butchery-Camp in Upper Egypt*. F. Wendorf, R. Schild, P. Baker, A. Gautier, L. Longo, and A. Mohamed, co-authors. Pp. 33 - 41. Dallas and Warsaw: Department of Anthropology (Institute for the Study of Earth and Man, Southern Methodist University) and Institute of Archaeology and Ethnology, Polish Academy of Sciences, 1997: 41.

[80] Juel Jensen, H. Functional Analysis of Prehistoric Flint Tools by High-Power Microscopy: A Review of West European Research. *Journal of World Prehistory*, 1988: 79.
Levi Sala, I. *A Study of Microscopic Polish on Flint Implements*. British Archaeological Reports International Series 629. Oxford: Tempus Repararum. 1996: 12.

[81] Cahen, D., L. H. Keeley, and F. Van Noten. Stone Tools, Toolkits, and Human Behavior in Prehistory. *Current Anthropology*, 1979: 681.

[82] Keeley, L. H. Hafting and "Retooling" at Verberie. In *La Main et routil: Manches et Emmanchements Prehistoriques*. D. Stordeur, ed. Pp. 89 - 96. Lyon: Travaux de la Maison de

TOrient, 1987: 91.

[83] Keeley, L. H. Hafting and "Retooling" at Verberie. In *La Main et rOutil: Manches et Emmanchements Prehistoriques*. D. Stordeur, ed. Pp. 89 – 96. Lyon: Travaux de la Maison de TOrient, 1987: 92.

[84] Mansur-Franchomme, M. E. Synthese: Emmanchements et traces d'utilisation. In *La Main et I 'Outil: Manches et Emmanchements Prehistoriques*. D. Stordeur, ed. Pp. 329 – 341. Lyon: Travaux de la Maison de l'Orient, 1987: 329 – 330.

[85] Unger-Hamilton, R., R. Grace, R. Miller, and C. Bergman. Drill Bits from Abu Salabikh, Iraq. In *La Main et l'Outil: Manches et Emmanchements Prehistoriques*. D. Stordeur, ed. Pp. 269 – 285. Lyon: Travaux de la Maison de l'Orient, 1987: 280.

[86] Frison, G., and B. Bradley. *The Fenn Cache: Clovis Weapons and Tools*. Santa Fe: One Horse Land and Cattle, 1999: 81 – 82.

[87] Levi Sala, I. *A Study of Microscopic Polish on Flint Implements*. British Archaeological Reports International Series 629. Oxford: Tempus Repararum, 1996: 70 – 71.

[88] Unger-Hamilton, R., R. Grace, R. Miller, and C. Bergman. Drill Bits from Abu Salabikh, Iraq. In *La Main et l'Outil: Manches et Emmanchements Prehistoriques*. D. Stordeur, ed. Pp. 269 – 285. Lyon: Travaux de la Maison de l'Orient, 1987: 280.

[89] Kay, M. Microwear Analysis of Some Clovis and Experimental Chipped Stone Tools. In *Stone Tools: Theoretical Insights into Human Prehistory*. G. H. Odell, ed. Pp. 315 – 344. New York: Plenum, 1996: 329 – 330.

[90] Juel Jensen, H. Functional Analysis of Prehistoric Flint Tools by High-Power Microscopy: A Review of West European Research. *Journal of World Prehistory*, 1988: 79.
Levi Sala, I. *A Study of Microscopic Polish on Flint Implements*. British Archaeological Reports International Series 629. Oxford: Tempus Repararum, 1996: 12, 20 – 21, 28.

[91] Clark, J. D., J. L. Phillips, and P. S. Staley. Interpretations of Prehistoric Technology from Ancient Egyptian and Other Sources. Part 1: Ancient Egyptian Bows and Arrows and Their Relevance for African Prehistory. *Pale'orient*, 1974.

走向细石器：从利凡特地区
看细石器技术的起源

迈克 P. 尼勒

（蒙大拿州立大学　波兹曼）

摘　要：晚更新世至早全新世期间细石器技术在全球大部分地区广泛分布。不同时空条件下的普遍存在正说明细石器在解决生存问题上的灵活性与重要性。从进化论的视角来看，利凡特地区细石器技术的起源可以视为一个长期变化过程的结果，涉及整个地区获取资源方式的变化，也可以视为一个以遗址为中心的短期行为的调整，代表当时人群流动策略的变化。研究结果表明细石器的出现与古人在资源获取与流动采食的行为变迁密切相关，同时也表明进化论的理论框架有助于了解这一过程。

晚更新世后期许多地方的考古材料中都出现了细石器技术。其出现意味着细石器这样的器物在社会与自然约束的环境中能够比之前的技术更有利于获取能量（食物资源）。如此多样的地理环境中、如此不同的时间点上出现细石器技术因素，都说明其灵活性与重要性，它有助于解决古人的生存问题。正是在这样的背景联系中，也就是作为解决生存难题的方法，我们来考察细石器技术。研究这一难题的视角基于进化论，这种方法适用于东地中海利凡特地区细石器技术起源的研究。本文运用利凡特地区的材料，从两个角度来审视细石器技术的演化过程。其一，将细石器技术视为一种获取动物食物资源的策略。这个角度的关键是生计策略的长期发展趋势，这些策略与当时狩猎采集者所具备的技术选择相关联。其二，从以遗址为中心的视角来看细石器技术,力图弄清短时间尺度里狩猎采集者的潜在选择或行为可能性。使用细石器技术的环境条件并不相同,考古遗存反映狩猎采集者多种可能的组合选择。就细石器技术而言,特别值得注意的是群体流动性与原料条件的影响。在细石器技术范畴内,原料的获取、生产与使用都存在着广泛的选择[1],成本变化多样。那些采用的选择应该能给人们带来短期的适应优势。运用进化论的模型能够更好地解释考古材料中所见的种种变化,这些变化给予采用者适应选择上的优势。

一、为什么是细石器?

石叶或长石片工业具有长期的使用历史,使用与放弃断断续续地存在着[2]。正如这些研究者所指出的,石叶技术并不总是比石片技术优越,尤其是面对不利于石叶技术使用的情况或难题的时候。就这方面而言,石叶技术只代表一种解决生存问题的途径——一种很可能跟特定的情况或是"历史偶然性"相关的途径[3]。不过,一旦晚更新世的人类选择了这类技术,可能跟捆绑技术的发展有关,随后我们看到了更小的石器产品——细小石叶。利凡特南部这种"细石器化"的过程跟旧石器时代晚期的小石叶(small blade)工业联系在一起。这类小石叶最早出现于距今 4 万年前,整个晚更新世一直都是当时人类仅有的几种技术选择之一[4]。旧石器时代晚期,与小石叶或细小石叶工业同时的阿玛连工业就是一种存在于利凡特地区的、以石片为主的奥瑞纳工业[5]。距今 1.8 万年前,细石器工业开始一统天下。这带来一个问题,为什么细石器如此流行?狩猎采集者的技术选择有限,他们最终都选择了细石器,这也就是说这种技术具有某种适应优势。后旧石器时代细石器依旧在利凡特地区的考古材料中占主导地位[6]。如果细石器在利凡特地区特定环境中不具有适应优势(也就是在选择上处在中间状态,既非有利也非不利),那么我们应该看到更多样的技术选择,考古材料中既应该有细石器,也应该有非细石器。另一个反对细石器不具有适应优势的理由是这一技术广泛的地理分布。类似于基因漂移,如果这是一种中立的特征,那么其空间分布应该要随机得多,而不是如此流行。

为什么细石器成为解决生存难题的良策呢?研究细石器技术效用的学者们提出众多的看法。第一种看法认为,细石器有助于提高狩猎采集者的流动性,因为这些器物容易搬运,解决了人们搬运笨重物品的麻烦[7]。第二种看法认为,细石器代表一种灵活的技术,通用的器形便于以不同的方式使用。细石器功能的解释非常多样,包括用作狩猎的标枪头、切割工具、植物加工工具[8]。第三种看法指出,细石器具有相对标准化的形制,这些可以替换的部件可以插入复合工具柄部的凹槽中,工具的维护更加便利高效[9]。这种替换的便利被克拉克[10]称为"拔出与插入"技术。第四种观点认为,细石器有助于避免高流动性条件下原料供给的短缺与不确定性。细石器可以在一个地方大量生产,在另一个地方使用,人们在工具使用、资源采集以及原料获取的地理位置上可以有更大的弹性。这种弹性可以从风险控制的角度来考虑,它可以抵消食物获取与技术选择的相关成本[11]。第五种也是最后一种观点认为,细石器的运用可以反映狩猎采集者狩猎策略的变化,或是特定动物资源条件的变化[12]。如此看来,细石器有助于提高资源获取的效率,尤其是跟其他技术相比。

上面所说的这些观点都表明细石器可能在许多方面具有优势。每一种观点都可以解释细石器的起源,基本都是从功能或适应的角度出发的,两者仅从概念上来说彼此独立。实际上,解释细石器的起源可能是上述许多因素相互作用与妥协的结果。本文的目的是以一个更加统一的角度来研究细石器,这个角度就是进化论。

二、进化论的方法

讨论细石器选择问题采用的视角来自考古学最近对进化论的强调。考古学与人类学中运用进化论思想有长期的历史。[13]不过,强调运用新进化论的方法还只是过去25年的事。考古学中在新达尔文主义进化论的名头下存在两个运用这些方法的分支——进化生态学与选择论[14]。后者可以追溯到罗伯特·邓尼尔[15]的研究,他提倡在考古学研究中运用以选择为中心的理论模型。尽管有邓尼尔的提倡,但是考古学家在本学科中接受进化论的解释潜力还是比较缓慢的,最近趋势有所改变,运用这种方法的研究著作在明显增加[16]。

这些进化论方法中有三项基本的主张。一是群体中本身就存在变化,变化的表现形式是表现型(phenotype)。考古学中表现型通过一定范围内可能的形态特征来表达。在特定的器物类型中(如陶器、石器),形态变化基本上是连续的,但基于主观的判断,这种连续的变化都会或多或少地分成若干独立的类型。例如,根据尺寸的大小,石制品中区分出石片、石叶以及细小石叶,这样的分类标准是主观设定的,用以区分连续的变化。二是变化的传递是从个体到个体,以非遗传的方式进行的。也就是说,变化是人与人之间的学习,跨越时空传递的。因此,这种变化的速度可能要比通过遗传的方式传递要快得多。三是从群体内特征变化的范围来看,某些特征比其他特征变化得更频繁,淘汰的过程如同自然选择。群体中存在的变化,通过个体往下传递,基于它们所含有的选择优势,变化的频率随之改变。选择的过程假定最终采用的特征具有某种选择优势。就选择而言,如果特征是中性的,那么形成特定表现型的趋势就只能指望随机选择的过程。

从进化的观点来看,特定表现型的长期存在意味着它相对于其他表现型存在某种选择的优势。我们现在认识到具有优势的表现型是有机体与社会和自然环境相互作用的产物,随着环境变迁,这些表现型可能不再具有相对其他表现型的选择优势。表现在考古学中,选择过程的结果可以通过考古材料中长期存在的表现型(器物)来了解。只有表现型在当地环境约束中表现出选择优势,它才会持续存在。在本文的讨论中,我们认为细石器工业的长期存在是由于它们所拥有的选择优势,适应特殊社会与自然环境条件。

三、利凡特地区的细石器选择

鉴于细石器的多功能,将之视为单一因素作用的结果是不现实的。相反,研究多种因素复杂的相互作用可能有助于我们了解所涉及的选择压力。为实现这个目的,这里提出两条线索,以利于深入的研究:(1)动物利用模式的变化,(2)石制品使用与废弃上的变化,它们反映了狩猎采集者不同的流动策略。前者涉及长期的变化,而后者关注更短期的变化。即便是衡量某一细石器技术的特征,由于选择压力的作用,仍然存在技术与行为上的差异。

(一)资源获取

一般说来,石器技术的改变反映资源获取方式的变化,因为石制品是食物资源获取与加工的技术手段。就此而言,石制品的运用有助于降低资源获取的风险。风险不仅可以包括成功或失败的概率,同时关系失败的连带成本[17]。显然,不同事件的失败成本以及导致的结果极其不同,器物生产与使用应该可以反映这些结果。除了失败的概率与成本,巴姆福斯与布雷德[18]就曾指出狩猎采集者必须明白技术选择的连带成本(他们称之为技术成本)。技术成本表示在石器原料获取、工具生产与使用过程中面临风险时所做的选择[19]。例如,我们可能看到一种情况,人们通过一次生产大批的石制品来降低时间安排上的冲突与技术成本。批量生产可以进一步降低资源获取成本(以失败的概率与失败的成本来表示),具体途径可以包括采用多种可替换的武器尖端部件,便于维修,形成更高程度的功能冗余。由此形成一种可靠的器物形式,关键时候能够用上,并且能够进行便捷地维护[20]。这样的话,把劳动分配到了器物制作开始阶段(获取原料与制作工具),有助于降低失败的成本。就器物形态而言,多样的器形有助于解决获取成本与时间安排上的难题;不过,特定表现型(如细石器)的长期存在可能指示某种选择优势。如果选择细石器技术降低资源获取的成本,我们应该可以从动物群材料的变化上找到某些证据。反映一种技术超越另一种技术的动物群材料特征包括所获取动物资源的丰富度(物种的数量)与均匀度(比例频率)的变化。丰富度与均匀度是动物群材料大致变化较为可靠的指标,鉴于保存条件与复原的水平,这个记录是粗线条的。高质量的材料组合,加上更加细致的分析,有助于发现潜在的地区模式,就像斯廷那等研究者所发现的那样[21]。为了更好地了解与资源获取相关的技术变化,有必要考虑更多代表不同时间阶段的石器技术。就本文的目的而言,动物群的材料不仅代表后旧石器时代早期的细石器组合,而且包括利凡特地区旧石器中晚期的动物考古材料[22]。这样我们就有了更大的时间尺度,可以更好地衡量变化的过程。

  研究物种丰富度与均匀度之间的关系,就会发现采用细石器技术存在三种可能的形态。第一种形态同时反映丰富度与均匀度的提高或减少(图3.1,A、B)。采用细石器与更大的物种多样性相关(更多物种,分布更均匀),或是多样性减少,强调利用特定的物种。动物组合的多样性的巨大变化可能受到一系列复杂因素的影响,包括人口密度与分布、技术、环境以及生计构成的变化。这些变化中的一个例子就是广谱革命,更新世之末南北半球许多地区的狩猎采集社会都受到它的影响[23]。第二种形态反映物种丰富度或是均匀度的变化,但不是同时的(图3.1,C、D)。此时食谱不是迅速扩充或是缩减,表明人类食物生境的变化并不剧烈,这可能是向食物多样性剧变的前兆。第三种形态反映丰富度与均匀度可能没有变化,表明选择细石器跟动物资源获取策略可能没有实质性的联系。像这样的形态需要我们重新思考细石器用作狩猎技术的可能性,细石器技术可能不是在动物资源获取上发挥优势(比如说细石器技术并没有导致更有效率的动物狩猎)。一个可能的领域是收割与处理植物资源,这是旧石器时代生计中一个经常被低估的方面,它超越了本文讨论的范围。细石器在这方面潜在的用途可以参见克拉克的研究[24]。细石器不是用于狩猎的说法可能会导致新的问题,即细石器在功能上是否可以等同于其他技术选择,是否选择细石器能够构成风格因素(就选择而言是中性的)。后

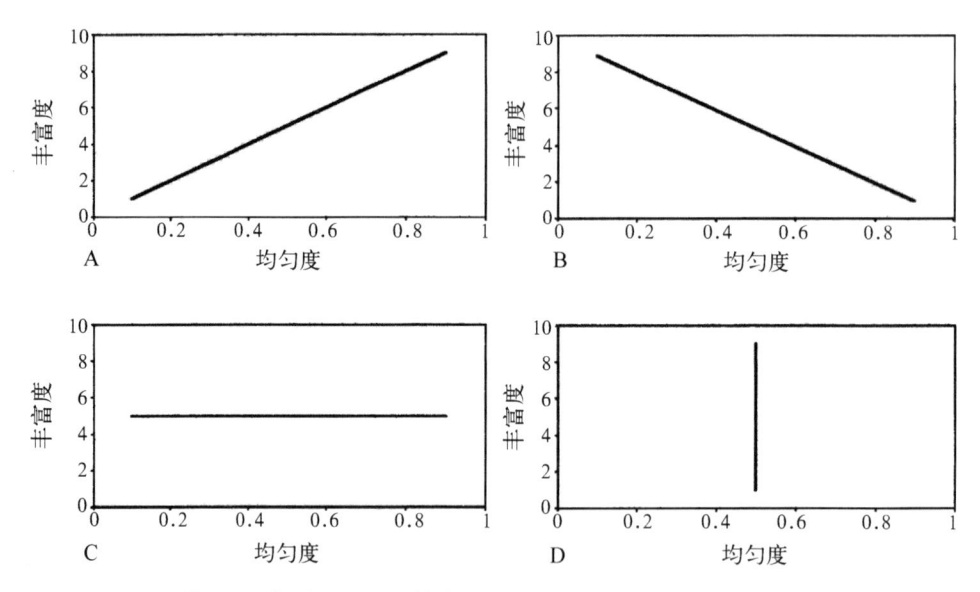

图 3.1　与采用细石器技术相关的动物群多样性的变化范围

（A. 丰富度与均匀度正相关的变化；B. 丰富度与均匀度负相关的变化；C. 丰富度变化与均匀度保持不变；D. 均匀度变化而丰富度不变。）

者几乎是不可能的，因为一种风格上完全中性的变化不可能长期存在，而且普遍分布，就像从细石器上观察的那样[25]。

尽管这一地区动物群材料一般都是粗线条的，但是某些代表考古材料形态特征的趋势还是可以看出来的。物种丰富度、相对均匀度的统计表显示物种的丰富度一直相对稳定，不过从旧石器时代中期到后旧石器时代早期物种均匀度在下降（图 3.2）。这种趋势跟第二种形态较为符合，它表明古人食谱的变化是渐进而非剧变的。随着细石器技术的流行，相关的优势可能包括狩猎策略的变化（如更强调群体狩猎，利用驱赶线路、风筝或是其他技术装备，以及如弓箭这样的投送系统的变化）。包括后旧石器时代晚期在内的分析显示，随着物种丰富度的提高，变化速率加速，与此同时，物种均匀度持续下降。此外，这种趋势跟广谱经济的发展联系在一起[26]。排除埋藏因素可能导致的偏差，这种趋势表明细石器技术的采用跟选择利用特定的物种有关，其利用存在不同的比例。换句话说，某些物种成为主要目标，也就是在特定环境条件下，通过利用细石器技术，这些物种更容易捕捉与处理。有意思的是，我们注意到动物群利用的变化最早出现在旧石器时代晚期，此时考古材料中细小石叶的生产与使用开始经常出现。

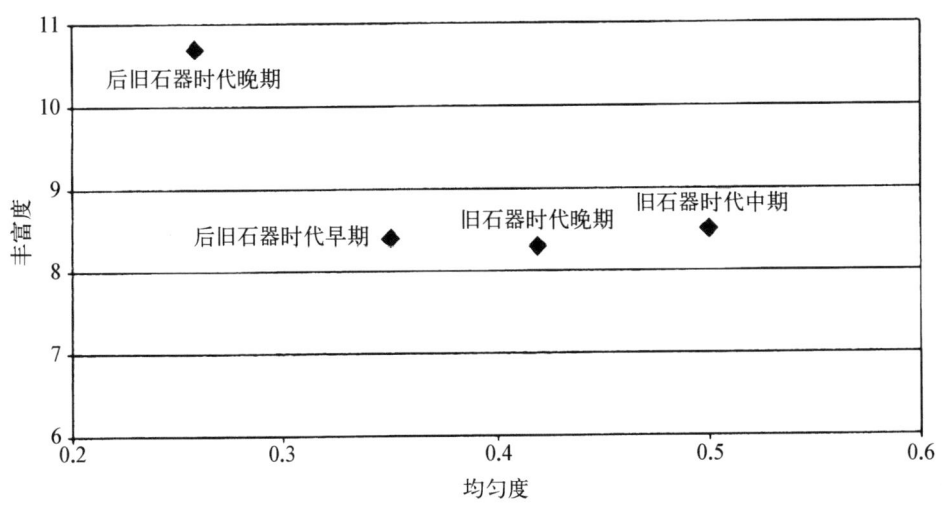

图3.2 利凡特地区古代动物群的丰富度与均匀度

（二）流动性与石器

除了可能应对动物狩猎长期策略的变化，采用细石器技术的优势之一就是有利于提高狩猎采集者的流动性。本文的基本观点也是这么认为的，相对于狩猎采集者所面对的自然与社会环境制约，不同的狩猎流动性策略可能具有选择意义，在这个意义上说，流动性有助于降低适应风险。然而，细石器技术所代表的流动性本身也有许多变化（各种各样的表现型），反映对不同环境约束的适应。因此，细石器技术不应看作静态的现象，而应看作动态的，通过不断修正、增补、变换以确保短时间内（也就是遗址居留期间）成功地完成工作。尤其是，流动性的变化应该对石料获取与工具生产的成本有所影响。因为这些地区时间与资源的约束，更高水平的流动性可能与更高成本密切相关，相反，低水平的流动性与低成本相关。石制品的使用与废弃可以指示不同种类的限制条件。就获取成本而言，废弃石核的密度与大小可能是最佳的标志。如果获取成本高，石核的密度与大小应该相对较低。如利凡特南部高质量的石料比较丰富[27]，流动性的高低应该在石料的获取过程中发挥更重要的作用。由于流动性的变化，原料的获取受到限制或是变化不定，尽管这里石料相对丰富。人们所采用获取策略的变化可能跟当地的自然环境差异与食物资源的时空分布相关。

就生产成本而言，细石器产品能够迅速生产，这就使得人们能够在短时间内生产大量的产品,进而具有时间优势。在高流动性的环境中,能够为将来的使用准备大量可用的产品无疑是最优的选择。由于细石器技术具有"拔出与插入"的特征,生产大量细石器能够为将来多样的使用方式提供足够的灵活性。生产细石器的活动之外,大量废弃的细石器可以指示镶嵌的过程——用新的部件更换使用过的或是不合适的部件。因此,生产与废弃过程紧密相连。需要提醒一下,流动性是一种适应策略,琢背与修理产品的比例可能与特定的环境条件相关。例如,在高流动性环境中,细石器相对非细石器产品的废弃比例应该是不平衡的(即细石器的比例应该更高)。基于细石器易于携带这样一个选择优势,高流动性环境中细石器应该比尺寸较大的非细石器产品更多。同样,那些大的石制品应该具有比细石器有更长的使用寿命,其废弃率相对更低。相反,在流动性降低的环境中,两者之间的比例应该反过来,或是更平均,因为没有必要生产高度适合携带的工具。除了更多非细石器产品,非细石器产品的大小应该相对更大,因为没有必要考虑携带的问题。某些这样的看法得到约旦后旧石器时代的托尔塔里奇遗址出土材料的支持。

(三)流动性:以利凡特南部为例

托尔塔里奇是一处有多个文化层的遗址,位于约旦中西部更新世古湖泊哈萨湖的岸边。遗址靠近一处化石泉堆积,由一系列短期利用的营地构成。1984年与1992年进行了发掘,发现有细石器工业,既有早期(非几何形的),也有晚期(几何形)类型[28]。从最早层位火塘边提取的材料放射性碳测年年代范围在距今16 900至15 580年前。文中所选的样本代表1992年发掘的三个层位(C2、B3、B5),三者不仅垂直分开,而且水平上也是分离的。

尽管细石器普遍见于所有层位,但是个同层位石核废弃的形态存在明显区别。基于石器所使用原料的范围基本相同,基本可以认为石器原料的供给是恒定的,石核废弃形态更多受到流动性变化的影响。所有层位都有细石器生产,石核的打片模式相对稳定。尽管某些变化可能跟终端产品的差异相关(几何形或非几何形细石器),但是都强调细石器技术,这把所有居住层统一起来。石核废弃与形态上的差别反映不同层位细石器生产的侧重点有所不同。B3层位含有最高密度的石核,石核的尺寸也最大(图3.3),表明这一层的流动性在时间与资源供给上受到限制较少。因此,从当地燧石资源条件来看,石核利用的强度相对较弱,石料获取也较容易。相反,B5层石核废弃形态很不同,所发现的石核更小,也更少。这可以解释为流动性更高,石料的获取机会更少。C2层处在两者之间,废弃的石核相对较大,但石核的密度仍然较低。这可能表明流动性较高,但原料的供给条件较好。

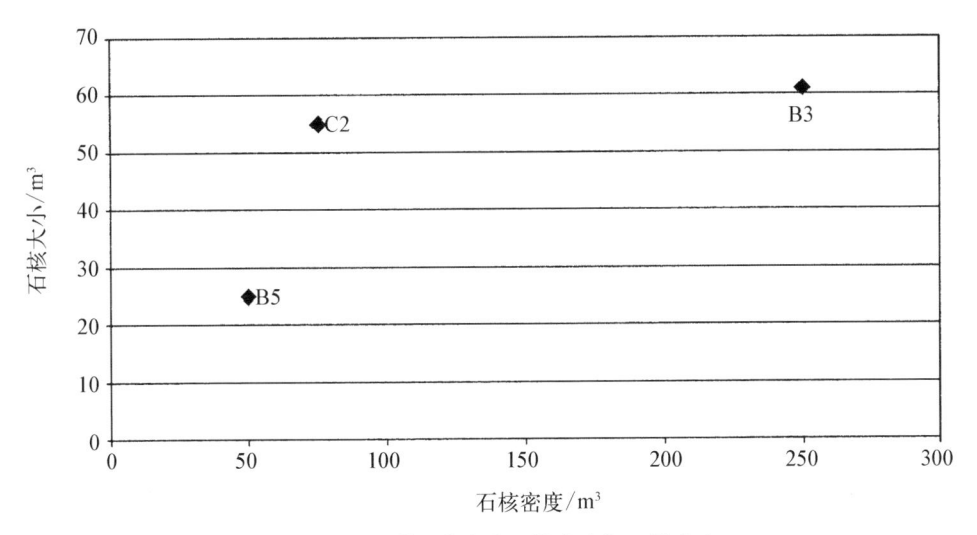

图 3.3 托尔塔里奇废弃石核大小与石核密度

石核废弃形态的区别可能反映原料获取成本的差异,成本的变化跟狩猎采集者流动性的大小相关。为了获取生产细石器的原料,狩猎采集者需要解决一些基本问题。他们需要采集合适的石器原料,预制石核以生产细石器,同时手边储存足够的原料以备将来不时之需。解决问题的办法显然多种多样。我们在这种关联中考虑流动性的变化,长时间的应用中某些解决方法或策略可能更有效。正如我在这个例子中所讲的,经由选择得来的解决方法受到流动性程度的影响。当流动性提高时,更经济地强化利用石核就有选择优势。相反,当流动性的约束降低,强化利用石核的需求也随之降低。从这个意义上来说,细石器技术不是一个简单的技术问题,而是对它所存在的特定环境难题一系列灵活且具有针对性的解决方法。

生产细石器的相关成本同时存在明显的层位差别。每个石核密度(每立方米堆积中石核的数量)中废弃细石器与非细石器的比例表明,相对于非细石器,B5 层细石器废弃的比例更高(图 3.4)。结合更小的石核与更低的石核密度,我们可以认为预期的流动性更高,资源更不确定。相对而言,石核密度高的 B3 层细石器与非细石器比例更加平均,表明相对降低流动性与提高的资源供给,尤其是从原料获取的证据来看。居住层之间的差异进一步得到非细石器大小的支持(图 3.5)。非细石器的有加工痕迹的石制品在高流动性的环境中应该是最笨重与最不方便的,B3层中出土的非细石器石制品比任何一个层位出土的都要大。废弃的非细石器大小指示源于流动降低相对低的生产成本。同时,这些区别可以认为是在特定流动性策略情形下具有优势的选择。

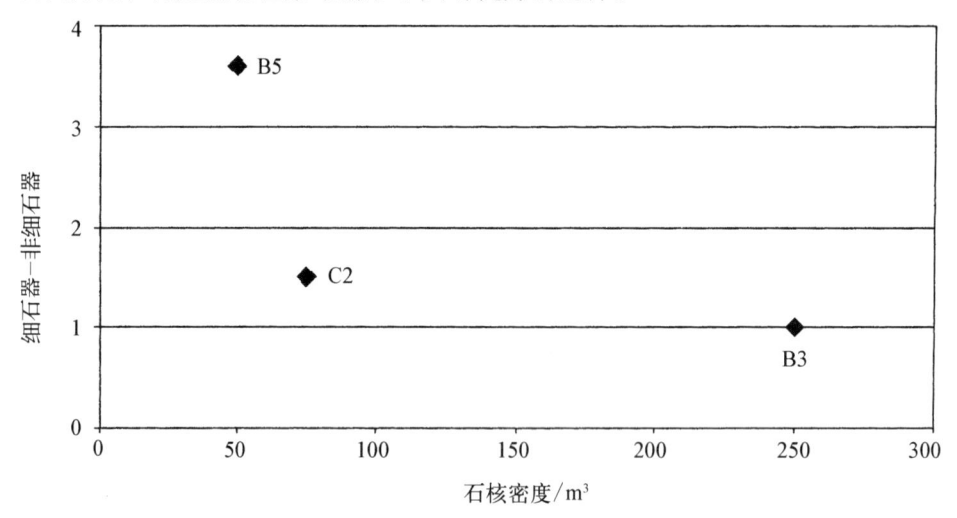

图3.4 托尔塔里奇遗址废弃细石器与非细石器的比值相对石核密度的分布

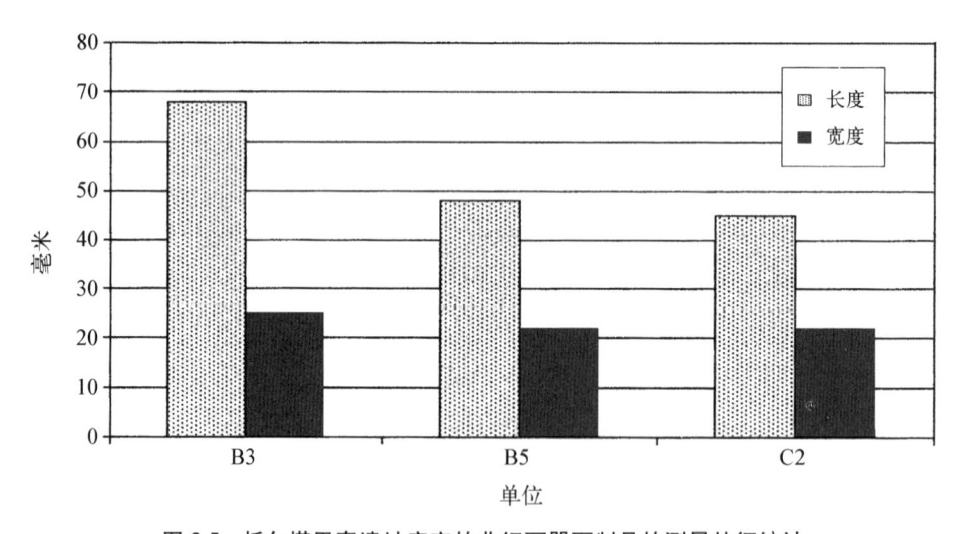

图3.5 托尔塔里奇遗址废弃的非细石器石制品的测量特征统计

可以将利凡特地区旧石器时代晚期到后旧石器时代的整个时期中细石器的解释都归因于流动性的变化么?很可能不是如此。尽管在此期间细石器在石器组合中的重要性不断提高,但是同时存在一个普遍的趋势,居住流动性在不断降低。流动性降低与细石器的生产在后旧石器时代晚期的纳吐芬文化时期都达到顶峰[29]。细石器与流动性的长期关系表明利凡特的细石器并不是解决工具携带问题的唯一具有优势的策略。不过，这是否必然会否定前面例子所得出的结论呢？此结论提出流动性是导致细石器生产与使用的关键因素。我认为这不会否定前面的结论，原因有几个方面。

首先，例子所涉及的时间与地理范围相对狭窄，讨论的只是约旦中西部地区单独一个地点后旧石器时代早期到中期的材料。从如此有限的时空框架来看，细石器生产与使用的层位很可能是特定条件所决定的，部分归因于环境与所用流动性组织策略的变化。因此，运用高居住流动性的狩猎采集者更可能将携带成本最小化，而携带成本对于较为稳定居住的群体来说就不那么重要。次之，选择细石器来解决跟流动性相关的潜在难题并不是一种单向发展的现象。也就是说，我们不大可能看到利凡特地区从旧石器晚期到后旧石器时代细石器的运用总是随流动性的变化而变化。纳吐芬工业中细石器成分显示这样的联系并不是简单对应的。有利于细石器的选择只是采食群体面对史前行为组织系统受到约束时解决问题的途径之一。

进一步说，我并不认为相对于旧石器时代晚期较少利用细石器的人群来说，后旧石器时代早期细石器出现频率就指示更高程度的居住流动性。似乎存在一个趋势，有利于选择利凡特组合的细石器表现型，而选择背后的因素可能非常多，而且没有必要在所有情况下都跟有利于流动性的优势联系在一起。纳吐芬文化也只是一个例子。纳吐芬工业跟更定居、更大遗址相关联，暗示更稠密的地区人口，以及可能更激烈的资源竞争[30]。人口提高的一个可能结果就是群体所占有领域范围缩小，人们需要在更有限的范围内获取必要的资源。这样的环境中居住流动性相对更早的时期受到更多的约束，细石器所谓加强流动性的手段于事无补。不过，细石器在加强流动性、降低携带成本之外还可能具有其他的优势。绑柄与工具维护相关的方面可能给细石器的使用者某种其他石器技术不具备的选择优势。此外，随着流动性受到约束，细石器可能在一种更依赖后勤组织文化系统中发挥优势，人们需要在受到约束的社会与自然环境中更有效地获取资源。

四、结语

在本文开头我就提出为什么细石器如此普遍的问题。为了回答这个问题，我认为利凡特地区细石器工业相关考古材料的形态可以运用进化过程的视角来解释。这种技术的广泛应用可能得益于其灵活性，可以广泛地运用许多活动中，这就赋予在利凡特南部流动采食的群体一种选择优势。为了讨论这个问题,我讨论了两个领域的狩猎采集者行为——流动性与资源获取。细石器在这两个方面都与人类行为的变化密切相关。能否建立因果联系还不得而知,因为考古材料中存在的这些形态很可能是一系列难以确定的因素作用的结果。这里我选择强调人类行为的两个重要方面,但是它们并非仅有的变化来源。鉴于人类狩猎采集者行为复杂的性质以及考古材料有限的细致程度,单因素的解释无疑不可能提供有关人类过去令人满意的解释。尽管研究的结果令人鼓舞,但是我们仍然需要了解是否相似的形态见于利凡特其他地区以及利凡特地区之外。我预计不同的地区在运用细石器应对当地不同问题时会显示出不同程度应用的证据。通过运用进化的方法考察一个地区的特定变化,我发现这种方法有助于理解晚更新世考古材料中为什么细石器能够脱颖而出,成为解决人类生存问题的重要手段。

注释:

[1] Bamforth, D. B., and P. Bleed. Technology, Flaked Stone Technology, and Risk. In *Rediscovering Darwin: Evolutionary Theory and Archeological Explanation*. CM. Barton and G. A. Clark, eds. Pp. 109 - 139. Archeological Papers of the American Anthropological Association, 7. Arlington, Va.: American Anthropological Association, 1997.

[2] Bar-Yosef, O., and S. L. Kuhn. The Big Deal about Blades: Laminar Technologies and Human Evolution. *American Anthropologist* 101: 322 - 338, 1999.

[3] Bar-Yosef, O., and S. L. Kuhn. The Big Deal about Blades: Laminar Technologies and Human Evolution. *American Anthropologist* 101: 331, 1999.

[4] Bar-Yosef, O., and A. Belfer. The Lagaman Industry. In *Prehistoric Investigations in Gebel Maghara*, Northern Sinai. O. Bar-Yosef and J. L. Phillips, eds. Pp. 42 - 84. Qedem 7. Jerusalem: Monographs of the Institute of Archaeology of the Hebrew University, 1977.

Gilead, I. The Upper Paleolithic Period in the Levant. *Journal of World Prehistory* 5: 105 - 154, 1991.

Marks, A., and C. R. Ferring. The Early Upper Paleolithic of the Levant. In *The Early Upper Paleolithic: Evidence from Europe and the Near East*. J. Hoffecker and C. Wolf, eds. Pp. 43 - 72. BAR International Series, 437. Oxford: British Archaeological Reports, 1988.

[5] Coinman, N. R. The Upper Paleolithic of Jordan. In *The Prehistoric Archaeology of Jordan*. D. O. Henry, ed. Pp. 39 - 63. BAR International Series, 705. Oxford: British Archaeological Reports, 1998.

[6] Bar-Yosef, O. The Epi-Paleolithic Complexes in the Southern Levant. In *Prehistoire du Levant*. J. Cauvin and P. Sanlaville, eds. Pp. 389 – 408. Paris: Centre National de la Recherche Scientifique, 1981.

Byrd, B. F. Late Quaternary Hunter-Gatherer Complexes in the Levant between 20 000 and 10 000 B. P. In *Late Quaternary Chronology and Paleoclimates of the Eastern Mediterranean*. O. Bar-Yosef and R. S. Kra, eds. Pp. 205 – 226. Tucson: Radiocarbon, 1994.

Goring-Morris, A. N. *At the Edge: Terminal Pleistocene Hunter-Gatherers in the Negev and Sinai*. BAR International Series, 361. Oxford: British Archaeological Reports, 1987.

Henry, D. O. *Prehistoric Cultural Ecology and Evolution: Insights from Southern Jordan*. New York: Plenum, 1995.

[7] Shott, M. Technological Organization and Settlement Mobility: An Ethnographic Examination, *Journal of Anthropological Research* 42: 15 – 51, 1986.

[8] Becker, M., and F. Wendorf. A Microwear Study of a Late Pleistocene Qadan Assemblage from Southern Egypt. *Journal of Field Archaeology* 20: 389 – 398, 1993.

Clarke, D. Mesolithic Europe: The Economic Basis. In *Problems in Economic and Social Archaeology*. G. de G. Sieveking, I. H. Longworth, and K. E. Wilson, eds. Pp. 449 – 481. London: Duckworth, 1976.

Odell, G. H. The Role of Stone Bladelets in Middle Woodland Society. *American Antiquity* 59: 102 – 120, 1994.

[9] Bar-Yosef, O., and S. L. Kuhn. The Big Deal about Blades: Laminar Technologies and Human Evolution. *American Anthropologist* 101: 322 – 338, 1999.

[10] Clarke, D. Mesolithic Europe: The Economic Basis. In *Problems in Economic and Social Archaeology*. G. de G. Sieveking, I. H. Longworth, and K. E. Wilson, eds. Pp. 457. London: Duckworth, 1976.

[11] Bamforth, D. B., and P. Bleed. Technology, Flaked Stone Technology, and Risk. In *Rediscovering Darwin: Evolutionary Theory and Archeological Explanation*. CM. Barton and G. A. Clark, eds. Pp. 109 – 139. Archeological Papers of the American Anthropological Association, 7. Arlington, Va.: American Anthropological Association, 1997.

Torrence, R. Retooling: Toward a Behavioral Theory of Stone Tools. In *Time, Energy and Stone Tools*. R. Torrence, ed. Pp. 57 – 66. Cambridge: Cambridge University Press, 1989.

[12] Myers, A. Reliable and Maintainable Technological Strategies in the Mesolithic of Mainland Britain. In *Time, Energy and Stone Tools*. R. Torrence, ed. Pp. 78 – 91. Cambridge: Cambridge University Press, 1989.

[13] Lyman, R. L., and M. J. O'Brien. The Concept of Evolution in Early Twentieth Century Americanist Archeology. In *Rediscovering Darwin: Evolutionary Theory and Archaeological*

Explanation. C M. Barton and G. A. Clark, eds. Pp. 21 - 48. Archeological Papers of the American Anthropological Association, 7. Arlington, Va.: American Anthropological Association, 1997.

[14] Broughton, J. M., and J. F. O'Connell. On Evolutionary Ecology, Selectionist Archaeology, and Behavioral Archaeology. *American Antiquity* 64: 153 - 165, 1999.

[15] Dunnell, R. C. Style and Function: A Fundamental Dichotomy. *American Antiquity* 43: 192 - 202, 1978. Evolutionary Theory and Archaeology. In *Advances in Archaeological Method and Theory*, vol. 3. M. B. Schiffer, ed. Pp. 35 - 99. New York: Academic. Bleed, P. Edwards, P. C, 1980.

[16] Barton, C. M., and G. A. Clark, eds. *Rediscovering Darwin: Evolutionary Theory and Archaeological Explanation*. Archeological Papers of the American Anthropological Association, 7. Arlington, Va.: American Anthropological Association, 1997.

Maschner, H. D. G. *Darwinian Archaeologies*. New York: Plenum, 1996.

O'Brien, M. J., ed. *Evolutionary Archaeology: Theory and Application*. Salt Lake City: University of Utah Press, 1996.

Teltser. P. A. *Evolutionary Archaeology: Methodological Issues*. Tucson: University of Arizona Press, 1995a.

[17] Torrence, R. Retooling: Toward a Behavioral Theory of Stone Tools. In *Time, Energy and Stone Tools*. R. Torrence, ed. Pp. 57 - 66. Cambridge: Cambridge University Press, 1989.

[18] Bamforth, D. B., and P. Bleed. Technology, Flaked Stone Technology, and Risk. In *Rediscovering Darwin: Evolutionary Theory and Archeological Explanation*. CM. Barton and G. A. Clark, eds. Pp. 117. Archeological Papers of the American Anthropological Association, 7. Arlington, Va.: American Anthropological Association, 1997.

[19] Bamforth, D. B., and P. Bleed. Technology, Flaked Stone Technology, and Risk. In *Rediscovering Darwin: Evolutionary Theory and Archeological Explanation*. CM. Barton and G. A. Clark, eds. Pp. 109 - 139. Archeological Papers of the American Anthropological Association, 7. Arlington, Va.: American Anthropological Association, 1997.

[20] Bleed, P. The Optimal Design of Hunting Weapons: Main-taxability or Reliability. *American Antiquity* 51 (4): 737 - 747, 1986.

[21] Stiner, M. C, N. D. Munro, and T. A. Surovell. Small-Game Use, the Broad-Spectrum Revolution, and Paleolithic Demography. *Current Anthropology* 41: 39 - 73, 2000.

[22] Neeley, M. P., and G. A. Clark. The Human Food Niche in the Levant over the Past 150 000 Years. In *Hunting and Animal Exploitation in the Later Palaeolithic and Mesolithic of Eurasia*. G. Larsen Peterkin, H. M. Bricker, and P. Mellars, eds. Pp. 221 - 240. Archeological Papers of the American Anthropological Association, 4. Arlington, Va.: American

Anthropological Association, 1993.

[23] Flannery, K. V. Origins and Ecological Effects of Early Domestication in Iran and the Near East. In *The Domestication and Exploitation of Plants and Animals*. P. J. Ucko and G. W. Dimbleby, eds. Pp. 73 – 100. London: Duckworth, 1969.

[24] Clarke, D. Mesolithic Europe: The Economic Basis. In *Problems in Economic and Social Archaeology*. G. de G. Sieveking, I. H. Longworth, and K. E. Wilson, eds. Pp. 449 – 481. London: Duckworth, 1976.

[25] Teltser. P. A. *Evolutionary Archaeology: Methodological Issues*. Tucson: University of Arizona Press, 1995a.

[26] Clark, G. A. From the Mousterian to the Metal Ages: Long-Term Change in the Human Diet of Northern Spain. In *The Pleistocene Old World: Regional Perspectives*. O. Soffer, ed. Pp. 293 – 316. New York: Plenum, 1987.

Neeley, M. P., and G. A. Clark. The Human Food Niche in the Levant over the Past 150 000 Years. In *Hunting and Animal Exploitation in the Later Palaeolithic and Mesolithic of Eurasia*. G. Larsen Peterkin, H. M. Bricker, and P. Mellars, eds. Pp. 221 – 240. Archeological Papers of the American Anthropological Association, 4. Arlington, Va.: American Anthropological Association, 1993.

Edwards, P. C. Revising the Broad Spectrum Revolution: Its Role in the Origins of Southwest Asian Food Production. *Antiquity* 63: 225 – 246, 1989.

[27] Bar-Yosef, O. Raw Material Exploitation in the Levantine Epi-Paleolithic. In *Raw Material Economies among Prehistoric Hunter-Gatherers*. A. Montet-White and S. Holen, eds. Pp. 235 – 250. Publications in Anthropology 19. Lawrence: University of Kansas, 1991.

[28] Clark, G. A., J. Lindly, M. Donaldson, A. N. Garrard, N. Coinman, J. Schuldenrein, S. Fish, and D. Olszewski. Excavations at Middle, Upper and Epipaleolithic Sites in the Wadi Hasa, West-Central Jordan. In *Prehistory of Jordan*. A. N. Garrard and H. G. Gebel, eds. Pp. 209 – 285. BAR International Series, 396. Oxford: British Archaeological Reports, 1988.

Neeley, M. P., J. D. Peterson, G. A. Clark. S. K. Fish, and M. Glass. Investigations at Tor al-Tareeq: An Epipaleolithic Site in the Wadi el-Hasa. Jordan. *Journal of Field Archaeology* 25: 295 – 317, 1998.

[29] Henry, D. O. *From Foraging to Agriculture: The Levant at the End of the Ice Age*. Philadelphia: University of Pennsylvania Press, 1989.

[30] Henry, D. O. *From Foraging to Agriculture: The Levant at the End of the Ice Age*. Philadelphia: University of Pennsylvania Press, 1989.

为什么是细石器？
利凡特地区的细石器化

安娜·贝尔福—科恩 尼基尔·格林—莫里斯
（希伯来大学 耶路撒冷）

摘　要：利凡特地区细石器的生产始于旧石器时代晚期。目前已知存在两种细石器生产技术：一种是连续齐整修理的（阿玛连）细小石叶，来自石叶或细小石叶打制技术；另一种为细小扭曲的"杜福尔"（利凡特的奥瑞纳）细小石叶，它是有意或无意的起脊（carination）修理的副产品。整个旧石器时代晚期扭曲的细小石叶或多或少地存在。连续齐整修理细小石叶最终占优势地位，并成为后旧石器时代成熟细石器技术的代表。旧石器时代晚期后段或后旧石器时代早期细石器技术发生了重要的变化。较早阶段的细石器具有既定的操作链，石器毛坯的形状与大小与成型细石器非常相似。后旧石器时代早期，石器的形状越来越受到毛坯修理的影响，修理的范围超越了边缘，有时还采用微雕刻器技术进行修理。到了后旧石器时代晚期，几乎所有细长的石片都刻意修理成细石器。这里细石器起源的可以归因于节省原料的考虑、石器的捆绑使用、投掷器技术的应用，以及功能上的多样化。这些变化或许可以解释为打片力量在下降，但细石器的使用效率与灵活性在提高。

地中海东部地区细石器有系统的生产持续了将近3万年，从旧石器时代晚期的阿玛连（Ahmarian）工业（它是紧接着当地旧石器时代中期莫斯特工业之后最早出现的旧石器时代晚期石器工业，从距今约4万至3.5万年前开始），一直延续到铜石并用/青铜时代早期，即距今约5 500年前[1]。

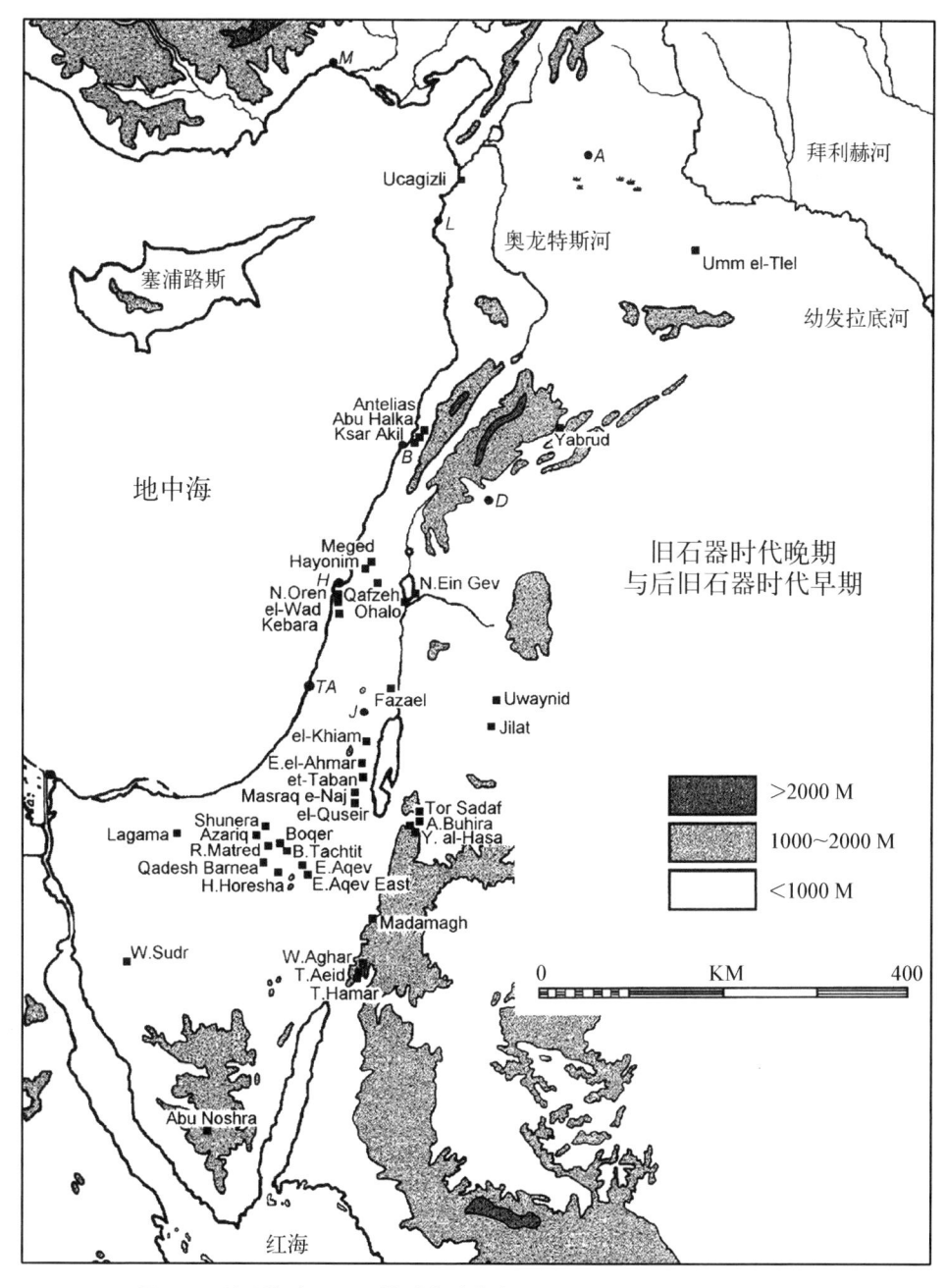

图 4.1 利凡特地区旧石器时代晚期与后旧石器时代早期的典型遗址

本文将考察与评论利凡特地区旧石器时代晚期(约距今4万至2万年前)细小石叶的演化发展以及接踵而至的后旧石器时代(约距今2万至1万年前)的状况(图4.1)。需要强调指出的是,跟其他许多研究利凡特旧石器时代的研究者一样,我们追随提克斯耶[2]对北非后旧石器时代石器组合的研究[a],采用他所定义的细小石叶(bladelets)与修理细小石叶(retouched bladelets)这两个术语。我们遵循目前广泛使用的利凡特地区旧石器时代晚期到后旧石器时代的石器分类学体系[3](同时参考其文献索引)(表4.1)。

表4.1 利凡特主要区域的文化遗存与其年代序列

距今年代 (未校正)	时 期		考 古 遗 存	
			地中海地区	草原&沙漠地区
~45.0 ka ~40.0	过渡期 旧石器时代晚期		埃米尔 阿玛连 利凡特的奥瑞纳 未命名的旧石器 晚期遗存	博克塔克提克 阿玛连/拉嘎玛 其他旧石器晚期遗存 (迪福尚/阿奇夫)
20.0~14.5	后旧石器时代	早期	马撒拉坎(阿玛连晚期) 克巴拉 尼扎那	马撒拉坎(阿玛连晚期) 勒贝肯 克巴拉 尼扎那
14.5~12.5		中期	几何形克巴拉	几何形克巴拉 穆沙边 莱蒙
12.5~10.2		晚期	纳吐夫	纳吐夫 哈利夫

进一步说,当我们谈到从陶鲁斯—扎格罗斯山到西奈南部与约旦的广大区域的一般趋势时,我们也明白不同地区的发展变化,以及半干旱地带与地中海地带之间的区别。石器原料跟细小石叶的起源、发展与出现频率之间的关系并不特别紧密;整个利凡特地区石器原料分布广泛,当然也有一些例外[4]。利凡特细石器出现频率的上升并不是线性的,其中有相当的变化存在,不同石器工业之间、某一石器工业特定石器组合之内都是如此。不过,这里我们主要讨论旧石器时代晚期、后旧石器时代石器组合(工具与毛坯)中细石器成分发展的一般趋势。

一、旧石器时代晚期的细石器

利凡特旧石器时代晚期早段,细小石叶开始出现,其中可以看到两条主要的

细石器生产途径:

1. 尖部修理、大多平直的细小石叶有时是石叶尖状器生产的末端产品,但不是所有时候都是如此。通过石器拼合以及两者不同大小的双峰分布可以推知有些石器组合中石叶与细小石叶的生产采用不同的打片程序[5]。不过其他旧石器时代晚期的石器组合中也有证据表明石叶/细小石叶的生产是单一模式的。因此,厄尔瓦德尖状器中有相当比例的产品属于细石器范畴的[6](图4.2,23、24)。大部分这样的材料被认为属于阿玛连组合,它们起源于以石叶/细小石叶为中心的石器打片程序。

2. "经典的"杜福尔细小石叶(交错或精细/半陡向修理),属于利凡特地区奥瑞纳类型(图4.2,9-13)。这些是有脊器物有意或无意加工的副产品[7]b。

从年代学的观点来看,阿玛连的石叶/细小石叶(图4.2,20~24)从观念上承袭了旧石器时代中期(反复出现的)勒瓦娄哇打制石叶的方法,它预先确定了毛坯形态与大小,在埃米尔尖状器的生产中达到顶峰[8](图4.2,25~27)。技术上讲,存在着一种转变,修理台面转向素台面,同时摩擦毛坯粗大端的腹面(图7、8)[9](图4.2,19)。似勒瓦娄哇的尖状器越来越窄,相对显得越来越长,无论是制作成投掷器的尖状器还是钻器[10]。因此,毛坯跟成品非常相似,侧面直或是向内弯曲,并有尖。细小石叶的毛坯来自一般的石叶生产程序,石核为素台面,运用间接打制或是软锤法生产(图4.2,14与19)。

所有旧石器时代晚期的细小石叶工具都有一个共同的特点,那就是修理简单(图4.2,1~7,9~13与20~24)。值得注意的是拉伽曼遗址(典型遗址为拉伽曼第7地点)的厄尔瓦德尖状器,其修理从非常精细(细密的)到精细,再到半陡向[11]。大部分半陡向的修理见于较大厄尔瓦德尖状器的尖部(采用相对较大石叶所制)。小的厄尔瓦德尖状器(大小属于细石器的范畴)很少有半陡向的修理(图4.2,23、24)。因此,通常修理出尖部的典型阿玛连细小石叶毛坯采用的是最少修理。

"经典的"杜福尔产品也很少有修理,修理常常是反向或是错向的(图4.2,9~13)。简单修理的绝对优势地位可能表明一种特殊装柄方法,每根柄或装配物上只安装一个器物。还有看法认为杜福尔产品用作鱼叉上成排的倒钩(与卡赞个人联系所知,1999;这样的工具显然具有空气动力学的考虑)。这些扭曲的(杜福尔)细小石叶少量存在于许多较晚的利凡特旧石器时代晚期石器组合中,大多是奥瑞纳以及其他"非阿玛连"以石片为中心的石制品组合,比如恩阿奇夫[12]或是哈尔霍里沙第1地点。

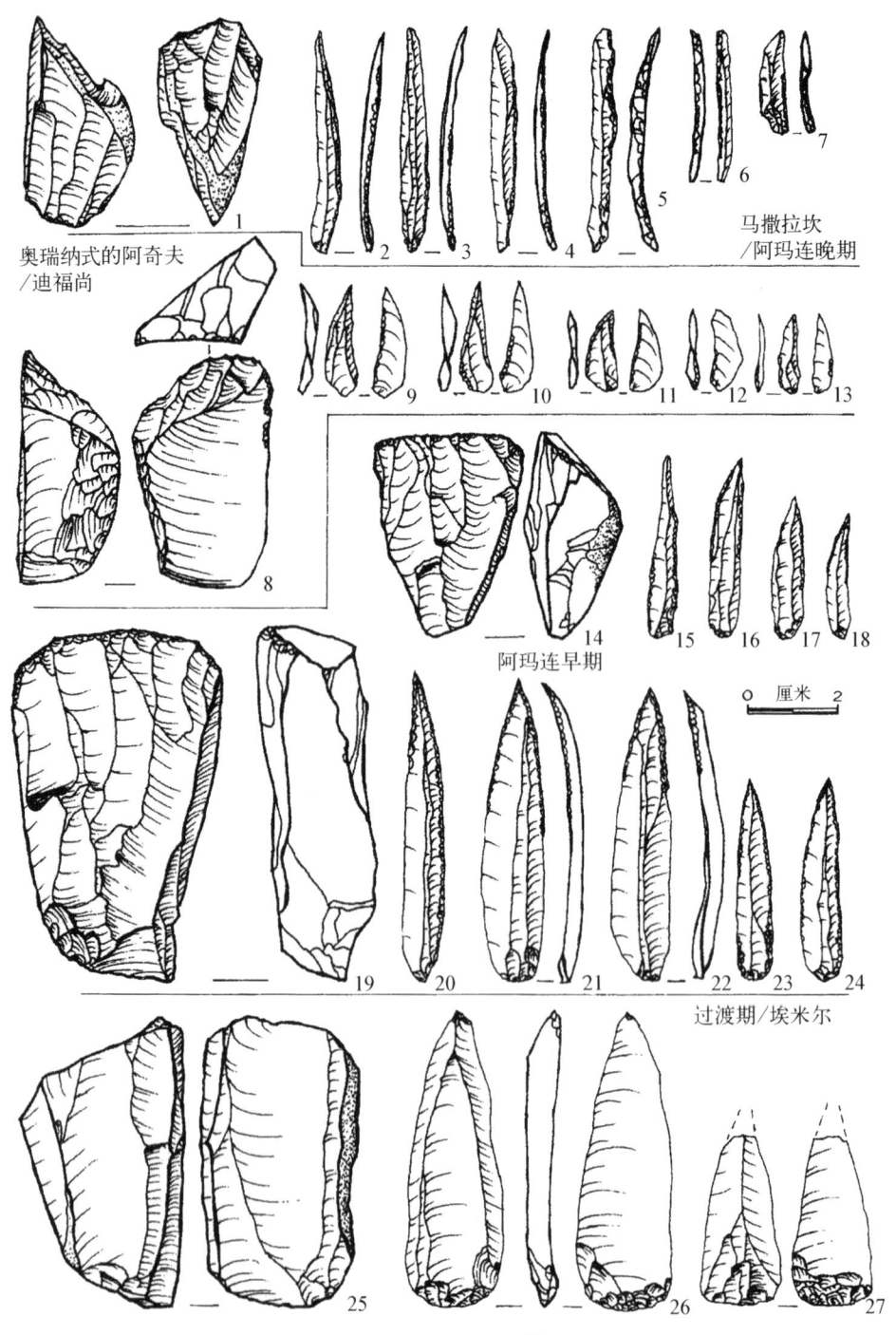

图 4.2　典型遗址石器图

（埃米尔尖状器（26~27）、埃尔—瓦迪尖状器（20~24）、杜福尔细小石叶（9~13）、奥恰塔塔修理与精细修理细小石叶（2~7、15~18）以及各自的石核类型。基于博克塔克提特遗址[13]、拉嘎玛 7 号与 11 号遗址[14]、伊恩卡迪斯 4 号遗址[15]、博克遗址[16]、伊恩阿奇夫遗址[17]、阿扎里克 13 号遗址、奥哈罗 2 号遗址[18]等遗址的考古报告重绘。）

不过还是马撒拉坎(阿玛连晚期)的平直类型最终主导了后旧石器时代细石器为主的石器组合[c]。按照菲林[19]的说法,阿玛连传统的末期(大约距今2.2万年前),存在一种技术转变,出现了多样的打片方法。生产[20]大石叶毛坯与生产大量细小石叶分别采用不同的技术路径。从类型学上来说,马撒拉坎组合以采用"奥恰塔塔"[21]与半陡向修理的细小石叶为主(图4.2,2~7),还有少量琢背细小石叶以及一些大石器。

此外,有些组合可以认为代表中间状态。例如,利凡特北部的乌姆厄尔特勒尔第2地点的2b层、2d层以及第1地点的4"b"层,三分之一的细小石叶是平直的,剩下的都是扭曲的[22]。当然,不考虑毛坯的形状,所有器物修理得都很精细,也就是说,实际上没有琢背或深入修理(invasive retouch)*。西奈半岛南部的阿布罗萨拉遗址的阿玛连组合也是如此[23]。

二、后旧石器时代的细石器

旧石器时代晚期与后旧石器时代的分界线在距今2.2~2.0万年,这主要是基于年代学划分的考虑。当然,两个时代之间也有一些区别,包括石器组合的构成在内都是如此。旧石器晚期较晚阶段的细石器与后旧石器时代细石器的关键区别主要跟修理方式相关。旧石器时代较晚阶段平直的细小石叶大多是简单修理,而后旧石器时代的细小石叶工具多是琢背修理(图4.3)。这不是说旧石器时代晚期的石器工业偶尔不会出现陡向修理;而是说,作为一个普遍的规律,其修理一般都是非常精细的,罕见陡向修理(图4.2,2~4,7,15~18)。修理方式的变化以及石叶(严格意义上的)数量的减少,可以视为新的技术革新,也就是复合工具引入的标志,复合工具很可能取代了大量旧石器时代晚期其他工具类型[24]。另一个特征是旧石器时代晚期细小石叶的修理通常只是部分的,稍稍改变器物的形状而已,而不是像后旧石器时代那样修理侧边以方便装柄[d]。

因此,在某些但不是所有后旧石器时代早期的石器工业(距今2.2~1.45万年,参见表4.1)中,成型工具的形制与大小标准化程度高,例如麦格德岩厦遗址(参考库恩等写作中的手稿),同时还包括特殊修理技术出现(如微雕刻器技术,参见图4.3)。尽管微雕刻器技术在后旧石器时代之初开始用于细石器工具的生产,最早见于勒贝肯遗址[25],但它在后来的使用中变化多端,直到后旧石器时代之末都是如此(比如说,这种技术通常不见于克巴拉、几何形克巴拉以及某些纳

---

* Invasive retouch 深度修理,指修理的疤痕超越器物的边缘,接近或超越了器物的中线。——译注

后旧石器时代晚期

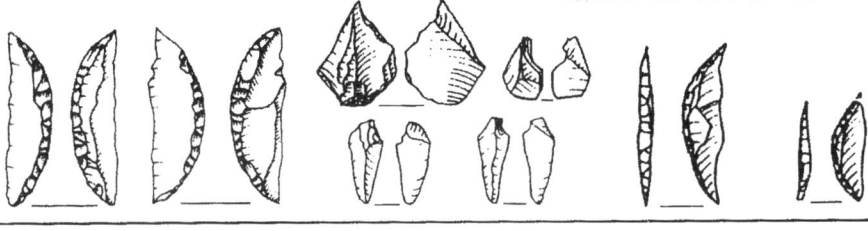

纳吐夫工业&(哈尔芬工业)

后旧石器时代中期

穆沙边工业或莱蒙工业

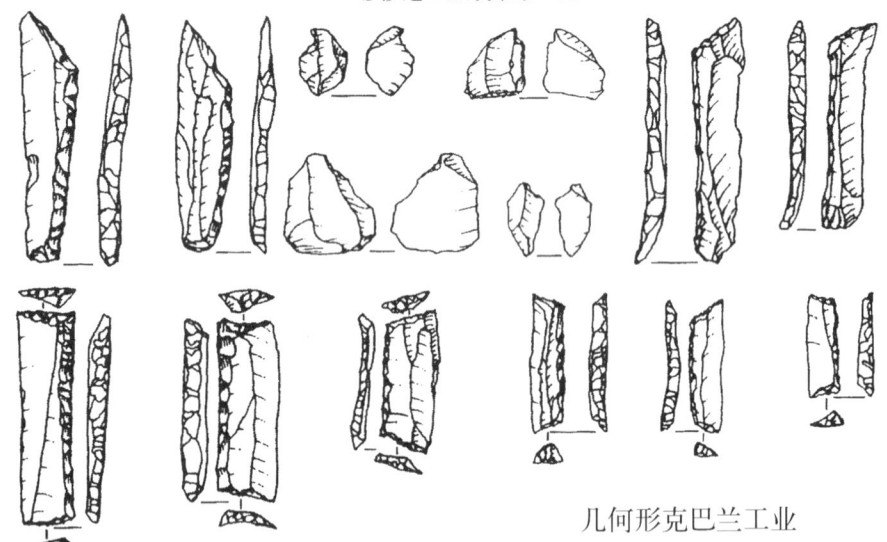

几何形克巴兰工业

后旧石器时代早期

巴扎那工业

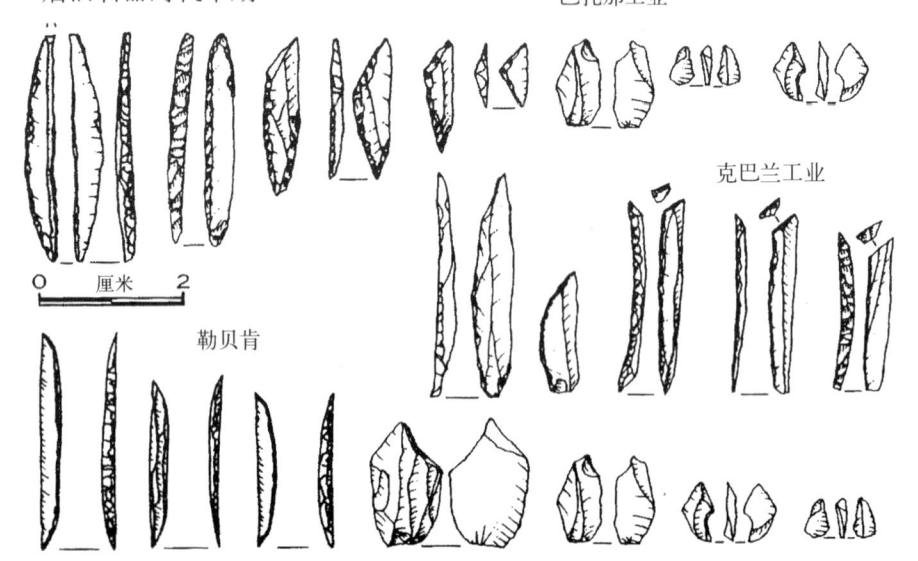

克巴兰工业

勒贝肯

图 4.3 利凡特中/南部各种后旧石器时代工业的
典型细石器类型与微雕刻器[26]

吐夫石器工业中[27]）。这跟大部分旧石器时代晚期的石器组合形成鲜明对比，旧石器时代晚期的细小石叶毛坯比修理工具相对更标准。后旧石器时代成品工具非常高的标准化程度反映了装柄的需要，以及维护工具的便利，也就是复合工具的出现。后旧石器时代中期（几何形克巴拉与穆沙边工业），尤其是后旧石器时代晚期（纳吐夫及其相关工业），几何形及其他细石器（图4.3）开始占主导地位，主要有琢背、截断长方形、新月—三角形等形态类型，毛坯原型与成品之间的联系非常严格。的确，尽管这些细石器毫无疑问是以石叶或细小石叶毛坯制作的，但是严格地说，情况并不总是如此的[28]。还存在细石器大小的整体下降，在纳吐夫晚期或最后阶段与哈利夫阶段的微月形器上达到顶峰，虽然这并不是一个完全单向的趋势[29]（以及其后的参考文献）。

三、讨论

过去后旧石器的定义主要基于细石器作为主要石器组合成分的出现[30]。不过现在我们知道不是细石器的出现与数量本身，而是复合工具装柄的需要，也就是，细石器的琢背修理与标准化，把"旧石器时代晚期"与"后旧石器时代"区分开来，至少是在石器组合上ᵉ。尽管旧石器时代晚期早段石器组合中偶尔也会有琢背器物发现，但是它们绝大多数还是在后旧石器时代石器工业中开始占据优势，并且成为后旧石器时代的标志。就细石器的基本形态类型而言，存在广泛的功能选择，它们可能用作投掷尖状器、石钻、倒钩、石刀或其他工具。功能的确定，如同微痕分析及相关研究所证明的，跟器物特定的加工类型没有什么联系。琢背修理的增加更可能跟装柄的新方法以及复合工具的流行（其出现相对比较突然）有关。的确，怀斯曼[31]就曾指出，几何形克巴拉工业多样的几何形外形反映了当时可能开始沿着细石器的长轴使用黏接剂，更早的时候库坎[32]也曾提出过。与此同时，从社会文化发展的一般规律来说，整个利凡特地区后旧石器时代早期，变化没有必要都是同时的，对此我们不应感到惊奇（比如说，勒比肯相对于马撒拉坎/阿玛连晚期）。

以琢背修理为主（陡向与两极修理，以及经常使用石砧）并非后旧石器时代早期唯一的重要变化。另一个重要的变化是加工细石器毛坯的方法。开始时，某些细石器组合（尤其是马撒拉坎/晚期阿玛连）仍然沿用"旧石器时代晚期"的预先确定的操作链。这导致细石器毛坯跟成品工具的形制与大小相当一致。而后旧石器时代真正的新复合工具概念有所不同，成品工具的形制主要来自后期的加工修理，或是采用更加深入修理/琢背修理，或是采用微雕刻器技术，或是同时采用两者。因此,毛坯的初始形态变得无关紧要,这也反映在石核的预制上。最近对纳吉夫西部将近 25 个旧石器时代晚期以及后旧石器时代的石器组合,尤其是后者的拼合研究充分说明了这一点[33](以及与马尔德个人联系,2002)。最后,到后旧石器时代晚期纳吐夫工业(距今 1.25~1.0 万年前)时,几乎是任何细长的石片都可以熟练地修理成细石器。

表面上来看,后旧石器时代晚期转向非标准化、不规则工具毛坯生产似乎可以解释成古人打片能力的下降。然而,如果仔细研究,就会注意到这样的变化更可能反映了工具生产效率与灵活性的整体提高(参见下文)[34]。这一过程的顶峰,如同纳吐夫工业所显示的,很可能跟定居、特化的狩猎采集生活的复杂性提高相关[35]。

欧洲细石器从中石器时代早期到晚期的变化涉及修理方式从简单向琢背修理的转变,修理的范围覆盖更大,更加标准化,如此等等。有观点认为这些现象可能反映了当时人们狩猎策略的变化[36]。中石器时代早期,细石器是大批量生产的,是为拦截式狩猎所需要的高可靠性工具系统而提前准备的,这是对一种特定环境条件的适应。这种环境中需要使用工具的时间很短,但失败的成本非常高昂,所以需要提前准备好。后来出现的琢背修理的细石器是小批量生产的,它是一种基于邂逅式的狩猎所需要的最佳选择,便于维护。这种工具系统适用于难以预测的环境,失败的成本不高,工具整年都需要。

欧洲模式并不必然适用于利凡特地区,因为这里从旧石器时代晚期到后旧石器时代并没有证据表明存在狩猎策略的重大变化以及不同区域内猎物构成上的变化。当然,利凡特地区所见的变化确实反映了流动性与聚落形态的转变[f]。从旧石器时代晚期到后旧石器时代的在广阔活动空间中流动的小游群,转向了后旧石器时代早期(勒比肯)多个游群季节性聚集,到后旧石器时代晚期纳吐夫时期形成了更大的定居社群[g]。这些趋势伴随着人口密度的稳步上升,形成更大程度相对拥挤的情况(可能跟普伦尼冰期*适于居住的地区减少有关)[37]。随着特定群体活动范围的减小,原料产地的利用强度加大,同时石核的打片也更彻底。勒比肯工业中可以看到这个过程的最初阶段,这一工业(几乎是完全的)分布于大裂谷东部高原地带,更早的旧石器时代晚期遗存罕见。勒比肯工业以前所未有的遗址群的形式出现,如阿扎拉克盆地(如吉拉特 6 与乌维尼德 14 遗址)[38](图 4.1)。随着地中海核心区定居生活的出现,人们每年生活的整体范围

---

* 普伦尼冰期(Pleniglacial),距今 2.2 万年至 1.6 万年之间,相当于末次冰期最盛期。——译注

更加局限,这导致包括燧石在内的原料利用的强度提高。复合装柄工具的大量生产需要结合更有效、更节省燧石原料的背景联系起来看。定居的纳吐夫人通过生产非标准化、不规则的工具毛坯最终实现节省劳动与原材料的目的。

最后,似乎可以这么说,利凡特石器工业中细石器成分的出现与发展与投掷尖状器的驱动方式、装柄技术、节省原料以及功能选择的共同发展相辅相成。这种长时段的变化无疑不仅仅是反映石器生产特定领域机械特征的变化。

需要指出的是,上文我们仅讨论了旧石器时代晚期、后旧石器时代石器毛坯生产与修理的大致形态。没有涉及细石器组合的风格问题,而利凡特地区考古遗存的区分基本依赖风格。正是在后旧石器时代开始时,风格因素(形态类型、微雕刻器技术的运用、琢背修理的类型等)日益明显,广泛用来确定不同时空多样的社会文化存在。

事实上,利凡特后旧石器时代社会文化的发展正体现在一定时空范围内石器组合中细石器成分的多样性与差异性上。当然,这些问题超出了本文讨论的范围。相反,本文主要关注的是细石器生产的广泛性与长时段的发展形态。我们希望这样一个宽广的框架,正如上文归纳的,将有助于区分与一般趋势相关的特征,以及区分那些代表特定考古遗存的特征。

注释一:

a. 提克斯耶对细小石叶的定义基于测量特征,即长不超过5厘米,同时/或者宽不超过12毫米,而修理过的细小石叶尺寸更小,宽小于或等于9毫米。当然,他也注意到这些标准因时因地可能有所改变,实际上具有新大陆背景的研究者不必采用同样的标准。

b. 这里我们采用的是杜福尔细小石叶的旧定义[39],更晚近的定义将之视为一种亚型,平直的细小石叶经过精细修理,甚至琢背修理[40],旧定义包含了它(参见图4.2,9~12,与2~7以及14~17对比)。琢背修理的细小石叶见于利凡特地区马撒拉坎工业(即晚阿玛连工业),是另外一种石核打片技术的产物(图4.2,8,与图4.2,1对比),而非如欧洲所见是起脊器物的副产品[41](参见图4.2,2~7)。

c. 例如,可以参考下列遗址:拉嘎玛10号遗址[42]、奥哈罗2号遗址[43]、法扎伊尔10号遗址[44]、东伊恩阿奇夫遗址[45]、阿扎里克13号遗址(格林—莫里斯的个人观察)、于提尔—阿尔—哈萨遗址[46]和伊恩埃尔—布西拉遗址(WHS 618)[47]。

d. 例如下列遗址:卡迪什巴尼601与9号遗址[48]、伊恩卡迪斯4号遗址[49]。厄尔瓦德尖状器有时在靠近基底的边缘修理出浅凹缺,很可能跟运用动物筋腱与麻线捆绑相关。

e. 即便是在旧石器时代中期运用黏胶捆绑的材料中,黏胶的位置也是在器物更厚的、呈现出

"自然"琢背修理的尾端[50]。从侧面固定黏胶痕迹见于几何形克巴拉及更晚的工业中[51]。

f. 但是有意思的是后旧石器时代早期的开始年代跟普伦尼冰期冷干的气候条件相对应。

g. 不管气候的波动,我们应该考虑到地中海与半干旱地带之间的区别。前者的植被总是相对茂密的,石器原料的可见度也相对受限。

注释二:

[1] Bar-Yosef, O. The Middle and Early Upper Palaeolithic in Southwest Asia and Neighbouring Regions. In *The Geography of Neandertals and Modern Humans in Europe and the Greater Mediterranean*. O. Bar-Yosef and D. Pilbeam, eds. Pp. 107 – 156. Peabody Museum Bulletin 8. Cambridge: Harvard University, 2000.

Coinman, N. R. The Upper Paleolithic of Jordan. In *The Prehistoric Archaeology of Jordan*. D. O. Henry, ed. Pp. 39 – 63. BAR International Series, 705. Oxford: British Archaeological Reports, 1998.

Gilead, I. The Micro-Endscraper: A New Tool Type from the Chalcolithic Period. *Tel Aviv* 11: 3 – 10, 1984.

The Chalcolithic Period in the Levant. *Journal of World Prehistory* 2(4): 397 – 443, 1988.

Goring-Morris, A. N., and A. Belfer-Cohen. The Articulation of Cultural Processes and Late Quaternary Environmental Changes in Cisjordan. *Paleorient* 23(2): 71 – 93, 1997.

Rosen, S. A. *Lithics after the Stone Age: A Handbook of Stone Tools from the Levant*. Walnut Creek, Calif.: Altamira, 1997.

[2] Tixier, J. *Typologie de l'Epipaleolithique du Maghreb*. Memoires du Centre de Recherches Anthropologiques, Prehistoriques et Ethnographiques 2. Paris: Arts et Metiers Graphiques, 1963.

[3] Bar-Yosef, O., and J. C. Vogel. Relative and Absolute Chronology of the Epi-Palaeolithic in the Southern Levant. In *Chronologies in the Near East*. O. Aurenche, J. Evin, and F. Hours, eds. Pp. 219 – 245. BAR International Series, 379. Oxford: British Archaeological Reports, 1987.

Belfer-Cohen, A., and O. Bar-Yosef. The Levantine Aurignacian: Sixty Years of Research. In *Dorothy Garrod and the Progress of the Palaeolithic*. W. Davies and R. Charles, eds. Pp. 118 – 134. Oxford: Oxbow, 1999.

Gilead, I. The Foragers of the Upper Paleolithic Period. In *The Archaeology of Society in the Holy Land*. T. E. Levy, ed. Pp. 124 – 140. London: Leicester University Press, 1995.

Goring-Morris, A. N., and A. Belfer-Cohen. The Articulation of Cultural Processes and Late Quaternary Environmental Changes in Cisjordan. *Paleorient* 23(2): 71 – 93, 1997.

Goring-Morris, A. N., and A. Belfer-Cohen, eds. *More than Meets the Eye: Studies on Upper Palaeolithic Diversity in the Near East*. Oxford: Oxbow, In press.

Marks, A. E. The Upper Palaeolithic of the Negev. In *Prehistoire du Levant*. P. Sanlaville and J. Cauvin, eds. Pp. 343 – 352. Paris: CNRS, 1981.

[4] Bar-Yosef, O. Raw Material Exploitation in the Levantine Epi-Paleolithic. In *Raw Material Economies among Prehistoric Hunter-Gatherers*. A. Montet-White and S. Holen, eds. Pp. 235 – 250. Publications in Anthropology 19. Lawrence: University of Kansas, 1991.

Goring-Morris, A. N. Square Pegs into Round Holes: A Critique of Neeley and Barton. *Antiquity* 70 (267): 130 – 135, 1996.

[5] Bar-Yosef, O., and A. Belfer. The Lagaman Industry. In *Prehistoric Investigations in Gebel Maghara, Northern Sinai*. O. Bar-Yosef and J. L. Phillips, eds. Pp. 42 – 84. Qedem 7. Jerusalem: Monographs of the Institute of Archaeology, Hebrew University, 1977.

Monigal, K. *Technology, Economy, and Mobility at the Beginning of the Levantine Upper Paleolithic*. Paper presented at the 65th Annual Meeting of the Society of American Archaeology, Philadelphia, 2000.

[6] Gilead, I., and O. Bar-Yosef. Early Upper Paleolithic Sites in the Kadesh Barnea Area, Northeastern Sinai. *Journal of Field Archaeology* 20: 265 – 280, 1993.

Jones, M., A. E. Marks, and D. Kaufman. Boqer: The Artifacts. In *Prehistory and Paleoenvironments in the Central Negev, Israel, vol. 3: The Avdat/Aqev Area, Part 3*. A. E. Marks, ed. Pp. 283 – 329. Dallas: Southern Methodist University Press, 1983.

Kerry, K. W. Jebel. Humeima: A Preliminary Analysis of an Ahmarian and Levantine Mousterian Site in Southwestern Jordan. In *The Prehistory of Jordan, II: Perspectives from 1997*. H. G. Gebel, Z. Kafafi, and G. O. Rollefson, eds. Pp. 125 – 136. SENEPSE 4. Berlin: ex oriente, 1997.

Williams, J. K. Tor Aeid, an Upper Paleolithic Site in Southern Jordan. In *The Prehistory of Jordan, II: Perspectives from 1997*. H. G. Gebel, Z. Kafafi, and G. O. Rollefson, eds. Pp. 137 – 148. SENEPSE 4. Berlin: ex oriente, 1997.

[7] Belfer-Cohen, A., and O. Bar-Yosef. The Aurignacian in Hayonim Cave. *Paleorient* 7(2): 19 – 42, 1981.

Lucas, G. Les lamelles Dufour du Flageolet I (Bezenac, Dordogne) dans le contexte Aurignacien. *Pale'o* 9: 191 – 219, 1997.

[8] Goring-Morris, A. N., O. Marder, A. Davidzon, and F. Ibrahim. Putting Humpty Dumpty Together Again: Preliminary Observations on Refitting Studies in the Eastern Mediterranean. In *From Raw Material Procurement to Tool Production: The Organisation of Lithic Technology in Late Glacial and Early Microlithization in the Levant 67 Postglacial Europe*. S. Milliken,

ed. Pp. 149 – 182. BAR International Series, 700. Oxford: British Archaeological Reports, 1998.

Marks, A. E., and D. Kaufman. Boqer Tachtit: The Artifacts. In *Prehistory and Paleoenvironments in the Central Negev, Israel, vol. 3: The Avdat/Aqev Area, Part 3*. A. E. Marks, ed. Pp. 69 – 125. Dallas: Southern Methodist University Press, 1983.

[9] Bourguignon, L. Un Mousterien tardif sur le site d'Umm el-Tlel (Bassin d'el Khowm, Syrie)? Exemples des Nivaux 11 Base' et I1I2A'. In *The Last Neandertals, The First Anatomically Modern Humans*. E. Carbonell and M. Vaquero, eds. Pp. 317 – 336. Barcelona: Universitat Rovira i Virgili, 1996.

[10] Becker, M. S. Reconstructing Prehistoric Hunter-Gatherer Mobility Patterns and the Implications for the Shift to Sedentism: A Perspective from the Near East. Ph. D. thesis, University of Colorado, Boulder, 1999.

[11] Bar-Yosef, O., and A. Belfer. The Lagaman Industry. In *Prehistoric Investigations in Gebel Maghara, Northern Sinai*. O. Bar-Yosef and J. L. Phillips, eds. Pp. 42 – 84. Qedem 7. Jerusalem: Monographs of the Institute of Archaeology, Hebrew University, 1977.

[12] Marks, A. E. Ein Aqev: A Late Levantine Upper Palaeolithic Site in the Nahal Aqev. In *Prehistory and Paleoenvironments in the Central Negev, Israel, vol. 1: The Avdat/Aqev Area, Part 7*. A. E. Marks, ed. Pp. 227 – 292. Dallas: Southern Methodist University Press, 1976.

[13] Marks, A. E., and D. Kaufman. Boqer Tachtit: The Artifacts. In *Prehistory and Paleoenvironments in the Central Negev, Israel, vol. 3: The Avdat/Aqev Area, Part 3*. A. E. Marks, ed. Pp. 69 – 125. Dallas: Southern Methodist University Press, 1983.

[14] Bar-Yosef, O., and A. Belfer. The Lagaman Industry. In *Prehistoric Investigations in Gebel Maghara, Northern Sinai*. O. Bar-Yosef and J. L. Phillips, eds. Pp. 42 – 84. Qedem 7. Jerusalem: Monographs of the Institute of Archaeology, Hebrew University, 1977.

[15] Goring-Morris, A. N. Upper Palaeolithic Occupation of the Ein Qadis Area on the Sinai/Negev Border. '*Atiquot* 27: 1 – 14, 1995b.

[16] Jones, M., A. E. Marks, and D. Kaufman. Boqer: The Artifacts. In *Prehistory and Paleoenvironments in the Central Negev, Israel, vol. 3: The Avdat/Aqev Area, Part 3*. A. E. Marks, ed. Pp. 283 – 329. Dallas: Southern Methodist University Press, 1983.

[17] Marks, A. E. Ein Aqev: A Late Levantine Upper Palaeolithic Site in the Nahal Aqev. In *Prehistory and Paleoenvironments in the Central Negev, Israel, vol. 1: The Avdat/Aqev Area, Part 7*. A. E. Marks, ed. Pp. 227 – 292. Dallas: Southern Methodist University Press, 1976.

[18] Goring-Morris, A. N. Complex Hunter-Gatherers at the End of the Paleolithic (20 000 – 10 000 BP). In *The Archaeology of Society in the Holy Land*. T. E. Levy, ed. Pp. 141 – 168. London: Leicester University Press, 1995a.

[19] Ferring, C. R. Technological Change in the Upper Paleolithic of the Negev. In *Upper Pleistocene Prehistory of Western Eurasia*. H. Dibble and A. Montet-White, eds. Pp. 333 – 348. University Museum Monographs, 54. Philadelphia: University of Philadelphia, 1988.

[20] Belfer-Cohen, A., and A. N. Goring-Morris. Har Horesha I: An Upper Palaeolithic Site in the Central Negev Highlands. Mitekufat Haeven — *Journal of the Israel Prehistoric Society* 19: 43 – 57, 1986.

[21] Tixier, J. Typologie de l'Epipaleolithique du Maghreb. Memoires du Centre de Recherches Anthropologiques, Prehistoriques et Ethnographiques 2. Paris: Arts et Metiers Graphiques, 1963: 115 – 117.

[22] Boeda, E., and S. Muhesen. Umm el-Tlel (el Kowm, Syrie): etude preliminaire des industries lithiques du Paleolithiques moyen et superieur 1991 – 1992. *Cahiers de l'Euphmte* 7: 47 – 91, 1993.

[23] Phillips, J. L. Refitting, Edge Wear and Chaines Ope'ratoires: A Case Study from Sinai. In *lingt-Cinq Ans d Etudes Technologiques en Prehistoire, Me Rencontre Internationales d'Archeologie et Histoire d'Antibes*. L. Meignen, ed. Pp. 305 – 317. Juan-les-Pins, France: Editions APDCA, 1991.

[24] Bar-Yosef, O. The Epi-Palaeolithic Cultures of Palestine. Ph. D. thesis, Hebrew University, Jerusalem, 1970.

Goring-Morris, A. N. *At the Edge: Terminal Pleistocene Hunter-Gatherers in the Negev and Sinai*. BAR International Series, 361. Oxford: British Archaeological Reports, 1987.

[25] Goring-Morris, A. N. Complex Hunter-Gatherers at the End of the Paleolithic (20 000 – 10 000 BP). In *The Archaeology of Society in the Holy Land*. T. E. Levy, ed. Pp. 141 – 168. London: Leicester University Press, 1995a.

Kirkbride, D. A Kebaran Rock Shelter in Wadi Madamagh near Petra, Jordan. *Man* 58: 55 – 58, 1958.

Tixier, J. L'Abri Sous Roche de Ksar Aqil: La Campagne de Fouilles 1969. *Bulletin de la Musee de Beyrouth* 33: 173 – 191, 1970.

[26] Byrd, B. F. Late Pleistocene Assemblage Diversity in the Azraq Basin. *Paléorient* 14(2): 257 – 265, 1988.

Goring-Morris, A. N. *At the Edge: Terminal Pleistocene Hunter-Gatherers in the Negev and Sinai*. BAR International Series, 361. Oxford: British Archaeological Reports, 1987.

[27] Bar-Yosef, O., and F. Valla. L'Evolution du Natoufien: Nouvelles Suggestions. *Paleorient* 5: 145 – 152, 1979.

[28] Belfer-Cohen, A. The Natufian Settlement at Hayonim Cave: A Hunter-Gatherer Band on the Threshold of Agriculture. Ph. D. thesis, Hebrew University, Jerusalem, 1988.

Olszewski, D. I. Tool Blank Selection, Debitage and Cores from Abu Hureya 1, Northern Syria. *Paleorient* 15(2): 29 – 37, 1989.

Valla, F. R. *Les Industries de Silex de Mallaha (Eynan) et du Natoufien dans le Levant.* Paris: Association Paleorient, 1984.

[29] Bar-Yosef, O. The Natufian Culture in the Levant, Threshold to the Origins of Agriculture. *Evolutionary Anthropology* 6: 159 – 177, 1998.

Byrd, B. F. Late Pleistocene Assemblage Diversity in the Azraq Basin. *Paléorient* 14(2): 257 – 265, 1988.

Goring-Morris, A. N. *At the Edge: Terminal Pleistocene Hunter-Gatherers in the Negev and Sinai.* BAR International Series, 361. Oxford: British Archaeological Reports, 1987.

Olszewski, D. I. A Reassessment of Average Lunate Length as a Chronological Marker. *Pale'orient* 12(1): 39 – 43, 1986.

Valla, F. R. The First Settled Societies: Natufian (12 500 – 10 200 BP). In *The Archaeology of Society in the Holy Land.* T. E. Levy, ed. Pp. 170 – 187. London: Leicester University Press, 1995.

[30] Bar-Yosef, O. The Epi-Palaeolithic Cultures of Palestine. Ph. D. thesis, Hebrew University, Jerusalem, 1970.

[31] Wiseman, M. F. Lithic Blade Elements from the Southern Levant: A Diachronic View of Changing Technology and Design Process. *Mitekufat Haeven — Journal of the Israel Prehistoric Society* 25: 13 – 102, 1993.

[32] Kukan, G. J. A Technological and Stylistic Study of Microliths from Certain Levantine Epipalaeolithic Assemblages. Ph. D. thesis, Department of Anthropology, University of Toronto, 1978.

[33] Davidzon, A., and A. N. Goring-Morris. *The End of the Upper Palaeolithic and the Transformation to the Epipalaeolithic in the Levant.* Paper presented at the 65th Annual Meeting of the Society of American Archaeology, Philadelphia, 2000.

Goring-Morris, A. N., O. Marder, A. Davidzon, and F. Ibrahim. Putting Humpty Dumpty Together Again: Preliminary Observations on Refitting Studies in the Eastern Mediterranean. In *From Raw Material Procurement to Tool Production: The Organisation of Lithic Technology in Late Glacial and Early Microlithization in the Levant 67 Postglacial Europe.* S. Milliken, ed. Pp. 149 – 182. BAR International Series, 700. Oxford: British Archaeological Reports, 1998.

Marder, O. Technological Aspects of Lithic Industries of Epipalaeolithic Entities in the Levant: Chaine Operatoire in the Ramonian of the Negev (Hebrew). M. A. thesis, Hebrew University, Jerusalem, 1994.

[34] Goring-Morris, A. N., O. Marder, A. Davidzon, and F. Ibrahim. Putting Humpty Dumpty

Together Again: Preliminary Observations on Refitting Studies in the Eastern Mediterranean. In *From Raw Material Procurement to Tool Production: The Organisation of Lithic Technology in Late Glacial and Early Microlithization in the Levant 67 Postglacial Europe*. S. Milliken, ed. Pp. 149 – 182. BAR International Series, 700. Oxford: British Archaeological Reports, 1998.

[35] Bar-Yosef, O. The Natufian Culture in the Levant, Threshold to the Origins of Agriculture. *Evolutionary Anthropology* 6: 159 – 177, 1998.

[36] Bleed, P. The Optimal Design of Hunting Weapons: Maintainability or Reliability. *American Antiquity* 51(4): 737 – 747, 1986.

Eerkens, J. W. Reliable and Maintainable Technologies: Artifact Standardization and the Early to Later Mesolithic Transition in Northern England. *Lithic Technology* – 23: 42 – 53, 1991.

[37] Rosenberg, M. Cheating at Musical Chairs: Territoriality and Sedentism in an Evolutionary Context. *Current Anthropology* 39(5): 653 – 681, 1998.

[38] Garrard, A. N., S. Colledge, C. Hunt, and R. Montague. Environment and Subsistence during the Late Pleistocene and Early Holocene in the Azraq Basin. *Paleorient* 14(2): 40 – 49, 1988.

[39] Brezillon, M. *La Denomination des Objects de Pierre Taille'e, Materiau. x pour un Vocabulaire de Prehistoriens de Langue Francaise*. IVe Supplement a Gallia Prehistoire. Bordeaux: CNRS. 66, 1968.

[40] Lucas, G. Les lamelles Dufour du Flageolet I (Bezenac, Dordogne) dans le contexte Aurignacien. *Pale'o* 9: 191 – 219, 1997.

Production experimentale de lamelles torses: Approche preliminaire. *Bulletin de la Societe Pre'historique Francaise* 96(2): 145 – 151, 1999.

[41] Ferring, C. R. Technological Change in the Upper Paleolithic of the Negev. In *Upper Pleistocene Prehistory of Western Eurasia*. H. Dibble and A. Montet-White, eds. Pp. 333 – 348. University Museum Monographs, 54. Philadelphia: University of Philadelphia, 1988.

[42] Gilead, I. Lagama X. In *Prehistoric Investigations in Gebel Maghara, Northern Sinai*. O. Bar-Yosef and J. L. Phillips, eds. Pp. 102 – 114. Qedem 7. Jerusalem: Monographs of the Institute of Archaeology, Hebrew University, 1977.

[43] Nadel, D. Ohalo II: The Third Season. Mitekufat Haeven. *Journal of the Israel Prehistoric Society* 24: 158 – 163, 1991.

[44] Goring-Morris, A. N. Upper Palaeolithic Sites from Wadi Fazael, Lower Jordan Valley. *Paléorient* 6: 173 – 191, 1980.

[45] Ferring, C. R. The Late Upper Paleolithic Site of Ein Aqev East. In *Prehistory and Paleoenvironments in the Central Negev, Israel, vol. 2: The Avdat/Aqev Area, Part 2 and the*

Har Harif. A. E. Marks, ed. Pp. 81 – 118. Dallas: Southern Methodist University Press, 1977.

[46] Olszewski, D. I., G. A. Clark, and S. Fish. WHS 784X (Yutil al-Hasa): A Late Ahmarian Site in the Wadi Hasa, West-Central Jordan. *Proceedings of the Prehistoric Society* 56: 33 – 49, 1990.

[47] Coinman, N. R. WHS 618-Ain el-Buhira: An Upper Paleolithic Site in the Wadi Hasa, West-Central Jordan. *Paléorient* 19(2): 17 – 37, 1993.

[48] Gilead, I., and O. Bar-Yosef. Early Upper Paleolithic Sites in the Kadesh Barnea Area, Northeastern Sinai. *Journal of Field Archaeology* 20: 265 – 280, 1993.

[49] Goring-Morris, A. N. Upper Palaeolithic Occupation of the Ein Qadis Area on the Sinai/Negev Border. *'Atiqot* 27: 1 – 14, 1995b.

[50] Boeda. E., J. Connan, D. Dessort, S. Muhesen, N Mercier, H. Valladas, and N. Tisnerat. Bitumen as a Hafting Material on Middle Paleolithic Artifacts. *Nature* 380: 336 – 338, 1996. Friedman, E., N. Goren-Inbar, A. Rosenfeld, O. Marder, and F. Burian. Hafting during Mousterian Times — Further Indications. *Mitekufat Haeven-Journal of the Israel Prehistoric Society* 26: 8 – 31, 1994 – 1995.

[51] Bar-Yosef, O., and A. Belfer. The Lagaman Industry. In *Prehistoric Investigations in Gebel Maghara, Northern Sinai.* O. Bar-Yosef and J. L. Phillips, eds. Pp. 42 – 84. Qedem 7. Jerusalem: Monographs of the Institute of Archaeology, Hebrew University, 1977.

选择小工具：有关西欧旧石器时代晚期至中石器时代细石器的思考

劳伦斯·G·施特劳斯

（新墨西哥大学 阿尔伯特基）

摘　要：欧洲旧石器时代晚期采用不同的技术加工细小石器，器物形制多样，细石器分布广泛，在器物组合中，无论绝对数量还是相对比例都是如此。旧石器时代晚期与中石器时代的重要文化地层单位概莫能外。细石器常用作投掷器，它的存在意味着装柄技术的应用。细石器（从杜福尔类型到琢背修理的细小石叶再到几何形细石器）可能成组镶嵌在木质或鹿角柄上，用作复合工具中可以替换的部件。细小轻薄的尖部或是倒刺会加重猎物的出血状况。不过，距今4万至6千年之间，安装细石器的标枪与单个整体的大型枪头（如格拉韦丁、方特—罗伯特、梭鲁特、特加特等类型）是交替"流行"的。迄今为止，我们还远未理解这些不同"猎杀技术"之间可能存在的功能差异，许多变化很可能并没有功能上的意义，不过是随机或"风格上的"特征。旧石器中期之后石器的轻量化显然正是阿贝·步日耶所谓"细石器时代"的标志。

尽管在整个石器时代石器技术发展的大框架中可以看到明显的宏观尺度的变化，甚至可以说是持续的进步与累积的发展（法语称之为"进化"），但是在解释人类物质文化变化方面还有许多其他现象同样重要。这些现象包括：

1. 不成功的实验；失败或是昙花一现；
2. 独立的发明；平行的、趋同的发展——时间与空间上既可能距离遥远也可能很靠近；

3. 解决方法的周期性；流行的风潮来来回回，几种可能的技术途径效率大致相当；

4. 基于社会习惯的选择。

我们首先需要知道的是：石器技术不是火箭科学。鉴于解剖学上的现代人的身体与大脑条件，鉴于对食物与容身之所的生理需要的确定范围，鉴于人类可用的原料（如石、骨、牙齿、皮、筋、木、植物胶）与可能驾驭的技术，在人类历史不同时间与地点上就类似的基本生存需要存在相似的解决方法，也就不足为奇。同样不足为奇的是，这些方法在效率上也相差无几（也是，"差不多"，所谓好的标准范围很大），因此，采用一种方法而不采用另一种方法并不必然就会导致生与死的区别，或是在种群竞争与替代中形成有差别的优势。鉴于一些相对简单的技术方法存在某种程度的相似性，于是在方法采用、保留或是放弃中存在一定的随机性，这也不足为奇。当然，作为"人类学的"或是"科学的"考古学家，这是我们部分考古学家希望了解的主要推动力（全球的、大洲的，或至少是地区的），这的确可能存在，它使得人类在特定的时间情形下放弃某些技术选择，而在其有限的可能性中选择了某些特定的方法，进而形成了生存优势。

从某种程度上说，发明类似于基因突变。有些方法，在一定的条件下，是"中性的"，但是随着条件的改变，一些方法变得"有利"，而另一些方法变得"不利"。所谓"有利"，意思是获取那些人人想要的东西，其途径更可靠、更高效、更有用、更丰富。因此，比那些选择"错"了（或是说没有得到"正确的"方法）的人们，这些技术的拥有者可能确实会活得长一些，留下更多的后代。也就是，物质文化选择可能确实会影响自然选择。从考古学上证明这一点，既不可能直接也不会简单，也不是这短短一篇文章能够说清楚的。

当然，分析发现似乎存在一些长的周期性循环，某些技术方法反复流行，目前还不清楚，其始终是否可以确实归因于已知的宏大原因（如气候变化、大范围的资源波动、急剧的人口变迁）。我们很难判断，史前史上的"潮流"究竟是来自传播（不管机制如何，比如访问、交易、通婚、迁徙等等），还是特定条件下（"被迫的"）不得不的选择，这个问题困扰着一代又一代考古学家。

石器（与骨器）的出现、消失与重新出现，都是为了满足狩猎采集者的基本技术需要，无论这样的"大"循环受到自然伟力的推动还是受到某些偶然原因的作用，考古学家都需要详细考察其存在的原因。考古学家经常把孤立出现的某些器物视为入侵、迁徙或是传播的证据，尤其时空上相对接近的时候。这样的幻觉导致产生了不少考古学上所谓的"传统",比如旧石器时代早期流行于非洲与欧亚的砾石工具组合,欧洲旧石器时代中晚期的石叶工业,以及欧洲与近东地区的奥瑞纳工业,都暗含着系统进化的意义。两个或多个不同时代与地区存在类似的石器(或骨器)通常解释为人群之间存在联系。某些人群迁移的证据(或是物品与观念)通常并不受重视,而是将相似性视为某种联系的证据(有时表面上看起来有可能,比如阿特林与梭鲁特工业之间的关联,但是有些则显得比较怪异,比如最近又复活的梭鲁特—克鲁维斯假说[*])。

贯穿整个第四纪,在世界范围内,你可以列出许多反复出现的"爆发",都可以说是"特殊"或复杂的石器发明:例如,旧石器时代中晚期以及新石器时代的棱柱状石叶技术,它也见于美洲阿兹特克文明中;旧大陆与新大陆许多地方多次出现过细石叶工艺;树叶形两面修理的石刀与尖状器见于撒哈拉以南非洲地区卢皮姆班的石器时代中期、莫斯特工业、米科克工业以及中东欧地区的斯泽勒特工业(严格意义上的)、西南欧的梭鲁特工业、美洲的古印第安技术组合、欧洲的铜石并用与青铜时代文化中;有铤与/或带凹缺的投掷尖状器见于新旧大陆地区各种各样的石器组合中,从北非的阿特林组合到伊比利亚半岛的梭鲁特工业,再到美国的林地文化。

我认为用形态相似性解释人类联系之前,考古学家应该首先排除独立发明的可能性(即便是同时代或接近同时代的发展),如果确实发生了联系,考古学家应该建立基于背景关联的、扎实可靠的实际模型——基于环境的、经济的、人口的条件,解释这些联系是如何发生的。考虑到理论视角的全面性,本文现实的目标是探讨西欧地区旧石器时代晚期材料中细石器的由来与消亡。

一、细石器

我所说的细石器是指所有有意修理的细小石器(2~3厘米长,通常更短),修理方式包括直接或间接的垂直修理(琢背修理)、简单修理(经常的)或压制修理,使用或不使用石砧。常用的修理有时可能比较深入(包括双面的或"赫尔文"类型),也可能是边缘的(波状的),向腹面修理(正常的),向背面修理(反向的),或是交错的。琢背修理可能单向(从毛坯背面或腹面开始),也可能是双向的。细石器一般由细小石叶(细石叶)毛坯所制,但是就概念而言,细小石叶处在小石叶与任何截断的石叶制品之间,难以发现其间的区别,截断石制品的长度

---

[*] 认为克鲁维斯尖状器技术来自梭鲁特工业,暗含最早的美洲人至少部分来自欧洲。——译注

显然也是主观的（我倾向于采用2厘米作为标准，但这是就西班牙北部这一地区长期工作之后的总结，这里大一点的燧石石块非常罕见）。几何形细石器是一种专门的细石器类型，有标准化的器形（半月形、长方形、等腰三角形、不等边三角形、菱形、梯形），通常用截断的细小石叶制作（经常采用"微雕刻器"技术或是采用制作凹缺然后折断的技术）。

我认为属于细石器的还包括杜福尔细小石叶、克里姆斯尖状器、琢背细小石叶、细小的格拉韦丁与阿兹连尖状器（其各自大小处在格拉韦丁与沙特尔佩龙尖状器的中间）、小矛头与标枪头以及各种非几何形的工具（如萨维特里安、塔德诺西安、宗霍芬尖状器）。可能还有人主张包括小型的边刮器（racelettes*）：它如同引火燧石，通常是方形的石片或是接近长方形的有多个琢背修理边缘的石片片段，还有拇指盖形端刮器，以及其他用小石片制作的端刮器，都可以视为细石器。就细石器长度范围较短的一头来说，许多诺阿耶（Noailles）雕刻器（多次截断，剥片时通常打出一个凹缺用以制动）与某些石锥当然也是细石器。

所有这些细石器的共同特点是曾经使用过，很可能是镶嵌使用的，或是单件或成组镶嵌在木质或骨质的柄梢上。不管解剖学上的现代人捏持的准确性，细石器大多太细小，不易使用，或者说是没有装柄的话根本就是不可能使用（例外可能还是有的，如用作穿孔的微型石锥或尖状器）。遗憾的是装柄的证据罕见。刻槽的鹿角片无疑适合镶嵌诸如琢背修理、一般修理或是未加修理的细小石叶与石片（或是片段），如宾斯凡特与圣马瑟尔的马格德林时期的出土标本所见的[1]。但是关于旧石器时代晚期的木柄，我们一无所知。许多尖状细石器上撞击痕迹的存在表明它们可能是轴向镶嵌的，用作投掷器的尖部，以及倒刺与侧边刃缘（以使猎物大出血）。这里问题的中心应该是那些"细石器"，它们可能常用于复合投掷武器上用于切割或刺穿的部件（基于微痕的证据以及常识）。

二、旧石器晚期早段：奥瑞纳

在佩里戈德旧石器时代晚期经典的综合研究中，丹妮丝·德索尼维尔—博尔德[2]注意到"典型的"奥瑞纳组合中存在边缘持续修理平整如波状的杜福尔细小石叶（数量或是比例通常都比较小）。当然，稀少的数量很有可能跟过时的

---

* Racelettes，按照博尔德的石器类型学的定义，它通常由薄石片制作，具有连续的精细的修理疤痕，通常是陡向的交错修理，修理有时不规则，呈锯齿状，跟使用石片的区别在于其修理疤痕连续。——译注

发掘技术有关。但是,即使是在佩里戈德现在的发掘材料(即细筛的)中,这些细石器的比例也是高度变化的[3]。

最近发表的奥布里帕图德材料支持这一观点,它有八个属于奥瑞纳技术组合的地层,其中一个水平层(第 8 水平层,为几个"中间"层位之一,距今 3.2 万年)含有相当数量的杜福尔细小石叶(44 件,占 10.8%);其他层位或是没有,最多的也仅 3 件[4]。此外,第 8 水平层不像帕图德遗址其他奥瑞纳层位那样含有若干其他类型的修理细小石叶。最近发掘的拉菲拉西遗址的组合形态与之非常相似:其中一个奥瑞纳层位(E1s 层:奥瑞纳晚期,距今 2.8 万年)含有相当数量的杜福尔细小石叶(11 件,占 9.7%),同时含有若干琢背修理或是其他类型修理的细小石叶[5]。这些材料可以表明杜福尔细小石叶具有特定的功能,虽然在居住遗存中数量有限,但代表相关活动的存在。按 F·德金德建[6]的多变量分析,富含杜福尔细小石叶的组合似乎构成奥瑞纳独特的"色彩"。当然,问题是哪些活动中用到了这些细小石叶?里古德最近指出它们是投掷武器复合工具的切割刃缘。里古德[7]援引 H·普利森对勒夫拉盖特的杜福尔细小石叶的微痕分析,支持这样的功能判断。他同时注意到奥瑞纳角质尖状器与杜福尔细小石叶之间存在反比关系,表明两者是可替代武器类型的组成部分。我还可以补充一点,其替代关系可以是严格意义上的等同(可能是"文化传统"的结果),也可以是根据猎物大小或投掷方法不同而形成功能差异。最后,里古德[8]提及杜福尔细小石叶与有脊端刮器的频繁共存可能意味着后者实际上只是生产前者的毛坯[9](或至少在其使用寿命的初期)。

佩里戈德之外的地区出现杜福尔细小石叶的频率也是高度变化的。例如我们最近发掘的勒托玛格丽特(位于比利时的瓦隆尼亚)遗址只是在距今 4 万与 3 万年的奥瑞纳层位中缺乏杜福尔细小石叶[10]。另一方面,杜福尔细小石叶是普罗旺斯[11]与意大利北部地区[12]某些特别早(或称"原初")的奥瑞纳石器组合的重要组成部分,某些器物呈现出高度专业化的特征。这样的组合曾见于西班牙的坎塔布连地区,但似乎不是这一地区奥瑞纳工业的普遍特征。坎塔布连地区的库瓦莫林是一处少有的完全采用现代技术发掘过的遗址,只是在第 9、8a、8b 以及第 6 水平层发现相当数量的杜福尔细小石叶,中间两层的频率较高(分别为 17 件,占 15.1%;25 件,占 21.1%)。后者(8b 水平层)与杜福尔细小石叶共出的还有一些修理过的细小石叶[13]。8a 与第 7 水平层的放射性碳测年年代为距今 2.8~2.9 万年。我们把第 9 到第 8 水平层称为"古奥瑞纳",第 6 到第 7 水平层称为"典型的奥瑞纳"与"进化的奥瑞纳"。第 5 层下部(可能带有底端劈开的骨质尖状器断片)与第7水平层只含有少量杜福尔细小石叶以及其他细小石叶。最近发掘的艾尔卡斯特罗第18水平层"古奥瑞纳"组合(距今3.8~4万年)中发现底端劈开的骨质尖状器与许多有脊刮削器,这些方面跟雨果·欧博梅尔的奥瑞纳时期的德尔塔地层联系起来。然而无论是老组合还是新组合都没有很多修理过的细小石叶:老组合中没有杜福尔细小石叶[14],新组合的初步描述也没有提及[15]。

库瓦莫林遗址发现的细石器明显不一致,这种状况同样见于最近发掘的岩厦遗址拉维纳(位于西班牙的阿斯图里亚斯)。基本描述显示第11、13以及13层下部只有"少量的"杜福尔细小石叶,不过第12层杜福尔细小石叶"丰富"。所有层位中都有较多的有脊刮削器/石核[16]。第13层下部测定年代为距今3.65万年;第13层(含有底端劈开骨质尖状器)年代为距今3.2万年[17]。另一方面,艾尔本多洞遗址(坎塔布里亚)数个经过现代发掘(即细致筛选,马格德林晚期以上层位明显采用了这一方法,阿兹连组合中含有相当丰富的琢背细小石叶及其他细石器),但未测年的奥瑞纳层位实际上不含有杜福尔细小石叶及其他修理过的细小石叶[18]。总之,坎塔布里亚地区奥瑞纳组合的任何阶段(即早中晚期)中细石器的出现频率是高度变化的,同时表明遗址使用中其功能可能存在较大的变化。

带尖的类似杜福尔的细小石叶(类似于克里姆斯尖状器)在葡萄牙的埃什特雷马杜拉地区有报道,可能是奥瑞纳(晚期的)时期的,尤其是佩戈多·迪亚波洞遗址(距今2.3~2.8万年)[19]。当然所有(非常少)组合都很小,即使是在迪亚波(第2水平层)遗址也只有11件修理工具,其中6件为杜福尔细小石叶(外加1件琢背细小石叶)。不过葡萄牙的前格拉韦丁时代似乎确实有细石器制的武器尖部。

三、格拉韦丁工业

许多奥瑞纳工具组合中都含有骨质的标枪头,而在"佩里戈德"(也就是西格拉韦丁工业,包括许多假定的亚文化,比如"瑙依兰"、"原马格德林或劳格林"、"方特罗伯特")工业中则要稀少得多,罕见的例外是德勒斯图里茨标枪头。相反,格拉韦丁富含石质武器尖头:格拉韦丁与微格拉韦丁工具、叶形尖状器、有肩尖状器以及有梃的方特—罗伯特尖状器。微格拉韦丁与更小的燕尾尖状器符合或接近细石器定义的范围。垂直琢背修理、直刃的格拉韦丁与微格拉韦丁工具在长度上具有过渡性,但按照定义后者的长度通常在3~3.5厘米之间[20]。

琢背细小石叶同样见于格拉韦丁工业中。

格拉韦丁工业中似乎存在其他的石器武器类型,或来自"地区文化传统",或来自习惯性的做法/武器投掷方法的需要。例如,采用现代技术发掘的麦瑟里斯—卡纳尔遗址(位于瓦隆尼亚,距今约2.8万年)出土有梃与单面叶形尖状器,各大约120件,另加10件有肩尖状器,没有格拉韦丁或微格拉韦丁工具,仅有4件琢背细小石叶的碎片[21]。我们自己的发掘与P.哈伊萨尔斯在瓦隆尼亚另一处重要的格拉韦丁旷野遗址胡科涅—黑米塔基(距今2.4~2.8万年)的发掘。他主以未经修理加工的废片为主,没有微格拉韦丁器物,只有一些格拉韦丁尖状器与有肩尖状器,35件琢背细小石叶,占主要遗址区域发现所有工具的21.5%[22]。假定用作武器尖头,两个遗址形成鲜明的对照,尽管两个遗址都靠近优质燧石原料地,显然都用作原料采集地(同时也有其他用途)。

奥布里帕图德遗址由H.L.莫维斯主持发掘。他以精细的田野工作以及详尽的资料发表而闻名,他的学生继承了他的工作[23]。这一遗址的发掘材料表明佩里戈德工业中格拉韦丁技术组合可能包含多样的武器尖头。所谓属于佩里戈德中期的第5层(距今约2.6~2.8万年)出土5 640件工具,实际上没有琢背细小石叶或有肩/有梃尖状器,但是确实有大量的格拉韦丁尖状器(占15.4%),以及相当数量的微格拉韦丁工具(9.6%)。同时还有少量的叶形尖状器,这可能是一种投掷用的尖状器,陡向修理成双尖叶形,偶尔接近细石器的大小(3~6厘米长,平均4.6厘米)[24]。所谓的瑙依兰(也就是佩里戈德Vc阶段)层(广义上的第4层,距今约2.6~2.7万年)实际上没有琢背细小石叶,也没有叶形尖状器、微格拉韦丁工具、有肩或有梃尖状器,只有非常少量的格拉韦丁尖状器[25]。狩猎可能不是当时主要的生计活动,或者说狩猎是采用其他完全不同的武器来完成的。相反,所谓佩里戈德VI阶段(第3层,距今约2.3~2.4万年)有大量的微格拉韦丁工具(181件,占13.8%),还能有许多格拉韦丁尖状器(85件,占6.5%),以及少量形态多样的琢背细小石叶(24件,占1.8%)。最后,也正相反,所谓"原马格德林"(也就是佩里戈德VII或称劳格林)的第2层(距今约2.0~2.2万年)有大量的琢背细小石叶(388件,占33.6%),但没有格拉韦丁尖状器或微格拉韦丁工具[26]。帕图德遗址的发现似乎表明格拉韦丁阶段不同时期所用的武器尖头非常多样,有时是大石器,有时是细石器。为什么格拉韦丁猎人采用如此多样的选择尚不得而知,但是这值得做进一步的功能分析,以确定不同的武器部件是否等同。

类似之,采用现代发掘的拉菲拉西遗址包含六个石器组合,属于佩里戈德

Va 阶段(距今 2.6~2.7 万年),带有中等数量(3%~14%)的有梃方特—罗伯特尖状器。同时含有大量格拉韦丁尖状器(9%~33%)、中等数量的微格拉韦丁工具(2%~8%),以及非常少量的琢背细小石叶[27]。可能运用不同武器尖头——大石器与细石器——的类似现象也见于最近发掘的佩里戈德时期的其他遗址如勒夫拉盖特,这个遗址含有几个佩里戈德层位,距今年代从 2.6 到 2.4 万年[28]。

坎塔布里亚地区最近发掘的格拉韦丁遗址很少确定有无疑的细石器(尤其是经过细致筛选的)。尽管不同遗址之间有细微的差别,不过莫林遗址属于格拉韦丁的第 4 层与 5 层上部(距今约 2.1 万年)只有少量的琢背细小石叶或是有肩的、微格拉韦丁或格拉韦丁尖状器(后者在第 5 层上部出人意料地达到 7.5%)。厄尔本多遗址格拉韦丁层位投掷器部件甚至更少,无论是大石器还是细石器。另一方面,经过精细发掘的拉维纳遗址的最晚期的格拉韦丁层位据说含有较为丰富琢背细小石叶/尖状器。

葡萄牙的埃斯特雷马杜拉地区所发现的格拉韦丁工业来自 1930 与 1940 年代 M.希伦罗的发掘,规模很大但质量不是太高,A.E.马克斯、J.吉尔豪及其同事最近还在发掘。吉尔豪[29]对两批发掘材料进行了详尽的分析,结果表明存在数量不等的微格拉韦丁与格拉韦丁尖状器,有时与当地一种数量众多、形制特殊的大石器共出,这种大石器称为卡萨尔杜菲力佩尖状器(一种由长三角形石叶所制的尖状器,仅作边缘修理,尖部锐利)。琢背细小石叶的比例高低不等,从极少到特拉杜曼努埃尔遗址的 13%。另一处旷野遗址方特桑塔(有观点认为属于格拉韦丁晚期,尽管热释光年代平均为距今 37 500±3 200 年)含有最高比例的卡萨尔杜菲力佩尖状器(31%),同时出土一些修理/琢背/截断的细小石叶以及少量的几何形细石器,但几何形细石器很可能是晚期居住(马格德林时代?)向下扰动混合的产物[30]。情况又是同样的,若干武器尖头类型(功能相同/相似或相异)共存,有时同属于同一时期,有时还共存于同一组合中。细石器无疑是格拉韦丁的组成部分,也曾是奥瑞纳的组成部分。但是否也见于梭鲁特工业呢?要知道梭鲁特主要以叶形与有梃的大尖状器而闻名。

四、梭鲁特工业

于法国的梭鲁特工业而言,传统典型的文化序列如劳格里—豪特欧斯特与厄斯特(佩里戈德地区的莱塞济距今约 2.1~1.95 万年)并非细石器工业,这种技术组合非常稳定,变化过程漫长。不论是在博尔德 1950 年代后半叶的发掘中,还是在佩罗尼 1920 年代的发掘中,这处规模巨大的岩厦遗址都没有发现多少琢背细小石叶(有意思的是,琢背细小石叶最多的层位居然来自最古老的组合之一:H′层,即"早期的"梭鲁特;总共发现25件,占石制品的2.6%)[31]。梭鲁特工业应该很少或没有琢背细小石叶,这种观点似乎早已深入人心(尽管佩罗尼在佩里戈德地区的弗诺杜戴贝尔遗址 Level I 层位丰富的石器组合中发现了178件细石器[占16%][32]),因此当我在西班牙的巴斯克—坎塔布连地区见到与梭鲁特尖状器共存的琢背细小石叶的时候,某位著名法国旧石器时代晚期的研究专家告诉我,这样的共存关系是靠不住的,很可能是发掘中搞混了地层。只应该得到相反的结论;也就是某些西班牙更早的发掘(尤其是德巴朗迪亚兰发掘的遗址)质量相对比较高,当时发现了细石器。而今法国某些梭鲁特石器组合中也发现有丰富的琢背细小石叶;这些遗址包括勒马尔帕斯(有15%~19%的琢背细小石叶)[33]、康贝索尼尔 I 层(有40%)[34],都位于佩里戈德地区。金尼斯特与佩里森[35]注意到梭鲁特尖状器(尤其是有肩尖状器)与琢背细小石叶(可能安装在鹿角标枪头上,康贝索尼尔遗址也有发现,距今约1.95~1.7万年)是交替使用的,可能用于狩猎不同的猎物或是采用不同的工具投掷。两组工具都发现了撞击破裂痕迹以及用于切肉所形成的痕迹。这些研究似乎进一步表明,除了康贝索尼尔与勒普拉卡德(位于夏朗德地区)确实存在投掷器之外[36],梭鲁特工业可能已经发明了弓箭,尤其是发射轻型有肩尖状器与嵌有琢背细小石叶的标枪头。这种可能性最近进一步得到证实,伊比利亚东部、南部与西部的梭鲁特工业中发现含有带梃的(一角有凹缺的)帕帕罗/卡萨达莫拉尖状器[37]。

西班牙巴斯克—坎塔布连(北部)地区梭鲁特工业以多样的叶形、有肩尖状器以及鹿角标枪头——还有琢背细小石叶为代表。不同区域、遗址与层位中梭鲁特尖状器与琢背细小石叶的比例变化甚大。琢背细小石叶指数从0到70%不等,5%到10%的器物比较典型[38]。实际上琢背细小石叶与梭鲁特尖状器之间大致存在反比的关系,这表明它们代表不同或是交替的武器尖部类型[39]。

类似比例范围的琢背细小石叶(大约可以达到25%)也见于艾尔·帕帕罗遗址(瓦伦西亚)的梭鲁特石器组合中,1929~1931年间佩里科特对该遗址进行了精细的发掘,遗址距今约2.05~1.8万年[40]。琢背细小石叶逐渐提高的趋势(同时见于坎塔布连梭鲁特组合中,如文化序列较长的拉里亚洞穴遗址,距今约2.05~1.7万年)也见于勒斯玛拉特(距今约2.1~1.65万年),跟艾尔·帕帕罗遗址相似。梭鲁特尖状器为细石器所取代被称为"除梭鲁特化"或称"马格德林化",但是很清楚的是,距今约1.7~1.65万年前,细石器成分并非完全是新的现象。琢背与边缘修理的细小石叶(最晚期的梭鲁特甚至出现少量的几何形细石器,距今约 1.65 万年)的增加同样见于安达卢西亚的安布罗西奥洞(阿尔梅里亚),这里某些有肩尖状器同样变得非常细小(小于 2 厘米),这也是西班牙地中海地区的一般趋势。

葡萄牙同样也发现各种梭鲁特尖状器、鹿角标枪头(某些具有纵向的沟槽)以及琢背细小石叶(比例不等)共存的证据[41]。葡萄牙有很多梭鲁特遗址,尤其是中南部地区(伊斯特利马杜拉),放射性碳测年年代范围在距今 2.05 到 1.8 万年之间。特别典型的材料来自洞穴遗址卡尔德罗、萨尔马斯、大布拉卡,以及旷野遗址瓦尔阿尔莫因哈、卡萨尔杜塞珀、大奥尔加。某些旷野遗址有较多的琢背细小石叶,某些没有,洞穴遗址的情况也是同样如此。

五、马格德林工业

当我们想到西欧旧石器时代晚期细石器的时候,通常是指其高峰阶段:马格德林与阿兹连工业(技术上可以称之为"后马格德林")。距今 1.7 万年到距今 9 千年的各个时段内,琢背细小石叶确实是马格德林与阿兹连石器组合的主要的,甚至是占绝对主导地位的器物类型。但是上文已经提及,这种细石器技术并非是在旧石器晚期的最后阶段重新出现的。解剖学上的现代人在制作复合(武器)工具的时候,有时采用细小的石制品用作工具的刃部,这种技术早在距今 3~4 万年就已经开始使用了。细石器的作用似乎在不断增长,旧石器时代晚期最后的大约 8 千年的时间里变得更加普遍,进入中石器时代还产生了新的形制。

马格德林的武器库继续包含许多梭鲁特工业的器物,但是明显更(重新出现的)强调鹿角标枪头(后来发展出有倒钩的鱼叉,这是一项新发明),当然不同的阶段、地区、遗址与地层有所差异。(尤其是就区域的游群传统、遗址功能与技术发展阶段而言,严格意义上的奥瑞纳、格拉韦丁、马格德林工业明显不同。事实上,某些专家因此将某些早期的材料称为"巴德格连",这个时段里法国与西班牙的地中海地区还有其他一些重要地区性的石器工业)。梭鲁特工业的深入修理的尖状器(叶形与有肩的)不见了,但马格德林技术组合中有方特—于维斯尖状器、特加特有梃尖状器、陡向加工的有肩尖状器以及直背(类似于格拉韦丁)与曲背(阿兹连工业)尖状器,以及标枪头。至少后两者可以归于细石器的范畴内。

佩里戈德地区马格德林工业开始相对较早,几何形细石器(特别是三角形的)首先出现,通常是数量稀少,但是偶尔也相当丰富,如佩里戈德的克拉比拉特遗址[42]。佩里戈德地区几何形细石器并不仅见于马格德林工业的遗址：我们最近在法国西南部加斯科涅最南端的杜弗尔遗址马格德林中期(距今约1.3万年)与晚期(距今约1.2万年)地层中发现了它们(主要是三角形的)，附近杜鲁西遗址同时期的文化层中也存在，这个遗址晚期马格德林层位中确实含有大量类型多样的几何形细石器[43]。艾尔米龙洞(坎塔布里亚)的早中期马格德林层位也有少量三角形细石器[44]。西班牙地中海地区的帕帕罗、内尔哈(马拉加地区)以及其他马格德林遗址中也有报道[45]。

当然，琢背细小石叶无疑是马格德林工业最主要的组成成分。理所当然还需要记住，由于细小石叶通常成行地镶嵌安装用作倒钩或是切割边刃，数件细石器(几何形的)才能相当于一件大投掷尖状器(宾斯凡特遗址就曾发现三个一组的琢背细小石叶组合[46])，所以非尖状器的细石器在数量统计投掷工具时不能等同于有肩、有梃、叶形或是剑形(如格拉韦丁)尖状器。从另一方面来说，尖部修理的细石器常被安装轻型投掷工具的尖部，因此他们又可以在数量上等同于较大尖状器。

为了表现马格德林晚期(距今1.3~1.1万年)琢背细小石叶的重要性，表5.1罗列了一组西欧最近发掘的较大的石器组合。当然，这些最近发掘的马格德林遗址中，不少遗址很少有琢背细小石叶或是其他类型的细石器，而在那些经过精细筛选的较大石器组合中通常含有较多与较高比例的细石器，表明当时强调生产轻型的复合投掷工具。此外，许多微痕研究[47]表明马格德林与阿兹连琢背细小石叶用作倒钩部件(带有纵向的条痕)，尖部修理的琢背细小石叶(如微格拉韦丁与阿兹连尖状器)用作投掷工具的尖部(通常带有撞击裂痕)。

表5.1　西欧部分马格德林晚期遗址琢背细小石叶的相对频率

遗址、层位或单位	地 理 位 置	%琢背细小石叶	资料来源
格勒尔斯多夫(北居住区)	德国莱茵兰	72	[48]
皮特斯福尔斯(P3,AH2)	德国西南部	46	[49]
博瓦斯莱特里(BSC+YSS水平层)	比利时瓦隆尼亚	20	[50]
沙洛克丝(5~6水平层)	比利时瓦隆尼亚	46	[51]
汉吉斯特伯里赫德(LUP遗址)	英国南部	0	[52]
霍特里夫—尚普里维耶尔斯(1区)	瑞士纽夏特	63	[53]
宾斯凡特(36区)	巴黎近郊	61	[54]

续　表

遗址、层位或单位	地　理　位　置	%琢背细小石叶	资料来源
韦尔布里(2地点)	巴黎近郊	27	[55]
马桑奇(I+II集合)	巴黎近郊	18	[56]
杜弗尔(4层)	法国加斯科尼	46	[57]
杜弗尔(3层)	法国加斯科尼	35	[58]
方特格拉斯(1~2水平层)	法国加斯科尼	26	[59]
拉里埃拉(24水平层)	西班牙阿斯图里亚斯	54	[60]
提托巴斯提洛(1a~b水平层)	西班牙阿斯图里亚斯	30	[61]
居维莫林(2水平层)	西班牙坎塔布里亚	15	[62]
埃卡恩(VI水平层)	西班牙巴斯克地区	49	[63]
内尔哈(16水平层)	西班牙安达卢西亚	39	[64]
德帕托马林霍(I层下部)	葡萄牙埃斯特雷马杜拉	11	[65]
卡尔内拉(II地点)	葡萄牙埃斯特雷马杜拉	20	同上

六、阿兹连/菲德尔梅萨工业

阿兹连工业是众多琢背尖状器"文化"之一(也包括西北欧的菲德尔梅萨组合、意大利与巴尔干地区最晚的后格拉韦丁传统、西班牙地中海地区与葡萄牙的细叶片形的后旧石器传统)。按照定义,这些石器工业很大程度上都是细石器的,不仅具有高比例的琢背细小石叶与微型尖状器,而且有小型端刮器(拇指盖刮削器),表明存在广泛地装柄使用方式。事实上,许多阿兹连组合很少有其他石器工具,除了法国—坎塔布里亚地区有扁平截面的鹿角鱼叉发现外,几乎没有骨制工具。原因可能是,随着森林的重新出现,木质工具开始用作箭头与标枪杆(差不多同时的德国西北部斯特尔摩尔的埃伦斯堡遗址也发现有鹿角鱼叉)。当然,西北欧与北欧平原地区更新世至全新世过渡期间有多种多样的有梃尖状器,是许多"文化"的特征器物,如汉堡文化、布罗姆文化、斯韦德林文化、马佐维亚文化等,这再次说明猎人为了同样或类似的目的具有多样的武器选择。一般说来,阿兹连组合本身不仅表明整体的细小化趋势(所有石器工具尺寸都变小),而且相对于马格德林晚期的工具组合更简单。没有必要强调后旧石器时代工业中阿兹连或其他叶片形细石器的重要性。正如我所发掘的两个主要的阿兹连遗址：拉里埃拉（第27水平层）与杜弗尔（第3层），分别含有44%与45%的琢背细小石叶。形制相当典型，但琢背细小石叶在比较专门化的居住层中比例更高，尽管不同遗址、不同层位的比例存在明显的变化。

尽管阿兹连工业不以几何形细石器闻名，但是其组合中偶尔也含有这些器物。例如皮拉戈（坎塔布里亚）的两个洞穴遗址分别含有2.5%与10%的几何形细石器（三角形的、截断的、长方形的以及圆形的），其多个层位均有分布，同时共出大量阿兹连尖状器、鱼叉，放射性碳测年年代为距今1.07~1.03万年[66]。实际上，人们早就知道这些中石器时代的"先驱"是阿兹连工业的组成部分，1909至1911年间希尔拉、欧贝梅尔、鲍伊索尼，与步日耶发掘埃尔维勒附近的洞穴时就发现大量几何形细石器（占残存工具组合的16%）[67]。

七、中石器时代的传统

几何形细石器（排除其他成型的修理工具类型，有些情况下排除端刮器）的突然"爆炸"见于西欧地区众多文献中，尤其是罗佐伊[68]的工作。再者，近年来各种各样的中石器时代研讨会文集多有讨论（爱丁堡、卢汶、格勒诺布尔、斯德哥尔摩）。一些遗址不仅含有大量几何形细石器（尺寸往往非常小），而且类型丰富，某些类型在整个西欧地区分布广泛或是"非常通用"，而某些类型只见于特定地区。这些特定的类型（同时还有具有地方特色的装饰品类型[69]）清楚地表明当时存在地区的社会群体与领地划分[70]。中石器时代几何形细石器可能不只是用作箭头，如罗佐伊[71]所认为的，弓箭的采用只是森林地带的产物。尽管某些箭支没有尖头，但是几何形细石器可以提供多样的箭头类型（锋利的、钝的）与倒钩，倒钩可以使得猎物伤口最大程度地流血，受伤更重，并且把箭头留在猎物身上（就像鹿角鱼叉，某些中石器时代"文化"中常见，如马格勒莫西文化）。

石器微痕分析证据、动物骨骼破损痕迹以及与动物骨骼共生的石器断片都表明中石器时代弓箭充分的有效性，尽管只是在箭支的尖部镶嵌一点细石器，或是把细石器用作倒钩[72]。中石器时代几何形细石器中是否存在空间的差异与时间上的变化还需要进一步的研究，我们还不知道如此多样的细石器尖状器是由于功能上考虑还是受到社会因素的影响，比如说，某些细石器更有效率，因此基于实用的目的而被选择；条件发生变化，新的武器类型变得更有优势；或者说只是一时的风尚，由于群体相互接触而扩散与消亡，这些难以把握的因素可能用以表达中石器时代社会关系网络中某些猎人或游群的威望；或者是在某些特定的时候与地方,箭头的形制风格带有象征意义；这跟社会领域边界与通婚圈的由开放走向封闭如何联系起来？长期来说,细石器的变化更可能是多种因素结合的结果。未来无论是功能主义还是社会考古学家仍将面临挑战。

  不应忘记的是中石器时代的石器技术中还有大石器,它们有时与细石器共出,有时则单独存在。沿加利西亚（西班牙西北部）与葡萄牙海岸存在某些了解比较清楚的海岸"文化",如坎塔布里亚地区的阿斯图林文化或类似的石器工业,还有苏格兰滨海地区的欧巴林文化。这些遗址与砾石制作的手镐、砍砸器、简单石片的关系还有争议,附近同时代早全新世遗址往往很少出其他器物：不同的文化,不同的活动（如采集软体动物还是狩猎）或是石器原料的不同,都可以看作最终形成差异的原因。有时大石器与小石器共存于同一遗址中。葡萄牙南部滨海与三角洲地带的中石器时代的某些遗址就是典型的例子（如姆格[73]与维迪加尔[74]的遗址）,这里不同石器原料用以制作不同种类的石器工具,这些工具反过来用于不同的目的,有时在单个遗址中存在空间上的分离：例如,非本地的燧石用于制作细石器的武器组成成分,用以狩猎,而本地的硬砂岩与石英岩用作权宜性的石片、手镐与砍砸器,用来采集与处理植物或是软体动物。然而,西班牙的坎塔布里亚地区大石器的阿斯图林文化的贝丘遗址是滨海遗址,而几公里外的内陆山区,同时代含细石器的遗址大多比较小,可能跟狩猎活动有关。

  最后,在几何形细石器一统天下的"文化"氛围中还可能存在非细石器组合的孤岛。如罗佐伊所说的分布于法国中北部与比利时中南部阿登连文化[75]。最近我们发掘了一处小型遗址：拉布里杜帕贝,符合阿登连文化的定义。这里细石器工具相当缺乏,阿登高原地区的遗址很大程度上缺乏适合制作细石器的原料,当然其他因素也有影响。有意思的是,附近的博伊斯·莱特里洞穴遗址发现一具中石器时代人骨遗存,没有石器随葬,人骨碳氮同位素的比例表明其饮食结构基本为素食：很少狩猎,几乎不用弓箭或是细石器[76]。如果这个结论得到证实,那么我们也许需要重新思考这些问题,为什么会有几何形细石器？为什么有时又没有呢？

八、结论

  西欧（以及其他地区）从旧石器时代晚期开始,杜福尔细小石叶出现。细石器一直是古人一个选项,它们是众多选项之一,尤其是制作武器的尖头或倒刺。旧石器时代晚期的各个阶段还存在深入修理与琢背修理的大型尖状器。这些器物底部可以进行各种修理以适合装柄。此外还有多样的角质、牙质、骨质与木质的尖状器。轻型的投掷器与重型打击武器平分秋色。随着旧石器晚期的发展，武器投掷方法也更加多样，包括刺杀标枪、用手投掷的标枪、用投掷器投掷的标枪，以及弓箭。弓箭的发明可能不止一次——伊比利亚的梭鲁特工业，随后更加普遍(?)。不同的发射方法可能同时共存，用于不同类型的狩猎或是狩猎不同的猎物(甚至是大鱼)。随着欧洲森林的重新出现以及喜群居的大型动物群(驯鹿、马、野牛)的消失，用手投掷的标枪或用投掷器投掷的标枪都变得没有效率并被淘汰，轻型的弓箭成为主要的武器，人们不断发明新的箭头类型。这种成功的技术(与各种几何形细石器)一直延续到新石器时代，铜石并用时代进一步改良，有些箭头就像是伊比利亚梭鲁特工业的回光返照，如果地层关系没有控制好的话，很容易搞混。三十年河东，三十年河西——至少就石器技术而言可以这么说！

注释：

[1] Leroi-Gourhan, A. Une tete de sagaie a armature de lamelles de silexa Pincevent. *Bulletin de la Societe Prehistorique Francaise* 80: 154 – 156, 1983.

[2] Sonneville-Bordes, D. de. *Le Paleolithique Superieur en Perigord*. Bordeaux: Delmas, 1960.

[3] Sonneville-Bordes, D. de. L'evolution des industries aurignaciennes. In *Aurignacien et Gravettien en Europe*. M. Otte, ed. Pp. 339 – 360. Etudes et Recherches Archeologiques de l'Universite de Liege 13(2). Liege, Belgium, 1982.

[4] Brooks, A. L'Aurignacien de l'Abri Pataud niveau 6 a 14. In *Le Paleolithique Superieur de l'Abri Pataud*. H. Bricker, ed. Pp. 167 – 222. Documents d'Archeologie Francaise 50. Paris, 1995.

[5] Delporte, H. L'Aurignacien de La Ferrassie. In *Le GrandAbri de la Ferrassie*. H. Delporte, ed. Pp. 145 – 234. Etudes Quaternaires 7. Paris, 1984.

[6] Djindjian, F. Les origines du peuplement aurignacien en Europe. In *Aurignacien en Europe et au Proche Orient*. L. Banesz and J. Kozlowski, eds. Pp. 136 – 153. Actesdu XII Congres International des Sciences Prehistoriques et Protohistoriques, vol. 2. Bratislava, 1993.

[7] Rigaud, J.-P. L'Aurignacien dans le Sud-Ouest de la France. In *Aurignacien en Europe et au Proche Orient*. L. Baneszand J. Kozlowski, eds. Pp. 183. Actes du XII Congres International des Sciences Prehistoriques et Protohistoriques, vol. 2. Bratislava, 1993.

[8] Rigaud, J.-P. L'Aurignacien dans le Sud-Ouest de la France. In *Aurignacien en Europe et au Proche Orient*. L. Baneszand J. Kozlowski, eds. Pp. 181 – 185. Actes du XII Congres

International des Sciences Prehistoriques et Protohistoriques, vol. 2. Bratislava, 1993.

[9] Sonneville-Bordes, D. de. *Le Paleolithique Superieur en Perigord*. Bordeaux: Delmas, 1960.

[10] Otte, M., and L. G. Straus. *Le Trou Magrite*. Etudes et Recherches Archeologiques de l'Universite de Liege 69. Liege, Belgium, 1995.

[11] Bazile, F. L'Aurignacien et Perigordien en Languedoc oriental. In *Aurignacien et Gravettien en Europe*. M. Otte, ed. Pp. 27 – 49. Etudes et Recherches Archeologiques de l'Universite de Liege 13(1). Liege, Belgium, 1983.

[12] Broglio, A. L'Aurignacien au sud des Alpes. In *Aurignacien en Europe et au Proche Orient*. L. Banesz and J. Kozlowski, eds. Pp. 193 – 202. Actes du XII Congres International des Sciences Prehistoriques et Protohistoriques, vol. 2. Bratislava, 1993.

[13] Bernaldo de Quiros, F. *Los Inicios del Paleolitico Superior Cantabrico*. Centro de Investigacion y Museo de Altamira, Monografias 8. Madrid, 1982.

[14] Bernaldo de Quiros, F. *Los Inicios del Paleolitico Superior Cantabrico*. Centro de Investigacion y Museo de Altamira, Monografias 8. Madrid, 1982.

[15] Cabrera, V., M. Lloret, and F. Bemaldo de Quiros. Materias primas y formas liticas del Aurinaciense arcaico de la Cueva del Castillo. *Espacio, Tiempoy Forma* Series I, 9: 141 – 158, 1996.

Cabrera, V., H. Valladas, F. Bemaldo de Quiros, and M. Hoy os. La transition Paleolithique moyen-Paleolithique superieur a El Castillo. *Comptes Rendus de l'Acadetnie des Sciences de Paris* Series I la, 322: 1093 – 1098, 1996.

[16] Fortea, J. Abrigo de la Vina. *Excavaciones Arqueologicasen Asturias* 3: 19 – 32, 1995.

[17] Fortea, J. Le Paleolithique superieur en Espagne: Galice et Asturies. In *UISPP, Congres de Forli Commission Paleolithique Superieur Bilan 1991 – 1996*. M. Otte, ed. Pp. 329 – 344. Etudes et Recherches Archeologiques de l'Universite de Liege 76. Liege, Belgium, 1996.

[18] Bernaldo de Quiros, F. *Los Inicios del Paleolitico Superior Cantabrico*. Centro de Investigacion y Museo de Altamira, Monografias 8. Madrid, 1982.

[19] Zilhao, J. O. Paleolitico Superior da Estremadura Portuguesa. Doctoral dissertation, Universidade de Lisboa, Lisboa, 1995.

[20] Bricker, H. Le Perigordien moyen de l'Abri Pataud niveau 5. In *Le Paleolithique Superieur de l'Abri Pataud*. H. Bricker, ed. Pp. 133 – 166. Documents d'Archeologie Francaise 50. Paris, 1995b.

Bricker, H., and N. David. Le Perigordien VI de l'Abri Pataud niveau 3. In *Le Paleolithique Superieur de l'Abri Pataud*. H. Bricker, ed. Pp. 89 – 104. Documents d'Archeologie Francaise 50. Paris, 1995.

Clay, B. Le Protomagdalenien de l'Abri Pataud niveau 2. In *Le Paleolithique Superieur de* l'Abri Pataud. H. Bricker, ed. Pp. 67 – 88. Documents d'Archeologie Francaise 50. Paris, 1995.

David, N. Le Noaillien de l'Abri Pataud. In Le Paleolithique Superieur de l'Abri Pataud. H. Bricker, ed. Pp. 105 – 132. Documents d'Archeologie Francaise 50. Paris, 1995.

[21] Otte, M. Le Paleolithique Superieur Ancien en Belgique. Monographies d'Archeologie Nationale 5. Brussels, 1979.

[22] Straus, L. G., M. Otte, A. Gautier, P. Haesaerts. I. Lopez Bayon, P. Lacroix. A. Martinez, R. Miller. J. Orphal, and A. Stutz. Late Quaternary Prehistoric Investigations in Southern Belgium. Prehistoire Europe'enne 11: 145 – 184, 1997.

Straus, L. G., M. Otte, and P. Haesaerts. La Station de I Hermitage a Huccorgne. Etudes et Recherches Archeologiques de l'Universite de Liege 94. Liege, Belgium, 2000.

[23] Bricker, H. Le Paleolithique Superieur de l'Abri Pataud. Selecting Small: Upper Paleolithic and Mesolithic of Western Europe 79 Documents d'Archeologie Française 50. Paris, 1995a.

Movius, H. L., ed. Excavation of the Abri Pataud. American School of Prehistoric Research Bulletin 30. Cambridge: Harvard University, 1975.

[24] Bricker, H. Le Perigordien moyen de l'Abri Pataud niveau 5. In Le Paleolithique Superieur de l'Abri Pataud. H. Bricker, ed. Pp. 133 – 166. Documents d'Archeologie Francaise 50. Paris, 1995b.

[25] David, N. Le Noaillien de l'Abri Pataud. In Le Paleolithique Superieur de l'Abri Pataud. H. Bricker, ed. Pp. 105 – 132. Documents d'Archeologie Francaise 50. Paris, 1995.

[26] Clay, B. Le Protomagdalenien de l'Abri Pataud niveau 2. In Le Paleolithique Superieur de l'Abri Pataud. H. Bricker, ed. Pp. 67 – 88. Documents d'Archeologie Francaise 50. Paris, 1995.

[27] Delporte, H., and A. Tuffreau. Les industries du Perigordien V de La Ferrassie. In Le Grand Abri de la Ferrassie. H. Delporte, ed. Pp. 235 – 248. Etudes Quaternaires 7. Paris, 1984.

[28] Rigaud, J.-P. Donnees nouvelles sur l'Aurignacien et le Perigordien en Perigord. In Aurignacien et Gravettien en Europe. M. Otte, ed. Pp. 289 – 324. Etudes et Recherches Archeologiques de l'Universite de Liege 13(2). Liege, Belgium, 1982.

[29] Zilhao, J. O. Paleolitico Superior da Estremadura Portuguesa. Doctoral dissertation, Universidade de Lisboa, Lisboa, 1995.

[30] Zilhao, J. O. Paleolitico Superior da Estremadura Portuguesa. Doctoral dissertation, Universidade de Lisboa, Lisboa, Pp. 11. 3, 1995.

[31] Smith, P. E. L. Le Solutreen en France. Bordeaux: Delmas, 1966.

[32] Smith, P. E. L. Le Solutreen en France. Bordeaux: Delmas, 1966.

[33] Montet-White, A. Le Malpas Rockshelter. University of Kansas Publications in Anthropology 4.

Lawrence, 1973.

[34] Geneste, J.-M., and H. Plisson. Le Solutreen de la Grotte de Combe Sauniere 1. *Gallia Prehistoire* 29: 9-27, 1986.

[35] Geneste, J.-M., and H. Plisson. Le Solutreen de la Grotte de Combe Sauniere 1. *Gallia Prehistoire* 22-24, 1986.

[36] Cattelain, P. Un crochet de propulseur de la Grotte de Combe Sauniere 1. *Bulletin de la Societe Prehistorique Francaise* 86: 213-216, 1989.

[37] Munoz, F. Algunas consideraciones sobre el inicio de la arqueria prehistorica. *Trabajos de Prehistoria* 56: 27-40, 1999.

[38] Straus, L. G. *El Solutrense l'asco-Cantabrico*. Centro de Investigation y Museo de Altamira, Monografias 10. Madrid, 1983.

Straus, L. G., and G. A. Clark. *La Riera Cave*. Anthropological Research Papers 36. Tempe, Arizona, 1986.

[39] Straus, L. G. The Original Arms Race: Iberian Perspectives on the Solutrean Phenomenon. In *Feuilles de Pierre*. J. Kozlowski. ed. Pp. 425-447. Etudes et Recherches Archeologiques de l'Universite de Liege 42. Liege, Belgium, 1990.

[40] Fullola, J. M. *Las Industrias Liticas del Paleolitico Superior Iberico*. Servicio de Investigacion Prehistorica, Trabajos Varios 60. Valencia, 1979.

[41] Zilhao, J. *O Solutrense da Estremadura Portuguesa*. Trabalhos de Arqueologia 4. Lisbon, 1987.

O Paleolitico Superior da Estremadura Portuguesa. Doctoral dissertation, Universidade de Lisboa, Lisboa, 1995.

[42] Sonneville-Bordes, D. de. *Le Paleolithique Superieur en Perigord*. Bordeaux: Delmas, 1960.

[43] Arambourou, R. *Le Gisement Prehistorique de Duruthy a Sorde-l'Abbaye*. Societe Prehistorique Francaise, Memoires 5. Paris, 1978.

[44] Straus, L. G., and M. Gonzalez Morales. 1998 Excavation Campaign in El Miron Cave. *Old World Archaeology Newsletter* 21(3): 1-9, 1999.

[45] Aura, J. E. *El Magdaleniense Mediterraneo*. Servicio de Investigación Prehistorica, Trabajos Varios 91. Valencia, 1995.

[46] Leroi-Gourhan, A., and M. Brezillon. L'habitation magdalenienne no. 1 de Pincevent pres Montereau. *Gallia Prehistoire* 9(2): 304, 1966.

[47] Audouze, F., D. Cahen, L. Keeley, and B. Schmider. Le site magdalenien du Buisson Campin a Verberie. Gallia Prehistoire 24: 99-143, 1981.

Moss, E. *The Functional Analysis of Flint Implements*. BAR Series 177. Oxford: British Archaeological Reports, 1983.

Moss, E., and M. Newcomer. Reconstruction of Tool Use at Pincevent. In *Taillerl Pour Quoi Faire*. D. Cahen, ed. Pp. 289 – 312. Studia Praehistorica Belgica 2. Tervuren, Belgium, 1982.

[48] Terberger, T. Les structures de l'habitat de Gönnersdorf, nouveaux résultats. In *Le Peuplement Magdalénien*. J.-P. Rigaud, H. Laville, and B. Vandermeersch, eds. Pp. 431 – 448. Paris: Comité des Travaux Historiques et Scientifiques, 1992.

[49] Albrecht, G. *Magdalénien-Inventare vom Petersfels*. TübingerMonographien zur Urgeschichte 6 Tübingen, Germany: Verlag Archaeologica Venatoria, 1979.

[50] Otte, M., and L. G. Straus. *La Grotte du Bois Laitehe*. Etudes et Recherches Archeologiques de l'Universite de Liege 80. Liege, Belgium, 1998.

[51] Otte, M. *Le Magdalénien du Trou de Chaleux*. Etudes et Recherches Archéologiques de l'Université de Liège 60. Liège, Belgium, 1994.

[52] Barton, R. N. E. *Hengistbury Head*, vol. 3: *The Late Upper Paleolithic and Early Mesolithic Sites*. Oxford University Committee for Archaeology, Monograph 34. Oxford, 1992.

[53] Leesch, D. *Hauterive-Champréveyres*, vol. 10. Archéologie Neuchâteloise 23. Neuchâtel, Switzerland, 1997.

[54] Leroi-Gourhan, A., and M. Brézillon. *Fouilles de Pincevent*. VII Supplément à Gallia Préhistoire. Paris: Centre National de la Recherche Scientifique, 1972.

[55] Audouze, F., D. Cahen, L. Keeley, and B. Schmider. Le site magdalénien du Buisson Campin à Verberie. *Gallia Préhistoire* 24: 99 – 143, 1981.

[56] Schmider, B. *Marsangy*. Etudes et Recherches Archéologiques de l'Université de Liège 55. Liège, Belgium, 1992.

[57] Straus, L. G. *Les Derniers Chasseurs de Renne du Monde Pyrénéen. L'Abri Dufaure*. Société Préhistorique Française, Mémoires 22. Paris, 1995.

[58] Arambourou, R. *Le Gisement Préhistorique de Duruthy à Sorde-l'Abbaye*. Société Prehistórique Française, Mémoires 5. Paris, 1978.

[59] Bazile, F. L'industrie lithique du site de plein air de Fontgrasse. In *Le Magdalénien en Europe*. J.-P. Rigaud, ed. Pp. 361 – 378. Etudes et Recherches Archéologiques de l'Université de Liège 38. Liège, Belgium, 1989.

[60] Straus, L. G., and G. A. Clark. *La Riera Cave*. Anthropological Research Papers 36. Tempe, Arizona, 1986.

[61] Moure, J. A., and M. Cano. *Excavaciones en la Cueva de Tito Bustillo*. Instituto de Estudios Asturianos, Oviedo, Spain, 1976.

[62] Gonzalez Echegaray, J., and L. G. Freeman. *Cueva Morin: Excavaciones 1966 – 1968*. Santander, Spain: Patronato de las Cuevas Prehistóricas, 1971.

[63] Altuna, J., and J. Merino. *El Yacimiento Prehistórico de la Cueva de Ekain*. San Sebastián, Spain: Sociedad de Estudios Vascos, 1984.

[64] Aura, J. E. *El Magdaleniense Mediterráneo*. Servicio de Investigación Prehistórica, Trabajos Varios 91. Valencia, 1995.

[65] Bicho, N. Technological Change in the Final Upper Paleolithic of Rio Maior, Portuguese Estremadura. Ph. D. dissertation, Southern Methodist University, Dallas, 1992.

[66] Garcia Guinea, M. A. Las Cuevas Azilienses de El Pielago y sus Excavaciones. *Sautuola* 4: 11 – 154, 1985.

[67] Fernandez Tresguerres, J. *El Aziliense en las Provincias de Asturias v Santander*. Centro de Investigacion y Museo de Altamira, Monografias 2. Santander, Spain, 1980.

[68] Rozoy. J.-G. *Les Derniers Chasseurs*. L'Epipale'olithique en France et en Belgique. Charleville, France: Societe Archeologique Champenoise, 1978.

[69] Newell, R., D. Kidman, T. Constandese-Westermann, W. van der Sanden, and A. van Gijn. *An Inquiry into the Ethnic Resolution of Mesolithic Regional Groups*. Leiden: Brill, 1990.

[70] Blankholm, H. P. Stylistic Analysis of Maglemosian Microlithic Armatures in Southern Scandinavia. In *Contributions to the Mesolithic in Europe*. P. Vermeersch and P. Van Peer, eds. Pp. 239 – 257. Leuven, Belgium: Leuven University Press, 1990.

Gendel, P. The Analysis of Lithic Styles through Distributional Profiles of Variation: Examples from the Western European Mesolithic. In *The Mesolithic in Europe*. C. Bonsall, ed. Pp. 40 – 47. Edinburgh: John Donald, 1989.

[71] Rozoy. J.-G. *Les Derniers Chasseurs*. L'Epipale'olithique en France et en Belgique. Charleville, France: Societe Archeologique Champenoise, 1978.

The Revolution of Bowmen in Europe. In *The Mesolithic in Europe*. C. Bonsall, ed. Pp. 13 – 28. Edinburgh: John Donald, 1989.

[72] Bratlund, B. A Study of Hunting Lesions Containing Flint Fragments on Reindeer Bones at Stellmoor, Schleswig-Holstein, Germany. In *The Late Glacial in North-West Europe*. N. Barton, A. Roberts, and D. Roe, eds. Pp. 193 – 207. CBA Research Report 77. London, 1990.

Dumont, J. Tool Form and Function: Aspects of the Mount Sandel and Star Carr Microwear Research in Relation to Other Comparable Studies. In *The End of the Paleolithic in the Old World*. L. G. Straus, ed. Pp. 31 – 45. BAR Series 284. Oxford: British Archaeological Reports, 1986.

Fischer, A. Hunting with Flint-Tipped Arrows. In *The Mesolithic in Europe*. C. Bonsall, ed. Pp. 29 – 39. Edinburgh: John Donald, 1989.

Noe-Nygaard, N. Mesolithic Hunting in Denmark Illustrated by Bone Injuries Caused by

Human Weapons. *Journal of Archaeological Science* 1: 217-248, 1974.

[73] Roche, J. Les amas coquillers (concheiros) mesolithiques de Muge (Portugal). In *Die Anfdnge des Neolithikums von Orient bis Sordeuropa*, vol. 7. J. Liming, ed. Fundamenta A3, Pp. 72-107. Koln: Bohlau Verlag, 1972.

[74] Straus, L. G., J. Altuna, and B. Vierra. The Concheiro at Vidigal. In *Contributions to the Mesolithic in Europe*. P. Vermeersch and P. Van Peer, eds. Pp. 463-474. Leuven: Leuven University Press, 1990.

[75] Rozoy, J.-G. La Roche-à-Fépin et al entre l'Ardennient et le Tardenoisien. In *Contributions to the Mesolithic in Europe*. P. Vermeersch and P. Van Peer, eds, Pp. 413-422. Leuven: Leuven University Press, 1990.

[76] Otte, M., and L. G. Straus. *La Grotte du Bois Laitehe*. Etudes et Recherches Archeologiques de l'Universite de Liege 80. Liege, Belgium, 1998.

细石器化的开拓者：
南欧"原奥瑞纳工业"

史蒂夫 L. 库恩

(亚利桑那大学　图森)

摘　要：欧亚大陆含大量细石器的石器组合主要见于更新世末期以及冰后期。更早的"原奥瑞纳工业"石器组合在南欧的几个遗址(克里姆斯、利帕罗莫奇、迪福曼岩厦、阿尔布利达洞)中有发现,距今 3.3 至 3.9 万年前。原奥瑞纳组合以相当数量的细石器为代表,主要是修理过的细小石叶。这种形态与更早的莫斯特工业以及更晚的典型奥瑞纳工业、格拉韦丁工业形成鲜明的对比。细石器组合的早期繁荣到后来的衰落(也见于西南亚与南非地区)具有一种不同的细石器化过程,我们必须区分更新世之末细石器技术全球性扩散过程中的普遍现象与历史特殊性。

晚更新世之时,也就是末次盛冰期(LGM,距今约 2 万年前)前后开始,细石器技术或"模式 5"技术[1]开始在欧洲、中亚与西南亚地区的考古材料中占主导地位。可能稍晚,细石叶技术开始在东亚地区出现[2],并且最终扩散到西北美地区[3]。晚更新世的细石器化趋势是目前已知旧石器时代石器技术演化阶段中最具有普遍性的文化现象。

为了解释细石器组合的出现与繁荣,有两个问题需要回答。第一个问题具有普遍性,"为什么细石器会出现",或是说,这种以生产细小、明显可替换部件为中心的石器技术体系有什么普遍的优势呢？第二个问题则具有历史特殊性：为什么如此之多的细石器组合出现于更新世之末？在专门研究晚更新世的论述中，两个问题常常合二为一。细石器技术相对所有其他石器生产技术体系具有明显优越性，模式5技术不可避免从早期萌芽到后来繁荣[4]。当然，也存在一些例外，那里的细石器技术出现相对较早，但是后来被放弃，没有扩散开来。考虑到这些情况有助于我们把与细石器化相关的普遍因素与历史特定因素区分开来。

目前我们知道欧亚地区旧石器晚期的最早阶段就有含相当比例细石器的石器组合出现。材料最清楚的一个例子就是南欧的"原奥瑞纳工业"。西班牙、意大利与奥地利的一系列石器组合表明存在一种生产细小石叶的成熟技术，修理过的细小石叶在修理工具中占相当的比重。这些早期组合赋予我们一种新的眼光，以重新审视晚更新世更晚阶段的细石器技术爆炸性的扩散。

一、两个定义

在正式开始讨论之前，有必要先澄清两个概念：细石器与细石器组合。广义上说，细石器就是一种细小的修理过石器，它太小，无法手持使用，推测用作复合工具的边刃（参见本书中卡洛斯的文章）。细石器的大小并没有一个绝对的边界，实际上建立这样一个边界也是徒劳的。基于细石器的尺寸，安柄使用是必须的，但是安柄并不足以构成细石器的定义。许多安柄的石器类型（标枪头、镶在柄中的刮削器）显然并非细石器。细石器通常以细小石叶为毛坯所制，但是也会使用石片。许多细石器是几何形的，通过两边或多边修理形成标准的形状，当然这并不是必需的。

单单细石器的存在并不能表明就是一个细石器组合。许多旧石器晚期石器组合，甚至是某些更早的石器组合中，都含有这种特殊的器物或是尺寸大小相当于细石器的器物类型。同样，缺少大型器物并不是细石器组合的本质特征。石器组合中往往都含有大型器物。为了便于讨论，文中所谓的细石器组合主观设定为其比例超过40%的石器组合。值得注意的是，一个考古样本中细石器的比例与它在镶嵌细石器组件的史前工具中的比例并没有必然联系。相对于大型石器来说，细石器组件的使用寿命可能很短，而且一件复合工具上可能镶嵌远不止一件细石器。所以，一个含有50%细石器的石器组合可能来自一个只有少量镶嵌细石器组件的史前工具组。

尽管有关细石器存在广泛而细致的类型学研究[5]，但是这些细小的修理过的石制品仅仅表面上符合"成型工具"的一般认识。绝大部分细石器是更大更复杂产品的组成部件。鉴于其大小与可能安装在某一工具上的方式（如部分为黏接剂或是胶所覆盖),细石器本身并不是很好地表达风格信息的媒介。另一方面,细石器的生产技术、形状、大小与复合工具的设计方案与装配复合工具边刃的传统密切关联。因此细石器可能带有更多有关技术流程方面的信息,而有关器物形制传统方面的信息较少。这并不是说细石器不涉及风格问题,而是它们更可能反映的是一种暗含的、难以检验的"技术风格"(?),而非那种形式或符号风格[6]。

很多研究讨论到镶嵌细石器的复合工具相对于简单石器或骨器的潜在优势。研究者认为这种复合工具更有效,不容易导致重大的失败,更容易修理,比单一的石器工具更少受到热胀冷缩效应的影响[7](本书中的数篇文章)。埃尔斯顿与班廷汉姆(见本书)认为镶嵌细石叶的投掷骨尖状器不仅非常"可靠",而且便于"维护",因此拥有布雷德[8]所说的技术连续体中的双重优势。与此同时,运用细小部件生产复合工具可以相对节约原料[9],尤其是当可用的石器原料由于地质方面的原因或是社会领域的限制而不易得到的时候,这就成了一个重要的优势。

当然,仅仅优势本身并不足以解释特定技术方法的出现、扩散与消亡。任何制作与维护器物的"选择"都有成本与劣势。复合工具的生产涉及多种原材料,黏接剂、捆绑用的绳索等加起来的成本比生产单一或两件简单组装的骨器或石器更高昂,尽管目前还很难准确地估计其成本。大多数细石器组件是功能多样的,也就是说它们可以安装在不同的工具上充当边刃[10],但是组装起来的工具却是相对专业化的。尤其是用以镶嵌细石器的有机工具很可能只有很窄的功能范围。因此,细石器技术很可能与专业化的器物生产相关联。

二、早期的细石器化:何时何地?

当然,细石器化一直被认为是一个旧石器时代晚期晚段(或是后旧石器时代)与中石器时代的现象,始于距今约 2 万年前。相反,更早旧石器时代晚期石器组合长期以来都被视为完全由大石片与石叶组成。这尤其是奥瑞纳工业的特征。有关奥瑞纳工业的教科书说法主要关注厚重的大石片与石叶工具(有脊的或有鼻[nosed]刮削器、修理过的石叶等),它们是奥瑞纳工业的标志性化石。杜福尔剥片石器(Lamelles Dufour)通常都非常小,多是深度修理或交叉修理、有点扭曲的细小石叶,许多奥瑞纳遗址中都有发现,但其数量一般较少(修理工具的比例小于5%~10%)。这些器物似乎来自习惯上称为雕刻器或端刮器的生产过程(至于它们是否还用作石核,抑或是说细小石叶不过是生产它们的副产品,这是另外一个问题）[11]。其他旧石器时代晚期早段石器工业也含有某些细石器成分，但同样很少在修理工具中占很高的比例。例如，意大利南部所谓的"进步的乌鲁齐安（evolved Uluzzian）"工业中，典型的弧形琢背石器有时就处在细石器的大小范围之内[12]。希腊与克里米亚的遗址也有类似的旧石器时代晚期早段遗址，包含少量形态上很典型的细石器[13]。

一般认为所有旧石器时代晚期早段的工业都是大石器工业，南欧所谓的原奥瑞纳工业代表一种例外的情况。这些石器工业，许多方面更像是旧石器时代晚期晚段的产品，广泛发现于从奥地利的克里姆斯—洪德施泰格[14]到西班牙东北部的阿尔布利达洞与里克劳韦弗尔遗址[15]等一系列遗址中。最集中的区域见于意大利北部，包括利帕罗莫奇遗址（利古里亚地区）的 G 层[16]、南阿尔卑斯山麓的迪福马林岩厦遗址的 A 与 D 层[17]、威尼托区的利帕罗·塔格丽恩特与帕伊那岩厦遗址的层位[18]（图6.1）。原奥瑞纳组合的绝对年代在距今3.3到3.9万年前之间（未校正的放射性碳测年年代），无疑属于西欧最早的旧石器时代晚期工业[19]。底部的年代（最早年代的层位）可以早到距今3.7到3.9万年前。最早的年代似乎出现在西部（阿尔布利达、里克劳韦弗尔）[20]，但鉴于缺乏统一年代校正[21]以及越古老的放射性碳对于微量的污染越敏感，因此所有这些测年应

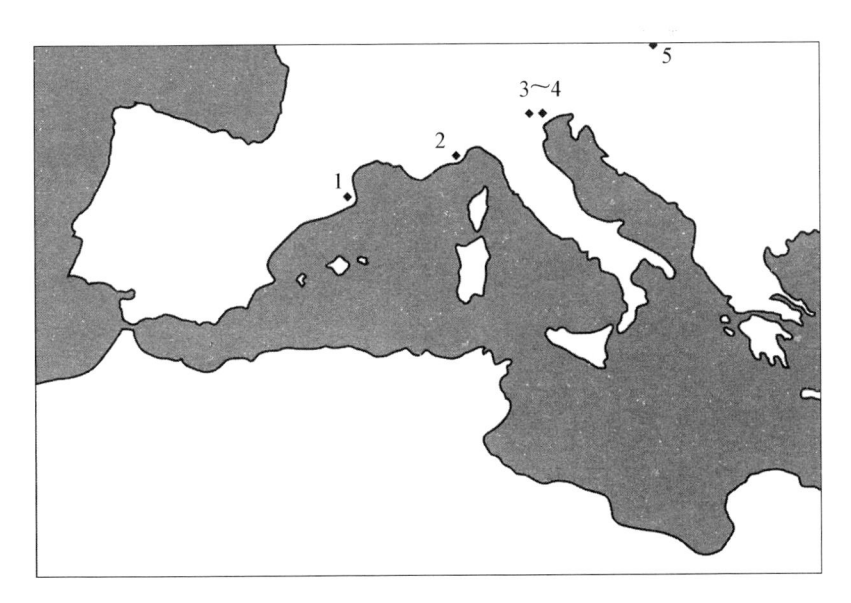

图6.1 欧洲地中海地区原奥瑞纳工业遗址

（1. 阿尔布利达洞；2. 利帕罗莫奇；3、4. 迪福曼岩厦，利帕罗·塔格林特；5. 克里姆斯—汉德斯特格）

该视为最晚的年代。在所有含有多个文化成分且有地层关联的遗址中,原奥瑞纳都是旧石器时代晚期现在已知最早的石器工业。正常情况下原奥瑞纳层位都在莫斯特晚期地层之上,有时两者之间有一段居住空白层位或是混合的层位。

原奥瑞纳石器组合鲜明的特征就是存在腹面或两面边缘修理的细小石叶。修理多见于侧边的边缘区域,不过克里姆斯遗址与福马林 A 层含有许多尖部修理的标本(图 6.2)。细小石叶毛坯平直或腹面凹陷[22]。尽管这些器物还不是几何形的,但是它们的大小与形态无疑是细石器的。原奥瑞纳细小石叶似乎并不是从所谓的有脊刮削器与成型雕刻器(busked burins)上打制下来的。相反,目前已有一些证据,表明成熟细小石叶打制技术包括棱柱状或近似棱柱状石核—有脊细小石叶与石核石板(core tablets)的来源(图 6.3)[23]。实际上,尽管已发表的报告中原奥瑞纳修理细小石叶通常是指杜福尔薄片。有些学者更愿意将这个概念限定于扭曲的类型,它来自有脊的刮削器石核,是奥瑞纳工业的典型器物[24]。

杜福尔薄片石器与原奥瑞纳修理细小石叶的另一个区别是后者数量更丰富。相反扭曲的杜福尔细小石叶很少占到奥瑞纳石器组合的5%以上,而原奥瑞纳工业中修理细小石叶占修理工具的绝大部分。修理细小石叶在阿尔布利达洞的 H 层中占石器组合的50%以上[25];按照比较保守的标准,利帕罗莫奇遗址中占到40%以上,这个石器组合较大(超过1 100件修理石制品)[26]。迪福马林岩厦遗址下部层位中修理细小石叶占到石器组合的70%以上[27](尽管该组合修理的定义可能比其他遗址更宽泛一些)。

除了修理细小石叶之外,早期的原奥瑞纳工业具有绝大部分典型旧石器时代晚期工业特征。含有多样的较大石器,包括端刮器、雕刻器、边刮器、凹缺刮器、锯齿刃器,雕刻器一般要比端刮器更丰富。有些组合如阿尔布利达洞 H 层、利帕罗莫奇遗址 G 层,"典型的"的奥瑞纳工具形制如有脊与有鼻刮削器以及成型雕刻器实际上相当罕见,这导致一个问题,原奥瑞纳工业如何才能跟典型的法国和利凡特奥瑞纳工业联系起来呢[28]?其他遗址如迪福马林岩厦中上述典型奥瑞纳工业的标志要常见得多。原奥瑞纳工业组合还含有多样的有机工具,包括一些底端分开的骨尖状器。利帕罗莫奇遗址[29]与迪福马林岩厦遗址[30]中还出土了大量的贝壳珠。

三、早期细小石叶工业对旧石器时代晚期细石器化的启示

尽管有证据表明原奥瑞纳工业一般都有很多细石器,跟后来的发展似乎有

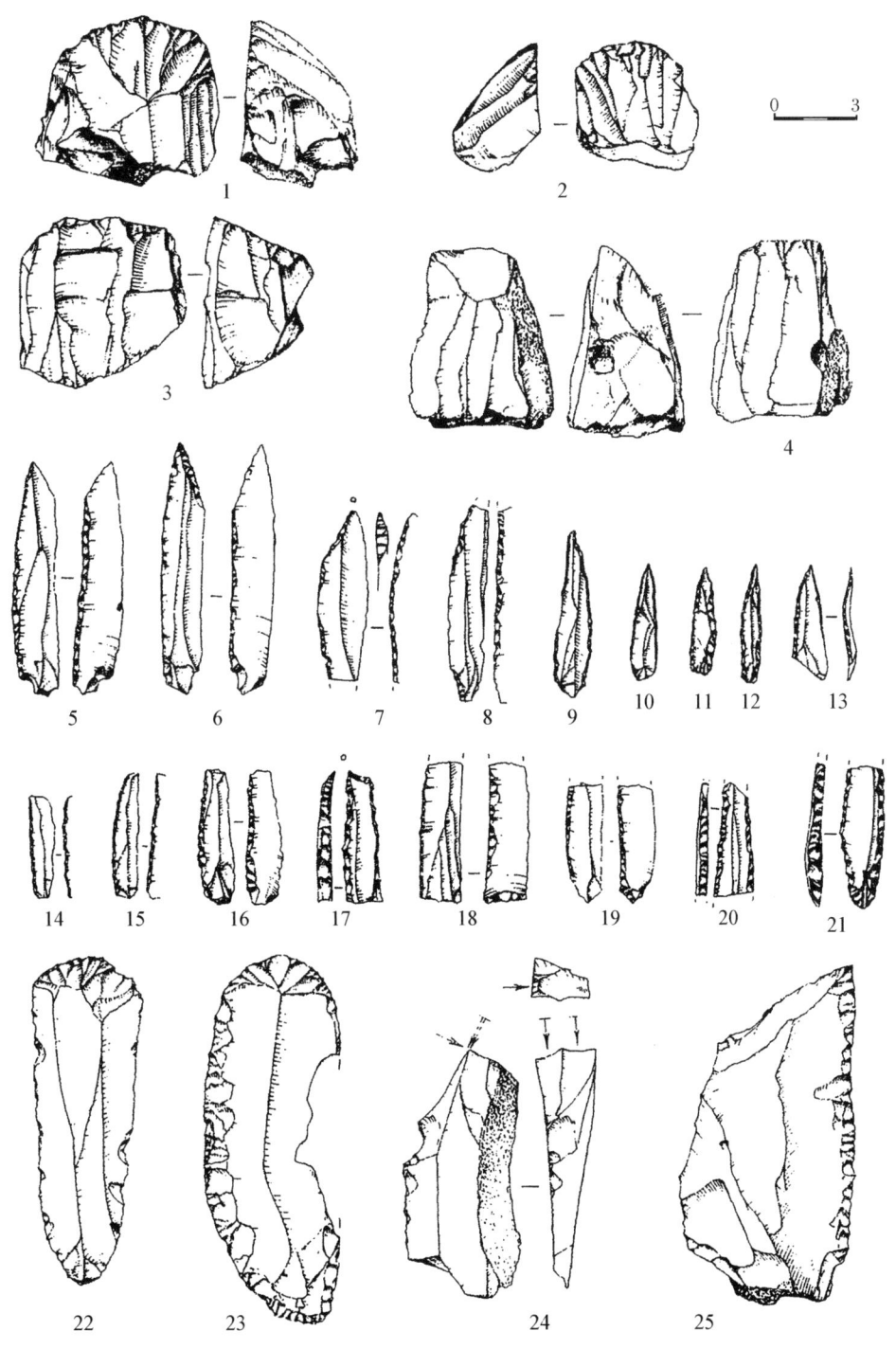

图 6.2 福马林 A 层出土较早的原奥瑞纳器物[31]

（1~2. 有脊刮削器或石核；3~4. 石核；5~21. 修理细小石叶；22~23. 端刮器；24. 雕刻器；25. 边刮器）

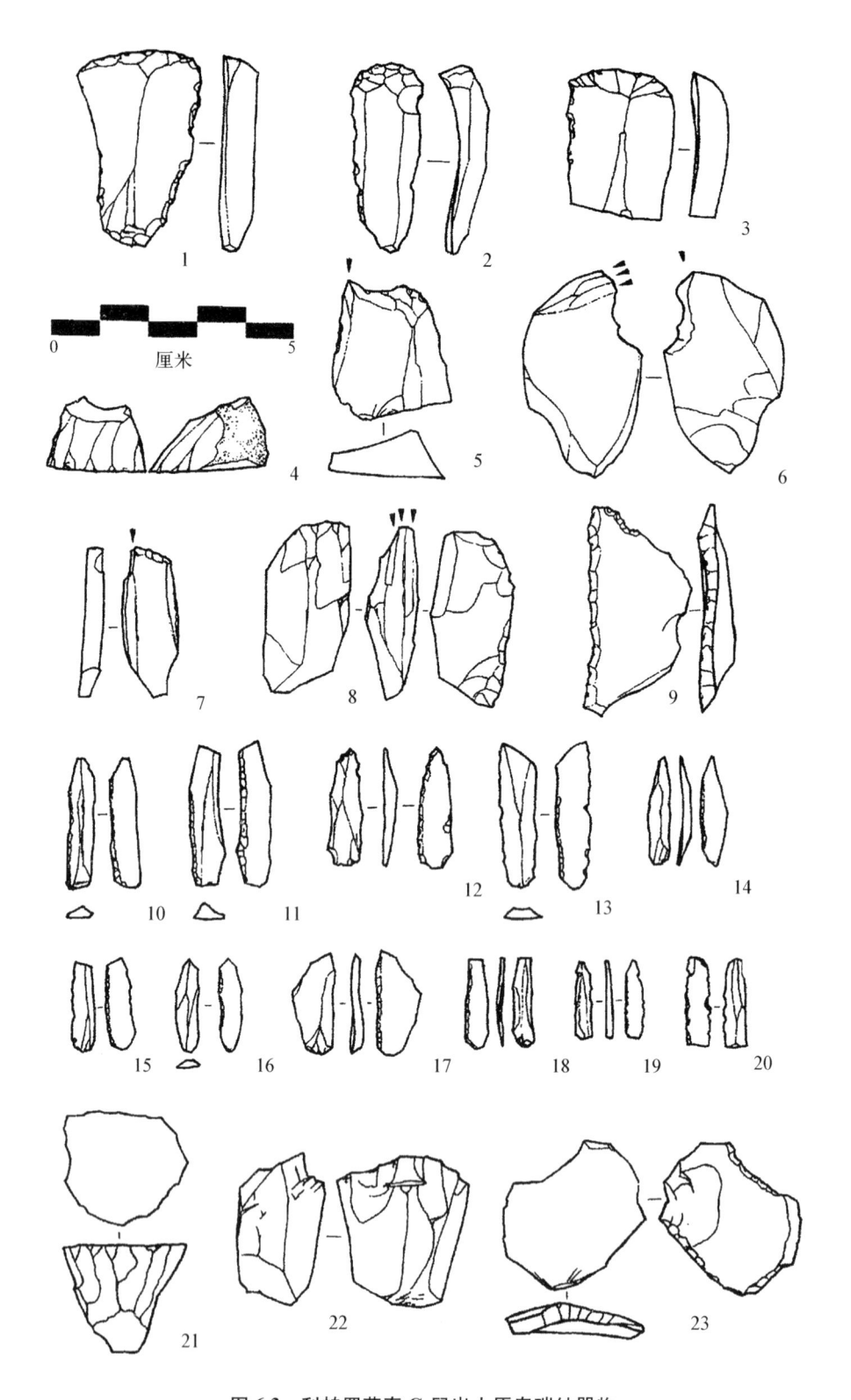

图 6.3 利帕罗莫奇 G 层出土原奥瑞纳器物

(1~3. 端刮器；4. 有脊刮削器或石核；5~8. 雕刻器；9. 边刮器；10~20. 修理的细小石叶；21~22. 细小石叶石核；23. 石核石板)

所关联,但是很难在旧石器时代晚期早段与晚段或后旧石器时代之间建立起直接且没有间断的技术联系。就我们讨论的地区而言,较晚的奥瑞纳工业的细小石叶生产逐渐衰落。利帕罗莫奇遗址属于奥瑞纳工业的F层(晚于3.2万年前)主要以重型奥瑞纳刮削器为主,同时含有少量的杜福尔薄片石器。迪福马林岩厦与阿尔布利达洞遗址的文化序列存在着同样的趋势,尽管不是那么突出。甚至这些地区的早期格拉韦丁工业并非典型的细小石叶工业。南欧的"原奥瑞纳工业"因此可以视为成功的细石器技术实验,它基于用作复合工具边刃的修理过的细小石叶。当然,更新世之末这个实验并没有持续不断,而是为更加典型奥瑞纳工业或其他非细石器旧石器晚期工业所替代。

从原奥瑞纳工业的例子中可以得出两个重要的结论。首先,晚更新世以细小石叶为中心的细石器技术的繁荣并不是由复合工具替代边刃技术的发明所触发的。在旧石器时代晚期此种技术有长期的历史。次之,晚更新世的细石器技术的迅速扩散并非基于其技术固有的优势。南欧地区早期技术采用许多细小修理细石器工具,随后大部分为更大石片或石叶工具所取代,如果不是所有的话。同样的状况也见于南部非洲地区,可能出现不止一次(阿姆布鲁斯的文章,见本书)[32]。显然,细石器技术所具有的优势无论多么大,都是局限的,取决于特定的背景条件。

本书的一个基本目标是要解释更新世之末细石器技术全球性的繁荣。原奥瑞纳工业似乎与旧石器时代晚期晚段的细石器组合没有直接的、文化传统上的联系。此外,其存在本身与晚更新世之末细石器技术繁荣的统一解释似乎有矛盾,也就是说它们本来就比其他石器工具的生产方式更有效率。当然,还需要考虑其他特征——除了存在许多小的部件外——似乎表明这些不同的石器组合可能存在共同的起源。一个有意思的可能性是:走向细石器技术的各种发展路线都是人类采食范围迅速扩大的副产品[33]。旧石器时代晚期早段生产空间的扩展可能与不同人类群体的相互影响相关,晚更新世之末人类食物的变化更可能是普遍提高的人口压力的结果,以及环境因素的影响。就我们研究的这个时期,动物考古学的材料提供了若干人类采食范围扩张的证据。

从各方面的证据来看,西欧地区的原奥瑞纳工业似乎是外来的[34]。无论它们来自哪里,这个技术组合的制作者似乎跟生活在欧洲的人类具有不同的进化路线。西班牙与意大利有很好的证据,表明原奥瑞纳工业与莫斯特晚期工业在时间上有所重叠[35],我们知道莫斯特工业很可能是尼安德特人的产品。遗憾的是,与原奥瑞纳工业共生的堆积中没有发现特征明显的可以断代的人类化石,尽管通常假定原奥瑞纳工业就是解剖学上现代人的产物。如果莫斯特晚期与原奥瑞纳工业的确代表不同的人类群体,那么当其中一个(与奥瑞纳工业相关的)扩张到南欧地区时,当他们发生接触的时候应该存在大量的竞争关系[36]。竞争并不意味都是直接冲突:为了食物、生存空间以及其他资源的间接竞争是更可能存在的形式。当然,间接竞争的共同结果之一是,一方或双方竞争者资源利用重心的改变。有意思的是,意大利的早期细石器技术的起源跟新的利用小动物资源的方式有关。旧石器时代晚期地层中发现强化利用鸟类的证据[37],这标志着这一地区人类食谱宽度前所未有的扩展。鸟类遗存也见于更早的考古动物遗存中,但是数量非常有限。而从原奥瑞纳工业开始,地表栖息的鸟类(主要是松鸡)成为重要的食物组成部分。

当然,许多研究者认为,末次盛冰期到冰期结束,人类人口增长迅速,地盘的划分日益严格,加之环境条件变化迅速,这些都促使人类生计基础扩大,引入多样的新资源,以及新的获取资源的技术[38]。这种趋势在所谓的广谱革命中达到高峰[39],并最终导致驯化的起源。当然,即便是在末次盛冰期时欧亚大陆也有人类食谱扩充的证据。正是在这个时期,兔形动物与其他繁殖迅速的小哺乳类动物以及鱼类,在欧亚大陆西部的人类食谱中开始占有重要的位置[40]。

旧石器时代晚期早晚段细石器技术可能受到同一个因素的影响,那就是生计的分化,不仅是在资源的种类上,而且在获取方法与采食技术上。技术分化就是指在人类进入新的采食与食物处理的生存环境时,产生适应辐射,形成新的技术形式,尤其是在发展的初期。细石器本身就是保存下来的最好的证据,表明平行发展的技术辐射,它与人类扩展的采食范围密切相关。在我们研究的时间段内,新的食物资源添加到了人类食谱中,鸟类与小型猎物的有效利用需要更多样武器、陷阱、网罗以及其他设施[41]。如上所述,相对通用的细石器——既可以充当切割刃,还可以充当尖头、利齿或是倒刺,非常适合用作各种各样专业化工具的组成部件,可以更好地利用新的动物(与植物)资源,更重要的是形成新的获取食物的方式。

当然,细石器技术长期的发展历史存在两个差异明显的阶段。就原奥瑞纳工业而言,这种技术策略最终被放弃了,取而代之一种以少量更大石器与骨器为中心的工具组合,而在晚更新世,细石器技术持续发展,直至农业发展的早期阶段。或认为旧石器时代晚期早段开始食谱多样化,然后收缩,实际情况可能并非如此:鸟类的利用一直持续到更新世最后阶段。当然,资源的获取确实在某个时段稳定下来,大致可以早到氧同位素第 2 阶段(末次盛冰期)。可能是经过一段新资源的尝试利用后,新的采食技术也稳定下来。近代狩猎采集者常用来捕鱼、捕小动物与飞鸟的网罗与陷阱可能成为大多数地区的技术选择[42]。这些装备不需要镶嵌细石器。相反,旧石器时代晚期后段存在很不一样的长期资源利用的过程。食谱扩充持续到全新世,最终转向需要高强度植物性食物资源的处理,如蔬果等。细石器继续用来捕猎小巧灵活的动物如兔子与鱼类。当然,细石器还可以镶嵌到镰刀、收割用石刀或其他与植物(最后驯化了)收割相关的工具中。有意思的是,新石器时代食谱多样性稳定下来后,细石器衰落,近东地区是代之以大石器制作的"镰刀片",尽管细石器还在某些地区继续使用[43]。经过一段时间尝试新的资源利用方式之后,技术多样性再一次缩小了。

四、结论

南欧地区原奥瑞纳工业中细石器技术起源很早,但随后放弃了,这挑战了传统的更新世之末才出现细石器化的认识。这些旧石器时代晚期早段的发现削弱了陈旧的观点:细石器技术固有某些优势,超越其他的石器生产技术形式,它在末次盛冰期后迅速扩散是必然的发展趋势。原奥瑞纳与旧石器时代晚期晚段/后旧石器时代工业中,细石器技术起源与利用小动物并且(最终)强调植物性食物的食谱扩充之间存在时间上的巧合。两种情况中都转向了镶嵌细石器部件组成复合工具的技术。如果统一的解释能够建立起来,那么就必须把技术分化与人类食谱的扩充联系起来。利用新资源支持发展新的采食技术与生计技术。细石器技术的一个主要优势就是它可用作边刃,能够适用于多样的工具。

这里强调的"生计辐射模型"为一组特定历史事件提供可能的解释,也就是细石器技术近乎全球性的起源。这个模型寻求解释在广大区域内发展并具有巨大时间尺度的技术趋势,而不大可能用于理解小时空尺度上的变化形态。研究细石器工业遗址间的、地区之间的以及短期年代变化,需要合适的尺度(如雷利的文章,本书)。功能的、策略的、经济的,或是社会的解释模型更有利于探讨细微的考古材料上的变化。

将细石器技术的起源解释为食谱的扩充基本能够得到欧亚大陆材料的支持,但是这种观点不能解释世界其他地区情况。全新世的大部分史前史上,澳大利亚与北美地区的狩猎采集者成功发展了多样化的采集经济,没有或是说极少依赖细石器技术来生产石器。当然,这些地区之间的发展差异可能与历史过程有关。欧亚地区旧石器时代晚期的采食者已经使用棱柱状石核技术生产石叶了,还生产骨角工具,以及复合/安柄工具。基于细小石叶的细石器技术显然就是在此基础上发展起来的。更新世之末澳大利亚与北美的石器技术分别以石片与两面器为中心,当采食策略需要分化的时候,两地因此形成不同的技术反应,也就不足为奇了。从另一个角度来说,澳大利亚与北美两地使用的细石器可能比我们想象的要多。无论是细小石叶还是细石叶都没有普遍存在于这些地区：北美地区细石叶的生产主要见于北极与太平洋西北海岸地带[44]。而我们知道澳大利亚部分地区把未经修理的石片镶嵌在标枪上形成倒刺[45]。由于没有修理,所以在考古材料中很难识别这些器物。

以上所归纳的假说只是解释更新世之末模式5技术繁荣的几种观点之一。本书的其他文章有相当不同的看法。显然,不管偏好何种解释,解释末次盛冰期后细石器技术爆炸性的发展都必须考虑历史发展过程。更新世中细石器技术的更早期的"实验"尤其重要。研究类似技术在全世界的出现与衰落的背景非常重要,它提供了必要的识别关联因素的视角,这些因素导致2万年后细小石器工业的繁荣与扩散。

注释：

[1] Clark, G. *World Prehistory: A New Outline*. Cambridge: Cambridge University Press, 1971: 29 – 32.

[2] Chen, C, and J. Olsen. China at the Last Glacial Maximum. In *The World at 18 000 BP*, Vol. 1: *High Latitudes*. O. Soffer and C. Gamble, eds. Pp. 276 – 295. NewYork: Plenum, 1990. Lie, D. L. The Microblade Tradition in China: Regional Chronologies and Significance in the Transition to Neolithic. *Asian Perspectives* 37: 84 – 112, 1998.

[3] Ackerman, R. Earliest Stone Industries on the North Pacific Coast of North America. *Arctic Anthropology* 29: 18 – 27, 1992.
Andrefsky, W. Diffusion and Innovation from the Perspective of Wedge Shaped Cores in Alaska and Japan. In *The Organization of Core Technology*. J. K. Johnson and C. A. Morrow, eds. Pp. 13 – 43. Boulder: Westview, 1987.
West, F. H. (ed.) *American Beginnings: The Prehistory and Paleoecology of Beringia*. Chicago: University of Chicago Press, 1996.

[4] Clark, G. Mesolithic Europe: The Economic Basis. In *Problems in Economic and Social Archaeology*. G. de G. Sieveking, 1. H. Longworth, and K. E. Wilson, eds. Pp. 457. London: Duckworth, 1976.

[5] Tixier, J. *Typologie de l'Epipaleolithique du Maghreb*. Memoires du Centre de Recherches

Anthropologiques, Prehistoriques et Ethnographiques 2. Paris: Arts et Metiers Graphiques, 1963.

[6] Weissner, P. Style and Social Information in Kalahari San Projectile Points. *American Antiquity* 48: 253-276, 1983.

[7] Clark, G. Mesolithic Europe: The Economic Basis. In *Problems in Economic and Social Archaeology*. G. de G. Sieveking. 1. H. Longworth, and K. E. Wilson, eds. Pp. 449-481. London: Duckworth, 1976.

[8] Bleed, P. The Optimal Design of Hunting Weapons: Maintainability or Reliability. *American Antiquity* 51(4): 737-747, 1986.

[9] Mitchell, P. *The Early Microlithic Assemblages of Southern Africa*. BAR International Series, 388. Oxford: British Archaeological Reports, 1988: 263.

[10] Clark, G. Mesolithic Europe: The Economic Basis. In *Problems in Economic and Social Archaeology*. G. de G. Sieveking. 1. H. Longworth, and K. E. Wilson, eds. Pp. 452-456. London: Duckworth, 1976.

[11] Lucas, G. Les lamelles Dufour du Flageolet I (Bezenac, Dordogne) dans le contexte Aurignacien. Paleo 9: 191-219, 1997.
Production experimentale de lamelles torses: Approche preliminaire. *Bulletin de la Societe Prehistorique Francaise* 96: 145-151. Marks, A., and K. Monigal In press Origins of the European Upper Paleolithic, Seen from Crimea: Simple Myth or Complex Reality? In *The Early Upper Paleolithic East of the Danube*. P. J. Brantingham, K. W. Kerry, and S. L. Kuhn, eds. Los Angeles: University of California Press, 1999.

[12] Palma di Cesnola, A. Paleolitico Superiore in Italia. Firenze, Italy: Garlatti and Razzai Editori, 1993: 93-99.

[13] Koumouzelis, M., B. Ginter, J. K. Kozlowski, M. Pawlikowski, O. Bar-Yosef, R. M. Albert, M. Litynska-Zajac. E. Stworzewicz, P. Wotjal, G. Lipecki, T. Tomek, Z. M. Bochenski, and A. Pazdur. The Early Upper Paleolithic in Greece: The Excavations in Klisoura Cave. *Journal of Archaeological Science* 28: 515-539, 2001. Marks, A., and K. Monigal. Origins of the European Upper Paleolithic, Seen from Crimea: Simple Myth or Complex Reality? In *The Early Upper Paleolithic East of the Danube*. P. J. Brantingham, K. W. Kerry, and S. L. Kuhn, eds. Los Angeles: University of California Press, in press.

[14] Laplace, G. L'Industrie de Krems Hundssteig et le probleme de l'origine des complexes Aurignaciens. In *Friihe Menschheit und Umwelt*. Pp. 242-297. Koln: Fundamenta Reihe, A2, 1970.

[15] Bischoff, J., N. Soler, J. Maroto, and R. Julia. Abrupt Mousterian/Aurignacian Boundary at c. 40 ka bp: Accelerator 14C Dates from L'Abreda Cave (Catalunya, Spain). *Journal of*

Archaeological Science 16: 563 - 576, 1989.

Soler, M., and J. M. Fullola. Cultural Change between Middle and Upper Paleolithic in Catalonia. In *The Last Neandertals, the First Anatomically Modern Humans*. E. Carbonelland M. Vaquero, eds. Pp. 219 - 250. Tarragona, Spain: Fundacio Catalana per la Recerca, 1996.

[16] Kuhn, S., and M. C. Stiner. The Earliest Aurignacian of Riparo Mochi (Liguria, Italy). *Current Anthropology* 39(supp): S175 - S189, 1998.

Laplace, G. II Riparo Mochi ai Balzi Rossi di Grimaldi (Fouilles 1938 - 1949): Les industries leptolithiques. *Rivista di Scienze Preistoriche* 32: 3 - 131, 1977.

[17] Bartolomei, G., A. Broglio, P. F. Cassoli, L. Cas-Clark, G. A., and L. Straus telletti, L. Cattani, M. Cremaschi, G. Giacobini, G. Malerba, A. Maspero, M. Presani, A. Sartorelli, and A. Tagliacozzo. La Grotte de Fumane. Un site Aurignacien au pied des Alpes. *Preistoria Alpina* 28: 131 - 179, 1992.

[18] Broglio, A. II Paleolitico Superiore del Friuli-Venezia Giulia. Atti della XXIX Riunione Scientifica del Istituto Italiano do Preistoria e Protostoria, Pp. 36 - 56. Firenze, Italy: IIPP, 1994.

Palma di Cesnola, A. *Paleolitico Superiore in Italia*. Firenze, Italy: Garlatti and Razzai Editori, 1993.

[19] Bischoff, J., N. Soler, J. Maroto, and R. Julia. Abrupt Mousterian/Aurignacian Boundary at c. 40 ka bp: Accelerator 14C Dates from L'Abreda Cave (Catalunya, Spain). *Journal of Archaeological Science* 16: 563 - 576, 1989.

Kuhn, S., and A. Bietti. The Late Middle and Early Upper Paleolithic in Italy. In *Interactions between Neandertals and Modern Humans*. O. Bar-Yosef and D. Pilbeam, eds. Pp. 49 - 76. Cambridge: Harvard University Press, 2000.

[20] Bischoff, J., N. Soler, J. Maroto, and R. Julia. Abrupt Mousterian/Aurignacian Boundary at c. 40 ka bp: Accelerator 14C Dates from L'Abreda Cave (Catalunya, Spain). *Journal of Archaeological Science* 16: 563 - 576, 1989.

Soler, M., and J. M. Fullola. Cultural Change between Middle and Upper Paleolithic in Catalonia. In *The Last Neandertals, the First Anatomically Modern Humans*. E. Carbonelland M. Vaquero, eds. Pp. 245. Tarragona, Spain: Fundacio Catalana per la Recerca, 1996.

[21] Koumouzelis, M., B. Ginter, J. K. Kozlowski, M. Pawlikowski, O. Bar-Yosef, R. M. Albert, M. Litynska-Zajac. E. Stworzewicz, P. Wotjal, G. Lipecki, T. Tomek, Z. M. Bochenski, and A. Pazdur. The Early Upper Paleolithic in Greece: The Excavations in Klisoura Cave. *Journal of Archaeological Science* 28: 515 - 539, 2001.

[22] Bartolomei, G., A. Broglio, P. F. Cassoli, L. Cas-Clark, G. A., and L. Straus telletti, L. Cattani, M. Cremaschi, G. Giacobini, G. Malerba, A. Maspero, M. Presani, A. Sartorelli,

and A. Tagliacozzo. La Grotte de Fumane. Un site Aurignacien au pied des Alpes. *Preistoria Alpina* 28: 131-179, 1992.

Kuhn, S., and A. Bietti. The Late Middle and Early Upper Paleolithic in Italy. In *Interactions between Neandertals and Modern Humans*. O. Bar-Yosef and D. Pilbeam, eds. Pp. 49-76. Cambridge: Harvard University Press, 2000.

Laplace, G. L'Industrie de Krems Hundssteig et le probleme de l'origine des complexes Aurignaciens. In *Friihe Menschheit und Umwelt*. Pp. 242-297. Koln: Fundamenta Reihe, A2, 1970.

[23] Kuhn, S., and M. C. Stiner. The Earliest Aurignacian of Riparo Mochi (Liguria, Italy). *Current Anthropology* 39(suppl): S175-S189, 1998.

[24] Lucas, G. Les lamelles Dufour du Flageolet I (Bezenac, Dordogne) dans le contexte Aurignacien. Paleo 9: 191-219, 1997.

[25] Soler, M., and J. M. Fullola. Cultural Change between Middle and Upper Paleolithic in Catalonia. In *The Last Neandertals, the First Anatomically Modern Humans*. E. Carbonelland M. Vaquero, eds. Pp. 228. Tarragona, Spain: Fundacio Catalana per la Recerca, 1996.

[26] Kuhn, S., and M. C. Stiner. The Earliest Aurignacian of Riparo Mochi (Liguria, Italy). *Current Anthropology* 39(suppl): S175-S189, 1998.

[27] Bartolomei, G., A. Broglio, P. F. Cassoli, L. Cas-Clark, G. A., and L. Straus telletti, L. Cattani, M. Cremaschi, G. Giacobini, G. Malerba, A. Maspero, M. Presani, A. Sartorelli, and A. Tagliacozzo. La Grotte de Fumane. Un site Aurignacien au pied des Alpes. *Preistoria Alpina* 28: 131-179, 1992.

[28] Kozlowski, J. The Evolution of the Balkan Aurignacian. In *Dorothy Garrod and the Progress of the Paleolithic*. W. Davies and R. Charles, eds. Pp. 97-117. London: O. xbow Books, 1999.

[29] Kuhn, S., and M. C. Stiner. The Earliest Aurignacian of Riparo Mochi (Liguria, Italy). *Current Anthropology* 39(suppl): S175-S189, 1998.

Stiner, M. Paleolithic Mollusk Exploitation at Riparo Mochi (Balzi Rossi, Italy): Food and Ornaments from the Aurignacian through Epigravettian. *Antiquity* 73: 735-754, 2000.

[30] Bartolomci, G., A. Broglio, P. F. Cassoli, L. Cas-Clark, G. A., and L. Straus telletti, L. Cattani, M. Cremaschi, G. Giacobini, G. Malerba, A. Maspero, M. Presani, A. Sartorelli, and A. Tagliacozzo. La Grotte de Fumane. Un site Aurignacien au pied des Alpes. *Preistoria Alpina* 28: 131-179, 1992.

[31] Bartolomei, G., A. Broglio, P. F. Cassoli, L. Cas-Clark, G. A., and L. Straus telletti, L. Cattani, M. Cremaschi, G. Giacobini, G. Malerba, A. Maspero, M. Presani, A. Sartorelli, and A. Tagliacozzo. La Grotte de Fumane. Un site Aurignacien au pied des Alpes. *Preistoria Alpina* 28: 131-179, 1992.

[32] Clark, J. D. The Microlithic Industries of Africa: Their Antiquity and Possible Economic Implications. In *Recent Advances in Indo-Pacific Prehistory*. V. N. Misra and P. Bellwood, eds. Pp. 95 – 103. New Delhi: Oxford and IBH, 1978.

Mitchell, P. *The Early Microlithic Assemblages of Southern Africa*. BAR International Series, 388. Oxford: British Archaeological Reports, 1988.

[33] Lie, D. L. The Microblade Tradition in China: Regional Chronologies and Significance in the Transition to Neolithic. *Asian Perspectives* 37: 84 – 112, 1998.

[34] Broglio, A. Discontinuity tra Musteriano e Protoaurignaziano mediterraneao nella Grotta di Fumane (Monti Lessini, Prealpi Venete). *Veleia* 12: 49 – 65, 1995.

Kozlowski, J. The Evolution of the Balkan Aurignacian. In *Dorothy Garrod and the Progress of the Paleolithic*. W. Davies and R. Charles, eds. Pp. 97 – 117. London: O. xbow Books, 1999.

[35] D'Errico, F., J. Zilhao, M. Julien, D. Baffler, and J. Pelegrin. Neanderthal Acculturation in Western Europe? A Critical Review of the Evidence and Its Interpretation. *Current Anthropology* 39(suppl): S1-S44, 1998.

Kuhn, S., and A. Bietti. The Late Middle and Early Upper Paleolithic in Italy. In *Interactions between Neandertals and Modern Humans*. O. Bar-Yosef and D. Pilbeam, eds. Pp. 49 – 76. Cambridge: Harvard University Press, 2000.

Straus, L. Continuity or Rupture; Convergence or Invasion; Adaptation or Catastrophe; Mosaic or Monolith: Views of the Middle to Upper Paleolithic Transition in Iberia. In *The Last Neandertals, the First Anatomically Modern Humans*. E. Carbonell and M. Vaquero, eds. Pp. 203 – 218. Tarragona, Spain: Fundacio Catalana per la Recerca, 1996.

[36] Pianka, E. *Evolutionary Ecology*. 2nd ed. New York: Harper and Row, 1978: 192 – 194.

[37] Stiner, M., N. Munro, T. Surovell, E. Tchernov, and O. Bar-Yosef. Paleolithic Population Growth Pulses Evidenced by Small Animal Exploitation. *Science* 283: 190 – 194, 1999.

Stiner, M. Paleolithic Mollusk Exploitation at Riparo Mochi (Balzi Rossi, Italy): Food and Ornaments from the Aurignacian through Epigravettian. *Antiquity* 73: 735 – 754, 2000.

[38] Clark, G. A., and L. Straus. Late Pleistocene Hunter-Gatherer Adaptations in Cantabrian Spain. In *Hunter-Gatherer Economies in Prehistory: A European Perspective*. G. Bailey, ed. Pp. 131 – 148. Cambridge: Cambridge University press, 1983.

Gamble, C. *The Paleolithic Settlement of Europe*. Cambridge: Cambridge University Press, 1986.

Klein, R. *The Human Career*. Chicago: University of Chicago Press, 360 – 388, 1989.

Stiner, M. Paleolithic Mollusk Exploitation at Riparo Mochi (Balzi Rossi, Italy): Food and Ornaments from the Aurignacian through Epigravettian. *Antiquity* 73: 735 – 754, 2000.

[39] Flannery, K. V. Origins and Ecological Effects of Early Domestication in Iran and the Near

East. In *The Domestication and Exploitation of Plants and Animals*. P. J. Ucko and G. \ \. Dimbleby, eds. Pp. 73 – 100. London: Duckworth, 1969.

[40] Stiner, M., N. Munro, T. Surovell, E. Tchernov, and O. Bar-Yosef. Paleolithic Population Growth Pulses Evidenced by Small Animal Exploitation. *Science* 283: 190 – 194, 1999.

Stiner, M. Paleolithic Mollusk Exploitation at Riparo Mochi (Balzi Rossi, Italy): Food and Ornaments from the Aurignacian through Epigravettian. Antiquity 73: 735 – 754, 2000.

[41] Clarke, D. Mesolithic Europe: The Economic Basis. In *Problems in Economic and Social Archaeology*. G. de G. Sieveking. 1. H. Longworth, and K. E. Wilson, eds. Pp. 449 – 481. London: Duckworth, 1976.

Hayden, B. Research and Development in the Stone Age: Technological Transitions among Hunter-Gatherers. *Current Anthropology* 22: 519 – 548, 1981.

Holliday, T. The Ecological Context of Trapping among Re92 Steven L. Kuhncent Hunter-Gatherers: Implications for Subsistence in Terminal Pleistocene Europe. *Current Anthropology* 39: 711 – 720, 1998.

[42] Hayden, B. Research and Development in the Stone Age: Technological Transitions among Hunter-Gatherers. *Current Anthropology* 22: 519 – 548, 1981.

Holliday, T. The Ecological Context of Trapping among Re92 Steven L. Kuhncent Hunter-Gatherers: Implications for Subsistence in Terminal Pleistocene Europe. *Current Anthropology* 39: 711 – 720, 1998.

Oswalt, W. *An Anthropological Analysis of Food-Getting Technology*. New York: John Wiley and Sons, 1976.

[43] Bar-Yosef, O., and R. Meadow. The Origins of Agriculture in the Near East. In *Last Hunters, First Farmers: New Perspectives on the Prehistoric Transition to Agriculture*. T. D. Price and A. B. Gebauer, eds. Pp. 39 – 94. Santa Fe: School of American Research Press, 1995.

Rosen, S. *Lithics after the Stone Age: A Handbook of Stone Tools from the Levant*. Walnut Creek, Calif.: Altamira, 1997.

[44] Ackerman, R. Earliest Stone Industries on the North Pacific Coast of North America. *Arctic Anthropology* 29: 18 – 27, 1992.

Andrefsky, W. Diffusion and Innovation from the Perspective of Wedge Shaped Cores in Alaska and Japan. In *The Organization of Core Technology*. J. K. Johnson and C. A. Morrow, eds. Pp. 13 – 43. Boulder: Westview, 1987.

[45] Flood, J. *Archaeology of the Dreamtime*. Honolulu: University of Hawaii Press, 1983: 190.

便宜、规范、可靠：日本晚更新世细石器技术设计差异的意义

彼得·布雷德

（内布拉斯加大学林肯分校）

摘　要：系统化生产的细石叶是日本列岛晚更新世之末有人类居住的标志。日本学者将细石叶生产地区差异解释成"文化的"差异。本文基于日本学者详细的技术分析，采用事件树分析方法分析荒谷、角二山以及福井洞石器组合，结果表明细石叶生产的主要区别来自不同的狩猎策略，反映了日本南北部之间的生态差异。

日本可能是世界上史前史研究最透彻的区域，这么开始话题并不能提供有关日本远古生活的详细信息。日本考古学家已经形成了非常强大的研究传统，揭示了极为翔实的有关日本列岛的考古材料。日本史前考古记录具有世界考古学家讨论的绝大部分材料，从亚洲人类的扩散，到定居生活、稳定社群与农业的起源，再到国家层面的政治体的形成。本文研究更新世之末狩猎者石器组合材料，有关信息都是日本研究者编就的。跟其他方面的研究材料相比，这些材料只是日本考古材料中非常小的一部分。但是，就研究更新世之末"细石器"工具组合的差异与决定因素而言，来自日本的证据是非常有用的。

广泛使用细石叶技术石器组合是日本旧石器时代结束的标志[1]。这些石器组合的年代属于更新世之末，日本学者高度关注其研究，至少基于两个原因。一是这些材料技术复杂，日本考古学家乐于研究其制作方式；二是它们可能与绳文文化传统的起源相关。因此，即使细石叶技术仅仅持续了大约2 000

年,而且也不如后来的材料那么引人注目,但是日本考古学努力且细致地研究了细石叶遗址与其石器组合。他们对石器组合的关注提供了有关"细石器"的丰富信息,有助于我们了解石器组合存在的种种差异性,这也是本书的中心。

有关日本细石叶组合的已有信息反映了日本考古学独特的方法以及日本地理的某些特殊之处。正如今村[2]最近所言,日本考古学分析以"坚韧的"实证主义为标志,非常强调细致的材料描述与分析,很容易回到原始材料。这意味着日本细石叶材料研究明显"没有理论",完全是描述性的,而且极其细致。其发掘技术非常精细,发表与报道也非常充分,因此能够让学者们非常准确地研究遗址的大小与结构。与此同时,大多数有关细石叶的分析注意到,不同遗址与地区组合都有独特的技术特征。这种研究当然强调特殊的器物类型,相对而言,很少有关于地区分布模式的讨论,而地区模式可能反映具有生态学意义的经济活动。了解这些遗址的生态条件有些困难,因为过去数千年前的历史已经很大程度上改变了日本的地表景观。最后,日本普遍分布的酸性火山土意味着这些遗址很少含有有机物。因此,尽管人们假定细石叶用于投掷器的倒刺与边刃,其特殊用法以及所射猎的动物依旧不为人所知。

日本考古学家用于分析细石叶组合的概念强调文化历史。细石叶组合分析所用的中心概念叫作"技法"(giho)。技法是重建楔形细石核制作与细石叶生产过程中所认识到的基本次序模型[3]。技法完全基于石器技术过程分析与拼合研究,日本考古学家将其解释为高度标准化的行为模式的反映。因为技法是如此标准化的,日本考古学家假定它们可以反映不同文化实体,可以视为习惯性行为并加以命名与研究。技法的分布分析清楚地表明日本列岛不同地区细石叶使用者采用不同的途径生产那些细小的工具。按照文化历史考古的术语,这种差异似乎表明更新世之末日本是一个族群多样的地区。这些差别同时还是另一重证据,日本南北人群与亚洲大陆不同地区具有文化关联。无须否认这些认识,日本细石叶组合的良好材料与分析表明,细石叶生产方式上的差异还可能反映其他方面的变化。也就是说,细石叶工艺的区别可能意味着古代日本狩猎者具有不同的设计考虑,采用了不同技术策略,这是需要研究的问题。

为了研究这些可能性,本文报道三个日本细石叶组合事件树分析的结果,两个来自本州中部,日本考古学家称之为细石叶分布的"北部"地区,第三个来自九州北部,它是细石叶生产南部圈的中心(图7.1)。我必须自豪地强调,我在这里所研究的石器组合包括两个日本最著名的旧石器遗址：北部的荒谷遗址与九州的福井洞遗址。承蒙芹泽长介与介川隆之助先生的帮助，我很荣幸看到了这些重要的材料。

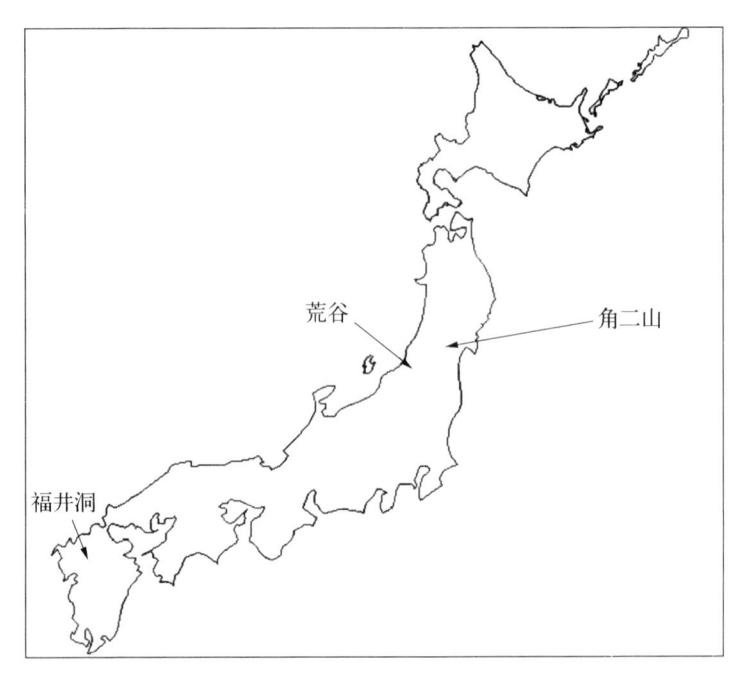

图 7.1　荒谷、角二山与福井洞遗址地理位置图

一、三种细石叶组合的事件树分析

事件树分析，或称 ETA，是一种确定技术活动中不同步骤的方法，用以了解特定步骤的成功与失败率。这种模型有助于描述特定工具类型的生产方式[4]，也有助于了解工具制作者的设计策略与技术组织。运用 ETA 方法分析考古材料最适合于活动高度程序化的材料，而且这些材料的获取与发表要非常精细。日本细石叶组合材料非常适合这些标准。

三个细石叶组合的事件树分析试图了解细石叶制作者采用的技术步骤，更重要的是，了解三个遗址细石叶生产技术的差异。我在其他文章中介绍过这些材料，所以这里我只是粗略提一下。

（一）荒谷

荒谷是本州地区最重要的细石叶组合之一，较为可靠的年代测定为更新世之末[5]。荒谷遗址位于新潟地区中部,坐落在海岸平原西部内侧边缘的残阶地上,俯瞰两条主要河流信浓川与鱼野川汇合处,历史上这里季节性鱼类资源丰富。遗址附近没有石料,石料可能是以大石片或是棕榈大小的两面器的形式带入遗址的,这些石料还用作石核与轻型砍砸工具。两面器是生产细石叶的起点。如图7.2的归纳,荒谷遗址制作石核的过程只有六个步骤。

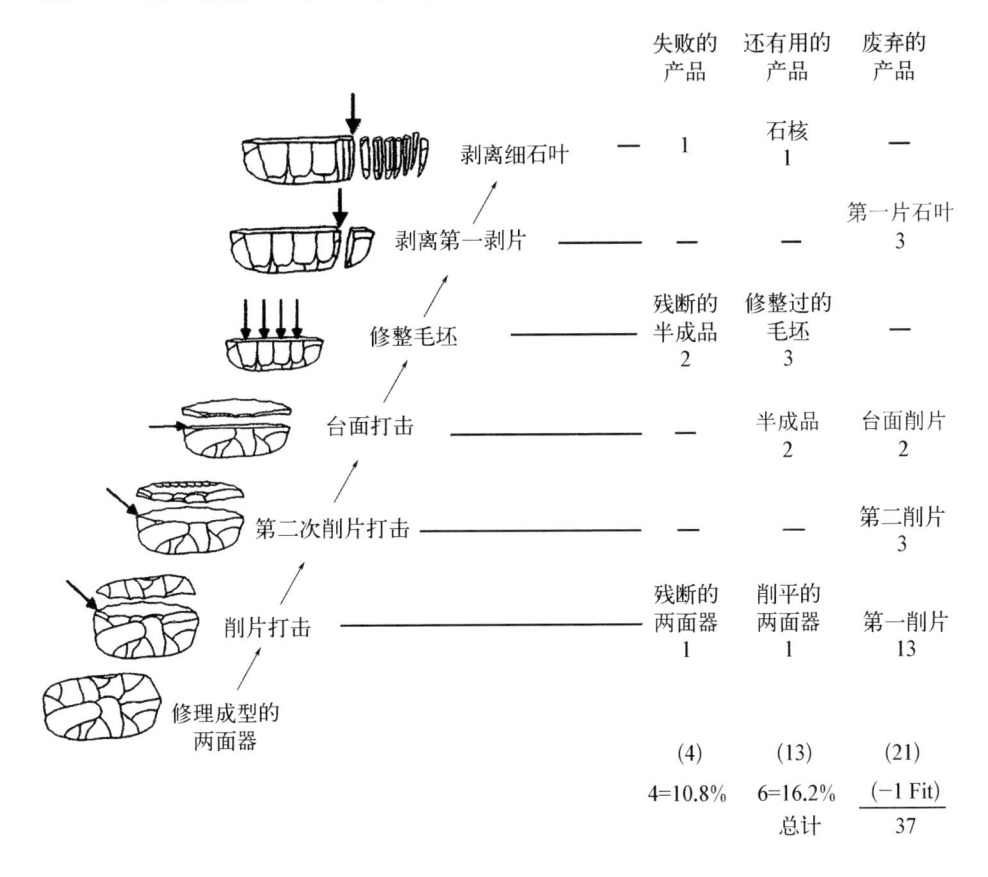

事件	失败的产品	还有用的产品	废弃的产品
剥离细石叶	1	石核 1	—
剥离第一剥片	—	—	第一片石叶 3
修整毛坯	残断的半成品 2	修整过的毛坯 3	—
台面打击	—	半成品 2	台面削片 2
第二次削片打击	—	—	第二削片 3
削片打击	残断的两面器 1	削平的两面器 1	第一削片 13
修理成型的两面器	(4) 4=10.8%	(13) 6=16.2%	(21) (−1 Fit)
总计			37

图 7.2 荒谷遗址细石叶生产的事件树模型

(左侧显示事件,右侧显示考古学上观察到的事件结果。失败的结果是残断的废弃品。待处理的结果显然还有用,有待进一步加工。废弃的结果为石核生产的副产品。图由斯坦·帕克斯与玛丽莎·邓尼所制)

1. 斜向打击两面器的边缘似乎总是过程的开端,即使并不是直接为了生产细石叶;

2. 经过一两次打击后,把两面器用作砍砸器;

3. 打出一个平台面来;

4. 细石叶毛坯形成;

5. 从一端剥离一片形态特殊的大"第一剥片",形成工作面;

6. 细石叶由此开始剥离。

除了技术步骤较为简单之外,生产细石叶的荒谷技法风险较低。石器组合中仅发现4件失败的标本,生产过程的失败率刚超过10%。加上废弃在遗址中未完成的标本,荒谷细石叶生产的整个失败率是27%。

由于荒谷遗址只有一件石核上具有不止一个石片,这似乎表明该标本的大部分加工工作都是其他地方做的。石核的所有加工阶段都是在遗址中进行的,但是发现许多首次、第二次与台面削片,比成品石核的数量多得多。这至少表明石核是在流动的状况下使用的,扔到了遗址之外。

(二)角二山

从类型学上来说,角二山遗址的细石叶组合与荒谷遗址基本相同,但两个遗址之间还是存在一些差异,可能是"设计"上的区别,反映两个社群按照他们自己的需要生产细石叶。

角二山遗址位于荒谷以东大约200公里的山形区北部[6]。跟荒谷遗址一样,角二山遗址也位于河流汇合处,历史时期是捕鱼的好地方。不过角二山与荒谷遗址的主要区别在于石器原料的便利程度。角二山遗址之下就是质量优良的硬页岩砾石,几乎用于制作遗址中所有的工具。石器组合中包括许多石锤、除皮石片、块状废片以及打片检验的砾石。

角二山遗址修理石核打制细石叶的基本过程如同荒谷遗址,见图7.3的归纳,两个遗址的技术之间存在三种明显的区别。首先,角二山遗址两面器削片、再削片、修平台面的过程相对不那么规范,荒谷遗址则非常严格地把两面器加工成石核毛坯。次之,经过初步的修形步骤后,角二山细石叶制作者采用多种多样的石核更新技术,延长石核使用寿命。这种活动不见于荒谷。这一过程的失败占角二山组合的大部分失败案例。最后,失败率的差别是两个遗址另一个不同点。角二山遗址的生产失败率为17%,比荒谷遗址略高。考虑到未完成的标本,整个失败率则上升到34%,还是比荒谷遗址高。如同荒谷遗址,两面器削片与修形残留石制品远远超过成型石核。

(三)福井洞

福井洞遗址跟上述两遗址非常不同,它是一处分层的岩厦遗址,位于远离南端的九州北部。这处遗址以出土距今1.27万年前的陶器而闻名,出土早期陶器

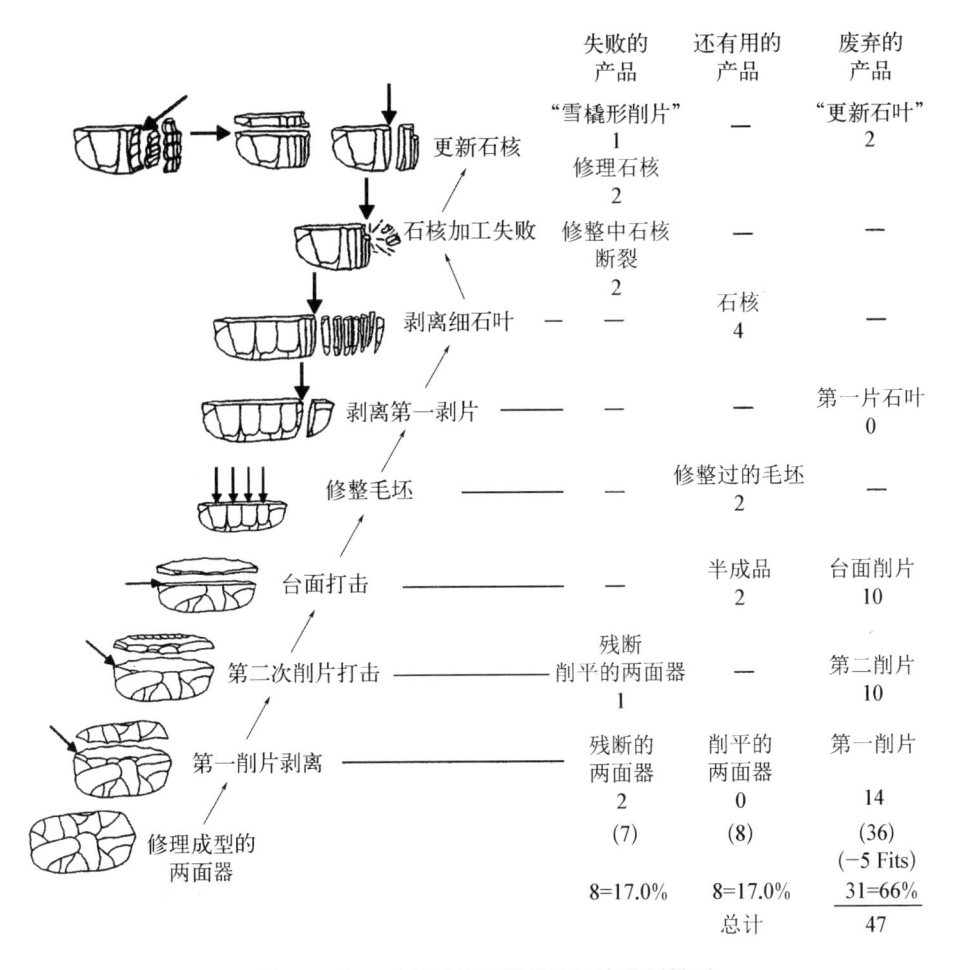

便宜、规范、可靠：日本晚更新世细石器技术设计差异的意义 ·149·

	失败的产品	还有用的产品	废弃的产品
更新石核	"雪橇形削片" 1 修理石核 2	—	"更新石叶" 2
石核加工失败	修整中石核断裂 2	—	—
剥离细石叶	—	石核 4	—
剥离第一剥片	—	—	第一片石叶 0
修整毛坯	—	修整过的毛坯 2	—
台面打击	—	半成品 2	台面削片 10
第二次削片打击	残断 削平的两面器 1	—	第二削片 10
第一削片剥离	残断的两面器 2	削平的两面器 0	第一削片 14
修理成型的两面器	(7)	(8)	(36) (−5 Fits)
总计	8=17.0%	8=17.0%	31=66% 47

图 7.3 角二山遗址细石叶生产的事件树模型

的层位同时也含有细石叶组合[7]。

福井的细石叶生产许多方面不同于上面所述的过程[8]。首先,它采用一种完全不同的石料。福井所有的石核都是由黑色黑曜石原料所制,这种原料多为相对较小的石块。次之,生产过程本身比较简单,仅仅涉及四个基本步骤(图 7.4)。

1. 福井洞石核是从 5 至 8 厘米长的杏仁形两面器开始制作的。没有证据表明这些两面器除了用作细石叶石核之外还有其他的用途;

2. 通过从一条长边上剥离一片特殊的"三面"石片,也就是"第一剥片",把雏形石核加工成石核毛坯;

3. 此时,细石叶的剥离可以开始了;

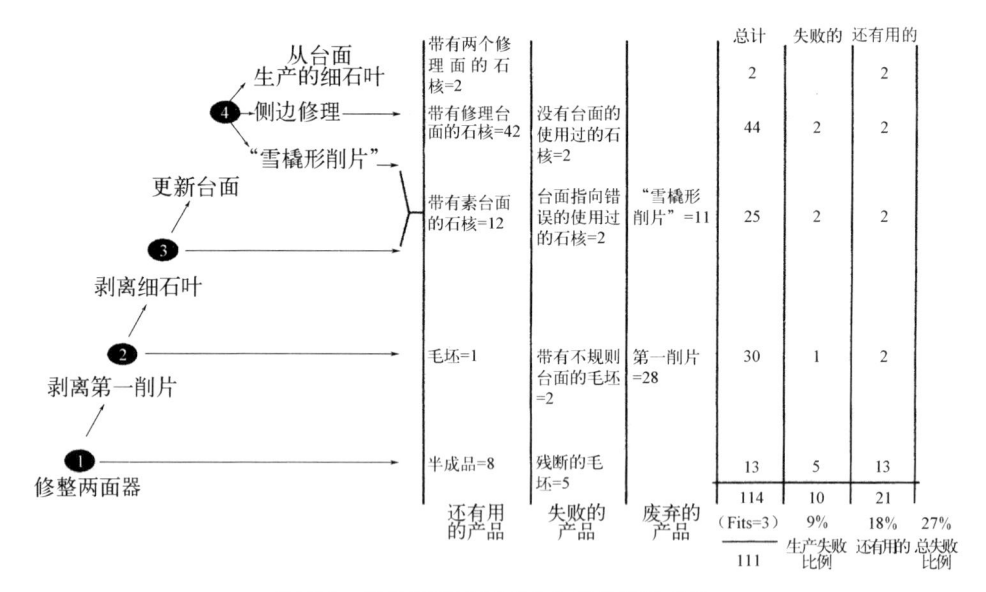

图7.4　福井洞遗址细石叶生产的事件总结

4. 石核是福井细石叶生产的基本组成部分，当时似乎运用了数种技术来调整石核打击台面，以延长其使用寿命。

福井的生产与总体失败率分别为9%与26%，跟荒谷遗址相近。遗留下来与耗尽石核的数量比第一削片的数量多得多。这表明遗址中加工过的石核始于其他地方。

二、为什么日本南北部细石叶组合不同？

三个细石叶组合在两个方面存在差异。第一个方面，也是最明显的，它们所涉及的步骤或是生产结构不同。除此之外，这些遗址的生产方式具有不同的生产风险水平。尽管它们之间看起来似乎没有联系，但是生产结构的差异与组合所反映的风险水平实际是紧密关联的。因此，可以提出这样一个观点，石器组合的明显区别来自"设计"，至少也是石器制作者合理的技术选择——如果不是"推断的"话。

（一）风险

若干有关石器工具组合的形制与构成影响因素的讨论都强调风险管理的重要性，它是指导古代单件与成套工具生产的主要因素。这些讨论非常有吸引力，但是考古学家很少有办法来测度史前技术生产活动所涉及的风险。事件树分析就提供了这样一个途径,分析生产过程中每一步所关联的风险以及失败发生的总体概率。由于我们很少有方法测度失败率,而且相关的材料也非常少,所以很难就这个问题展开讨论。当然,这里三个石器组合失败率的差别似乎表明生产失败率某种程度上是由工具制作者控制的。

荒谷与福井洞遗址的生产失败率基本上都是10%左右。角二山遗址的比例稍高,达到17%,因此把遗址中失败与废弃的细石叶石核都包括在内时,整体比例超过了三分之一。

如何解释这些区别呢?这些生产失败比例上的差别可能来自荒谷与福井遗址都远离石器原料产地,相反角二山遗址实际就位于原料产地上。由于原料近在咫尺,角二山的石器制作者由于可能会打制质地较差的石料,承担更大的风险,或是用这个遗址来练习或是教授打制石器的技艺。任何一种这样的做法都会导致角二山遗址打制失败的石制品更常见。荒谷遗址的细石叶制作者可能已经拥有发达的制作工艺,不需要更新石核。当然,这样的技巧对于远离石料产地的人们来说是非常合适的。因此,荒谷与角二山遗址之间的主要区别就是技艺水平。

如果石器的制作技巧有助于减少失败的风险,在优质石料罕见的情况下,就像荒谷石器制作者的例子,人们会倾向磨砺技巧,提高石器打制的水平。我认为这种情况带来许多有趣的、尚待研究的问题,如"技巧"是何时以及如何发展起来的,还有是如何接受与传递,又如何通过考古材料来研究它们。

(二) 生产结构

上述三个遗址细石叶生产的步骤各不相同,跟各个遗址不同的情况相适应。

福井洞遗址的细石叶生产方式独特,非常直接。发现于遗址中用于制作细石叶的两面器似乎只有这样一个功能。两面器修理加工成细石叶毛坯,采用的方式相对简单。当然,尽管过程简单,但是生产细石叶的方式还是多样的,同时采用了不少石核更新技术,于福井洞遗址而言也是必需的,因此形成了福井洞遗址细石叶生产特殊的质量特点。福井洞石核非常细小,几件石核与需要剥离细石叶工具可以放在一个小包里携带。

福井洞遗址的许多毛坯是从其他地方开始加工的,这里成型石核的数量(60件)是第一削片(28件)数量的两倍多。这种情况下,我们有理由相信日本南部的细石叶生产是由在许多遗址之间流动的人们生产的,生产过程可能稳定持续。

日本北部的遗址,荒谷与角二山,情况则非常不同。这里细石叶生产是一个更复杂的过程,包括更庞杂的石器生产方式。细石叶石核由较大的两面器制作,两面器同时用作两种通用的工具。也就是,既用作生产石片的石核,还在成为细石核之前用作石斧。这些遗址的细石叶生产是一种专业化的活动,这一活动也是规范的再循环体系的终点。严格的规范,辅之以高超的技术技巧,似乎最合适描述荒谷的细石叶生产过程。

日本北部遗址刚开始打制的石核相对于已完成打制的石核的比例与福井洞遗址的状况差不多正好相反。荒谷与角二山遗址,削片与打平台面的遗存数量远超成型石核的数量。这些遗址可能具有不同的专门目的,但是也存在这样的可能,北部遗址中的石核也是按计划制作的,要携带到其他地方使用。

最后,即便经过整形,北部遗址的石核依然是相当大块的石料。与其他生产细石叶的工具一道,几件这样的石核就会形成一个体积相对较大的工具组合。

三、结论

我们基本不知道日本细石叶是如何使用的。当然,如同世界其他地区一样,我们可以假定它们是复杂精致武器的组成部件,可能具有平行的两种用途,用作多种倒刺以及用作比较确凿的功能,也就是充当"可替换的"模块化尖头部件。一般说来,这些武器具有可靠技术体系的特征,在任何需要的时候发挥作用。某些情况下这些设计特征更有优势,因此它们具有某些含义,指示更新世之末日本列岛群体的狩猎形态。这些信息增加并扩充了材料的解释潜力。

日本北部,细石叶制作者采用明显具有通用形式的工具组合——石片、石核,以及未安柄的斜刃石斧,其用途可能非常固定与专门。至少是在荒谷遗址,其制作过程具有相当的技巧。可能是一些"专家"确立了日本北部细石叶的生产技巧与规范。北部石器组合中明显存在的技巧与规范与成批处理的行为一致。成批处理具有若干优势。它可以降低装备成本,使生产者"容易进入最佳工作状态",而且,也是最重要的,这有助于安排"休息时间",不跟其他机会冲突。正如所强调的,石器组合的构成进一步表明人们在不同地方制作与使用细石叶石核,自然时间也不同。所有这些都是可靠技术体系的典型特征。

这些特征与福井洞组合形成鲜明的对照。那里细石叶由专门"工具"制作,但基本过程简单,可能由在福井洞及其他遗址之间流动的单个弓箭制作者所为,操作中略有变化。福井洞遗址所用技术的关键部件非常细小,易于携带。所有这些都是可维护技术体系的典型特征,易于修理或调整,能够在短时间内满足多样的用途。

这些操作区别表明日本北部更新世之末的狩猎者生活的环境与生计节律更固定,比生活在南部的群体受到更多关键条件的约束。

这些细石叶组合同时使得我们有机会考察可靠性、可维护性等设计理念的意义与作用。[9] 显然,没有一个日本石器组合仅仅是"可靠的"或"可维护的"。相反,就其构成部件与运用而言,可以运用这些术语来衡量石器组合。这种做法使得我们可以探寻那些最有意思的问题,"何种情况下才有意义"?

可靠性与可维护性的概念有助于考古学家思考工具制作者所具有的选择。当然,不宜将它们具体化为固定的对立面或类别,或是特征。运用这些概念帮助考古学家认识与解释考古材料,以及得到分析技术体系所需要的可操作变量。

注释:

[1] Chard, C. S. *Northeast Asia in Prehistory*. Madison: University of Wisconsin Press. Imamura, K, 1974: 110-113.

Imamura, K. *Prehistoric Japan: New Perspectives of Insular East Asia*. Honolulu: University of Hawaii Press, 1996: 34-38.

[2] Imamura, K. *Prehistoric Japan: New Perspectives of Insular East Asia*. Honolulu: University of Hawaii Press, 1996: x.

[3] Bleed, P. Trees or Chains, Links or Branches: Conceptual Alternatives for Consideration of Sequential Activities. *Journal of Archaeological Method and Theory* 8(1): 101-127, 2001.

[4] Bleed, P. Operations Research and Archaeology. *American Antiquity* 56(1): 19-35, 1991.

[5] Bleed, P. Risk and Cost in Japanese Microblade Production. *Lithic Technology* 21: 95-107, 1996.

Sutoh, T. *The Araya Site: Results of the Second and Third Term Excavations*. Department of Archaeology, Tohoku University, Sendai, Japan, 1990.

[6] Bleed, P. Risk and Cost in Japanese Microblade Production. *Lithic Technology* 21: 95-107, 1996.

Uno, S., and S. Ueno. Kakuniyama. In *Nihon no Kyuseki Bunka*, vol. 2: *Iseki to Ibutsu*. Y. Aso, S. Kato, and T. Fujimoto, eds. Pp. 96-112. Tokyo: Oyama, 1983.

[7] Bleed, P. Risk and Cost in Japanese Microblade Production. *Lithic Technology* 21: 95-107, 1996.

[8] Bleed, P. Wedge-Shaped Cores from Fukui Cave and the Organization of Japanese Terminal Paleolithic Technology. In *Senshigaku to Kanrenkagaku*. S. Chiba, ed. Pp. 25-36.

Sapporo, 1993.

Risk and Cost in Japanese Microblade Production. *Lithic Technology* 21: 95–107, 1996.

[9] Bleed, P. The Optimal Design of Hunting Weapons: Maintainability or Reliability. *American Antiquity* 51(4): 737–747, 1986.

北亚的细石器技术：旧石器时代晚期与早全新世的风险最小化策略

罗伯特·G·埃尔斯顿　　P·杰夫·班廷汉姆
（银城　内华达）　　（加利福尼亚大学　洛杉矶）

摘　要：从晚更新世到更新世至全新世过渡期，甚至更晚，细石叶技术在整个北亚地区狩猎采集者的适应中占有非常重要的地位。迄今为止，这一地区大多数有关研究主要关注细石叶技术的起源、技术源流以及文化历史。相反，我们的关注重心有所不同，通过分析器物的设计与风险，我们研究细石器技术在北亚地区狩猎采集者的适应策略与解决生存难题上的作用。我们首先讨论亚洲细石叶的功能，与纯粹有机尖状器与石质打制尖状器比较，归纳出镶嵌了细石叶的有机尖状器的成本与效益，以及楔形细石核与砾石对劈（split-pebble）细石核的相对优势，并以 Z–score 模型来表示。我们的结论是，细石器技术是北亚地区极地与亚极地大动物狩猎者的风险最小化策略，文章同时还指出进一步研究的线索。

晚更新世的较晚阶段到更新世与全新世过渡期间以及更晚的时候，整个北亚地区狩猎采集者的适应中细石叶技术占有重要的地位[1]。迄今为止，大多数有关这一地区的研究者主要关注文化历史问题，其中文化起源与类型学研究又是重中之重[2]。因此，我们看到的一系列石器类型，区分或是归纳为考古学文化，从来不解释为什么——总有某些组合或年代处在普遍的分布形态之外。不能把考古材料划归这些类别并不是因为我们的发掘或是类型学研究的技巧不够。而是说，它是过去人类行为变化不可避免的结果，这些行为不是类别的，而且条件的产物。细石器技术的分布与变化仍旧是需要探索的重要内容,不过我们的主要关注点是研究适应策略上细石器技术的作用。换句话说,细石器技术能够为北亚狩猎采集者解决哪些重要的问题？回答这个问题将有助于解释北亚地区细石器技术的起源、扩散与长期存在。

我们从器物设计优势的角度[3],以及运用 Z-score 模型进行风险分析来研究这个问题[4]。首先我们将讨论亚洲细石叶的功能,并且归纳出细石器技术三个方面的成本收益优势:(1)镶嵌了细石叶的有机尖状器相对于纯粹有机尖状器和石质打制尖状器的优势;(2)两面器与细石叶生产的相对效率;(3)基于 Z-score 模型来衡量楔形细石核与砾石对劈细石核的相对优势。我们认为细石器技术的出现跟北亚地区晚更新世环境加剧的变化相关,最后,文章指出未来研究的方向。

一、亚洲细石叶的功能

亚洲旧石器时代晚期的细石器技术是用来生产石质镶嵌物的,生产出来的细石叶镶嵌在有机材料如骨、角、牙齿上,构成复合工具的刃部。迄今为止,中国还没有发现复合工具的有机物部件,但是西伯利亚已知旧石器时代晚期的带镶嵌物的投掷尖状器[5]。西伯利亚与中国东北新石器时代都发现有复合工具制作的尖状器与小刀[6]。安装在端部经过修理的细石叶有时也用作刮削器、石钻、小刀以及投掷尖状器。没有证据表明中国新石器时代把镶嵌石刃的工具用作镰刀[7],这一功能由带有锯齿刃的磨制石器、骨器或蚌器承担了[8]。

因此,这里我们赞同[9]其他研究者的认识,大部分亚洲新石器时代之前的细石叶是用于骨、角、齿投掷尖状器的边刃。在本文中,我将没有镶嵌物的尖状器称为有机尖状器[10],将带有镶嵌物的有机尖状器称为镶嵌尖状器。通过与有机尖状器、石质打制尖状器的比较,能够最有效地理解镶嵌尖状器的成本收益。

二、有机尖状器与石质打制尖状器的运用状况

通过实验复制与使用,我们基本了解了有机与石质打制尖状器的应用特征,民族学材料也有反映。最近海蒂·卡内奇[11]与克里斯托弗·伊利斯[12]的论文包括这两个方面的研究。他们的发现简要归纳如下(表8.1)。

表 8.1　有机与石质打制尖状器的操作特征

有机的尖状器	石质的尖状器
材料限制了形制 需要相当多的时间去生产 造成的肌肉组织伤害较小 更耐用 　·不受寒冷气候的影响 　·携带中很少损坏 　·使用中很少损坏 容易修理/重新磨尖 不大可能使用前杆 可反复使用	形制更多变化 可以相对较迅速地制作 造成肌肉组织伤害大,流血多 不耐用 　·寒冷气候中更脆 　·携带中容易损坏 　·射偏后容易折断 　·射中猎物后容易碎断 很难或不可能修理 使用前杆更常见 消耗品

　　石质尖状器相对更脆,使用中更可能失败,后果严重。当石质尖状器落到地面上,或是撞到树木、岩石上尤其容易断裂。更重要的是,石质尖状器在严寒中会明显变脆,更容易损坏。带有石质尖头的标枪与箭矢构成复合工具,石质部件用于消耗[13],损坏也可能是意料之中的事。按民族志记载,有些猎人认为石质尖状器在刺穿猎物时可能断裂,其杀伤力反而更强,因为断片会扩大伤口,使猎物流血更多。相比生产柄杆、修出安装缺口或是投掷标枪的凹槽、安装羽翼、捆扎,制作石质尖状器要更便宜、快捷。带石质尖头的投掷器本来就设计了可替换的尖头部件,无须重新制作整个工具。采用脱柄的前杆有助于保护主杆,同时降低尖头部件更换的难度。当然,为石质尖状器准备前杆,并把石质尖头安装在上面,这增加了生产成本,而且采用前杆的武器较之带整根杆部的武器更不结实。

　　有机尖状器通过劈开骨、角,然后刮削、磨制成形。有机尖状器比石质尖状器更耐用,使用中更不容易断裂,如果变钝或是断裂了,也更容易修理。制作一件有机尖状器的时间比制作绝大多数石质尖状器要长。当然,有机尖状器的使用寿命更长,人们可能需要花更多的时间生产一系列要消耗的石质尖状器才相当于一件有机尖状器[14]。有机尖状器的杀伤力可能不如石质尖状器,后者锋利的刃缘会制造更大的伤口,让猎物流血更多。

　　如表 8.2 所归纳的,伊利斯[15]调查了超过 100 个民族学案例,然后评估选择石质或有机尖状器的影响因素。他发现石质箭头或标枪头几乎毫无例外地用于狩猎大而危险的猎物(熊与大型食草类),以及用于战争,置敌人于死地。不过,带石质尖头的投掷标枪更多限于对使用者没有什么危险的情况下,或是有大量替代武器可用的情况。有机尖状器用于刺杀更小的猎物,没有替代武器时捕猎危险的动物的时候也会用到,还有在战争中需要多次刺杀的时候,寒冷天气(此时石质枪头更脆易断)需要箭头的时候以及在茂盛的植被中投掷标枪的时候,有机尖状器就有了用武之地。

表 8.2　民族志中有机与石质打制尖状器的使用状况

使用有机的尖状器的情况	使用石质的尖状器的情况
不用前杆直接刺杀成群的动物 没有替代武器时抵御大型/危险的动物 近身格斗时用作刺杀工具 寒冷气候中用作箭头 植被茂盛的地方用作投掷标枪	狩猎大动物的时候 攻击危险的落单猎物(熊) 危险较小时进行刺杀 远距离击杀敌人

伊利斯收集的民族志材料表明多种因素影响到有机或是石质尖状器的选择,包括周围环境的气温与猎物类型。影响不同情况下决定的主要因素似乎是与武器失败相关的成本或风险[16]。潜在成本相对较低的时候,更倾向于采用石质尖状器。而在失败成本较高的时候,就需要更可靠的武器了(某种意义上[17]),此时更可能采用有机尖状器。

三、镶嵌尖状器的成本与收益

制作镶嵌尖状器涉及一个包括生产、使用与维护等工具在内的复杂工具组合,其中我们可能发现硬锤、软锤、压制工具、固定工具、石砧、楔裂工具、砺石、刮削器、开槽工具(雕刻器、刻刀、锯),以及黏接剂[18]。制作石质或有机尖状器的工具组合中种类要少得多。

武器系统中采用镶嵌尖状器是成本高昂的。它需要大量的投入,学习如何生成宽厚一致的细石叶,以及如何在田野条件下尽可能迅速地满足当时的需要[19]。同等数量石料时,打制细石叶比生产两面器要更耗时[20]。把细石叶毛坯制作成合适的镶嵌刃,并把它安装到已开槽的有机尖状器的侧边还需要时间。学会制作宽度、深度一致的槽的成本可能同样高昂,需要耗费不少时间来生产。

伊利斯[21]没有引用民族志中使用镶嵌尖状器的案例。不过,他对使用有机与石质尖状器民族志材料的回顾表明,镶嵌尖状器结合了两者的优点。它给猎物造成的伤口与出血情况跟石质尖状器差不多,更不容易折断:两者的杀伤力都很强(图 8.1)。镶嵌尖状器可以多次使用,避免频繁更换尖头与使用前杆的麻烦。与此同时,镶嵌尖状器便于维护,仅仅需要更换丢失或破损的刃缘,偶尔修理尖部使其更锋利。批量生产的镶嵌刃缘能够满足不时之需[22]。

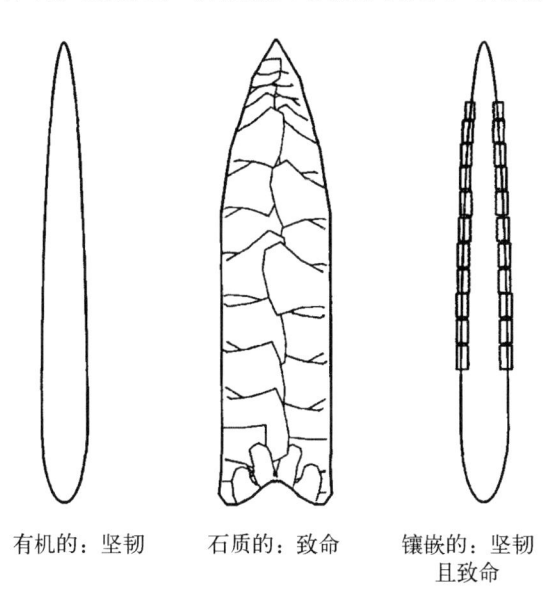

有机的:坚韧　　石质的:致命　　镶嵌的:坚韧且致命

图 8.1　有机、石质与镶嵌石刃的有机尖状器的比较

不过,如上所言,生产镶嵌尖状器的成本比生产有机或石质尖状器成本更高。平衡镶嵌尖状器高成本的因素就是灾难性或致命性的失败成本:需要多次使用,没有替代品,此时猎物至关重要,必须在有限的时间内获取,猎物非常危险或是敌人近在咫尺,还有武器使用的环境非常寒冷,这些状况使得镶嵌尖状器的制作有利可图。

四、两面器与细石叶在提供边刃上的相对效率

获取原料之后,准备各种楔形石核的第一步都涉及某种程度的两面器生产(参见本书布雷德的文章)。因此,我们需要假定所有史前制作细石叶的石器打制者可能生产了两面器,如果需要使用的时候会用作工具。某些地方的石器组合中确实存在两面器用作工具与尖头部件的情况(西伯利亚的久克太洞,日本的上ノ平与荒,中国的虎头梁与鸽子山盆地),另有一些地方,单面修理的石片(西伯利亚的阿方托瓦戈拉-2遗址)与大石叶(西伯利亚的科科里沃-2遗址)的功能同于两面加工的石刀与尖状器。

这样的变化无疑是多维的,我们通过比较生产两面器与细石叶的成本收益,

研究了其中的几个方面。我们的分析采用的是弗兰尼肯[23]的实验材料(表8.3)。为了比较两种技术在时间与原料耗费上的差别,弗兰尼肯的实验通过复制久克太两面器石核生产细石叶,以及制作两面器。从毛坯的打制开始,他选择差不多大小的大石片同时生产楔形石核与两面器。弗兰尼肯[24]从实验中得出结论,两面器的生产在运用石料上很不经济,因为生产的细石叶(每个石核平均生产101片)可以占到预制石核重量的41.6%,而两面器成品只占到毛坯重量的29.5%。不过,我们的分析表明这个结论可能并不正确,因为弗兰尼肯显然没有计算毛坯生产过程中浪费的比例,同样他也没有包括细石叶生产最后的生产步骤。

表8.3 细石叶与两面器的制作实验,基于弗兰尼肯[25]的材料

打片阶段	平均重量(g)	前面的阶段	前面阶段的比例
细石叶			
最初的石片	没有		
第2阶段的两面器	219.1		
两面修理的预制石核(雪橇形削片剥离)	158.8	第2阶段两面器	72.48
耗尽的细石核	33.4	预制石核	21.03
预制的细石核重量减去耗尽的细石核重量	125.4		
每个石核平均有101件可用细石叶	没有		
每个预制石核生产的细石叶(等于41.6%的预制石核重量)	66.06	第2阶段两面器	30.15
细石叶生产的嵌刃	33.0	第2阶段两面器	15.06
两面器			
最初的石片	没有		
第2阶段的两面器(跟细石叶生产的路径相似)	219.1	第2阶段两面器	
完成的两面器	64.6		29.5

弗兰尼肯[26]没有报道用于打制实验的石片毛坯的平均重量。不过,用第2阶段两面器的平均重量作为出发点,通过报道出来的产品与废片的比例追溯生产过程,我们能够估计出来关键产品的重量,以及副产品的重量。弗兰尼肯所说

第2阶段用于生产细石叶石核的两面器"毛坯"平均重量为219.1克。我们假定弗兰尼肯所谓生产两面器的"毛坯",也就是第2阶段的两面器。这个假定很重要,也是合理的,因为(1)每次用于打制实验的石片大小都差不多;(2)弗兰尼肯报道的细石叶石核(第2阶段的两面器)与正式的两面器("毛坯")开始的重量是相等的。

基于上述假定的等同性所进行的比较表明,多达69.85%的原材料在生产细石叶石核的预制、打制与维护的过程中浪费了,仅有30.15%的原料转化成了细石叶。完整两面器生产浪费了70.5%的原材料;29.5%的重量还留在成品上。

这个比较表明两种技术在原材料的节省程度上并没有明显的区别。不过还存在与技术相关的潜在成本与收益。值得注意的是,相当一部分细石叶不过是石碴,并不堪用。用于镶嵌的细石叶通常需要打掉细石叶毛坯的两端,这大致要占到完整细石叶重量的三分之一到二分之一。因此,弗兰尼肯实验中每个石核生产的66克细石叶只有33克可以用于镶嵌,仅占最初毛坯重量的15.06%,不到成型两面器产量的一半。弗兰尼肯还指出细石叶的生产更耗时,他生产大约100片细石叶平均要花费51分钟,每个石核(不包括热处理的时间)要耗费两倍于生产两面器的时间。因此,跟细石叶生产相比,两面器生产似乎耗费时间更少,原料利用上更节省。

与此同时,我们要知道两面器与细石叶可能代表两种不同技术形式,并不能通过诸如原料重量这样的标准进行比较。注意我们讨论的中心是镶嵌细石叶与石质尖状器相对的使用特征。石质尖状器由于有锋利的刃缘而杀伤力更强。如果我们假定可用边刃的长度是需要最大化的目标[27],生产时间是需要最小化的成本,那么我们就有了比较的共同标准。弗兰尼肯实验的两面器平均长度15厘米,因此最大边刃长度30厘米(如果装柄的话,长度就要短一些)。平均每个石核生产101件细石叶,假如每片细石叶长度2厘米,那么每个石核就能生产202厘米长的边刃,差不多七倍于实验两面器的边刃长度,而花费的时间只有两倍,原料成本则是一样的。

但是,也许有人认为两面器能够反复修理,这会增加它的使用价值。一件两面器确实可以用作刮削器或是刀子,能够反复修理多次,使用寿命比较长,而一件两面器的投掷尖状器使用最多几次就可能彻底报废[28]。大多数石质两面器尖状器不可能反复修理到堪比细石叶石核的程度,要知道平均每个石核能生产202厘米细石叶边刃。在成为细石叶石核之前,两面器可以用作工具,日本[29]与中国[30]就看到这样的例子,两面器削薄石片与预制细石叶石核的雪橇形削片还可以用作工具或是工具毛坯,这都增加了细石叶石核的用途。这种循环使用的方式能够减少原料的需求,并能提供额外的边刃[31],这不需要标准的镶嵌细石叶来提供,也不用作投掷尖状器的边刃。通过实验复制与模拟分析成本收益似乎已经成熟。

五、船底形细石核与楔形细石核的效率比较

亚洲细石叶石核经常分成许多类型[32],成(Seong)[33]做了项有意义的工作,将这些杂乱的类型简化为四个基本类型。本文中我们只区分为两种基本的制作方法:对劈砾石所制的船底形石核,以及通过两面器毛坯制作的楔形石核(图8.2,A、B)[34]。

A → 两面器毛坯　　台面打制　　剥离细石叶

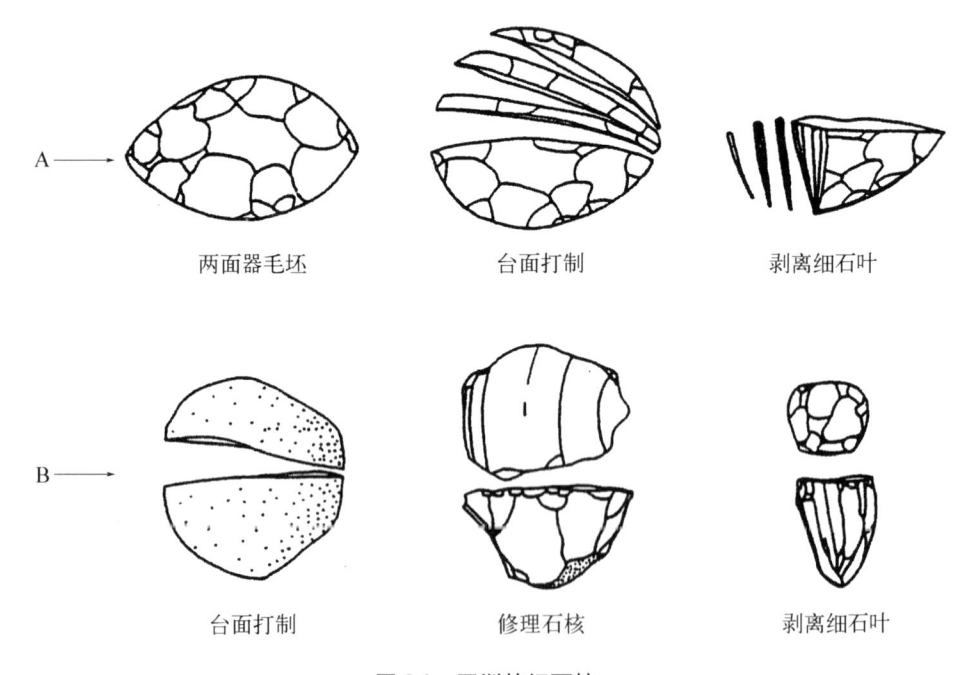

B → 台面打制　　修理石核　　剥离细石叶

图8.2　亚洲的细石核

(A. 从两面器毛坯生产的楔形细石核;B. 通过对劈砾石毛坯制作的船形细石核)[35]

利用船底形石核只需少量步骤就可以生产细石叶[36]。船底形石核的一个主要优势就在于它通常可以利用砾石大小的原石来制作,而这种石料许多地方都能得到。预制船底形石核只需要非常少的几个步骤,这样可以得到很高比例的砾石毛坯用以生产细石叶[37]。预制过程的步骤越少,石核加工失败的风险也就越低,因为几乎不可能出错。相反,以加工两面器的方式预制楔形石核需要更大的原石,当地不一定出产。楔形石核的预制是在两面器加工完成后开始的,首先剥离一条边刃(也就是雪橇形的削片),形成台面,然后调整台面的边缘,使其切合固定装置,再后就是剥离一条冠状石叶,剥片面成形(参见图8.2,A,本书布雷德的文章[38])。

尽管我们现在还没有实验材料的支持,但是我们可以认为楔形石核相对于船底形石核的优势在于它生产的细石叶更加规整。楔形石核上生产的细石叶宽度、厚度变化小,腹面与侧边更平直,截面多呈梯形,所有这些特点都有助于用作嵌刃有机工具的边刃。比如,QG3出土一批细石叶,这个中石器时代遗址位于中国宁夏鸽子山盆地[39]。其细石叶可以分为两类。一类为生产型细石叶,用于镶嵌;另一类为维护型细石叶,用于调整石核半径,维护石核的最佳的形状。QG3遗址生产型细石叶与维护型细石叶的比例表明,每得到一片生产型的细石叶,就会产生超过一片的维护型细石叶。前者更宽、更薄,两边更平行,腹面更平直,偶尔还会修理。注意表8.4中QG3遗址生产型的细石叶的厚度平均值与标准差都更小。这表明QG3的石器打制者注意将生产型细石叶的厚度限定在一个狭窄的适合镶嵌的范围内。

表8.4 中国宁夏QG3遗址生产与维护细石叶的宽度与厚度

	数量	平均宽	标准差	平均厚	标准差
生产	81	6.00	1.79	1.56	0.69
维护	130	5.23	1.58	1.76	1.68

楔形石核控制细石叶差异的方式可以通过一个简单的石核几何形模型来说明(图8.3),其关系由三个变量来表示:石核工作面(也就是细石叶剥离的剥片面)的半径,剥离细石叶的厚度与宽度。

可以先把石核的工作面想象成一个圆柱体,其平面形状(从台面上往下看)就像一个圆半径为 r 的弧(图8.3,b)。剥离细石叶的宽就相当于弦 c ,细石叶的厚度也就是 x 。x 与 c 垂直相交。

根据勾股定理:

$$r^2 = (r-x)2 + \left(\frac{c}{2}\right)^2 \tag{1}$$

以 c 为中心重组方程

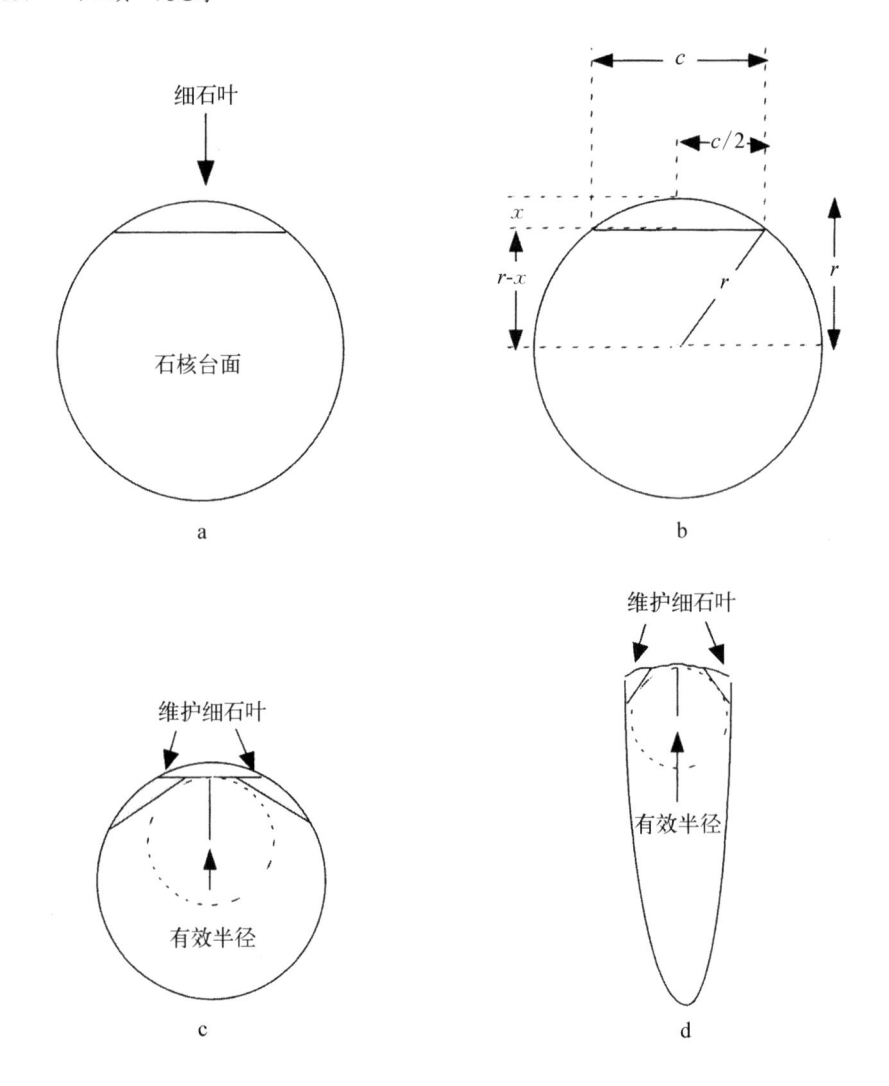

图 8.3 石核几何图形的简化模型

（a. 石核台面与细石叶；b. 几何关系；c. 维护石叶不断缩小的有效半径；d. 楔形石核的有效半径更小）

$$c = 2\sqrt{2(rx) - x^2} \qquad (2)$$

石核工作面的维护对所有细石叶石核来说都是必要的，因为细石叶的剥离会不断提高 r（细石叶宽度对应的圆的半径）（图 8.3，c）。当 r 能够随意提高的时候，维护工作面宽的石核的效率就比较低，而楔形石核较窄的工作面能将 r 限制在一定范围内时，其维护更有效率（图 8.3，d）。楔形石核只需要剥离很少的材料(即更小的维护型细石叶)就可以达到维护的目的。

为了说明 c 与 x 的关系。图 8.4 显示根据方程 2 所得细石叶宽度 c 与 r 的关系,其中厚度 x 是个常数(采用 QG3 遗址生产型细石叶的平均值 1.56 毫米),r 在 2 毫米至 40 毫米之间变化。随着 r 变大,宽度 c 也增大,但是增加的速率递减。因此可以说,当 r 较小时(小于 10 毫米),对石核的微小调整都将对细石叶的宽度 c 产生较大的影响。

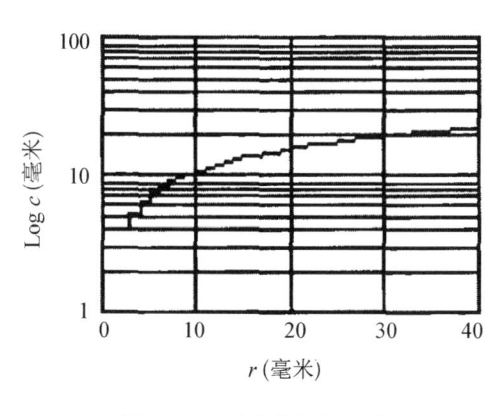

图 8.4 石核半径与细石叶宽度对数的梯状图

以 r 为中心重组方程(1):

$$r = \frac{1}{2}\left(\frac{x^2 + \frac{1}{4}c^2}{x}\right) \tag{3}$$

QG3 遗址生产型细石叶平均宽为 6.00 毫米,平均厚为 1.56 毫米(表 8.4)。根据方程 3,似乎可以说 QG3 的石器制作者采用的是工作面半径为 3.7 毫米的细石核,比 BB 弹稍大。鉴于这个值小于遗址中发现的任何适合的宽度,我们假定古代石器制作者可能已经通过剥离维护型细石叶,以及用其他方式在生产型细石叶剥离之前消除了生产型细石叶的台面限制,从而形成了当地有效半径较小的特征。而在较宽的圆柱形石核上(图 8.3,c),这一过程可能导致更多的变化,比较窄的楔形石核更浪费原料(图 8.3,d)。

六、风险与细石叶技术

考古材料表明船底形石核与楔形石核不是前后发展或是进化的关系。日本首先出现的是船底形石核,后来为楔形石核所取代[40];但是,朝鲜半岛首先出现的是楔形石核,后来出现的是船底形石核[41]。中国的情况是船底形石核最早,但是楔形石核出现后,船底形石核还在使用[42]。西伯利亚地区,最早的细石叶是由微型棱柱状或锥形石叶石核生产的;随后,真正的细石核包括船底形石核与楔形石核出现[43]。就此而言,石器组合中船底形石核对楔形石核的比例似乎反映许多条件因素。某些情况下,标准一致是首重的目标;另外的情况下,则又不是。某些这样的变化来自原料的供给状况[44],但大多情况下可能跟规避风险有关。

温特豪尔德等[45]将风险定义为"某一行为结果中难以预测的变化",跟适合度或实用性相关。鉴于结果是非线性的,所以行为分析中用到一种风险敏感的模型,也就是 Z-score 模型[46]。风险敏感分析要求首先确定或估计每个行为的概率结果,明确其实用性或适合度的量值与结果。大多数风险敏感性研究表明人与动物都惯于规避风险,食物选择中的冒险行为常常与可怕的短缺相关。

Z-score 模型计算资源短缺的概率,它以短缺阈值(r_{min})与期望收益的平均值(μ)与标准差(σ)的距离来衡量:

$$Z = \frac{r_{min} - \bar{\mu}}{\bar{\sigma}} \quad (4)$$

当平均期望收益低于短缺阈值(r_{min})的时候,变化范围更大的行为(更高的 Z)的概率就会提高,超越短缺阈值,最终减小整体的风险。如图 8.5 所示,行为 a 与行为 b 的平均值都在 r 之下,但是模型预测行为 b(具有更大的标准差 σ)应该更受偏好。相反,当平均期望收益高于 r 的时候,Z 将是负的,变化范围更小的行为(更低的 σ)风险更小。图 8.5 中,行为 c 与 d 的平均值都在 r 之上,行为 c

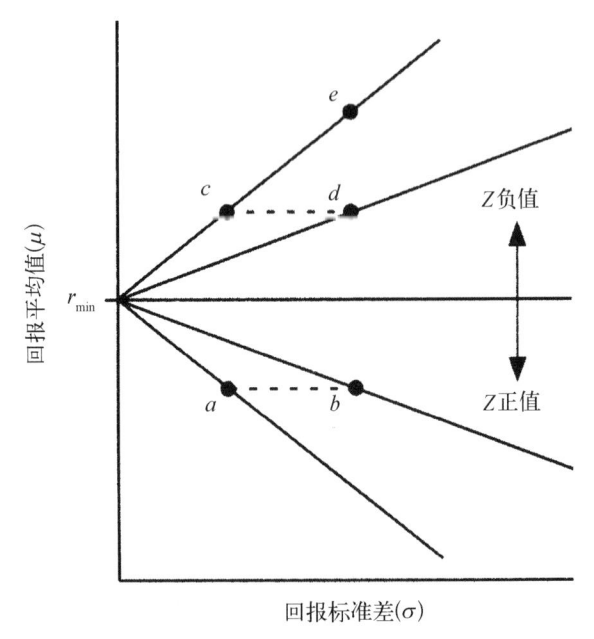

图 8.5 风险敏感的 Z-score 模型的等值图[47]

的 Z 值更小,应该比行为 d 更受偏好。如果两点落在同一线上,即 Z 值相同,觅食者的选择就不在意选择哪一个了(如图 8.5 中的行为 c 与行为 e)。

就细石叶技术而言,楔形石核与船底形石核在生产细石叶上很可能各自具有不同概率分布。尽管我们还不能确定它们的概率,但是我们怀疑楔形石核降低细石叶产品的变化范围。如果准确性与规整程度是细石叶生产所必需的,Z-score 模型就可以提供一个普遍的预测框架。

图 8.6 模拟了这些关系,其纵轴表示可能的收益值;狩猎收益短缺阈值用水平的断线表示,低于这个阈值就很可能发生饥饿;楔形石核(W)与船底形石核(B)细石叶生产的平均值和标准差以点、线表示。这里行为 W 与行为 B 的平均值相同,但是行为 B 的标准差更大一些。为了便于表述,让我们假定不同的技术行为影响狩猎成功的概率。当期望收益高于这个阈值时,失败的成本就高(如冬季远离中心营地狩猎),狩猎者需要做出选择,降低行为的变化范围。当短缺阈值等于 $r_{min}a$ 时,行为 W 与行为 B 的平均值都高于它,图 8.6 中表示了这种情况。通过楔形石核(W)生产细石叶就是更好的选择,因为船底形石核的范围可能落在 $r_{min}a$ 之下。

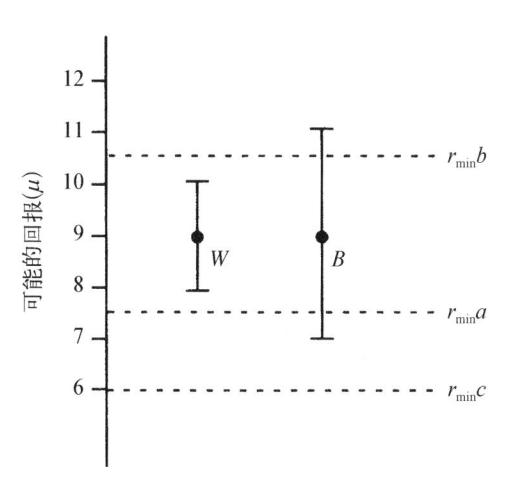

图 8.6 细石叶生产采用楔形石核(W)与船形石核(B)的选择模型以及与假定的生产短缺阈值($r_{min}a$–c)的关系

(黑点与垂直线段分别代表 W 与 B 的平均值与标准差。对风险 $r_{min}a$ 而言,选择楔形石核将可以降低落在阈值之下的风险;而在 $r_{min}b$ 时,选择船形石核将更可能碰到阈值。当阈值在 $r_{min}c$ 时,无论采用楔形还是船形石核都不存在落在阈值之下的风险;居于其中选择更多考虑的是非风险因素)

此种情况下,船底形石核(B)如果可能的话,就不应该使用。如果把楔形石核同时部分用作携带的狩猎工具,从而保证高质量替代部件的供给,那么变化与风险还能够进一步降低。狩猎者可能在出发的地方批量生产了细石叶,携带过程可能带来磨损与断裂[48]。进一步说,携带的补给可能不足以应付所有不时之需。因此许多情况下(但不是所有的),携带石核更有利于减小收益的变动。

如果同样这些猎人发现所需要的细石叶超过楔形石核所能生产的,那么怎么办呢?图 8.6 中,短缺阈值等于 $r_{min}b$ 时涉及这种情况。行为 W 与行为 B 的平均值相等,都位于$r_{min}b$之下,但模型预测狩猎者应该采用能够得到的材料生产细石叶,包括对劈砾石的船底形石核(B)。这种方法至少有一线机会超越短缺阈值($r_{min}b$)。此时,可用细石叶相对于废料的比例相对较低,即便产品的变化程度较大,其影响也有限,因为成本很小。图8.6同时帮助我们想象短缺阈值($r_{min}c$)在两种细石叶生产技术平均值之下的情况。此时觅食者从降低风险的角度来看,可以不必在意究竟采用船底形还是楔形石核,但是其他偶然因素可能会有影响。比如,如果猎物的组成结构随季节变化,为关键性狩猎准备的生产在某些季节可能用不上。或者某些类型的个体倾向于采用产品变化更大的技术,这样的话,在细石叶生产技术中我们可能看到船底形石核用于训练孩子,或者女性在营地周围采用船底形石核制作自己需要的工具。

问题不是上述的哪种方案能够真实反映史前人类的行为,而是包括 Z‑score 模型在内的风险敏感性模型有助于确定石器变化的范围,以不同于类型学的方式更有效地实现这一目的。原则上,Z‑score 模型在研究细石叶组合上的作用是非常直接的。模型表明风险应该制约细石叶大小、原料、石核大小以及生产技术上的变化。可以评估史前时代不同情况下的相对风险(参见本书 Bleed 的文章),将之按照等级排列,一头代表时间非常紧急的大动物如驯鹿的狩猎,另一头可能是夏季居住营地的狩猎。检验假说需要测量石器组合细石叶以及细石核生产过程中的废品,这些石器组合要大小足够、保存完整。遗憾的是北亚地区符合上述标准的石器组合材料凤毛麟角。以后的研究中应该坚持使用细筛并注意在组合分析中进行细致的测量。

七、北亚细石器技术的起源

尽管我们认为北亚地区采用嵌刃尖状器是有条件与偶然的,但是我们现在只能够把它的用途与最一般性的环境特征结合起来。细石器技术与纬度的关系非常密切,它主要分布于北纬33°到70°之间[49],从中国最西部、西伯利亚到太平洋海岸、库页岛以及日本列岛。这种偏北的分布特征表明亚洲细石器技术与嵌刃武器有可能是为了解决漫长而严酷的冬季狩猎资源贫乏且难以捕猎的难题,一旦不能狩猎到足够的猎物,就可能会有致命的后果[50]。

这一假说进一步得到细石器技术出现时间的支持,戈贝尔(本书)做了相关的总结。北亚狩猎采集者可能在末次盛冰期时已经开始试验使用细石器技术了,尽管还不像冰后期那么流行,它的高峰最有可能是在距今 17 000 至 18 000 年前。生产细石叶所需要的许多技巧与知识在西伯利亚旧石器时代晚期早段就已具备,但是中国除了水洞沟遗址短时间出现过之外[51],其他地区并无分布。间接打击技术与运用专用的工具精确压制石叶技术使得石器打制者能够克服工具原石大小的限制。细石器技术的发明与发展总的来说很可能是减小觅食风险的关键策略。

以上方案目前仍然只能看作是假说,还需要进一步的检验。中国发现的动物遗存非常少。西伯利亚倒是有不少动物群信息(戈贝尔,本书中的文章),表明细石叶可能用于狩猎驯鹿。然而,现在还没有可以用来评估食谱宽度、不同部位利用率、猎物群体变化以及季节性的详细动物遗存信息。

晚更新世该地区普遍的资料是气候干冷,冰后期变化加剧,对人类来说冬季并没有因此而更好过些。进一步说,气候变暖导致"猛犸象动物群"[52]的分布北移,剩下的动物也不得不寻找适宜的栖息地。例如,中国的鄂尔多斯与腾格尔沙漠地区大湖重新出现[53],但是我们怀疑大动物能否在这些"绿洲"边栖息,狩猎压力很快就能耗光这里的资源。西伯利亚的情况可能也是如此,鲍尔斯[54]称这种环境为"超级生态带"(hyperzonal),这个地带缺乏我们今天看到的植被,但是它被分割成许多小型的资源斑块,包括草原、森林与苔原。这帮助我们解释某些晚更新世考古遗址中丰富多样的动物遗存,对狩猎者的影响很可能是他们不得不提高流动性,因为某些小"优质斑块"可能很快会被耗尽。如果此时人口还在增长的话,就会进一步提高对已经萎缩的动物群资源的压力,导致狩猎的收获变化不定。细石器技术可以视为人们强化大动物狩猎策略的组成部分,它可以帮助应对日益加剧的季节变化与关键资源的不确定性。

更新世至全新世过渡期大动物狩猎还很重要,嵌刃尖状器还在继续使用,都表明动物仍然是关键的资源。不过,此时猎物的短缺与高度的变化不再只是季节性的,而是持续存在着。大约从距今14 000年开始,人们开始采用新的技术以利用更低级别的食物资源如植物种子,南西伯利亚、蒙古与中国等地出现磨制石器与陶器就是标志[55]。随着新技术在这里的应用,新石器时代农业最终解决了这一系列的生计难题,人们一般使用的技术中细石叶减少[56]。细石叶逐步仅残存于北亚与新大陆的部分地区,这里农业出现较晚,或是不可行;在某些环境斑块中,狩猎对于保障越冬来说虽然具有风险,但仍然是不可或缺的生计策略。当然,正如本书所说明,作为用以应对寒冷气候大动物狩猎风险的策略,并不能解释世界其他地区的细石器技术与复合工具,这些地区的气候并不寒冷,也不狩猎大型动物(如西南亚、澳大利亚)。不过,运用细石器与复合工具可能有助于减少狩猎采集者面对的其他风险(利用时间非常有限的关键资源、仇敌等)。

八、结论

本文的目标是想从适应策略与风险管理的角度思考细石器技术,而不是继续研究起源与类型学问题。我们相信这一方法有助于我们理解细石叶在北亚狩猎采集者的经济生活中所扮演的多重角色。风险与作用的形式模型(如 Z-score 模型、运输成本模型、石器获取模型、工具作用模型)与复制实验相结合将可以解释当地与大范围区域石器组合上的变化[57]。不过,如果没有更好的动物群材料的话,这些模型不可能形成可以完全检验的假说。尽管大部分西伯利亚动物群组合的材料还需要运用现代动物考古学方法来分析,但是这些材料毕竟还在那里。中国的情况更不理想,这里很少有晚更新世的遗址为人所知,有动物群清单的遗址更少。我们希望通过证明这种方法的作用,让更多的考古学家对运用它感兴趣。

注释:

[1] Chard, C. S. *Northeast Asia in Prehistory*. Madison: University of Wisconsin Press, 1974.

Chen, C. The Microlithic of China. *Journal of Anthropological Archaeology* 1(3): 79–115, 1984.

Chen, C, and X. Wang. Upper Paleolithic Microblade Industries in North China and Their Relationships with Northeast Asia and North America. *Arctic Anthropology* 26(2): 144–145, 1989.

Derev'anko, A. P., ed. *The Paleolithic of Siberia*. Urbana: University of Illinois Press, 1998.

Gai, P. Microlithic Industries in China. In *Paleoanthropology and Paleolithic Archaeology in the People's Republic of China*. R. Wu and J. Olsen, eds. Pp. 225–242. New York: Academic, 1985.

Goebel, T. The Record of Human Occupation of the Russian Subarctic and Arctic. *Byrd Polar Research Center Miscellaneous Series* M–335: 41–46, 1995.

Goebel, T., M. R. Waters, I. Buvit, M. V. Konstantinov, and A. V. Konstantinov. Studenoe-2 and the Origins of Microblade Technologies in the Transbaikal, Siberia. Antiquity 74: 567–575, 2000.

Goebel, T., and S. B. Slobodin. The Colonization of Western Beringia: Technology, Ecology, and Adaptations. In *Ice Age Peoples of North America: Environments, Origins, and Adaptations of the First Americans*. R. Bonnichsen and K. L. Turnmire, eds. Pp. 104–155. Corvallis: Oregon State University Press, 1999.

Hoffecker, J. F., W. P. Powers, and T. Goebel. The Colonization of Beringia and the Peopling of the New World. *Science* 259: 46 – 53, 1993.

Kobayashi, T. Microblade Industries in the Japanese Archipelago. *Arctic Anthropology* 7(2): 38 – 58, 1970.

Kuzmin, Y. V., and L. A. Orlova. Radiocarbon Chronology of the Siberian Paleolithic. *Journal of World Prehistory* 12(1): 1 – 53, 1998.

Lu, T. L. D. The Microblade Tradition in China: Regional Chronologies and Significance in the Transition to Neolithic. *Asian Perspectives* 37(1): 85 – 112, 1998.

Seong, C. Microblade Technology in Korea and Adjacent Northeast Asia. *Asian Perspectives* 37 (2): 245 – 278, 1998.

[2] Seong, C. Microblade Technology in Korea and Adjacent Northeast Asia. *Asian Perspectives* 37 (2): 245 – 278, 1998.

[3] Bamforth, D. B., and P. Bleed. Technology, Flaked Stone Technology, and Risk. In *Rediscovering Darwin: Evolutionary Theory and Archeological Explanation*. C. M. Barton and G. A. Clark, eds. Pp. 109 – 139. Archeological Papers of the American Anthropological Association, 7. Arlington, Va.: American Anthropological Association, 1997.

Bleed, P. The Optimal Design of Hunting Weapons: Maintainability or Reliability. *American Antiquity* 51 (4): 737 – 747, 1987.

Ellis, C. J. Factors Influencing the Use of Stone Projectile Tips. In *Projectile Technology*. H. Knecht, ed. Pp. 37 – 74. New York: Plenum, 1997.

Knecht, H. Early Upper Paleolithic Approaches to Bone and Antler Projectile Technology. In *Hunting and Animal Exploitation in the Later Paleolithic and Mesolithic of Eurasia*. G. L. Peterkin, H. M. Bricker, and P. Mellars, eds. Pp. 33 – 47. Archeological Papers of the American Anthropological Association, 4. Arlington, Va.: American Anthropological Association, 1993.

Projectile Points of Bone, Antler, and Stone: Experimental Explorations of Manufacture and Use. In *Projectile Technology*. H. Knecht, ed. Pp. 191 – 212. New York: Plenum, 1997.

[4] Bettinger, R. L. *Hunter-Gatherers: Archaeological and Evolutionary Theory*. New York: Plenum, 1991.

Stephens, D. W. The Logic of Risk-Sensitive Foraging Preferences. *Animal Behavior* 26: 628 – 629, 1981.

Stephens, D. W., and E. L. Charnov. Optimal Foraging: Some Simple Stochastic Models. *Behavioral Ecology and Sociobiology* 10: 252 – 263, 1982.

Winterhalder, B. P., F. Lu, and B. Tucker. Risk-Sensitive Adaptive Tactics: Models and Evidence from Subsistence Studies in Biology and Anthropology. *Journal of Archaeological*

Research 7(4): 301 – 348, 1999.

[5] Chard, C. S. *Northeast Asia in Prehistory*. Madison: University of Wisconsin Press, 1974: fig.1.16.

Derev'anko, A. P., ed. *The Paleolithic of Siberia*. Urbana: University of Illinois Press, 1998: figs.87, 127.

[6] Chard, C. S. *Northeast Asia in Prehistory*. Madison: University of Wisconsin Press, 1974: fig.2.14, 2.16.

Guo, D. S. Hongshan and Related Cultures. In *The Archaeology of Northeast China: Beyond the Great Wall*. S. M. Nelson, ed. New York: Routledge, 1995: fig.1.11.

Lu, T. L. D. The Microblade Tradition in China: Regional Chronologies and Significance in the Transition to Neolithic. Asian Perspectives 37(1): 92, 1998.

[7] Elston, R. G., C. Xu, D. B. Madsen, K. Zhong, R. L. Bettinger, J. Li, P. J. Brantingham, H. Wang, and J. Yu. New Dates for the North China Mesolithic. *Antiquity* 71: 985 – 993, 1997.

Gai, P. Microlithic Industries in China. In *Paleoanthropology and Paleolithic Archaeology in the People's Republic of China*. R. Wu and J. Olsen, eds. Pp. 225 – 242. New York: Academic, 1985.

Lu, T. L. D. The Microblade Tradition in China: Regional Chronologies and Significance in the Transition to Neolithic. Asian Perspectives 37(1): 92, 1998.

Madsen, D. B., R. G. Elston, X. Chen, R. L. Bettinger. Z. Kan, J. Brantingham, and A. L. Jingjen. The Loess/Paleosol Record and the Nature of the Younger Dryas Climate in Central China. *Geoarchaeology* 13(8): 847 – 869, 1998.

[8] Chang, K. C. *The Archaeology of Ancient China*. 4th ed. New Haven: Yale University Press, 1986: figs.49, 52, 126.

Shih, X. The Discovery of the Pre-Yangshao Culture and Its Significance. In *Pacific Northeast Asia in Prehistory*. C. M. Aikens and S. N. Rhee, eds. Pp. 125 – 132. Pullman: Washington State University Press, 1992: figs.8, 9.

Underhill, A. P. Current Issues in Chinese Neolithic Archaeology. *Journal of World Prehistory* 11(2): 103 – 160, 1997: fig.4.

[9] Lu, T. L. D. The Microblade Tradition in China: Regional Chronologies and Significance in the Transition to Neolithic. Asian Perspectives 37(1): 92, 1998.

[10] Knecht, H. Projectile Points of Bone, Antler, and Stone: Experimental Explorations of Manufacture and Use. In *Projectile Technology*. H. Knecht, ed. Pp. 191 – 212. New York: Plenum, 1997.

[11] Knecht, H. Early Upper Paleolithic Approaches to Bone and Antler Projectile Technology. In

Hunting and Animal Exploitation in the Later Paleolithic and Mesolithic of Eurasia. G. L. Peterkin, H. M. Bricker, and P. Mellars, eds. Pp. 33 – 47. Archeological Papers of the American Anthropological Association, 4. Arlington, Va.: American Anthropological Association, 1993.

Projectile Points of Bone, Antler, and Stone: Experimental Explorations of Manufacture and Use. In *Projectile Technology*. H. Knecht, ed. Pp. 191 – 212. New York: Plenum, 1997.

[12] Ellis, C. J. Factors Influencing the Use of Stone Projectile Tips. In *Projectile Technology*. H. Knecht, ed. Pp. 37 – 74. New York: Plenum, 1997.

[13] Bamforth, D. B., and P. Bleed. Technology, Flaked Stone Technology, and Risk. In *Rediscovering Darwin: Evolutionary Theory and Archeological Explanation*. C. M. Barton and G. A. Clark, eds. Pp. 129. Archeological Papers of the American Anthropological Association, 7. Arlington, Va.: American Anthropological Association, 1997.

[14] Knecht, H. Projectile Points of Bone, Antler, and Stone: Experimental Explorations of Manufacture and Use. In *Projectile Technology*. H. Knecht, ed. Pp. 191 – 212. New York: Plenum, 1997.

[15] Ellis, C. J. Factors Influencing the Use of Stone Projectile Tips. In *Projectile Technology*. H. Knecht, ed. Pp. 37 – 74. New York: Plenum, 1997.

[16] Bamforth, D. B., and P. Bleed. Technology, Flaked Stone Technology, and Risk. In *Rediscovering Darwin: Evolutionary Theory and Archeological Explanation*. C. M. Barton and G. A. Clark, eds. Pp. 109 – 139. Archeological Papers of the American Anthropological Association, 7. Arlington, Va.: American Anthropological Association, 1997.

Torrence, R. Retooling: Toward a Behavioral Theory of Stone Tools. In *Time, Energy and Stone Tools*. R. Torrence, ed. Pp. 57 – 66. Cambridge: Cambridge University Press, 1989.

[17] Bleed, P. The Optimal Design of Hunting Weapons: Maintainability or Reliability. *American Antiquity* 51 (4): 737 – 747, 1987.

[18] Flenniken, J. J. The Paleolithic Dyuktai Pressure Blade Technique of Siberia. *Arctic Anthropology* 24(2): 117 – 132, 1987.

Tabarev, A. V. Paleolithic Wedge-Shaped Microcores and Experiments with Pocket Devices. *Lithic Technology* 22(2): 139 – 149, 1997.

[19] Bamforth, D. B., and P. Bleed. Technology, Flaked Stone Technology, and Risk. In *Rediscovering Darwin: Evolutionary Theory and Archeological Explanation*. C. M. Barton and G. A. Clark, eds. Pp. 132. Archeological Papers of the American Anthropological Association, 7. Arlington, Va.: American Anthropological Association, 1997.

[20] Flenniken, J. J. The Paleolithic Dyuktai Pressure Blade Technique of Siberia. *Arctic Anthropology* 24(2): 117 – 132, 1987.

[21] Ellis, C. J. Factors Influencing the Use of Stone Projectile Tips. In *Projectile Technology*. H. Knecht, ed. Pp. 37 – 74. New York: Plenum, 1997.

[22] Bamforth, D. B., and P. Bleed. Technology, Flaked Stone Technology, and Risk. In *Rediscovering Darwin: Evolutionary Theory and Archeological Explanation*. C. M. Barton and G. A. Clark, eds. Pp. 132. Archeological Papers of the American Anthropological Association, 7. Arlington, Va.: American Anthropological Association, 1997.

Kuhn, S. L. A Formal Approach to the Design and Assembly of Mobile Toolkits. *American Antiquity* 59(3): 426 – 442, 1994.

[23] Flenniken, J. J. The Paleolithic Dyuktai Pressure Blade Technique of Siberia. *Arctic Anthropology* 24(2): 117 – 132, 1987.

[24] Flenniken, J. J. The Paleolithic Dyuktai Pressure Blade Technique of Siberia. *Arctic Anthropology* 24(2): 122 – 132, 1987.

[25] Flenniken, J. J. The Paleolithic Dyuktai Pressure Blade Technique of Siberia. *Arctic Anthropology* 24(2): 122 – 132, 1987.

[26] Flenniken, J. J. The Paleolithic Dyuktai Pressure Blade Technique of Siberia. *Arctic Anthropology* 24(2): 117 – 132, 1987.

[27] Kuhn, S. L. A Formal Approach to the Design and Assembly of Mobile Toolkits. *American Antiquity* 59(3): 426 – 442, 1994.

[28] Rondeau, Michael F. When Is an Elko? In *Stone Tools: Theoretical Insights into Human Prehistory*. George H. Odell, ed. Pp. 229 – 243. New York: Plenum, 1996.

[29] Bamforth, D. B., and P. Bleed. Technology, Flaked Stone Technology, and Risk. In *Rediscovering Darwin: Evolutionary Theory and Archeological Explanation*. C. M. Barton and G. A. Clark, eds. Pp. 109 – 139. Archeological Papers of the American Anthropological Association, 7. Arlington, Va.: American Anthropological Association, 1997.

[30] Lu, T. L. D. The Microblade Tradition in China: Regional Chronologies and Significance in the Transition to Neolithic. *Asian Perspectives* 37(1): 85 – 112, 1998.

[31] Kelly, R. L. The Three Sides of a Biface. *American Antiquity* 53(4): 717 – 734, 1988.

Kuhn, S. L. A Formal Approach to the Design and Assembly of Mobile Toolkits. *American Antiquity* 59(3): 426 – 442, 1994.

[32] Chen, C, and X. Wang. Upper Paleolithic Microblade Industries in North China and Their Relationships with Northeast Asia and North America. *Arctic Anthropology* 26(2): 144 – 145, 1989.

Morlan, R. E. Technological Characteristics of Some Wedge-Shaped Cores in Northwestern North America and Northeast Asia. *Asian Perspectives* 19(1): 96 – 106, 1976.

[33] Seong, C. Microblade Technology in Korea and Adjacent Northeast Asia. *Asian Perspectives* 37

(2): 245-278, 1998.

[34] Kobayashi, T. Microblade Industries in the Japanese Archipelago. *Arctic Anthropology* 7(2): 38-58, 1970.

[35] Kobayashi, T. Microblade Industries in the Japanese Archipelago. *Arctic Anthropology* 7(2): 38-58, 1970.

[36] Morlan, R. E. Technological Characteristics of Some Wedge-Shaped Cores in Northwestern North America and Northeast Asia. *Asian Perspectives* 19(1): 96-106, 1976.

[37] Seong, C. Microblade Technology in Korea and Adjacent Northeast Asia. *Asian Perspectives* 37(2): 272-274, 1998.

[38] Flenniken, J. J. The Paleolithic Dyuktai Pressure Blade Technique of Siberia. *Arctic Anthropology* 24(2): 117-132, 1987.

Tabarev, A. V. Paleolithic Wedge-Shaped Microcores and Experiments with Pocket Devices. *Lithic Technology* 22(2): 139-149, 1997.

[39] Elston, R. G., C. Xu, D. B. Madsen, K. Zhong, R. L. Bettinger, J. Li, P. J. Brantingham, H. Wang, and J. Yu. New Dates for the North China Mesolithic. *Antiquity* 71: 985-993, 1997.

Madsen, D. B., R. G. Elston, X. Chen, R. L. Bettinger. Z. Kan, J. Brantingham, and A. L. Jingjen. The Loess/Paleosol Record and the Nature of the Younger Dryas Climate in Central China. *Geoarchaeology* 13(8): 847-869, 1998.

[40] Aikens, C. M., and T. Higuchi. *Prehistory of Japan*. New York: Academic, 1982.

Andrefsky, W., Jr. Diffusion and Innovation from the Perspective of Wedge Shaped Cores in Alaska and Japan. In *The Organization of Core Technology*. J. K. Johnson and C. A. Morrow, eds. Pp. 13-43. Boulder: Westview, 1987.

Kobayashi, T. Microblade Industries in the Japanese Archipelago. *Arctic Anthropology* 7(2): 38-58, 1970.

[41] Seong, C. Microblade Technology in Korea and Adjacent Northeast Asia. *Asian Perspectives* 37(2): 272-274, 1998.

[42] Chen, C. The Microlithic of China. *Journal of Anthropological Archaeology* 1(3): 79-115, 1984.

Chen, C, and X. Wang. Upper Paleolithic Microblade Industries in North China and Their Relationships with Northeast Asia and North America. *Arctic Anthropology* 26(2): 144-145, 1989.

Lu, T. L. D. The Microblade Tradition in China: Regional Chronologies and Significance in the Transition to Neolithic. *Asian Perspectives* 37(1): 85-112, 1998.

[43] Derev'anko, A. P., ed. *The Paleolithic of Siberia*. Urbana: University of Illinois Press, 1998.

Goebel, T. The Record of Human Occupation of the Russian Subarctic and Arctic. *Byrd Polar Research Center Miscellaneous Series* M − 335: 41 − 46, 1995.

Goebel, T., M. R. Waters, I. Buvit, M. V. Konstantinov, and A. V. Konstantinov. Studenoe − 2 and the Origins of Microblade Technologies in the Transbaikal, Siberia. *Antiquity* 74: 567 − 575, 2000.

Goebel, T., and S. B. Slobodin. The Colonization of Western Beringia: Technology, Ecology, and Adaptations. In *Ice Age Peoples of North America: Environments, Origins, and Adaptations of the First Americans*. R. Bonnichsen and K. L. Turnmire, eds. Pp. 104 − 155. Corvallis: Oregon State University Press, 1999.

Hoffecker, J. F., W. P. Powers, and T. Goebel. The Colonization of Beringia and the Peopling of the New World. *Science* 259: 46 − 53, 1993.

[44] Seong, C. Microblade Technology in Korea and Adjacent Northeast Asia. *Asian Perspectives* 37 (2): 272 − 274, 1998.

[45] Winterhalder, B. P., F. Lu, and B. Tucker. Risk-Sensitive Adaptive Tactics: Models and Evidence from Subsistence Studies in Biology and Anthropology. *Journal of Archaeological Research* 7(4): 302, 1999.

[46] Bettinger, R. L. *Hunter-Gatherers: Archaeological and Evolutionary Theory*. New York: Plenum, 1991.

Stephens, D. W., and E. L. Charnov. Optimal Foraging: Some Simple Stochastic Models. *Behavioral Ecology and Sociobiology* 10: 252 − 263, 1982.

Winterhalder, B. P., F. Lu, and B. Tucker. Risk-Sensitive Adaptive Tactics: Models and Evidence from Subsistence Studies in Biology and Anthropology. *Journal of Archaeological Research* 7(4): 301 − 348, 1999.

[47] Winterhalder, B. P., F. Lu, and B. Tucker. Risk-Sensitive Adaptive Tactics: Models and Evidence from Subsistence Studies in Biology and Anthropology. *Journal of Archaeological Research* 7(4): fig.2, 1999.

[48] Ellis, C. J. Factors Influencing the Use of Stone Projectile Tips. In *Projectile Technology*. H. Knecht, ed. Pp. 37 − 74. New York: Plenum, 1997: 58.

[49] Bamforth, D. B., and P. Bleed. Technology, Flaked Stone Technology, and Risk. In *Rediscovering Darwin: Evolutionary Theory and Archeological Explanation*. C. M. Barton and G. A. Clark, eds. Pp. 109 − 139. Archeological Papers of the American Anthropological Association, 7. Arlington, Va.: American Anthropological Association, 1997.

Bettinger, R. L., D. B. Madsen, and R. G. Elston. Prehistoric Settlement Categories and Settlement Systems in the Alashan Desert of Inner Mongolia, PRC. *Journal of Anthropological Archaeology* 13: 74 − 101, 1994.

Derev'anko, A. P., ed. *The Paleolithic of Siberia*. Urbana: University of Illinois Press, 1998.

Elston, R. G. Toward Understanding the Spatial and Temporal Distribution of Microlithic Technology in Northeast Asia and Eastern Beringia. In *Entering America: Northeast Asia and Beringia before the Last Glacial Maximum*. D. B. Madsen, ed. Salt Lake City: University of Utah Press, 2002.

Kuzmin, Y. V., and L. A. Orlova. Radiocarbon Chronology of the Siberian Paleolithic. *Journal of World Prehistory* 12(1): 1-53, 1998.

Kuzmin, Y. V., and K. B. Tankersley. The Colonization of Eastern Siberia: An Evaluation of the Paleolithic Age Radiocarbon Dates. *Journal of Archaeological Science* 23(4): 577-585, 1996.

Lu, T. L. D. The Microblade Tradition in China: Regional Chronologies and Significance in the Transition to Neolithic. *Asian Perspectives* 37(1): 85-112, 1998.

The Transition from Foraging to Farming and the Origin of Agriculture in China. BAR International Series, 774. Oxford: British Archaeological Reports, 1999.

Morlan, R. E. Wedge-Shaped Core Technology in Northern North America. *Arctic Anthropology* 7-2: 17-37, 1970.

[50] Bamforth, D. B., and P. Bleed. Technology, Flaked Stone Technology, and Risk. In *Rediscovering Darwin: Evolutionary Theory and Archeological Explanation*. C. M. Barton and G. A. Clark, eds. Pp. 109-139. Archeological Papers of the American Anthropological Association, 7. Arlington, Va.: American Anthropological Association, 1997.

Torrence, R. Time Budgeting and Hunter-Gatherer Technology. In *Hunter-Gatherer Economy in Prehistory*. G. Bailey, ed. Pp. 11-22. Cambridge: Cambridge University Press, 1983.

Retooling: Toward a Behavioral Theory of Stone Tools. In *Time, Energy and Stone Tools*. R. Torrence, ed. Pp. 57-66. Cambridge: Cambridge University Press, 1989.

[51] Brantingham, P. J. Astride the Movius Line: Late Pleistocene Lithic Technological Variability in Northeast Asia. Ph. D. dissertation, Department of Anthropology, University of Arizona, Tucson, 1999.

Madsen, D. B., J. Li, P. J. Brantingham, X. Gao, R. G. Elston, and R. L. Bettinger. Dating Shuidonggou and the Upper Paleolithic Blade Industry in North China. *Antiquity* 75: 706-716, 2001.

[52] Powers, W. R. Siberia in the Late Glacial and Early Postglacial. In *Humans at the End of the Ice Age: The Archaeology of the Pleistocene-Holocene Transition*. L. G. Straus, B. V. Eriksen, J. M. Erlandson, and D. R. Yesner, eds. Pp. 229-242. New York: Plenum, 1996.

[53] Madsen, D. B., R. G. Elston, X. Chen, R. L. Bettinger. Z. Kan, J. Brantingham, and A. L. Jingjen. The Loess/Paleosol Record and the Nature of the Younger Dryas Climate in Central

China. *Geoarchaeology* 13(8): 847-869, 1998.

[54] Powers, W. R. Siberia in the Late Glacial and Early Postglacial. In *Humans at the End of the Ice Age: The Archaeology of the Pleistocene-Holocene Transition.* L. G. Straus, B. V. Eriksen, J. M. Erlandson, and D. R. Yesner, eds. Pp. 229-242. New York: Plenum, 1996.

[55] Elston, R. G., C. Xu, D. B. Madsen, K. Zhong, R. L. Bettinger, J. Li, P. J. Brantingham, H. Wang, and J. Yu. New Dates for the North China Mesolithic. *Antiquity* 71: 985-993, 1997.

Fairservis, W. A. *The Archaeology of the Southern Gobi — Mongolia.* Durham, N. C.: Carolina Academic, 1993.

Kuzmin, Y. V., A. J. T. Jull, Z. S. Lapshina, V. E. Medvedev. Radiocarbon AMS Dating of the Ancient Sites with Earliest Pottery from the Russian Far East. *Nuclear Instruments and Methods in Physics Research B* 123: 496-497, 1997.

Lu, T. L. D. *The Transition from Foraging to Farming and the Origin of Agriculture in China.* BAR International Series, 774. Oxford: British Archaeological Reports, 1999.

Maringer, J. *Contribution to the Prehistory of Mongolia.* Stockholm: Statens Etnografiska Museum, 1950.

Zhuschchikhovskaya, I. On Early Pottery-Making in the Russian Far East. *Asian Perspectives* 36(2): 159-174, 1997.

[56] Lu, T. L. D. *The Transition from Foraging to Farming and the Origin of Agriculture in China.* BAR International Series, 774. Oxford: British Archaeological Reports, 1999.

[57] Elston, R. G., and D. Zeanah. Modeling Pre-Archaic Diet Breadth and Patch Choice in the Great Basin of North America. *World Archaeology* 34(1): 103-130, 2002.

Kuhn, S. L. A Formal Approach to the Design and Assembly of Mobile Toolkits. *American Antiquity* 59(3): 426-442, 1994.

Metcalfe, D., and K. R. Barlow. A Model for Exploring the Optimal Trade-Off between Field Processing and Transport. *American Anthropologist* 94(2): 340-356, 1992.

Zeanah, D.. J. A. Carter, R. G. Elston, and J. E. Hammett. *An Optimal Foraging Model of Hunter-Gatherer Land Use in the Carson Desert.* Report to U.S. Fish and Wildlife Service and U.S. Department of the Navy. Silver City, Nev.: Intermountain Research, 1995.

"细石叶适应"与晚更新世晚段西伯利亚的重新殖民

泰德·戈贝尔

(内华达大学 里诺)

摘　要：迄今为止,西伯利亚地区缺乏距今2.2到1.8万年前的遗址,这表明人们无法应对末次盛冰期的极端气候,放弃了该地区。之后,随着冰川的消退,树线逐渐向北推进,使用细石叶技术的人们重新殖民了亚洲北部地区,距今1.1万年前最终到达北极地区。本文重新梳理这次重新殖民事件的时间进程,总结超过20处遗址的技术、生计与居址材料,重建旧石器时代晚期晚段西伯利亚地区狩猎采集者的适应状况。结果表明末次冰期生产细石叶的人群为高度流动的狩猎者,他们生活在短期利用的居址中,狩猎较为单一的物种。

广义上说西伯利亚是俄罗斯亚洲部分的一片广大区域,西起乌拉尔山脉,东到太平洋,南起阿尔泰山与萨彦岭,北到北冰洋(图9.1)。按照这个定义,西伯利亚覆盖了超过1 000万平方公里的北方地区,五条大河流淌其中:鄂毕河、叶尼塞河、安加拉河与阿穆尔河。末次冰期之初,距今1.8到1.4万年前,西伯利亚的景观以"苔原—草原"为主,动物群组合以大型食草动物为代表,包括猛犸象、野牛、野马、马鹿与驯鹿。末次冰期的最后阶段,距今1.4至1.1万年前,苔原—草原逐渐让位于北方针叶林与森林草原,森林动物增加,包括驼鹿与狍子[1]。

西伯利亚可以考古的时代与末次冰期的气候与环境变化同时,通常称为旧石器时代晚期晚段(或最后阶段)[2]。旧石器时代晚期晚段由一系列地区文化传统组成,包括雅库特地区的久克太文化[3]、叶尼塞河上游盆地的阿方托瓦—科

·180· 小工具 大思考

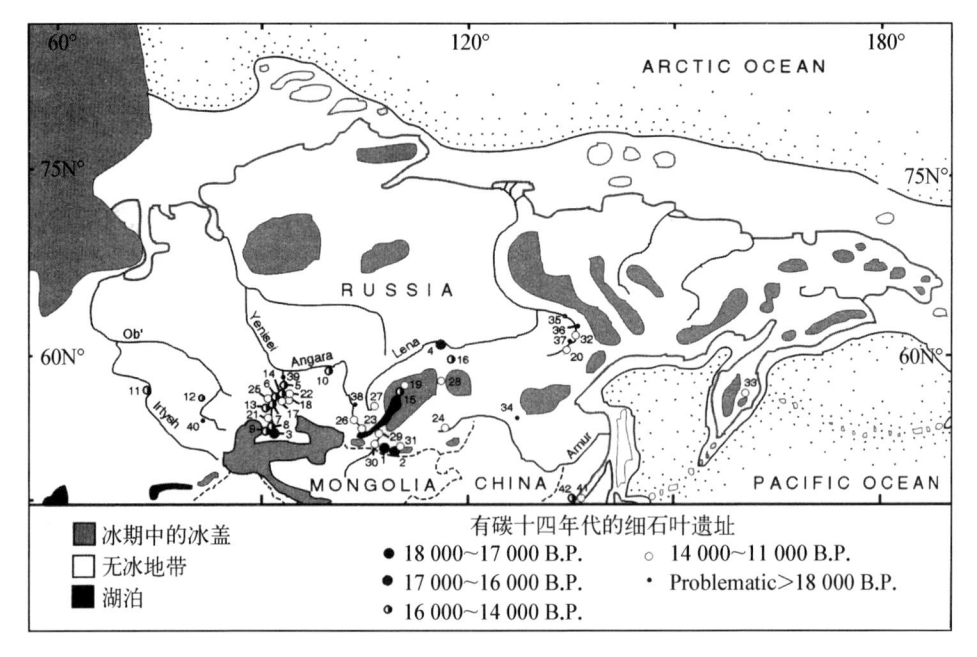

图 9.1 西伯利亚与俄罗斯远东旧石器时代晚期晚段遗址的位置以及大致年代

（1. 斯图德诺伊-2；2. 乌斯太—梅尔瓦-2；3. 东梅林斯卡娅；4. 卡尔盖斯洞；5. 利斯特芬卡；6. 诺沃瑟洛沃-7；7. 科科里瓦-4b；8. 奥赞那切诺伊-1；9. 梅林斯卡娅主地点；10. 乌斯太—科夫；11. 切尔诺奥泽里-2；12. 沃尔卡亚·格里瓦；13. 塔施提克-4；14. 库尔塔克-3；15. 库尔拉-6；16. 阿芙德卡；17. 科科里瓦-2；18. 科科里瓦-1；19. 库尔拉-3；20. 久克太洞；21. 哥鲁巴尼-1；22. 科科里瓦-3；23. 维克霍伦斯卡娅戈拉；24. 索卡廷-4；25. 苏沃瑟洛沃-6；26. 乌斯太—贝拉索；27. 马尔罗沃-2；28. 波尔肖伊—伊艾科尔-1；29. 奥舒尔科沃；30. 乌斯太—卡呀卡塔-17；31. 乌斯太—门萨-1；32. 乌斯太—米尔斯-2；33. 乌斯基-1；34. 乌斯太—厄尔曼-1；35. 乌兹因-2；36. 伊赞伊斯；37. 维肯尼·特洛伊斯卡娅；38. 卡拉斯诺威—伊艾尔-1；39. 阿方托瓦戈拉-2；40. 莫格奇诺-1；41. 苏沃罗沃-4；42. 格尔巴特卡-3）

科里沃文化[4]。鉴于所有这些文化的年代与技术一致，所以可以归为统一的一个技术组合。一般说来，西伯利亚旧石器时代晚期工业距今1.8至1.1万年前，流行从特殊预制的楔形石核上剥离细石叶（典型的细石叶不到2厘米长、1厘米宽）的技术，这些楔形石核以两面器或是由相对较薄的石片制作的小型"末端"石核为毛坯[5]（图9.2）。旧石器时代晚期晚段的石器组合中，较大的棱柱状石叶石核、砸击石核，以及其他简单预制的石片石核也都比较常见。进一步的修理主要见于单面修理与雕刻器打制技术中。西伯利亚西部的大部分地区两面器技术罕见，但在雅库特、外贝加尔以及俄罗斯远东地区较为流行[6]。雕刻器的形制多样，但横截雕刻器边刃最常见。其他的石器类型还包括较大的边刮器，通常由带天然石皮的石片所制，还有用细小石叶制作的小型端刮器、刻刀（graver）以及

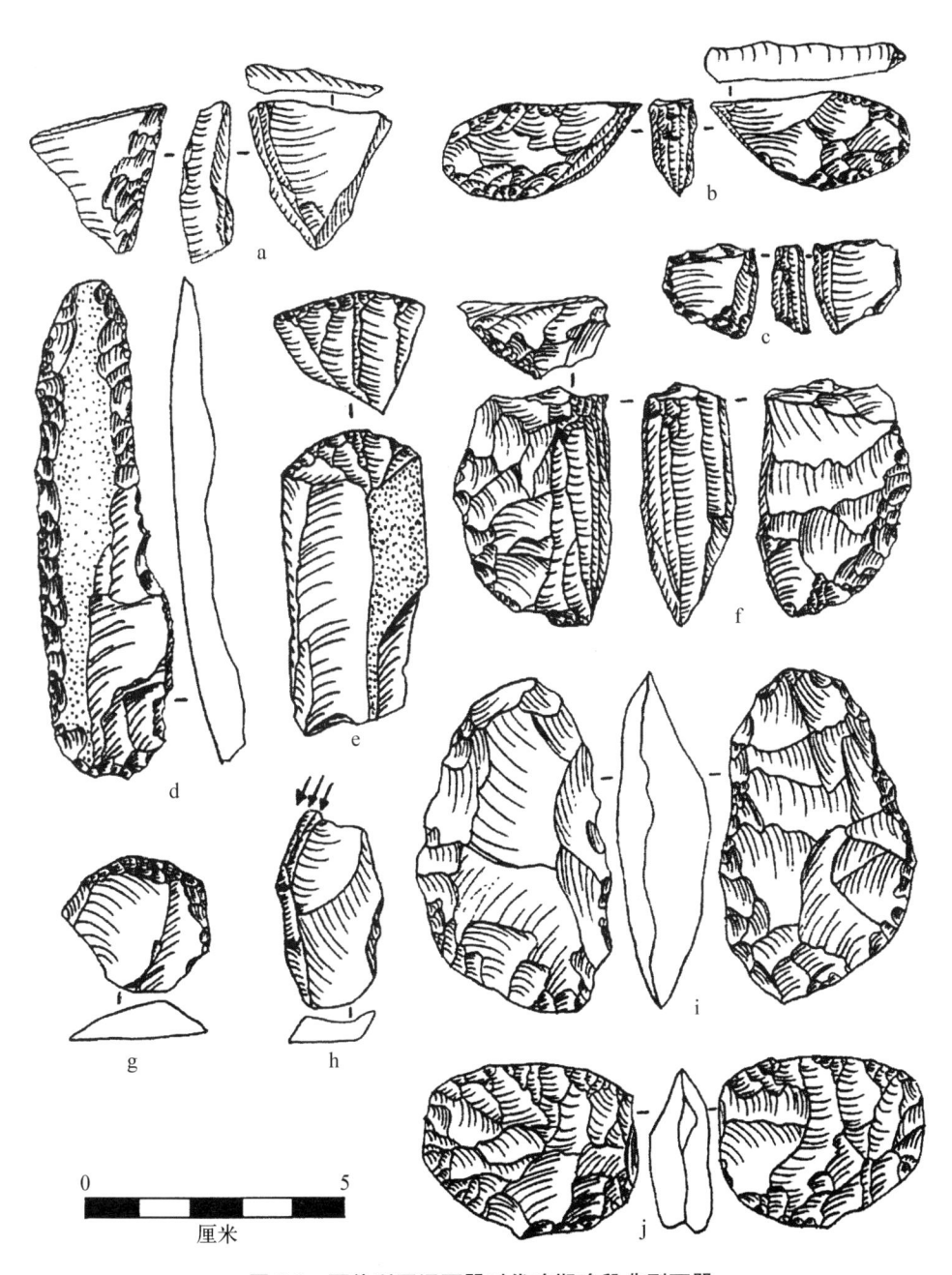

图 9.2 西伯利亚旧石器时代晚期晚段典型石器

(a、c. 末端细石叶石核;b、f. 楔形细石叶石核;d. 边刮器;e、g. 端刮器;h. 雕刻器;i、j. 两面器;索斯诺维伊波尔:a,b,g,h,i,j;科科里沃-3:c,e;诺沃瑟洛沃-6:d,f)

修理石片。旧石器时代晚期晚段的骨制品加工技术主要指生产开槽嵌石刃的骨角与象牙尖状器与刀子。雕刻器可能用于开槽[7],细石叶则被镶嵌在槽中。目前发现了不少保存这种复合投掷技术的完整标本[8]。

本文中关于西伯利亚旧石器时代晚期晚段的讨论,我主要考虑三个基本问题:(1)西伯利亚的细石叶技术何时出现的?(2)西伯利亚细石叶技术的源头在哪里?(3)西伯利亚末次冰期时人类适应的特征如何?

一、西伯利亚细石器技术何时起源的?

关于西伯利亚旧石器时代晚期晚段最早细石叶工业的年代目前还有许多疑问。问题在于最早的细石叶技术的年代究竟是在末次盛冰期之前还是之后。有些学者提出细石叶技术的出现可以早到距今 3.0～2.5 万年前[9];然而,其他学者,包括我在内,认为细石叶工业确定无疑的碳十四最早年代要晚得多,可能晚到距今 1.8～1.7 万年前[10]。争议源于那一系列早期考古遗址有问题的地层、不连续的碳十四年代,或是单个未经证实的碳十四年代。这些遗址包括莫格奇诺-1、阿方托瓦戈拉-2、克拉斯诺伊—伊艾尔-1、乌斯太—科瓦、库尔拉-3、索卡提诺-4、雅库特的"原久克太"遗址,以及乌斯太—厄尔曼-1 遗址。

莫格奇诺-1 遗址位于西伯利亚西部鄂毕河边。1970 年代的发掘发现了丰富的楔形石核与细石叶,同时还发现了猛犸象、野马、驯鹿、披毛犀、野牛与狐狸等动物遗存[11]。一件骨骼标本运用传统碳十四方法进行了年代测定,得到一个年代数据,距今 20 150±240 年(SOAN－1513),但遗址的发掘者佩廷认为这个年代"有点偏老",出土细石叶工业的年代很可能距今 1.7～1.6 万年前[12]。含细石叶层位与下部中更新世晚期的砂层不整合,并受到泥流作用与融冻作用的严重影响,上面覆盖着一层再堆积的"腐殖泥"(如泥炭),运用传统碳十四技术得到两个测年数据,距今 27 300±400 年(GIN－1701)与 34 200±1 300 年(GIN－1702)[13]。我赞同佩廷的观点,我们不能太快接受单个骨骼断代数据,由此就断定旧石器时代晚期晚段文化遗存的年代,不仅因为传统骨骼测年技术的问题,也因为遗址本身的地层有问题。不过,遗址中披毛犀的存在(它在西伯利亚地区末次冰期初期灭绝)确实表明莫格奇诺-1 文化遗存的年代可能属于末次冰期的初期。

西伯利亚中南部的叶尼塞盆地地区有最早碳十四年代的楔形石核工业发现于阿方托瓦戈拉-2 遗址,它位于叶尼塞河沿岸卡拉斯诺亚斯卡郊区。格拉莫夫于 1912 年发现该遗址。他与奥尔芭卡、索斯诺夫斯基于 1923～1925 年间进行了大规模的发掘,揭露出两个旧石器时代晚期含细石叶的文化层以及绝灭的动物遗存[14]。1962 年的一次地质考察中,从遗址一处暴露的剖面上采集到一块碳样,并用传统碳十四技术测定了年代,为距今 20 900±300 年(GIN -117),切特林[15]因此认为其下文化层的年代早于末次盛冰期。但是阿巴拉莫娃等[16]认为这个碳测年样本并不能肯定出自哪个文化层,基于与叶尼塞盆地其他遗址的比较,下文化层的细石叶很可能是末次冰期之后形成的,大约距今 1.6 万年前。

安加拉地区也有几处细石叶工业遗存被认为早于距今 1.8 年前。其中位于南安加拉河沿岸克拉斯诺伊—伊艾尔-1 遗址最著名。这个遗址有多个文化层,位于分层清楚的河流堆积中,包括有两组含细石叶的文化层。上面一组(文化层 I~IV)与一层古土壤层关联,地层学上属于科科里沃间冰期,其年代距今约 1.4~1.3 万年前。下面一组(文化层 V~VII)与冰缘冲积层关联,属于末次盛冰期堆积,距今 1.9~1.8 万年前[17]。这个较早的年代还得到共存披毛犀遗存的支持,第 VI 层还有一个碳测年年代,距今 19 000±100 年(GIN - 5530)[18]。梅德韦杰夫[19]称第 VI 层出土的器物组合在西伯利亚中部"独一无二",因为它含有大型石英岩石核与刮削器,以及鸵鸟蛋壳装饰品,还因为这里出土年代相当早的楔形细石叶石核技术,比安加拉地区任何其他地方都要早。他谨慎地认为卡拉斯诺伊—伊艾尔-1 的早期组合比较"贫乏"、"形制不明确"[20]。安加拉地区其他所谓早期细石叶遗址还包括乌斯太—科瓦(上部组合)与库尔拉-3(第 2 文化层)。

库兹明与奥尔洛娃[21]报道一个新的基于木炭的碳十四数据,将乌斯太—科瓦的细石叶工业年代确定在距今 19 540±90 年(SOAN - 1900),但是这明显跟同一组合的另一个木炭测年数据距今 14 220±100 年(LE - 1372)不符合[22]。库尔拉-3 遗址(第 2 层)细石叶工业只有一个碳十四数据(从非常少的木炭样品中测得的)为距今 24 060±5 700 年(SOAN - 1397),但标准差如此之大使得这个测年没有参考价值[23]。乌斯太—科瓦与库尔拉-3 遗址的细石叶很可能都比碳十四的年代要晚,不过卡拉斯诺伊—伊艾尔-1 的早期文化层可能确实早到距今 19 000 年前,表明南安加拉地区细石叶工业出现在末次冰期的高峰阶段。当然,还需要更多的测年数据来证实这一点。

索卡提诺-4 遗址位于外贝加尔东部地区赤塔市附近,1970 年代由克里洛夫发掘[24]。他的发掘揭露出丰富的楔形石核、细石叶与两面器遗存,并与多样的动物遗存共存,其中包括猛犸象、狍、马鹿、驼鹿[25]。目前已报道了两个传统碳十四数据：一个用骨头测定，为距今 11 900±130 年(SOAN－841)；另一个用木炭，为距今 26 110±200 年(SOAN－1138)。尽管奥克拉德尼科夫与克里洛夫[26]偏向更老的那个数据，但是我赞同阿巴拉莫娃[27]的观点，石器工业中丰富的两面器，以及通常生活于森林环境的驼鹿与狍的存在，都表明这一工业更可能晚于末次冰期的最后阶段，也就是距今 12 000 年之后。

莫查诺夫[28]曾经指出细石叶技术起源于东雅库特地区，时间是在末次盛冰期之前，这种观点基于三个主要遗址的证据：艾肯因-2、乌斯太—米尔斯-2、伊赞提斯。但是这些"原久克太"遗址出土材料在俄罗斯与美国考古学文献中受到反复的批评[29]。简言之，这些遗址都出自次生堆积，因此石器工业与碳十四年代的关系并不可靠，就乌斯太—米尔斯-2 与艾肯因-2 遗址而言，出土石器组合非常细小，并没有包含明确无误可称为细石叶工业的石制品。维肯尼·特洛伊斯卡娅遗址出土少量确定无疑的细石叶组合，碳十四年代为距今 18 000 年[30]，表明雅库特地区细石叶技术起源于末次冰期早段，然而即便是这个遗址，很可能也出自次生堆积，所以相关碳十四年代也要小心对待。

俄罗斯远东地区最古老的细石器工业来自乌斯太—厄尔曼-1 遗址。它位于谢列姆贾河沿岸，这条河是阿穆尔河北部的一条主要支流。遗址有一个传统碳十四年代数据，距今 19 360±65 年(SOAN－2619)，测年材料为木炭[31]。这是该遗址唯一的测年数据，细石叶出自很浅的地层(<1 米)。要全面弄清遗址的年代，还需要更多测年样本与相关文化遗存材料，以及更多的碳十四年代测定。因此，目前早于末次盛冰期的楔形石核与细石叶技术的证据是贫乏的。确定属于早期遗址的年代都还不能确定，或是因为碳十四年代不连续，或是地层有问题，或是仅有一个碳十四年代数据，显然还需要更多的数据。因此，我认为我们需要考虑一个更保守一点的年代序列，基于多个连续的碳十四年代数据，并且相关联的文化特征确定无疑地属于楔形石核与细石叶工业。考虑到这些限制因素，西伯利亚细石叶的年代就会缩短许多。确切地说，没有楔形石核与细石叶工业早于距今 18 000 年(图 9.3)。

根据上面所说更短的年代表，西伯利亚地区确定无疑的最早的楔形石核与细石叶工业来自贝加尔地区南部。证据来自两个遗址，乌斯太—门萨-2 与斯图德诺伊-2，它们位于奇科河沿岸，这是色楞格河(流入贝加尔湖)的一条主要支流。乌斯太—门萨-2 由康斯坦丁诺夫于 1980 年代到 1990 年代早期发掘，发现了一系列旧石器时代晚期的文化遗存，上覆河流泛滥的堆积，分层良好。上文化层的碳十四年代为距今 16 900 至 14 800 年，而两个最下部的层位碳十四年代分

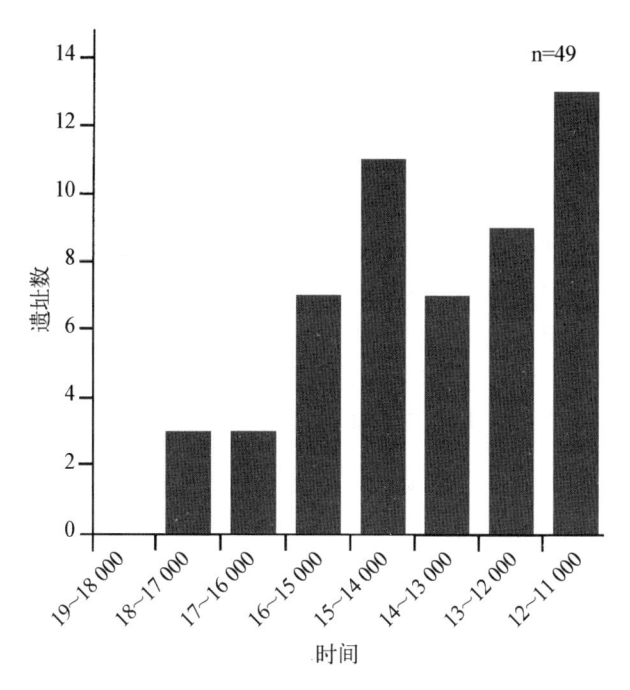

图9.3　旧石器时代晚期晚段考古遗址数量直方图

（以一千年为间隔,注意距今19 000到18 000年之间缺乏遗址,距今18 000至16 000年间数量较少,距今16 000至11 000年间数量较多）

别为距今17 600±250、16 980±150[32]。采用的是传统碳十四测年法,材料为出自火塘的木炭,与楔形石核与细石叶的共存关系明确。最近,康斯坦丁诺夫的团队发掘了斯图德诺伊-2遗址,这处遗址也有一系列地层清楚的文化遗存,时间跨越末次冰期。迈克·瓦特斯、伊恩布维特与我参加了1996年的发掘工作,随后参与到遗址的地质考古与断代工作中。加速器碳十四断代将该遗址早期细石叶工业的年代确定在距今17 165±115年(AA-23657)(第5文化层)、17 885±120年(AA-23653)(第4、5文化层之间)。测年材料来自居住遗址火塘中的木炭[33]。因此,与蒙古中部相邻的贝加尔南部地区,楔形石核与细石叶技术出现的确切年代为距今17 500年,正好在末次盛冰期之后。

随着远离南贝加尔地区,确切的最早细石叶技术也就越晚(图9.1)。叶尼塞盆地年代确定的最早细石叶遗址是梅林斯卡娅东地点(第5层),碳十四年代为距今16 500年[34]。其他遗址(如,梅林斯卡娅主地点、诺沃瑟洛沃-7、科科里沃-4b、库尔塔克-3、奥赞那切诺伊-1)都处在距今15 500至15 000年之间[35]。再往西到鄂毕盆地,最早的细石叶甚至更晚,切尔诺奥泽里-2遗址测定年代为距今 14 500 年后(该遗址的年代很可能接近距今 12 000 年)。类似之,往东到俄罗斯远东的阿穆尔/普利莫尔地区,真正带有细石叶工业年代最早的遗址可能包括苏沃罗沃-4(距今 15 000 年)和格尔巴特卡-3(晚于距今 13 500 年)[36]。同样的分布形态也见于北部地区雅库特与白令地区。就雅库特地区而言,如果不考虑特洛伊斯卡娅遗址与"原久克太"遗址,那么年代可靠的最早细石叶工业晚到距今 16 000 年,甚至更晚。这些遗址包括卡尔盖斯洞(距今 16 000 年)[37]、久克太洞(距今 14 000~13 000 年)[38]与阿芙德卡(距今 13 000 年)[39](图 9.1)。最后,在白令地区,细石叶工业出现于末次冰期的最后阶段,勘察加(乌斯基遗址)与中阿拉斯加地区(戴尔溪遗址)的年代大约距今 10 700 年[40]。

这些所说较短的年代表明北亚地区细石叶技术首先出现于南贝加尔湖地区,正在末次盛冰期之时或稍晚,距今 18 000 至 17 000 年。之后不久,距今 16 000 至 14 000 年间,细石叶向西到了叶尼塞地区,向东到了阿穆尔地区,向北到了雅库特地区。距今约 11 000~10 000 年,这种技术最终出现在白令地区,全新世早期扩散到整个阿拉斯加与加拿大西北地区[41]。距今 18 000 至 11 000 年之间细石叶技术的扩散可能代表现代人在末次盛冰期之后重新拓殖西伯利亚的过程。

二、西伯利亚细石叶技术源头是什么?

西伯利亚细石叶的起源问题基本上有两种答案。西伯利亚细石叶的源头或是在某些西伯利亚当地更早的文化中,或是来自邻近的东亚或中亚地区(即蒙古、中国或东亚海岸地带)。最可能的当地源头是西伯利亚旧石器晚期中段组合,包括玛尔塔、伊格特伊斯基·罗格、乌伊-1 与卡萨坦卡等遗址,所有年代都位于距今约 25 000 至 20 000 年间。这些遗址存在一种细石器化的趋势,以从小型棱柱状石核上剥离的狭窄细小石叶为代表[42]。这些遗址中发现的某些细小石叶很像是晚期细石叶的缩小版;当然,旧石器时代晚期中段的小石核与石叶更可能是高强度石核打制的结果,为了节省原料,而不是旧石器时代晚期晚段独特技术体系的结果。尽管旧石器时代晚期晚段的楔形石核与细石叶技术最终可能从棱柱状石叶打制技术演化而来,但是还有其他证据表明它们来自西伯利亚以外的地区,在末次盛冰期之后传入该地区。

如果我们考察西伯利亚地区距今 35 000 至 11 000 年间有碳十四年代的旧石器时代晚期遗址的分布频率,很容易发现距今 19 000~18 000 年间有段空白,恰好是末次盛冰期时(图 9.3)[43]。这段空白很关键,因为它差不多是成熟细石叶技术出现的时间。目前只有三处遗址的碳十四的年代在距今 19 000~18 000 年的范围内,分别是托姆斯卡、什伦卡、塔拉奇卡。托姆斯卡是一个多世纪前发掘的,仅有的传统碳十四年代为距今 18 000±1000 年,测年材料是一块 1896 年收集并存档的木炭[44]。木炭与可能在托姆斯卡杀死的猛犸象的关联并不是很清楚。什伦卡只有一个文化层,四个碳十四年代距今 22 800 至 17 600 年间;只有一个年代数据落在距今 19 000 至 18 000 年间[45]。遗址的真实年代很可能接近距今 20 000 年。塔拉奇卡有两个年代数据——距今 19 800±180 与距今 18 900±320 年,两者可能比距今 19 000 年早几百年[46]。因此,末次盛冰期时西伯利亚似乎没有人类居住,旧石器时代晚期晚段细石叶工业晚于末次盛冰期,这种现象表明西伯利亚后来由外来人群重新拓殖。这些人群的确切源头尚不清楚,但是最近的源头可能就是蒙古中部地区,紧邻贝加尔湖南部,这里似乎是西伯利亚细石叶技术的最早源头(本文的前面已讨论过)。不过,对蒙古中部地区旧石器时代我们几乎一无所知,所以这个方案也没有得到充分支持。

三、我们如何确定西伯利亚"细石叶适应"的特征?

西伯利亚地区发掘、发表了大约 20 处旧石器时代晚期遗址,并做了碳十四测年。空间分布、石器技术与工具形制以及遗址所出动物遗存的研究,都表明西伯利亚旧石器时代晚期晚段的人群是高度流动的狩猎采集者,他们主要利用大型哺乳动物资源。

典型的旧石器时代晚期晚段遗址都比较小。保存下来的遗迹与器物分布表明其是短期居留。不过,大多数遗址有多个文化层(如利斯特芬卡、梅林斯卡娅遗址),或是不止一个地点(如科科里沃、乌斯太—门萨),表明当时的人们对关键地点的反复光顾。叶尼塞河上游盆地地区,大部分年代属于末次冰期的遗址只有非常小的火塘,相关文化堆积很薄,绝大多数遗址都没有发现储藏坑[47]。居住遗迹同样罕见,不过在乌伊-2 与利斯特芬卡确实有发现,弧形的石圈中间是火塘[48]。或认为是轻型地表帐篷的遗迹[49],但也可能是风挡设施。外贝加尔地区,若干旧石器时代晚期晚段的遗址(如乌斯太—门萨-2、斯图德诺伊-2 遗址)中发现了保存完好的居住遗迹[50]。为环形到椭圆形的石圈,一般直径 4 至 5 米,中间有石头围成的火塘,居住面很薄(不足 1 厘米厚),文化堆积稀少[51]。同样缺乏明确的储藏坑。库茨勒佐夫[52]认为这些遗存是地表茅草屋的遗迹,居留的时间比较短,可能仅仅是在某个季节。不过基于这些遗址动物遗存的季节性研究还没有开展,所以我们还不能轻易地指出人们在居住营地的季节,以及居留的时间长度。不过,小型营地遗址的反复光顾、储藏设施遗存的缺乏以及保存下来的居留遗迹的稀薄程度,都表明旧石器时代晚期晚段的西伯利亚人是高度流动的——比更早期的人群更加流动(如玛尔塔组合),更早期的人群通常修建了近乎半定居的大型居所,挖掘了很深的储藏坑,居住营地的规模更大,居住的时间也更长[53]。

石制品研究能够提供有关石器原料获取与居址流动性的重要信息,但是西伯利亚地区旧石器时代晚期晚段的石器组合从来没有做过这样的分析[54]。我们对原料的获取、工具的携带、不同类型石器的功能,都知之甚少,大多数情况下我们甚至不知道有修理使用痕迹的工具与石片、石叶之间的比例(因为西伯利亚的发掘并不总会系统收集废片)。不过,大多数遗址还是报告工具类型比例的,因此我们能够计算成型与非成型工具的相对数量,这是一个可以表示流动性高低或居留时间长短的变量[55]。成型工具指那些存在有意、深入修理的石器工具,表明是使用之前提前准备好的(如两面加工的尖状器与石刀、刮削器、刻刀),而非成型工具指权宜性的、边缘修理的工具,根据需要临时加工而成(如修理加工的石片与石叶)。高比例的成型工具至少在某些情况下代表更短的居留时间以及更高程度的居住流动性。我曾经计算过一系列西伯利亚旧石器时代晚期晚段遗址成型工具与非成型工具的比例(表 9.1),并把它们与旧石器时代晚期早段的遗址相比较。旧石器时代晚期晚段的遗址显然比旧石器时代晚期早段的遗址有更高比例的成型工具。这很好地反映了旧石器时代晚期晚段更高的流动性。

表 9.1 西伯利亚旧石器时代晚期晚段遗址成型与非成型工具的频率

遗 址	非成型工具的频率 n	%	成型工具的频率* n	%	总工具数 n	参考文献
旧石器时代晚期晚段						
索斯诺维伊波尔,5 组	21	30.9	47	69.1	68	本研究
塔施提克-1,3 组	26	18.7	113	81.3	139	[56]
塔施提克-1,2 组	10	12.8	68	87.2	78	同上
科科诺沃-2	76	32.9	155	67.1	231	同上
梅林斯卡娅,3 组	44	32.6	91	67.4	135	[57]

续 表

遗 址	非成型工具的频率 n	非成型工具的频率 %	成型工具的频率* n	成型工具的频率* %	总工具数 n	参考文献
梅林斯卡娅,4组	21	18.8	91	81.3	112	同上
总计	198	26.0	565	74.0	763	
旧石器时代晚期早段						
索斯诺维伊波尔,6组	20	57.1	15	42.9	35	[58]
卡拉—波姆	113	48.9	118	51.1	231	同上
奥利姆波夫斯基	17	37.0	29	63.0	46	同上
马卡罗沃	191	71.8	75	28.2	266	同上
瓦尔瓦里纳戈拉	52	37.4	87	62.6	139	同上
托尔巴加	259	42.3	354	57.7	613	同上
总计	652	49.0	678	51.0	1330	

* 不包括砾石工具与石楔,它们可能是石核。

有些研究者还考虑到,流动的狩猎采集者通常会生产高比例具有多用途的成型工具。北美的古印第安石器组合中,两面器就属于这类工具。它们既充当石核,还用作刀子[59]。西伯利亚旧石器时代晚期晚段工具组合中楔形细石叶石核可能充当类似的角色。楔形石核通常由劈开或断裂的两面器来生产,两面修理的边缘常常带有修理与使用痕迹,很可能是用作刀子使用的结果[60]。不过,剥离细石叶时将石核固定在卡扣工具中可能也会导致楔形石核底部的磨损痕迹[61],但是没有证据表明旧石器时代晚期晚段的石器制作者如此使用卡扣工具。类似之,许多"末端"(或称 tortsovyi)石核(即以石片为毛坯制作的细石叶石核)有清晰的单面刮削器修理所形成的反锋(图 9.2,c)。因此,细石叶石核似乎常用作多功能的工具,这可能进一步指示旧石器时代晚期晚段的流动性。

西伯利亚旧石器时代晚期晚段另一个有趣的特征是完全缺乏便携的艺术品。目前发现有几件带刻划图案的开槽骨尖状器与骨锥[62],少量带条痕或刻划痕迹的象牙盘状器,可能是挂件的毛坯[63],梅林斯卡娅遗址还出土一件黏土制作的人形塑像[64]。不过,这些旧石器时代晚期晚段的艺术品很难跟更早期的玛尔塔文化所出土的相提并论[65]。这也可能表明旧石器时代晚期晚段的流动性更高，或至少表明在居址中停留的时间更短。

我们有关旧石器时代晚期晚段生计的信息大多来自西伯利亚中南部叶尼塞地区，主要基于艾尔莫洛娃[66]的研究。卡拉斯诺亚斯卡与阿巴坎市之间叶尼塞河沿岸的米努辛斯克盆地，旧石器时代晚期晚段动物群组合以驯鹿为主（图9.4）。科科里沃-2遗址第2、3层，驯鹿骨骼占到动物群组合的63%，个体数的30%[67]，诺沃瑟洛沃-6与诺沃瑟洛沃-7遗址中，驯鹿骨骼占到动物群组合的98%。沿着叶尼塞河上游往南，在萨彦岭地区驯鹿并不常见。例如，梅林斯卡娅遗址每个文化层的动物群组合中代表性的大型哺乳动物都不同——西伯利亚山羊、马鹿或是野牛。外贝加尔地区乌斯太—门萨与斯图德诺伊遗址的动物群组合的简报显示旧石器时代晚期晚段的人们主要狩猎马鹿[68]。因此，狩猎鹿类动物似乎是旧石器时代晚期晚段生计的重要方面，虽然大多数遗址中也有野牛与马。

旧石器时代晚期晚段遗址中猛犸象遗存并不常见。事实上，我仅知道六个有碳十四年代的南西伯利亚旧石器时代晚期晚段遗址曾经出土过猛犸象遗存：沃尔卡亚·格里瓦、什卡伊维卡-2、利斯特芬卡、科科里沃-2、阿方托瓦戈拉-2、索斯诺维伊波尔。沃尔卡亚·格里瓦遗址位于西南西伯利亚巴拉宾草原地区，发掘出土超过1 000件猛犸象骨骼，但是与之共存的仅有两件石片、四件细小石叶[69]。利斯特芬卡遗址的遗存还没有详细描述过，但已有简报显示大部分层位中只有象牙[70]；索斯诺维伊波尔遗址的情况也一样[71]。遗址中存在的象牙可能来自收集。仅有科科里沃-2与什卡伊维卡-2遗址出土较多层位关系清楚的猛犸象骨骼。科科里沃-2遗址的动物群组合中至少有七个猛犸象个体，占到遗址所发现动物骨骼的30%（图9.4）[72]，什卡伊维卡-2遗址中两头猛犸象似乎是被猎杀的，并部分屠宰[73]。后者可能是西伯利亚旧石器时代晚期晚段唯一有记录的猛犸象猎杀遗址。

西伯利亚旧石器时代晚期晚段另一个有趣特征是野兔（*Lepus* sp.）成为重要的猎杀动物。几乎所有叶尼塞地区的遗址都有野兔标本存在，科科里沃-4b遗址中野兔的骨骼与所代表的个体超过大多数大型哺乳动物（仅有驯鹿的数量较多）（图9.4）。其他经常出现于许多遗址中的小型动物包括红狐、狼（或狗）、獾、北极狐，科科里沃-1、科科里沃-2、科科里沃-4b、梅林斯卡娅遗址还发现鸟类遗存[74]。这些遗址中都没有鱼的遗存，其出现直到旧石器时代晚期晚段之末，距今12 000年之后见于奥舒尔科沃、乌斯太—贝拉亚、乌斯太—卡呀卡塔-17等遗址[75]。

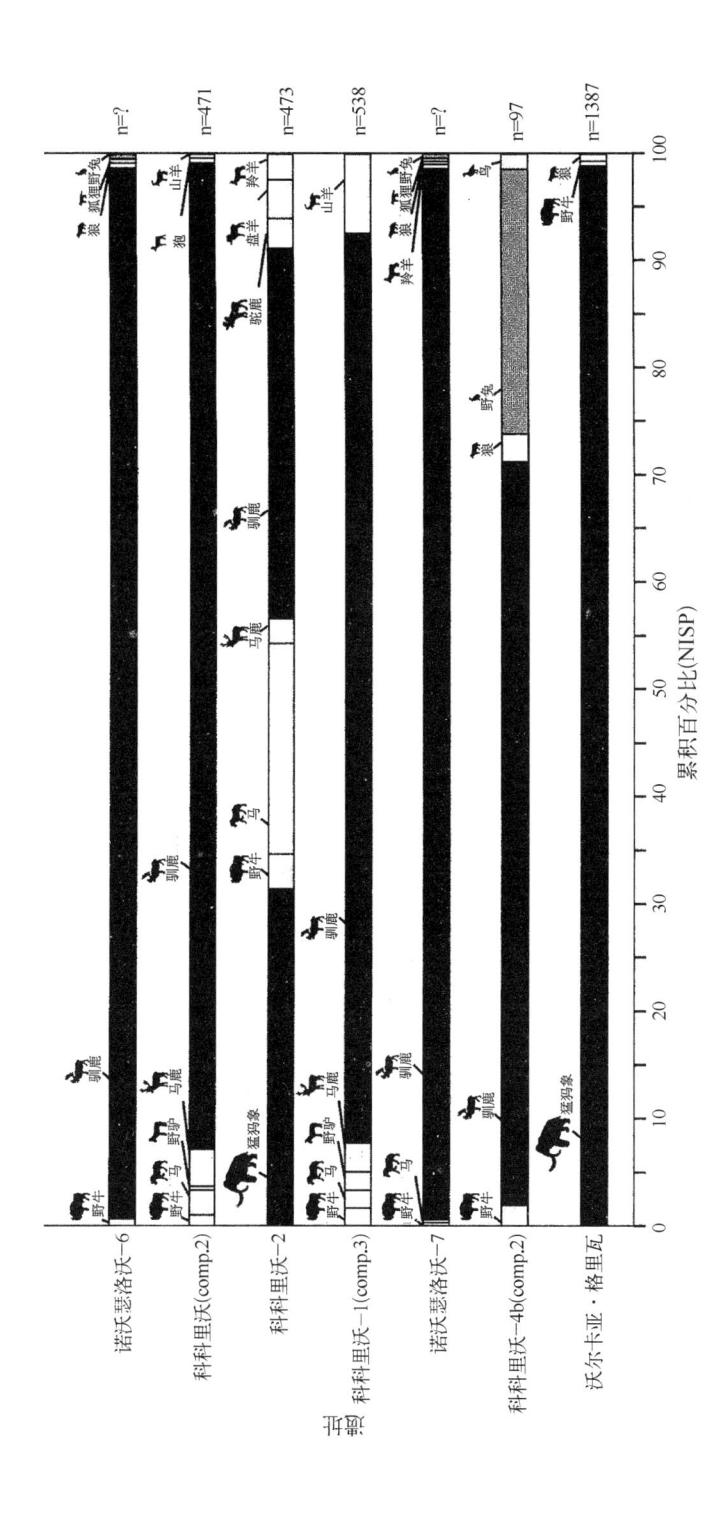

"细石叶适应"与晚更新世晚段西伯利亚的重新殖民 · 191 ·

图 9.4 西伯利亚旧石器时代晚期晚段遗址动物遗存的相对频率

[（参见图 9.1 了解这些遗址的地理位置与大致年代）；材料显示单件标本的数量（NISP）；最小个体数（MNI）的材料并非每个遗址都有，所以这里没有列出来；参考文献见文中]

总体上,旧石器时代晚期晚段遗址的内在布局、器物组成、技术方法以及动物遗存都表明存在一种高度流动的适应方式。细石叶石核可能经常用作多用途的工具,旧石器时代晚期晚段石器组合中成型工具占绝对优势,这代表流动狩猎采集者可能经常储藏工具。几乎所有的遗址都是以单一哺乳动物为主,许多已知的遗址可能只是短期居址。没有储藏坑、没有房基,以及几乎没有艺术品,都表明这些遗址不是长期使用的中心营地,而是流动的觅食群体所留下的短期居住营地。他们为利用季节性资源如迁徙的驯鹿而反复利用同一地方。

我们能否将旧石器时代晚期晚段狩猎采集者的流动性进一步区分后勤类型*与居住类型呢[76]?就这一点而言,我的回答是否定的。我们需要更多不同遗址比较的信息,从而确定石器组合、遗迹、活动方式以及居留时间长度的变化范围。没有这些材料,我们就不能确定遗址的类型,也不能确定旧石器时代晚期晚段居址布局的特征。再者,末次冰期时西伯利亚的环境不同地区是高度变化的,并且还在不断变化中,这就使得狩猎采集者的土地利用方式很可能随之变化。

欧洲地区末次冰期时细石器技术分布广泛,考古学家已经反复证明了旧石器时代晚期晚段生计、居址与社会组织的性质。一方面,德国西南部马格德林狩猎采集者运用的是后勤类型的流动方式,在春夏与秋冬营地之间进行短期的季节性迁居,可能是为了应对相对短暂的驯鹿迁徙时间[77]。而另一方面,法国西南部马格德林驯鹿狩猎者的流动性非常高,"区域上广泛分布"[78],巴恩[79]甚至认为马格德林居址流动跨越数百公里,广泛分布于佩里戈德与比利牛斯地区之间。类似之,巴黎盆地的宾斯凡特与韦尔布里广泛分布的旧石器时代晚期晚段遗址可能代表马格德林狩猎者散布的迁徙营地[80]。显然,如果中西欧地区旧石器时代晚期晚段的考古记录中存在这样的变化,那么西伯利亚可能也如此。旧石器时代晚期晚段的西伯利亚人比末次盛冰期之前的人群流动性更高,这里所提及的材料支持这一观点,但是体现高流动适应特征的详细信息还需要进一步分析相关的石器技术与遗址布局。

四、结论

通过以上对西伯利亚旧石器时代晚期晚段研究的回顾,根据现有材料形态,

---

* Logistical mobility 是指那种有中心营地与临时营地区别的流动方式,人们在临时营地利用某些特定的资源,然后将部分采集到资源带回到中心营地中去。Residential mobility 则没有这种明显的区分,人们的营地整体迁移,在每个营地停留时间都差不多。前者更加复杂,通常会涉及食物与工具的储藏、搬运,以及成批处理某些食物资源。——译者注

我提出以下结论：

1. 西伯利亚细石叶技术是一个末次冰期现象,最早年代确定的楔形石核与细石叶工业距今17 500年出现于南贝加尔地区。那些年代超过距今18 000年含细石叶的遗址地层关系不佳,碳十四年代不连续,或者仅有一个年代,还需要重复检验。

2. 西伯利亚地区细石叶技术的起源是在末次盛冰期之后,代表末次冰期人类重新利用北亚地区。考古材料中距今19 000至18 000年之间的空白表明末次盛冰期时人类离开了西伯利亚,细石叶技术起源于亚洲温带地区,可能是蒙古的中东部地区。

3. 短期居址的反复利用以及长期村落或中心营地的缺乏表明西伯利亚末次冰期的殖民者是高度流动小群体的狩猎采集者,他们频繁迁徙,追随重要的动物资源。废弃堆积少,居留时间短暂,关键地点反复利用。

4. 旧石器时代晚期晚段的石器工业有利于流动性。旧石器时代晚期晚段石器工具组合以高比例的成型工具为代表,细石叶石核可能用作多功能的工具。

5. 动物遗存材料表明旧石器时代晚期晚段的人们主要以狩猎大中型动物为生。尽管遗址中通常不止一种动物存在,但动物群组合一般只以某一种动物为主,比如驯鹿、马鹿、野牛,表明一定程度的狩猎特化。距今12 000年后,渔猎出现,表明随着末次冰期的结束,资源利用范围的扩大。

这些结论应该被视作假说,希望能够引发一些讨论与持续的研究。显然,就西伯利亚旧石器时代晚期晚段还需要更深入细致的研究。那些原来认为早于或处在末次盛冰期的早期细石叶遗址需要再进一步考察与重新断代。为了检验是否存在末次盛冰期中的遗址,以及揭示细石叶技术起源,应该启动蒙古中东部旧石器时代晚期晚段遗址的调查工作。最后,为了了解末次冰期时人类生态与适应的问题,还需要完成石器与动物遗存材料新的详细分析。西伯利亚旧石器时代晚期晚段的狩猎采集者采取的是后勤类型还是居址类型的流动方式？没有遗址之间材料详细的比较,就不能回答这一问题。如果我们希望全面了解末次冰期西伯利亚地区人类适应的演化与重新殖民的过程,我们就需要更多了解旧石器时代晚期晚段石器原料的获取方式与技术流程,以及季节性的生计与居住行为。要想全面了解"细石叶适应",我们需要看到考古材料的各个方面,不管是多么细微,注意单个考古遗址及其特定生态联系。换句话说,我们需要大思考。

注释：

[1] Guthrie, R. D. *Frozen Fauna of the Mammoth Steppe: The Story of Blue Babe*. Chicago：

University of Chicago Press, 1990.

Powers, W. R. Siberia in the Late Glacial and Early Postglacial. In *Humans at the End of the Ice Age: The Archaeology of the Pleistocene-Holocene Transition*. L. G. Straus, B. V. Eriksen, J. M. Erlandson, and D. R. Yesner, eds. Pp. 229 – 242. New York: Plenum, 1996.

Ukraintseva, V. V. *Vegetation Cover and Environment of the "Mammoth Epoch" in Siberia*. Hot Springs: The Mammoth Site of Hot Springs, South Dakota, 1993.

[2] Goebel, T. Pleistocene Human Colonization of Siberia and Peopling of the Americas: An Ecological Approach. *Evolutionary Anthropology: Issues, News, and Reviews* 8(6): 208 – 227, 1999.

Kuzmin, Y. V., and L. A. Orlova. Radiocarbon Chronology of the Siberian Paleolithic. *Journal of World Prehistory* 12(1): 1 – 53, 1998.

Vasil'ev, S. A. The Upper Palaeolithic of Northern Asia. *Current Anthropology* 34(1): 82 – 92, 1993.

[3] Mochanov, Y. A. *Drevneishie Etapy Zaseleniia Chclovekom Severo-Vostochnoi Azii*. Novosibirsk, U.S.S.R.: Nauka, 1977.

[4] Abramova, Z. A. Paleolit Eniseia: Afontovskaia Kul'tura. Novosibirsk, U. S. S. R.: Nauka, 1979b.

Paleolit Eniseia: Kokorevskaia Kul'tura. Novosibirsk, U.S.S.R.: Nauka, 1979c.

[5] Abramova, Z. A. Paleolit Eniseia: Afontovskaia Kul'tura. Novosibirsk, U. S. S. R.: Nauka, 1979b.

Paleolit Eniseia: Kokorevskaia Kul'tura. Novosibirsk, U.S.S.R.: Nauka, 1979c.

Flenniken, J. J. The Paleolithic Dyuktai Pressure Blade Technique of Siberia. *Arctic Anthropology* 24(2): 117 – 132, 1987.

Mochanov, Y. A. *Drevneishie Etapy Zaseleniia Chclovekom Severo-Vostochnoi Azii*. Novosibirsk, U.S.S.R.: Nauka, 1977.

[6] Derev'anko, A. Selemdzha and the Eastern Siberian, Far Eastern, and Beringian Records. In *The Paleolithic of Siberia: New Discoveries and Interpretations*. A. P. Derev'anko, ed. Pp. 285 – 286. Urbana: University of Illinois Press, 1998.

Mochanov, Y. A. *Drevneishie Etapy Zaseleniia Chclovekom Severo-Vostochnoi Azii*. Novosibirsk, U.S.S.R.: Nauka, 1977.

[7] Guthrie, R. D. *Frozen Fauna of the Mammoth Steppe: The Story of Blue Babe*. Chicago: University of Chicago Press, 1990.

[8] Abramova, Z. A., S. N. Astakhov, S. A. VasiPev, N. M. Ermolova, and N. F. Lisitsyn. *Paleolit Eniseiia*. Leningrad: Nauka, 1991.

Drozdov, N. L., V. P. Chekha, S. A. Laukhin, V. G. Kol'tsova, E. V. Akimova, A. V.

Ermolaev, V. P. Leont'ev, S. A. Vasil'ev, A. F. Iamskikh, G. A, Demidenko, E. V. Artem'ev, A. A. Bikulov, A. A. Bokarev, I. V. Foronova, and S. D. Sidoras. *Khrono-Stratigrafiia Paleoliticheskikh Pamiatnikov Srednei Sibiri: Bassein R. Enisei*. Novosibirsk, U.S.S.R.: Nauka, 1990.

Petrin, V. T. *Paleoliticheskie Pamiatniki Zapadno-Sibirskoi Ravniny*. Novosibirsk, U.S.S.R.: Nauka, 1986.

[9] Derev'anko, A. Selemdzha and the Eastern Siberian, Far Eastern, and Beringian Records. In *The Paleolithic of Siberia: New Discoveries and Interpretations*. A. P. Derev'anko, ed. Pp. 285 – 286. Urbana: University of Illinois Press, 1998.

Mochanov, Y. A. *Drevneishie Etapy Zaseleniia Chclovekom Severo-Vostochnoi Azii*. Novosibirsk, U.S.S.R.: Nauka, 1977.

Stratigraphy and Absolute Chronology of the Paleolithic of Northeast Asia. In *Early Man in America from a Circum-Pacific Perspective*. A. L. Bryan, ed. Pp. 54 – 66. Edmonton, Canada: Archaeological Researches International, 1978.

Morlan, R. E. The Pleistocene Archaeology of Beringia. In *The Evolution of Human Hunting*. M. H. Nitecki and D. V. Nitecki, eds. Pp. 267 – 308. New York: Plenum, 1987.

West, F. H. Beringia and New World Origins II: The Archaeological Evidence. In *American Beginnings: The Prehistory and Palaeoecology of Beringia*. F. H. West, ed. Pp. 537 – 559. Chicago: University of Chicago Press, 1996.

[10] Abramova, Z. A. Paleolit Severnoi Azii. In *Paleolit Kavkaza I Severnoi Azii*. Pp. 143 – 243. Leningrad: Nauka, 1989.

Goebel, T. Pleistocene Human Colonization of Siberia and Peopling of the Americas: An Ecological Approach. *Evolutionary Anthropology: Issues, News, and Reviews* 8(6): 208 – 227, 1999.

Medvedev, G. Upper Paleolithic Sites in South-Central Siberia. In *The Paleolithic of Siberia: New Discoveries and Interpretations*. A. P. Derev'anko, ed. Pp. 122 – 137. Urbana: University of Illinois Press, 1998.

Vasil'ev, S. A. The Upper Palaeolithic of Northern Asia. *Current Anthropology* 34(1): 82 – 92, 1993.

[11] Petrin, V. T. *Paleoliticheskie Pamiatniki Zapadno-Sibirskoi Ravniny*. Novosibirsk, U.S.S.R.: Nauka, 1986.

[12] Petrin, V. T. Paleoliticheskie Pamiatniki Zapadno-Sibirskoi Ravniny. Novosibirsk, U.S.S.R.: Nauka, 1986: 102, 117.

[13] Petrin, V. T. Paleoliticheskie Pamiatniki Zapadno-Sibirskoi Ravniny. Novosibirsk, U.S.S.R.: Nauka, 1986: 80.

[14] Abramova, Z. A., S. N. Astakhov, S. A. VasiPev, N. M. Ermolova, and N. F. Lisitsyn. *Paleolit Eniseiia*. Leningrad: Nauka, 1991: 97.

[15] Tseitlin, S. M. *Geologiia Paleolita Severnoi Azii*. Moscow: Nauka, 1979.

[16] Abramova, Z. A., S. N. Astakhov, S. A. VasiPev, N. M. Ermolova, and N. F. Lisitsyn. *Paleolit Eniseiia*. Leningrad: Nauka, 1991.

Abramova, Z. A. Paleolit Eniseia: Afontovskaia Kul'tura. Novosibirsk, U. S. S. R.: Nauka, 1979b.

[17] Tseitlin, S. M. *Geologiia Paleolita Severnoi Azii*. Moscow: Nauka, 1979.

[18] Medvedev, G. Upper Paleolithic Sites in South-Central Siberia. In *The Paleolithic of Siberia: New Discoveries and Interpretations*. A. P. Derev'anko, ed. Pp. 122 – 137. Urbana: University of Illinois Press, 1998.

[19] Medvedev, G. Upper Paleolithic Sites in South-Central Siberia. In *The Paleolithic of Siberia: New Discoveries and Interpretations*. A. P. Derev'anko, ed. Pp. 131. Urbana: University of Illinois Press, 1998.

[20] Medvedev, G. Upper Paleolithic Sites in South-Central Siberia. In *The Paleolithic of Siberia: New Discoveries and Interpretations*. A. P. Derev'anko, ed. Pp. 137. Urbana: University of Illinois Press, 1998.

[21] Kuzmin, Y. V., and L. A. Orlova. Radiocarbon Chronology of the Siberian Paleolithic. *Journal of World Prehistory* 12(1): 1 – 53, 1998.

[22] Vasil'evskii, R. S., V. V. Burilov. and N. I. Drozdov. *Arkheologicheskie Pamiatniki Severnogo Priangar'ia*. Novosibirsk, U.S.S.R.: Nauka, 1988.

[23] Kuzmin, Y. V., and L. A. Orlova. Radiocarbon Chronology of the Siberian Paleolithic. *Journal of World Prehistory* 12(1): 1 – 53, 1998.

[24] Okladnikov, A. P., and I. I. Kirillov. *Iugo-Vostochnoe Zabaikal'e v Epochu Kamnia I Rannei Bronzy*. Novosibirsk, U.S.S.R.: Nauka, 1980.

[25] Okladnikov, A. P., and I. I. Kirillov. *Iugo-Vostochnoe Zabaikal'e v Epochu Kamnia I Rannei Bronzy*. Novosibirsk, U.S.S.R.: Nauka, 1980: 51.

[26] Okladnikov, A. P., and I. I. Kirillov. *Iugo-Vostochnoe Zabaikal'e v Epochu Kamnia I Rannei Bronzy*. Novosibirsk, U.S.S.R.: Nauka, 1980: 51.

[27] Abramova, Z. A. *Paleolit Severnoi Azii*. In *Paleolit Kavkaza I Severnoi Azii*. Pp. 220. Leningrad: Nauka, 1989.

[28] Mochanov, Y. A. *Drevneishie Etapy Zaseleniia Chclovekom Severo-Vostochnoi Azii*. Novosibirsk, U.S.S.R.: Nauka, 1977.

Stratigraphy and Absolute Chronology of the Paleolithic of Northeast Asia. In *Early Man in America from a Circum-Pacific Perspective*. A. L. Bryan, ed. Pp. 54 – 66. Edmonton, Canada:

Archaeological Researches International, 1978.

[29] Abramova, Z. A. O Vozraste Paleolita Aldana. *Sovetskaia Arkheologiia* 4: 5 – 14, 1979a.
Paleolit Severnoi Azii. In *Paleolit Kavkaza I Severnoi Azii*. Pp. 143 – 243. Leningrad: Nauka, 1989.
Hopkins, D. M., J. V. Matthews, Jr., C. E. Schweger, and S. B. Young. Synthesis. In *Paleoecology of Beringia*. D. M. Hopkins, J. V. Matthews, Jr., C. E. Schweger, and S. B. Young, eds. Pp. 425 – 444. New York: Academic, 1982.
Kuzmin, Y. V., and L. A. Orlova. Radiocarbon Chronology of the Siberian Paleolithic. *Journal of World Prehistory* 12(1): 1 – 53, 1998.
Kuzmin, Y. V., and K. B. Tankersley. The Colonization of Eastern Siberia: An Evaluation of the Paleolithic Age Radiocarbon Dates. *Journal of Archaeological Science* 23(4): 577 – 585, 1996.
Yi, S., and G. Clark. The "Dyuktai Culture" and New World Origins. *Current Anthropology* 26(1): 1 – 20, 1985.

[30] Mochanov, Y. A. *Drevneishie Etapy Zaseleniia Chclovekom Severo-Vostochnoi Azii*. Novosibirsk, U.S.S.R.: Nauka, 1977.

[31] Derev'anko, A. Selemdzha and the Eastern Siberian, Far Eastern, and Beringian Records. In *The Paleolithic of Siberia: New Discoveries and Interpretations*. A. P. Derev'anko, ed. Pp. 285 – 286. Urbana: University of Illinois Press, 1998.

[32] Konstantinov, M. V. *Kamennyi Vek Vostochnogo Regiona Baikal'skoi Azii*. Ulan-Ude and Chita, Russia: Rossiiskaia Akademiia Nauk, Sibirskoe Otdelenie, 1994.

[33] Buvit, I. The Geoarcheology and Archeology of Stud'onoye, an Upper Paleolithic Site in Siberia. M. A. thesis. Department of Anthropology, Texas A&M University, College Station, 2000.
Goebel, T., M. R. Waters, I. Buvit, M. V. Konstantinov, and A. V. Konstantinov. Studenoe – 2 and the Origins of Microblade Technologies in the Transbaikal, Siberia. *Antiquity* 74: 567 – 575, 2000.
Konstantinov, M. V. *Kamennyi Vek Vostochnogo Regiona Baikal'skoi Azii*. Ulan-Ude and Chita, Russia: Rossiiskaia Akademiia Nauk, Sibirskoe Otdelenie, 1994.

[34] Drozdov, N. I., V. P. Chekha, S. A. Laukhin, V. G. Kol'tsova, E. V. Akimova, A. V. Ermolaev, V. P. Leont'ev, S. A. Vasil'ev, A. F. Iamskikh, G. A, Demidenko, E. V. Artem'ev, A. A. Bikulov, A. A. Bokarev, I. V. Foronova, and S. D. Sidoras. *Khrono-Stratigrafiia Paleoliticheskikh Pamiatnikov Srednei Sibiri: Bassein R. Enisei*. Novosibirsk, U.S.S.R.: Nauka, 1990.

[35] Abramova, Z. A., S. N. Astakhov, S. A. VasiPev, N. M. Ermolova, and N. F. Lisitsyn. *Paleolit Eniseiia*. Leningrad: Nauka, 1991.

Drozdov, N. L, V. P. Chekha, S. A. Laukhin, V. G. Kol'tsova, E. V. Akimova, A. V. Ermolaev, V. P. Leont'ev, S. A. Vasil'ev, A. F. Iamskikh, G. A, Demidenko, E. V. Artem'ev, A. A. Bikulov, A. A. Bokarev, I. V. Foronova, and S. D. Sidoras. *Khrono-Stratigrafiia Paleoliticheskikh Pamiatnikov Srednei Sibiri: Bassein R. Enisei*. Novosibirsk, U.S.S.R.: Nauka, 1990.

[36] Kuzmin, Y. V., L. A. Orlova, L. D. Sulerzhitsky, and A. J. T. Jull. Radiocarbon Dating of the Stone and Bronze Age Sites in Primorye (Russian Far East). *Radiocarbon* 36(3): 359 – 366, 1994.

[37] Kostiukevich, V. V., and O. V. Dneprovskaia. Radiouglerodnye Dannye Laboratorii Geokhimii Instituta Merzlotovedeniia SO AN SSSR. *Biulleten' Komissiipo Izucheniiu Chetvertichnogo Perioda* 59: 180 – 182, 1990: 182.

[38] Mochanov, Y. A. *Drevneishie Etapy Zaseleniia Chclovekom Severo-Vostochnoi Azii*. Novosibirsk, U.S.S.R.: Nauka, 1977.

[39] Mochanov, Y. A. Stratigraphy and Absolute Chronology of the Paleolithic of Northeast Asia. In *Early Man in America from a Circum-Pacific Perspective*. A. L. Bryan, ed. Pp. 54 – 66. Edmonton, Canada: Archaeological Researches International, 1978: 64.

[40] Dikov, N. N. *Arkheologicheskie Pamiatniki Kamchatki, Chukotki i Verkhnei Kolymy*. Moscow: Nauka, 1977.

Goebel, T., and S. B. Slobodin. The Colonization of Western Beringia: Technology, Ecology, and Adaptations. In *Ice Age Peoples of North America: Environments, Origins, and Adaptations of the First Americans*. R. Bonnichsenand K. L. Turnmire, eds. Pp. 104 – 155. Corvallis: Oregon State University Press, 1999.

Hamilton, T. D., and T. Goebel. Late Pleistocene Peopling of Alaska. In *Ice Age Peoples of North America: Environments, Origins, and Adaptations of the First Americans*. R. Bonnichsen and K. L. Turnmire, eds. Pp. 156 – 199. Corvallis: Oregon State University Press, 1999.

Powers, W. R., and J. F. Hoffecker. The Pleistocene Settlement in the Nenana Valley, Central Alaska. *American Antiquity* 54(2): 263 – 287, 1989.

[41] Hoffecker, J. F., W. R. Powers, and T. Goebel. The Colonization of Beringia and the Peopling of the New World. *Science* 259: 46 – 53, 1993.

[42] Goebel, T., and S. B. Slobodin. The Colonization of Western Beringia: Technology, Ecology, and Adaptations. In *Ice Age Peoples of North America: Environments, Origins, and Adaptations of the First Americans*. R. Bonnichsenand K. L. Turnmire, eds. Pp. 104 – 155. Corvallis: Oregon State University Press, 1999.

Vasil'ev, S. A. The Upper Palaeolithic of Northern Asia. *Current Anthropology* 34(1): 82 – 92, 1993.

[43] Goebel, T. Pleistocene Human Colonization of Siberia and Peopling of the Americas: An Ecological Approach. *Evolutionary Anthropology: Issues, News, and Reviews* 8(6): 208 - 227, 1999.

[44] Tseitlin, S. M. *Geologiia Paleolita Severnoi Azii*. Moscow: Nauka, 1979.

[45] Vasil'ev, S. A. The Late Paleolithic of the Yenisei: A New Outline. *Journal of World Prehistory* 6(4): 337 - 383, 1992.

[46] Kuzmin, Y. V., and L. A. Orlova. Radiocarbon Chronology of the Siberian Paleolithic. *Journal of World Prehistory* 12(1): 1 - 53, 1998.

[47] Abramova, Z. A., S. N. Astakhov, S. A. VasiPev, N. M. Ermolova, and N. F. Lisitsyn. *Paleolit Eniseiia*. Leningrad: Nauka, 1991.

Vasil'ev, S. A. *Pozdnii Paleolit Verkhnego Eniseiia: Po Materialam Mnogosloinykh Stoianok Raiona Mainy*. St. Petersburg: Russian Academy of Sciences, 1996.

[48] Abramova, Z. A., S. N. Astakhov, S. A. VasiPev, N. M. Ermolova, and N. F. Lisitsyn. *Paleolit Eniseiia*. Leningrad: Nauka, 1991.

Drozdov, N. L, V. P. Chekha, S. A. Laukhin, V. G. Kol'tsova, E. V. Akimova, A. V. Ermolaev, V. P. Leont'ev, S. A. Vasil'ev, A. F. Iamskikh, G. A, Demidenko, E. V. Artem'ev, A. A. Bikulov, A. A. Bokarev, I. V. Foronova, and S. D. Sidoras. *Khrono-Stratigrafiia Paleoliticheskikh Pamiatnikov Srednei Sibiri: Bassein R. Enisei*. Novosibirsk, U.S.S.R.: Nauka, 1990.

Vasil'ev, S. A. *Pozdnii Paleolit Verkhnego Eniseiia: Po Materialam Mnogosloinykh Stoianok Raiona Mainy*. St. Petersburg: Russian Academy of Sciences, 1996.

[49] Vasil'ev, S. A. *Pozdnii Paleolit Verkhnego Eniseiia: Po Materialam Mnogosloinykh Stoianok Raiona Mainy*. St. Petersburg: Russian Academy of Sciences, 1996.

[50] Goebel, T., M. R. Waters, I. Buvit, M. V. Konstantinov, and A. V. Konstantinov. Studenoe - 2 and the Origins of Microblade Technologies in the Transbaikal, Siberia. *Antiquity* 74: 567 - 575, 2000.

Konstantinov, M. V. *Kamennyi Vek Vostochnogo Regiona Baikal'skoi Azii*. Ulan-Ude and Chita, Russia: Rossiiskaia Akademiia Nauk, Sibirskoe Otdelenie, 1994.

[51] Konstantinov, M. V. *Kamennyi Vek Vostochnogo Regiona Baikal'skoi Azii*. Ulan-Ude and Chita, Russia: Rossiiskaia Akademiia Nauk, Sibirskoe Otdelenie, 1994.

Kuznetsov, O. V. Kharakter Kurturno-khoziaistvennoi Adaptatsii Pozdnepaleoliticheskogo Naseleniia Zapadnogo Zabaikal'ia. In *100 Let Gunnskoi Arkheologii: Nomadizm Proshloe, Nastoiashchee v Global nom Kontekste i Istoricheskoi Perspektive*. Pp. 34 - 37. Ulan-Ude, Russia: Russian Academy of Sciences, Siberian Division, 1996.

[52] Kuznetsov, O. V. Kharakter Kurturno-khoziaistvennoi Adaptatsii Pozdnepaleoliticheskogo

Naseleniia Zapadnogo Zabaikal'ia. In *100 Let Gunnskoi Arkheologii: Nomadizm Proshloe, Nastoiashchee v Global nom Kontekste i Istoricheskoi Perspektive*. Pp. 34 – 37. Ulan-Ude, Russia: Russian Academy of Sciences, Siberian Division, 1996.

[53] Goebel, T. Pleistocene Human Colonization of Siberia and Peopling of the Americas: An Ecological Approach. *Evolutionary Anthropology: Issues, News, and Reviews* 8(6): 208 – 227, 1999.

[54] Bamforth, D. B. Technological Efficiency and Tool Curation. *American Antiquity* 51: 38 – 50, 1986.

Kuhn, S. L. *Mousterian Lithic Technology: An Ecological Perspective*. Princeton: University of Princeton Press, 1995.

Odell, G. H. Economizing Behavior and the Concept of "Curation." In *Stone Tools: Theoretical Insights into Human Prehistory*. G. H. Odell, ed. Pp. 51 – 80. New York: Plenum, 1996.

Parry, W. J., and R. L. Kelly. Expedient Core Technology and Sedentism. In *The Organization of Core Technology*. J-K. Johnson and C. A. Morrow, eds. Pp. 285 – 304. Boulder: Westview, 1987.

Shott, M. J. Technological Organization and Settlement Mobility: An Ethnographic Examination. *Journal of Anthropological Research* 42: 15 – 51, 1986.

[55] Andrefsky, W., Jr. *Lithics: Macroscopic Approaches to Analysis*. Cambridge: Cambridge University Press, 1998.

Parry, W. J., and R. L. Kelly. Expedient Core Technology and Sedentism. In *The Organization of Core Technology*. J-K. Johnson and C. A. Morrow, eds. Pp. 285 – 304. Boulder: Westview, 1987.

Torrence, R. Time Budgeting and Hunter-Gatherer Technology. In *Hunter-Gatherer Economy in Prehistory*. G. Bailey, ed. Pp. 11 – 22. Cambridge: Cambridge University Press, 1983.

[56] Abravova, Z. A. *Paleolit Eniseia: Afontovskaia Kul'tura*. Novosibirsk, U. S. S. R.: Nauka, 1979b.

[57] Vasil'ev, S. A. *Pozdnii Paleolit Verkhnego Eniseiia: Po Materialam Mnogosloinykh Stoianok Raiona Mainy*. St. Petersburg: Russian Academy of Sciences, 1996.

[58] Goebel, T. *Middle to Upper Palaeolithic Transition in Siberia*. Ann Arbor, Mich.: University Microfilms, Bell and Howell, 1993.

[59] Kelly, R. L. The Three Sides of a Biface. *American Antiquity* 53(4): 717 – 734, 1988.

[60] Dikov, N. N., and N. A. Kononenko. Rezul'taty Trasologicheskogo Issledovaniia Klinovidnykh Nukleusov iz Shestogo Sloia Stoianok Ushki I-V na Kamchatke. In *Drevnie Pamiatniki Severa Dal'nego Vostoka (Novye Materialy i Issledovaniia Severo-Vostochno-Aziatskoi Kompleksnoi*

Arkheologicheskoi Ekspeditsii). Pp. 170 – 175. Magadan, U. S. S. R: Akademiia Nauk SSSR, 1990.

[61] Flenniken, J. J. The Paleolithic Dyuktai Pressure Blade Technique of Siberia. *Arctic Anthropology* 24(2): 117 – 132, 1987.

[62] Abramova, Z. A., S. N. Astakhov, S. A. VasiPev, N. M. Ermolova, and N. F. Lisitsyn. *Paleolit Eniseiia*. Leningrad: Nauka, 1991.

Okladnikov, A. P., and I. I. Kirillov. *Iugo Vostochnoe Zabaikal'e v Epochu Kamnia I Rannei Bronzy*. Novosibirsk, U.S.S.R.: Nauka, 1980.

[63] Medvedev, G. Upper Paleolithic Sites in South-Central Siberia. In *The Paleolithic of Siberia: New Discoveries and Interpretations*. A. P. Derev'anko, ed. Pp. 122 – 137. Urbana: University of Illinois Press, 1998.

[64] Vasil'ev, S. A. *Pozdnii Paleolit Verkhnego Eniseiia: Po Materialam Mnogosloinykh Stoianok Raiona Mainy*. St. Petersburg: Russian Academy of Sciences, 1996.

[65] Goebel, T. Pleistocene Human Colonization of Siberia and Peopling of the Americas: An Ecological Approach. *Evolutionary Anthropology: Issues, News, and Reviews* 8(6): 208 – 227, 1999.

Medvedev, G. Upper Paleolithic Sites in South-Central Siberia. In *The Paleolithic of Siberia: New Discoveries and Interpretations*. A. P. Derev'anko, ed. Pp. 122 – 137. Urbana: University of Illinois Press, 1998.

[66] Medvedev, G. Upper Paleolithic Sites in South-Central Siberia. In *The Paleolithic of Siberia: New Discoveries and Interpretations*. A. P. Derev'anko, ed. Pp. 122 – 137. Urbana: University of Illinois Press, 1998.

[67] Medvedev, G. Upper Paleolithic Sites in South-Central Siberia. In *The Paleolithic of Siberia: New Discoveries and Interpretations*. A. P. Derev'anko, ed. Pp. 122 – 137. Urbana: University of Illinois Press, 1998.

[68] Kuznetsov, O. V. Kharakter Kurturno-khoziaistvennoi Adaptatsii Pozdnepaleoliticheskogo Naseleniia Zapadnogo Zabaikal'ia. In *100 Let Gunnskoi Arkheologii: Nomadizm Proshloe, Nastoiashchee v Global nom Kontekste i Istoricheskoi Perspektive*. Pp. 34 – 37. Ulan-Ude, Russia: Russian Academy of Sciences, Siberian Division, 1996.

[69] Petrin, V. T. *Paleoliticheskie Pamiatniki Zapadno-Sibirskoi Ravniny*. Novosibirsk, U.S.S.R.: Nauka, 1986.

[70] Akimova, E. V., V. P. Chekha, V. G. Kol'tsova, N. D. Ovodov, and L. D. Sulerzhitskii. Pozdnepaleoliticheskaia Stoianka Listvenka. In *Arkheologiia, Geologiia i Paleogeografiia Paleoliticheskikh Pamiatnikov Iuga Srednei Sibiri (Severo-Minusinskaia Vpadina, Kuznetskii Alatau i Vostochnyi Saian)*. Pp. 34 – 47. Krasnoiarsk, Russia: Russian Academy of Sciences,

Siberian Division, 1992.

[71] Lezhnenko, 1. L.. G. 1. Medvedev. and G. N. Mikhniuk. Issledovaniia Paleoliticheskikh i Mezoliticheskikh Gorizontov Stoianki Sosnovyi Bor na Reke Beloi v 1966 – 1971 Gg. In *Paleolit i Mezolit Iuga Sibiri*. Pp. 80 – 107. Irkutsk, U.S.S.R.: Izdatel'stvo lrkutskogo Universiteta, 1982.

[72] Ermolova, N. M. *Teriofauna Doliny Angary v Pozdnem Antropogene*. Novosibirsk, U.S.S.R.: Nauka, 1978.

[73] Petrin, V. T. *Paleoliticheskie Pamiatniki Zapadno-Sibirskoi Ravniny*. Novosibirsk, U.S.S.R.: Nauka, 1986.

[74] Abramova, Z. A., S. N. Astakhov, S. A. VasiPev, N. M. Ermolova, and N. F. Lisitsyn. *Paleolit Eniseiia*. Leningrad: Nauka, 1991.

Ermolova, N. M. *Teriofauna Doliny Angary v Pozdnem Antropogene*. Novosibirsk, U.S.S.R.: Nauka, 1978.

Vasil'ev, S. A. *Pozdnii Paleolit Verkhnego Eniseiia: Po Materialam Mnogosloinykh Stoianok Raiona Mainy*. St. Petersburg: Russian Academy of Sciences, 1996.

[75] Tashak, V. I. K Voprosu o Vozniknovenii Rybolovstva na Iuga Zapadnogo Zabaikal'ia. In *100 Let Gunnskoi Arkheologii: Nomadizm Proshloe, Nastoiashchee v Global'nom Kontekste I Istoricheskoi Perspektive*. Pp. 61 – 64. Ulan-Ude, Russia: Russian Academy of Sciences, Siberian Division, 1996.

[76] Binford, L. R. Willow Smoke and Dogs' Tails. *American Antiquity* 45: 4 – 20, 1980.

[77] Eriksen, B. V. Resource Exploitation, Subsistence Strategies, and Adaptiveness in Late Pleistocene-Early Holocene Northwest Europe. In *Humans at the End of the Ice Age: The Archaeology of the Pleistocene-Holocene Transition*. L. G. Straus, B. V. Eriksen, J. M. Erlandson, and D. R. Yesner, eds. Pp. 101 – 128. New York: Plenum, 1996.

Weniger, G.-C. Magdalenian Settlement Patterns and Subsistence in Central Europe: The Southwestern and Central German Cases. In *The Pleistocene Old World: Regional Perspectives*. O. Soffer, ed. Pp. 201 – 216. New York: Plenum, 1987.

[78] Straus, L. G. The Archaeology of the Pleistocene-Holocene Transition in Southwest Europe. In *Humans at the End of the Ice Age: The Archaeology of the Pleistocene-Holocene Transition*. L. G. Straus, B. V. Eriksen, J. M. Erlandson, and D. R. Yesner, eds. Pp. 95. New York: Plenum, 1996.

[79] Bahn, P. Seasonal Migration in South-West France during the Late Glacial Period. *Journal of Archaeological Science* 4: 245 – 257, 1977.

[80] Audouze, F. The Paris Basin in Magdalenian Times. In *The Pleistocene Old World: Regional Perspectives*. Olga Soffer, ed. Pp. 183 – 200. New York: Plenum, 1987.

细石叶与迁徙：移民美洲的族群与经济模型

戴维·R·耶斯纳　　　　　乔治·皮尔森
（阿拉斯加大学　安克雷奇）（堪萨斯大学　劳伦斯）

摘　要：因为跟最早美洲人问题相关，大白令地区早期细石叶组合一直是主要的研究重心。尽管早在距今20 000年前细石叶已经在东北亚地区出现，其生产的高峰还是在更新世之末，跟白令地区最早确切的有人居住年代重合。阿拉斯加地区细石叶生产主要见于全新世的最早阶段，有种观点认为它是最早进入美洲（古印第安人）之后移民美洲的特定族群（纳—德内人）的标志性器物。另一种观点认为它是适应北极寒冷地带狩猎生活的技术，这里石料相对较少，特别是在冬天。折中的观点则认为早期群体较少利用这一技术，随着大动物的绝灭，北美驯鹿越来越重要，细石叶技术也越来越普遍。冰盖以南地区缺乏细石叶，细石叶没有进入北美腹地，这种状况支持细石叶代表特定族群的观点。

当前最早美洲人的问题跟75年前发现古印第安人时一样，仍然是一个充满争议的问题。时间、路线、移民的机制，甚至是人的来源都受到各个角度的批评。即使是白令陆桥，这个40年前就已经得到承认的基本迁徙线路也受到了攻击[1]，不再被看作是人类进入美洲最可能的线路[2]。然而，尽管参与者改变了，许多基本问题还是跟1960年代惊人相似。那些支持人类较早（即早于距今12 000年）进入美洲的研究者较少怀疑那些年代较早的少量碳十四测年数据，尽管有时还存在地层关系问题，他们倾向支持"前投掷尖状器阶段"这个概念,早期殖民者是小群的狩猎者,还不是很了解石器技术[3]。相反,那些支持更晚进入美洲的研究者对碳十四年代与地层关系持高度怀疑的态度,并且认为最早的殖民者是高度熟练的狩猎者,他们装备有良好的武器系统。

那些支持人类在新大陆大动物灭绝过程中发挥了重要作用的研究者倾向于支持更晚进入的方案[4],但是那些支持更晚进入方案的研究者有时又将气候改变视为动物灭绝的主要原因[5]。按照某些持更早进入观点的研究者的说法,这里存在着一种转变,从"大动物狩猎"的范式过渡到另一种范式,把最早殖民者视为一般化的觅食者。这尤其适用于南美,这里较晚的古印第安人与古代期的狩猎采集者之间的差异要小于更北方的草原环境地带[6]。当然,更晚进入观点热心支持者偏好的"克鲁维斯最早"模型也逐渐让位,从专门狩猎大动物的模型变为更强调生计多样性的模型,即使在草原环境中也是如此[7]。

一个最近流行的方案是所谓"海岸迁徙假说",最早的殖民者拥有足够熟练航海技术以及利用海洋资源的生计方式,沿着从前未曾探索的海岸线持续向前迁徙数千公里[8]。这意味着半定居的海岸聚落形态可能早到距今15 000年前就已经出现了,人们从中心营地出发去获取海豹、海鸟、鱼、贝类,东北亚或白令地区可能也存在这样的方式。这个假说存在若干问题:(1)俄罗斯远东地区类似的遗址没有早于距今6 500年的,最相似的遗址就是日本北部的绳文早期遗址;(2)阿拉斯加最早海岸生活方式的证据,即使是在板块抬升或等高区域,都没有超过全新世最早期(距今10 000年);(3)早期用小舟跨越阿拉斯加西海湾是非常危险的,生计资源很可能局限于环斑海豹、海象与北极熊,需要复杂的技术与社会组织才能有效地狩猎;(4)加州与秘鲁的早期海岸遗址(测年年代距今11 000年前)主要反映的是近岸利用,人们狩猎海鸟,在近岸环境中采集贝类,它们不是熟练的航海者;(5)从阿拉斯加到智利南部的海岸人群中没有证明存在遗传学上的联系,无论是基于人骨遗存还是基于器物,部分原因可能是后者的两类证据在早期遗址中都非常罕见。

阿拉斯加与北方考古学家基于他们在北方生活的经验,一般都倾向于认为人类最早进入美洲需要的条件相当严格。在他们看来,早期的移民至少需要拥有一套完善的能够应对极端寒冷气候条件的工具,缝制暖和的皮服,具有冬季大范围行动的设备,甚至应该具有良好的信号传递方式。他们需要拥有多样的狩猎策略,包括找到各种各样的动物,能进行单人与群体狩猎,以及尸食。可能还需要多样的工具以及投掷方法,以及就地取材满足技术需要的能力。

另一个热点问题是最早的北美殖民者的族属,这一问题始于有关北美西北部早全新世人骨遗存生物学联系的争论[9]。半个世纪前我们就知道发现于北美各地的古印第安人人骨材料跟晚期的人群特征有所不同,其颅骨更长更窄。无论是因为趋同还是因为源于同一祖先,他们与阿伊努人及其他东北亚古亚洲人有相似性。这一现象既与微进化过程有关,也与全新世新的基因输入有关。如果是后者,一种主要的可能来自圆颅的"典型蒙古人种"的基因,显然这与爱斯基摩—阿留申祖先人群跨越白令陆桥的晚期移民有关。此外,从基因标志、牙齿形态、语言学特征上来看,还有第三波移民纳—德内人[10]。纳—德内人包括阿拉斯加与加拿大西部的特林基特人、海达人与北阿萨帕斯康人,美国西南部的南阿萨帕斯康人(阿帕奇人)以及俄勒冈与加州西北部太平洋沿海的少数族群。

就阿拉斯加与整个北美最早人类移民而言,细石叶技术于其中起到怎样的作用呢?晚更新世到早全新世从西伯利亚中部、中国东北到北美西北部的乔治亚—普格特桑德湾地区,细石叶技术广泛分布。跨越从海岸到内陆的广阔地区,这种分布特征表明这些工业之间或者存在"遗传学上的"联系,或是普遍采用一种技术组合,以有效解决极北地区某些共同的难题。

阿兰·布莱恩[11]是最早注意到阿拉斯加与加拿大西部细石叶工业与古印第安人工业截然不同的研究者之一,冰盖南部可能会发现更早的工具组合。在他与其他研究者看来,细石叶制作者是较晚移民的后代,比南部地区制作克鲁维斯(以及前克鲁维斯?)工具组合的移民更晚。北部地区许多"前—投掷尖状器"组合是南部地区克鲁维斯的先驱,从不列颠山组合到色地纳溪的"器物"到特里尔溪、老克罗的骨齿角工业,以及最近莱米山洞的早期材料[12]。北方地区早期人类遗存稀少,阿尔伯塔发现的塔贝尔小孩与育空地区老克罗遗址发现的稍晚的下颌骨代表更新世人类进入美洲的可能证据。然而几乎所有这样的遗址如今都被否定了,基于大量已接受的遗址材料,最早的证据定在距今 12 000 年,可能早到距今 14 000 年。根据我们现有的材料,细石叶技术占什么样的地位呢?它跟最早美洲人这个大问题有着怎样的关系呢?

一、东北亚的细石叶工业

东北亚(俄罗斯、蒙古、中国、朝鲜、日本)旧石器时代晚期石器工业的年代受到许多问题的困扰,不论是洞穴还是旷野遗址[13],但某些阶段的主要形态还是明显的。石叶工业标志旧石器时代晚期的开端,西伯利亚西部与阿尔泰地区跟欧洲一样早,其年代可以早到距今40 000~44 000年前[14]。西伯利亚中部(如叶尼塞河地区)的年代稍晚一些,最早的年代在距今32 000年左右[15]。再向东,外贝加尔地区与西伯利亚东部的勒拿河盆地,年代更晚。尽管有些遗址(如托尔巴加与瓦尔瓦里纳戈拉)的年代在距今35 000年前后,但绝大多数年代都集中在距今28 000至20 000年之间,正好在末次盛冰期之前(很少有年代在距今20 000年至18 000年之间,这可能与末次盛冰期寒冷气候有关,西伯利亚东部无人居住或是放弃了[16])。向南,石叶工业也见于蒙古与中国北方旧石器时代晚期早段石器组合中,尤其是鄂尔多斯高原地区,但是这些遗址的年代测定不佳。不过,石叶工业在日本北部与朝鲜半岛的出现较为清楚,俄罗斯远东阿穆尔河口以南的遗址如乌斯提诺夫卡也不错,其年代都在末次盛冰期之后,不早于距今20 000年。石叶工业整体的分布特征确实表明存在从西向东的迁徙或传播,时间还不是非常清楚。

　　细石叶工业通常被看作是"旧石器时代晚期晚段"的标志,实际年代可能更晚,许多都是末次盛冰期之后出现的。尽管其分布形态还不完全清楚,但还是有些理由认为细石叶组合存在由西向东年代递减的趋势。最早的细石叶组合实际上集中于外贝加尔地区与中国西北,正好在末次盛冰期之后(距今18 000~16 000年左右[17])。某种程度上说,细石叶的分布不仅向西(西伯利亚中部)年代递减,出现年代在距今16 000至14 000年间,向东(西伯利亚东部、俄罗斯远东、中国东北与日本),出现年代在距今15 000至13 000年间[18]。俄罗斯远东沿海省份与日本,发现有细石叶与更早的石叶工业之间叠压地层关系,细石叶出现于距今15 000年左右。俄罗斯远东地区,阿穆尔河盆地往南,细石叶在早全新世中石器时代遗址中还在使用,新石器时代早期遗址中还能见到一些,与陶器共存。类似之,日本绳文早期中石器工业继续使用细石叶,也与早期陶器共存。还值得注意的是,不同的技术用来生产细石叶,既包括锥形石叶,也包括楔形石核(后者从前称为戈壁或校园石核)。尽管整个东北亚地区两种石核技术都存在,包括两到三种不同形制的楔形细石核生产,向西锥形石核更常见,而楔形石核多见于东部(从北海道到北美西北太平洋沿岸)。

　　如何解释这些材料呢?为了方便讨论起见,如果我们假定这些技术确实某个层面上反映族群性质,那么一个可能的解释就是,石叶工业反映解剖学上的现代人的欧洲群体向东推进到贝加尔地区,最终达到俄罗斯远东,而细石叶技术基本上反映解剖学现代人北亚地区特有群体,也来到同一地区,最终分布于中国东北、日本、朝鲜半岛以及俄罗斯远东地区。还有一种观点视细石叶就是基本由亚洲居民发明的东西,随后为欧洲人群所采用,继续向东迁徙,并且可能进入了新大陆。这种观点可能对于某些人有政治上的吸引力,但它几乎没有考古或生物学事实的支持。

西伯利亚东北角(楚科奇与勘察加地区)的情况又如何呢?长期以来这里都被视作移民阿拉斯加与北美的出发地点。位于这一地区西北角上的布里勒克遗址,以及这一地区东南角上的乌斯基遗址,具有晚更新世的年代。布里勒克遗址中晚更新世猛犸象遗存与器物的共存关系还存有疑问,但碳十四年代数据位距今 11 800 至 13 400 年。少量"似石叶石片"为原地埋藏,但发现于遗址中的细石叶石核则不是原地埋藏[19]。乌斯基遗址中细石叶层位(图 10.1)年代为距今 10 800 年左右,年代比较可靠。这一层位之下是一层含带梃尖状器的文化层,跟东北亚任何地区都没有清楚的联系,还发现有一些石叶与雕刻器,但没有细石叶的发现报道[20]。不过,鲍尔斯[21]注意到这个较老的层位中发现有少量细石叶,但没有细石核,其年代为距今 14 300 年前后。

最后,值得注意的是,整个东北亚地区,大两面器既跟石叶共出,也跟细石叶工业共出,很少有明确关联形式。许多两面器可能就是毛坯或是半成品,剩下的可能是石刀或其他两面器,既不能反映族群形制,也很少能反映环境(即用此类工具狩猎特定的物种)。

二、阿拉斯加的细石叶组合:时间进程与关联

(一)阿拉斯加晚更新世的细石叶?

目前已发现某些细石叶确实与阿拉斯加以及育空地区某些最早的遗址相关(图 10.2)。育空地区北部布鲁费希 2 号洞穴发现有少量细石叶(图 10.3),但没有发现细石核,它们与遗址中更新世大动物群的关联可能也有问题,动物群年代超过距今 13 000 年。阿拉斯加内陆地区塔纳那河流域的黑利湖遗址最底部层位发现近 100 件细石叶以及楔形细石核[22]。这些层位提供了两个年代,距今 11 000 年与距今 11 400 年;大部分年代处在距今 8 000 年至 10 500 年间,可能存在地层混杂的问题。还是在塔纳那流域,斯旺角遗址最底部层位同样发现了大

厘米

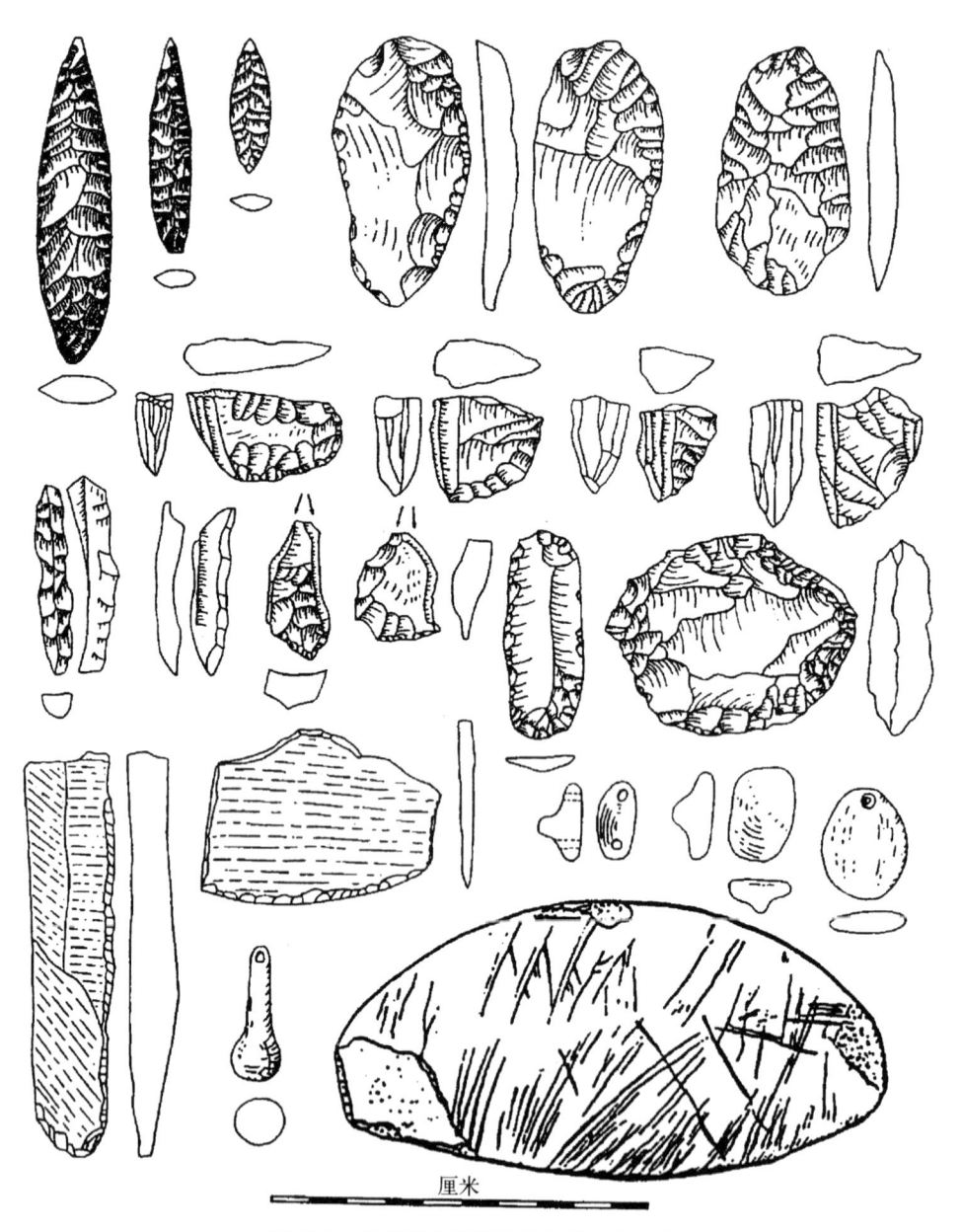

图 10.1　乌斯基 I 遗址第四层的文化组合

（经允许采用[23]）

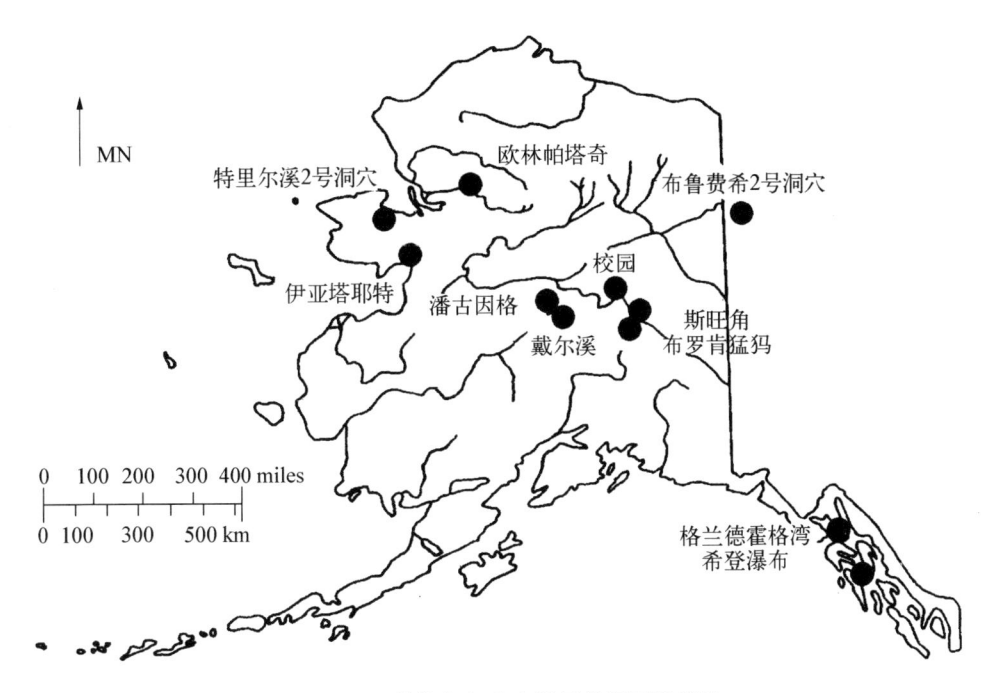

图 10.2 阿拉斯加与育空地区的细石叶遗址

量细石叶(图 10.4),年代距今 11 700 年左右[24](与霍尔默斯个人联系,2002),但与之共存的只有一些不典型的细石叶(非楔形细石核)。阿拉斯加北部的梅萨遗址也发现少量细石叶,但因为缺乏地层关系,所以很难与古印第安人联系起来。再者,遗址的十多个年代中仅有两个属于晚更新世,含细石叶的火塘没有直接测年。

因此,阿拉斯加与育空地区遗址出土的早期(即更新世)细石叶数量相对较少,地层关系与年代多有问题,很少共存有细石核。例如,斯旺角遗址出土的许多细石叶最多只能称为"似石叶石片",附近布罗肯猛犸遗址最底部层位出土的石制品也是如此。一般说来,这些遗址最底部层位出土的石器材料,所用原料质量较为粗劣,很可能采自河卵石。这跟较晚的(早全新世)组合形成鲜明对照,晚期组合中不仅含有丰富的、经过精致加工的细石叶,而且还有相当数量的楔形细石核。

戈贝尔、霍菲克、鲍尔斯把阿拉斯加内陆地区最早的石器工业命名为勒纳那组合[25],理由是勒纳那流域的戴尔溪、驼鹿溪、瓦尔克路及其他一些遗址厚层黄土底部发现了这些工业明确的地层关系。尽管这一技术组合的主要特征

厘米

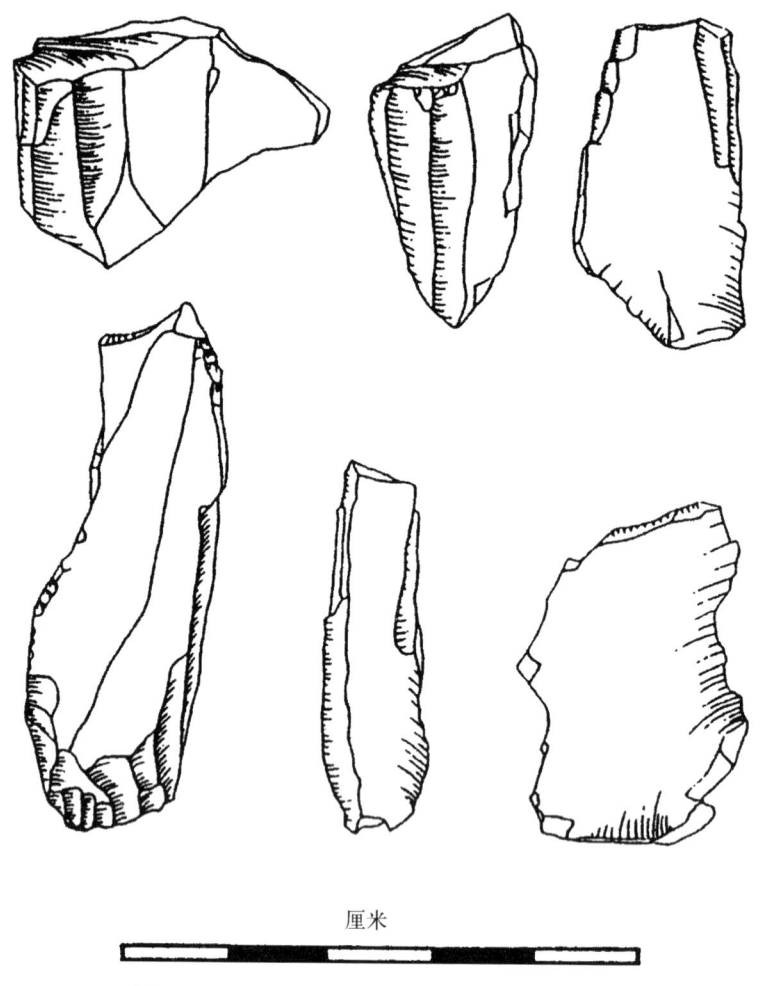

图 10.3 育空地区布鲁费希洞 2 号遗址出土的细
石核、细石叶与角雕刻器[26]
（经允许使用）

是包括大量的平凸刃刮削器与其他典型工具,两个代表性的特征是存在石叶,没有细石叶。就此而论,其组成与晚更新世俄罗斯远东地区乌斯提诺夫卡工业相似。不过,不少研究者不大能接受将缺乏典型工具类型视为石器组合的特征。

（二）古北极与白令传统：勒纳那与德纳里组合

阿拉斯加内陆地区发现的细石叶工业是最早的证据之一,表明与西伯利亚早

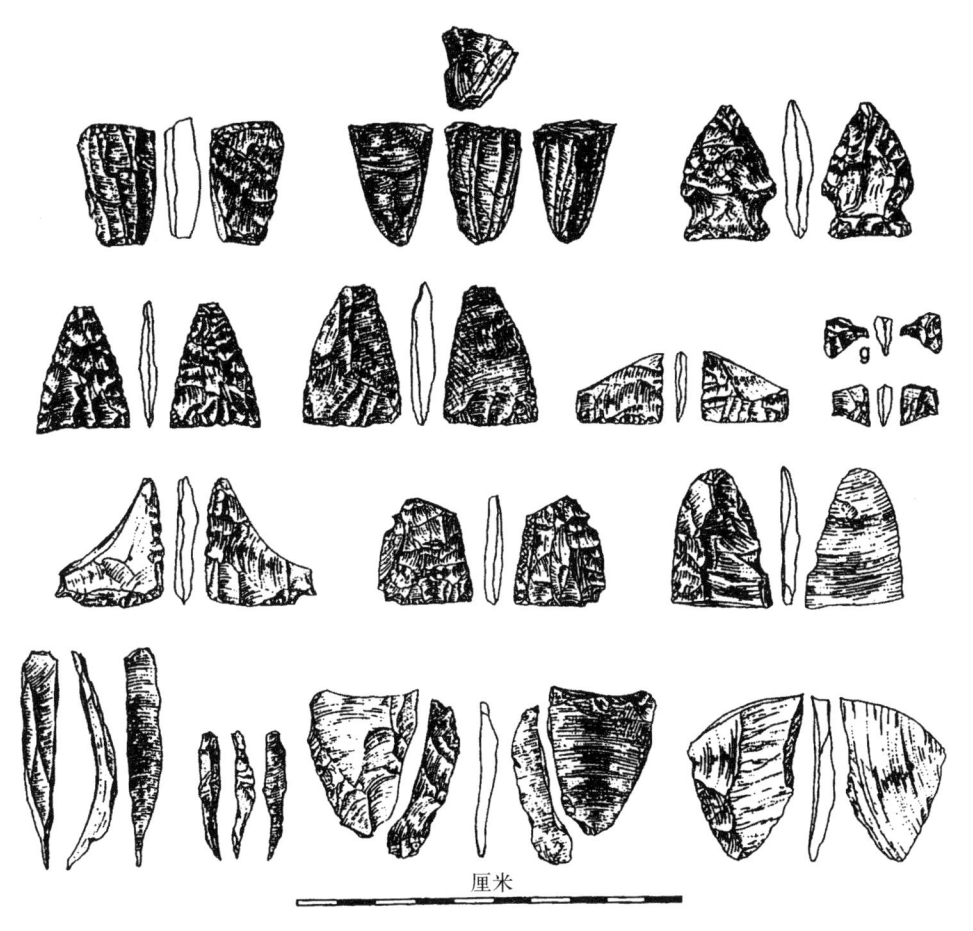

图 10.4　斯旺角的器物，包括下文化层出土的"细石叶预制石片"[27]

期考古的直接联系[28]。发现于阿拉斯加大学法尔班克斯的校园遗址也位于塔纳那流域，出土楔形细石叶与细石叶，跟东北亚相似（图10.5）。这个遗址存在地层扰动与混杂的严重问题，塔纳那流域其他遗址包括黑利湖遗址中最终发现更多这样的器物以及少量较早的年代，似乎支持其年代为晚更新世至早全新世。不过，1950至1960年代，由于路易斯·吉登斯与他的学生道格拉斯·安德森在科布克与诺阿塔克流域的细致工作，研究中心转向了阿拉斯加西北部。他们在欧林帕塔奇遗址发现了距今8 000年的细石叶与两面器工业证据[29]（图10.6），之前是一种较早的含石叶而没有细石叶的工业，他们称之为"阿克马克"。尽管这些较早的工业没有确切的年代，安德森认为它们是北美驯鹿狩猎群体的后裔，居住在白令陆桥的

厘米

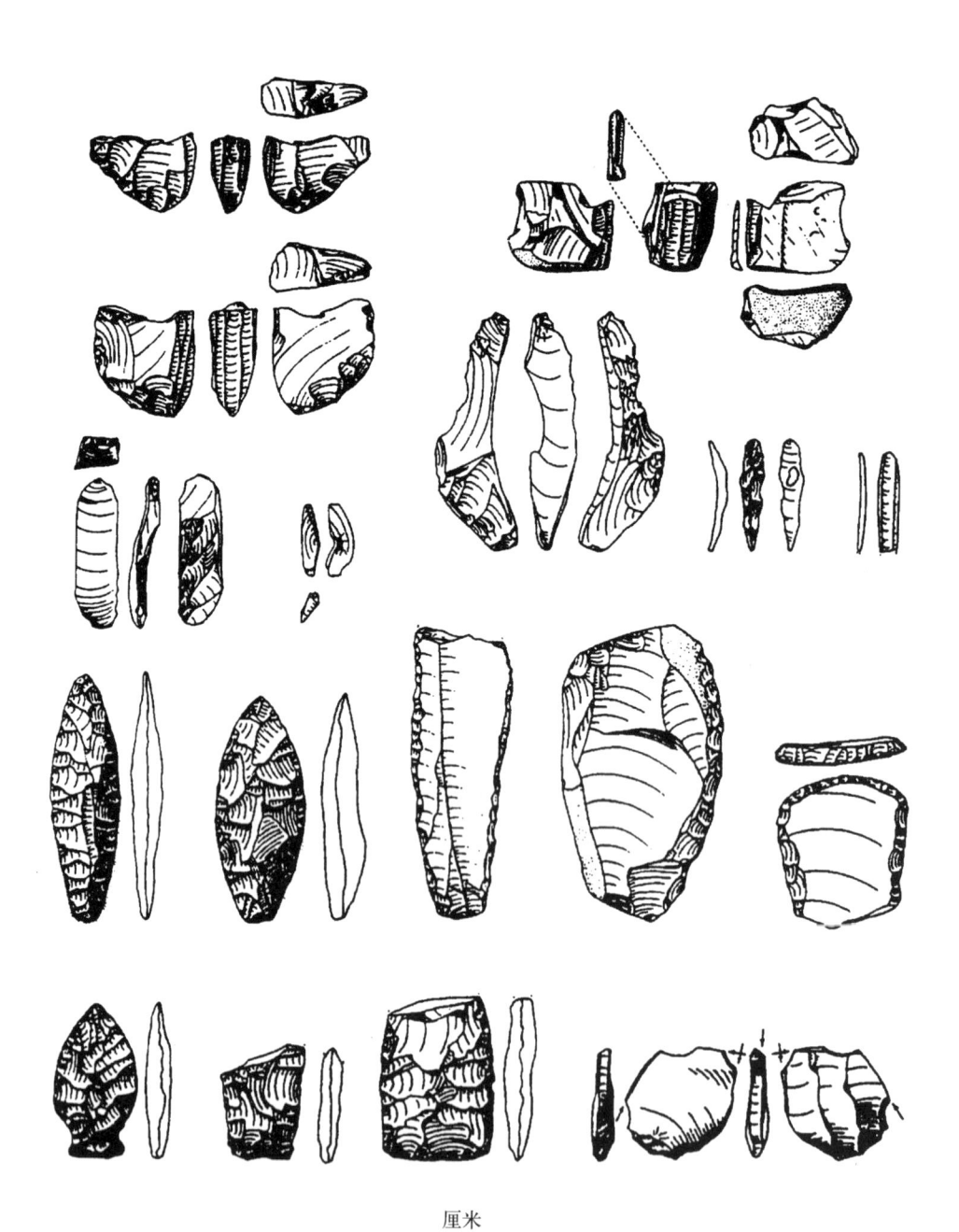

图 10.5 塔纳那流域坎帕斯遗址出土器物
（经允许采用[30]）

厘米

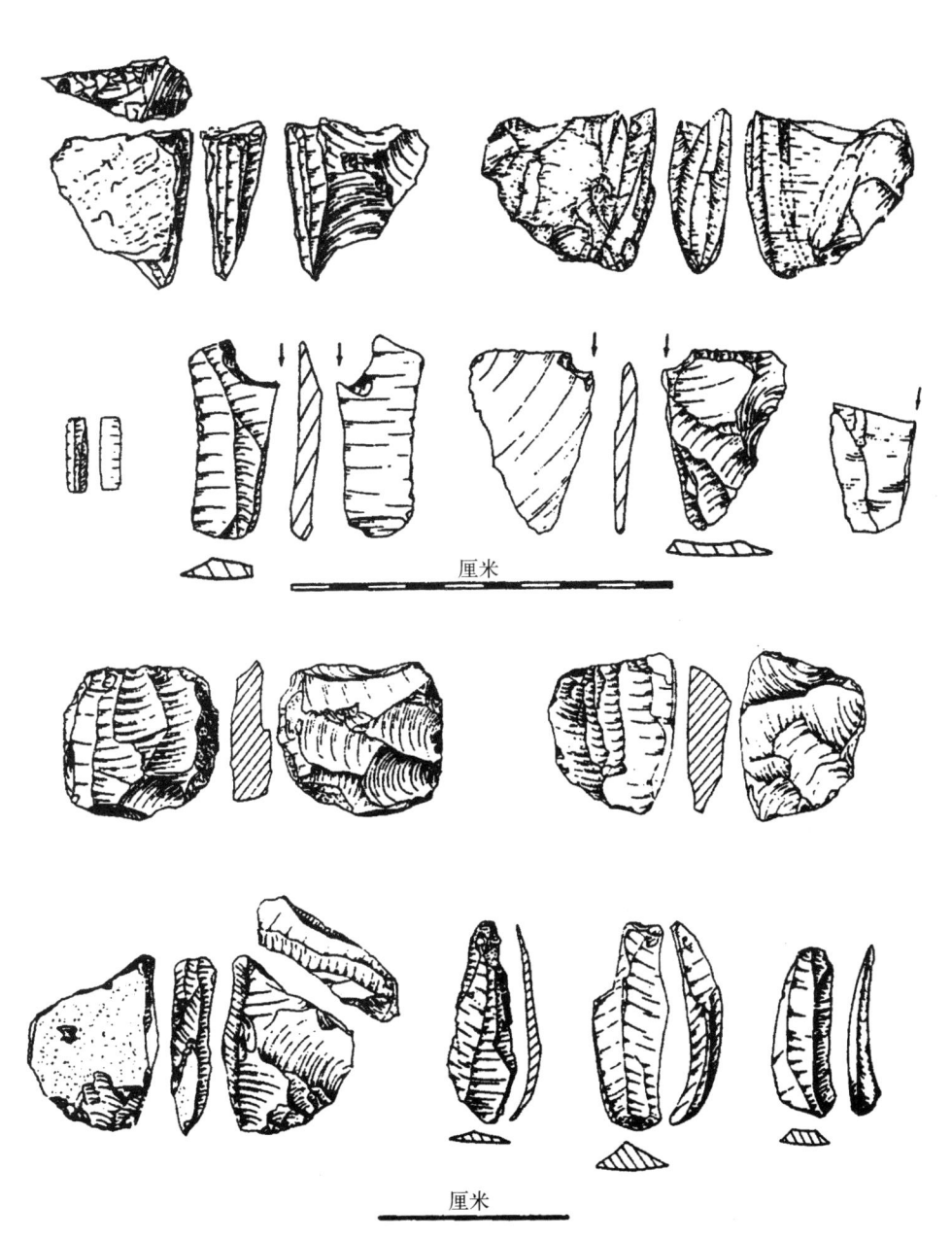

厘米

图 10.6 欧林帕特奇遗址阿克马克与科布克组出土的器物

（经允许采用[31]）

内陆地区,可以早到距今 15 000 年。这是一种确实含有西伯利亚来源的北美古北极文化的组成部分。同时,发现于阿拉斯加北坡地区的细石叶工业,大多来自地表采集,没有碳十四年代或好的地层关系。

由于弗雷德·哈德雷格·维斯特的工作,研究中心再一次转向了阿拉斯加内陆地区的坦格勒湖地区,它位于塔纳那流域西南部,处在阿拉斯加山脉环抱中。晚更新世时这里曾经是冰川覆盖区域,早期石器工业发现于近地表地层中,土壤发育很薄,几乎没有可以测年的材料,地层关系也很差。原来认为属于晚更新世,现在看来这一地区最早的人类居住不会早于距今 10 500 年。阿姆菲希尔特山组合含有大两面器,可能是半成品或毛坯,跟采集当地一处重要的燧石产地的原料有关。德纳里组合分布更广泛,维斯特[32]认为它包含有大两面器、细石叶、楔形细石核(图 10.7)。许多研究者试图把这些细石叶工业跟安德森所说的美洲古北极文化联系起来。

勒纳那与塔纳那流域随后的工作在很大程度上帮我们弄清楚了德纳里组合的内涵,但也产生了新的问题,不仅在时空分布上,还包括适应环境方面。勒纳那流域的遗址如戴尔溪出土数量较大的德纳里组合材料,比较早的勒纳那组合材料丰富。戴尔溪遗址出土的德纳里组合材料包括丰富的细石叶以及至少 21 件楔形细石叶(图 10.8)。这个组合有一个距今 10 700 年的年代,这使得它成为最早的德纳里组合之一[33],仅比同一遗址勒纳那组合的年代晚 500 年。实际上,戴尔溪遗址存在地层年代颠倒的问题,可能发生了混杂,以及受到该地区煤炭中化石炭的污染(与罗伯特·索尔森个人联系,1999)。不过,附近驼鹿溪遗址发现两个细石叶地层,较老的那个年代距今 10 500 年,较年轻的距今 5 700 年[34]。此外,塔纳那流域下游格力斯特尔河采石场遗址最近发现的细石叶组合含有一个距今 10 500 年左右的火塘(与查尔斯·霍尔默斯个人联系,2000)。

勒纳那流域的潘古因格溪遗址也出土了德纳里组合材料(图 10.9),包含 150 件细石叶与 10 件石核,距今 7 000 至 8 000 年。遗址较早的组合距今 9 800 至 10 200 年,还没有确定属于哪一个文化传统,但它的年代与技术与布罗肯猛犸遗址第 3 层的发现类似,我们认为它可能代表较晚阶段的勒纳那组合[35]。类似之,塔纳那流域的恰格瓦特遗址发现了约 30 件细石叶,遗址位于法尔班克斯正南,1980 年代早期发掘,"暂时"有两个碳十四年代,距今 9 000 与距今 9 500 年[36]。

(三)"持续存在的"与衍生的细石叶工业:阿拉斯加内陆地区及其他地区

与此同时早期细石叶工业还包括塔纳那流域遗址如恰格瓦特、黑利湖以及

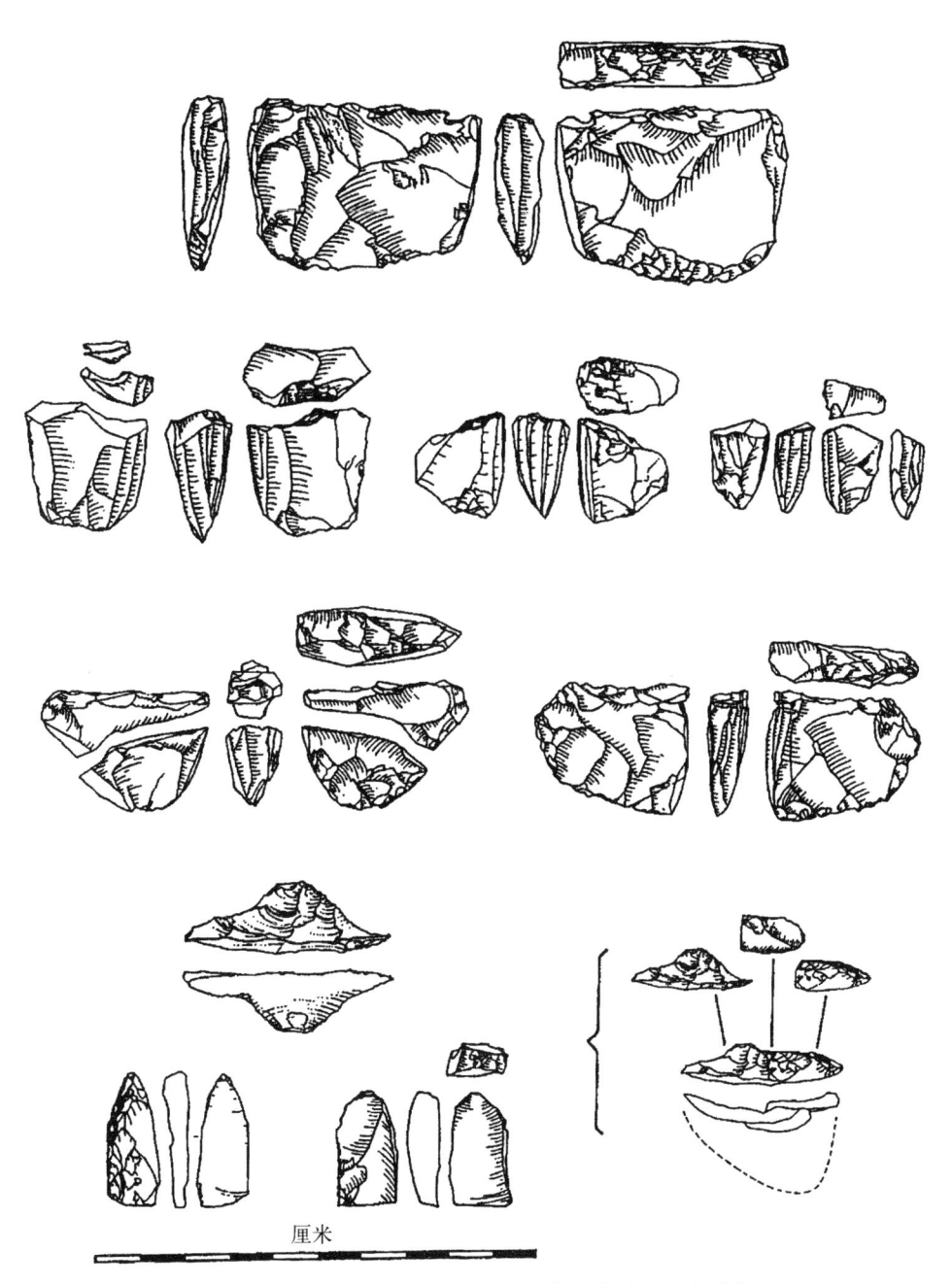

细石叶与迁徙：移民美洲的族群与经济模型 ·215·

厘米

图 10.7 坦格勒湖地区菲普斯遗址出土德纳里组合器物
（经允许使用[37]）

厘米

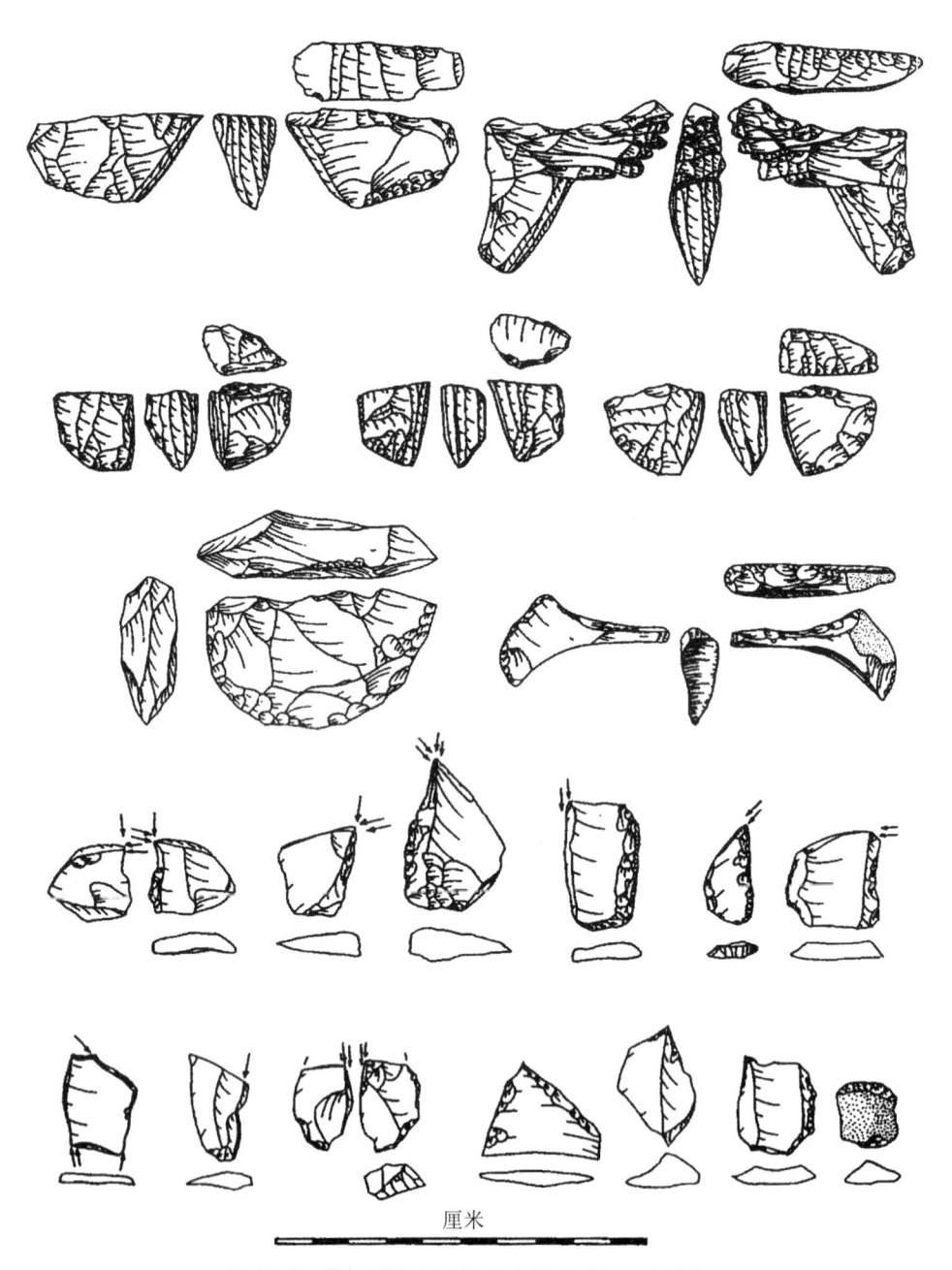

图 10.8　戴尔溪遗址 II 组出土的德纳里组合器物

（经允许使用[38]）

厘米

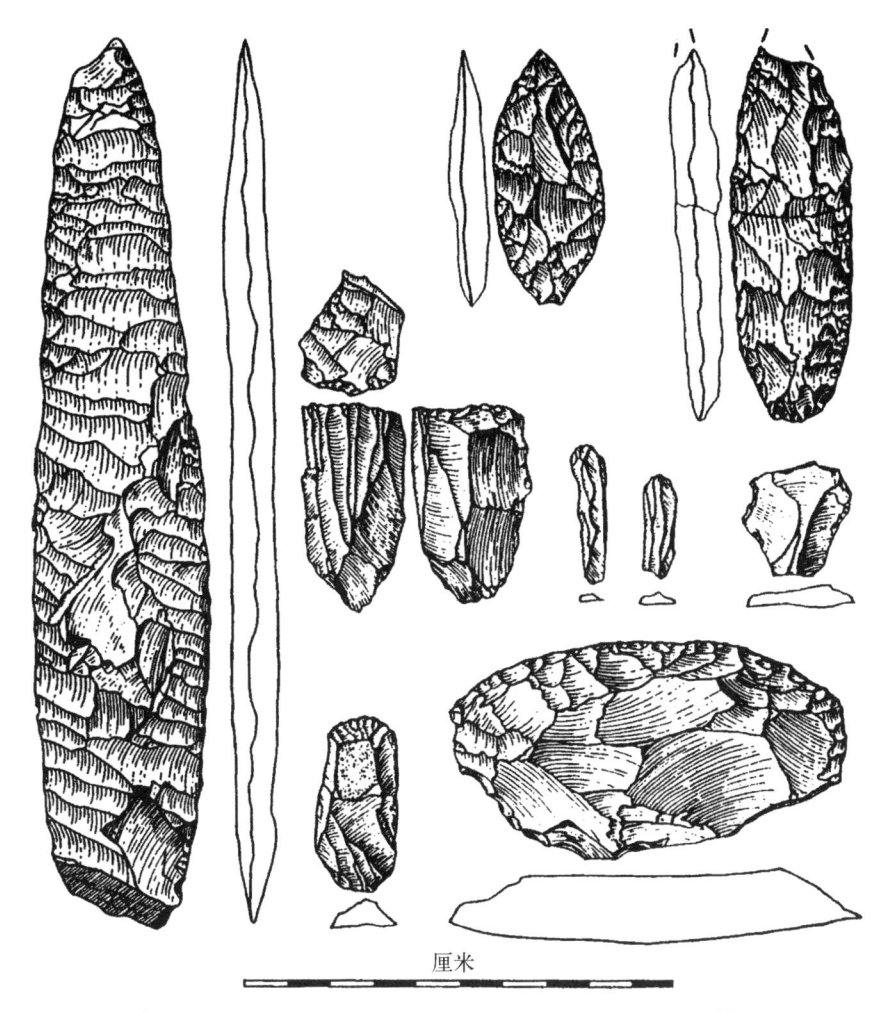

图 10.9　潘古因格溪遗址出土器物，包括细石叶与细石核

（经允许使用[39]）

德尔塔河支流的多个遗址，现在逐渐清楚的一点是，这一地区的细石叶组合一直持续到晚全新世。为了弄清晚德纳里组合的内涵，查尔斯·莫布里重新分析了坎帕斯遗址，这个遗址曾经出土超过 600 件细石叶，至少 40 件细石核，但是年代不清楚。莫布里[40]测定了三个年代，距今 2 725 至 3 500 年，它认为这就是细石叶的年代。最近皮尔森与鲍尔斯[41]重新发掘了这个遗址，得到了可靠的年代，但至少有一个年代是早全新世的。

某种程度上说，南部塔纳那流域中游最近的发掘澄清了晚德纳里组合相关的问题。从 1989 年起，塔纳那河流域中游萧溪地区的工作发现了大量晚更新世至早全新世的考古材料。这个遗址地层深厚。这些遗址位于塔纳那河流域与育空—塔纳那高地结合部的基岩突起上,为厚厚的黄土覆盖,基本避免了大量生物扰动的问题。布罗肯猛犸遗址 2 米厚的黄土覆盖层下发现两个不同的文化层,一个测定年代为距今 11 800 至 11 000 年,另一个为 10 500 至 10 000 年。两个文化层中所包含的石器组合可能跟勒纳那组合相关,包括平凸刃大刮削器、石叶,以及大量单面与两面修理工具类型。遗址中也有德纳里组合,但是与下部勒纳那组合的材料之间有一段至少 80 厘米的没有文化遗存的黄土层。类似的现象也见于附近的米德遗址,位于东北方向大约 2 公里远的地方。两个遗址(以及斯旺角遗址)中有一个年代距今大约 7 500 年的文化层,文化面貌还不清楚。布罗肯猛犸遗址的这个文化层跟遗址台地后部的一个大型火塘共存,很少有直接关联的器物发现。有段时间研究者假定布罗肯猛犸遗址的细石叶材料可能与这个年代相关,似乎相当于其他遗址的早全新世年代。不过,目前很清楚的是,这些材料通常的年代为距今 2 000 至 4 500 年,证实它们属于晚德纳里组合。这导致我们可以推断,在阿拉斯加许多地区已经放弃细石叶技术之后,它们在阿拉斯加中东部地区还持续了数千年。

此外,还有一个问题。自从早期吉登斯在阿拉斯加西北部开展工作以来,我们已经知道,阿拉斯加内陆地区带凹缺尖状器工业出现于全新世中期,大约距今 6 500 至 4 000 年。这些带凹缺尖状器组合跟冰盖以南加拿大与北美地区带凹缺尖状器为主的组合相似,基于此,它们被称为古北方工业(Northern Archaic),或是命名为古舍尔德、古劳伦泰等。刚开始研究者认为这可能反映了晚更新世森林环境替代了苔原或苔原草原。不过,新近的材料表明,云杉最晚距今 8 000 年已经侵入到阿拉斯加北坡,森林环境与带凹缺尖状器工业之间关系并不像是以前认为的那样。更有意思的是,已知的古北方工业遗址中,超过 50%的遗址也含有细石叶工业(与本·波特个人联系,1999)。这种分布形态最早见于阿拉斯加内陆地区的明楚米纳湖,霍尔默斯[42]在此发现这些工业在较晚的带凹缺尖状器遗址中共存。一个明显的证据是塔纳那流域中游的米德遗址,年代距今 4 000 年左右,它表明阿拉斯加内陆地区细石叶技术的残留是一个相当复杂的现象。

细石叶组合还继续存在于阿拉斯加西部海岸许多地点中,白令海地区的特里尔溪的洞穴中发现了用于镶嵌细石叶(图 10.10)的带凹槽骨尖状器[43]。北极小石器传统阿拉斯加地方类型中细石叶与雕刻器也很常见,吉登斯[44]最早从诺顿桑德地区的遗址群中识别出登比格组合(Denbigh Complex)(图

10.11)。登比格组合,距今大约4000年,通常认为是来自西伯利亚东部的移民文化,跟新石器时代楚科奇文化有关联,常常认为代表爱斯基摩早期或原爱斯基摩文化。这些细石叶技术随后在可能属于所谓诺顿传统的后续文化中消失了。

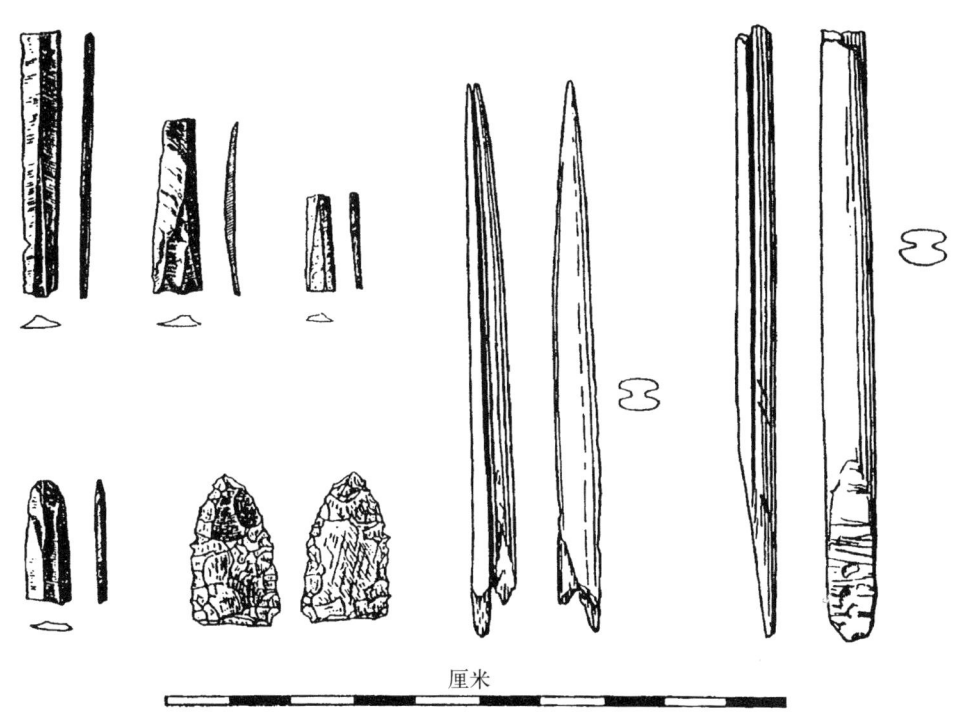

图10.10 西瓦尔德半岛特里尔溪2号洞III层及以下层位出土器物
(经允许采用[45])

再往南到太平洋海岸地区,细石叶工业年代早到距今9000年,见于阿拉斯加半岛北部的尤加史克纳罗斯、格拉威亚德角。类似的细石叶遗址在阿拉斯加东北部克奈半岛(如朗德山),库克湾北部(如贝卢加角)、马丹卢思卡流域(如拉万湖),但都没有直接的测年材料。科迪亚克岛与阿拉斯加半岛东部,石叶工业早于距今8000年,后让位于细石叶工业,这些细石叶工业是奥辛湾传统的最早类型,通常认为是阿鲁提克或太平洋爱斯基摩人的祖先。再往北,细石叶工业不见于较晚的奥辛湾传统遗址中。两个地区中,细石叶技术消失后,磨制石板技术开始占主导地位,尽管爱斯基摩南部地区更常见;而在北部地区,其他打制石器继续流行。阿留申群岛地区,文化序列始于年代超过距今8000年的石叶遗址,包括安南古拉遗址[46],以及杜蒙德与克勒奇特最近发掘的霍格岛遗址。他

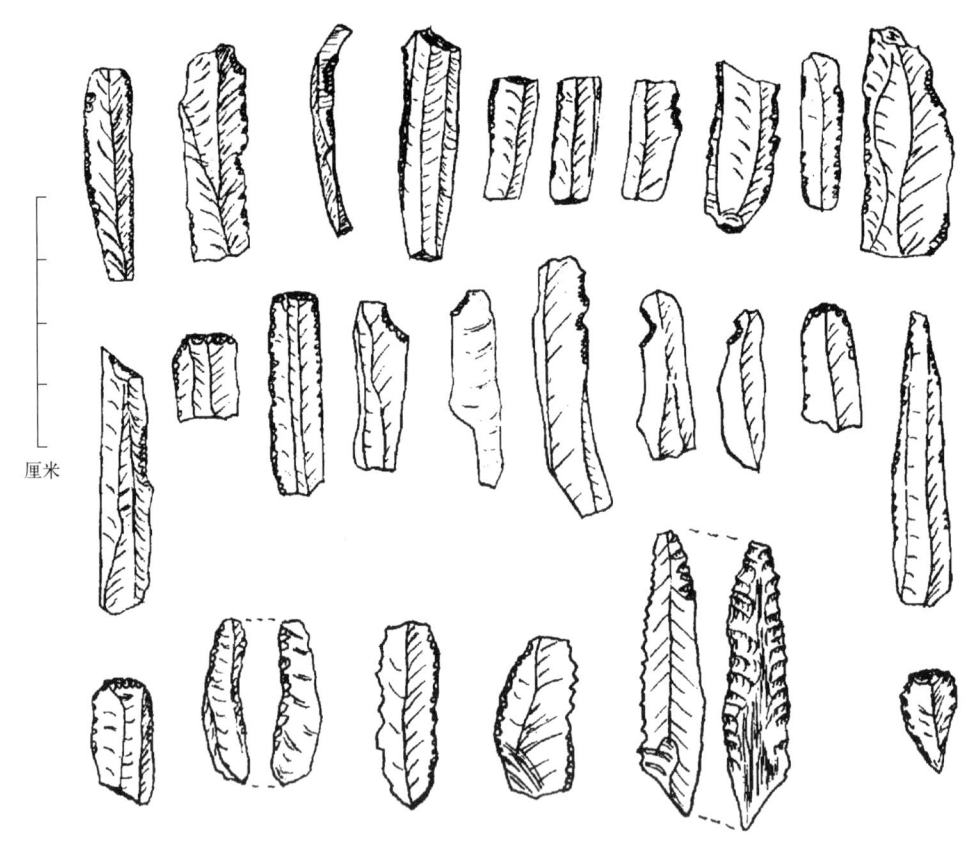

图 10.11　阿拉斯加伊亚塔耶特角登比格组合（北极小石器传统）的细石叶[47]

们[48]认为所发现的石叶工具的大小存在明显的双峰分布，将近50%的器物应该归为细石叶。尤纳拉斯卡岛全新世中期过渡文化中石叶与似石叶石片持续存在，玛格丽特湾与阿玛克纳克遗址中有发现[49]，阿留申文化晚期消失（即距今2 000年）。

最后，全新世早期细石叶文化在阿拉斯加中南部与东南部以及不列颠哥伦比亚海岸地区广泛分布[50]。许多年来，这些遗址的年代分布已经很清楚。阿拉斯加东南部，遗址的年代可以早到距今10 500年，例如格兰德霍格湾（图10.12）、希登瀑布（图 10.13）、恰克湖、昂尤里斯洞等遗址；不列颠哥伦比亚海岸北部地区年代早到距今9 000年，例如那慕尔遗址，到夏洛特女王群岛年代为距今9 500年，如罗恩角遗址。尽管年代的分布特征部分要归因于海岸上升的差异，以及板块运动与平衡作用导致的下沉，但是其整体的趋势至少可能反映了细石叶使用者的从北向南的迁徙过程。

厘米

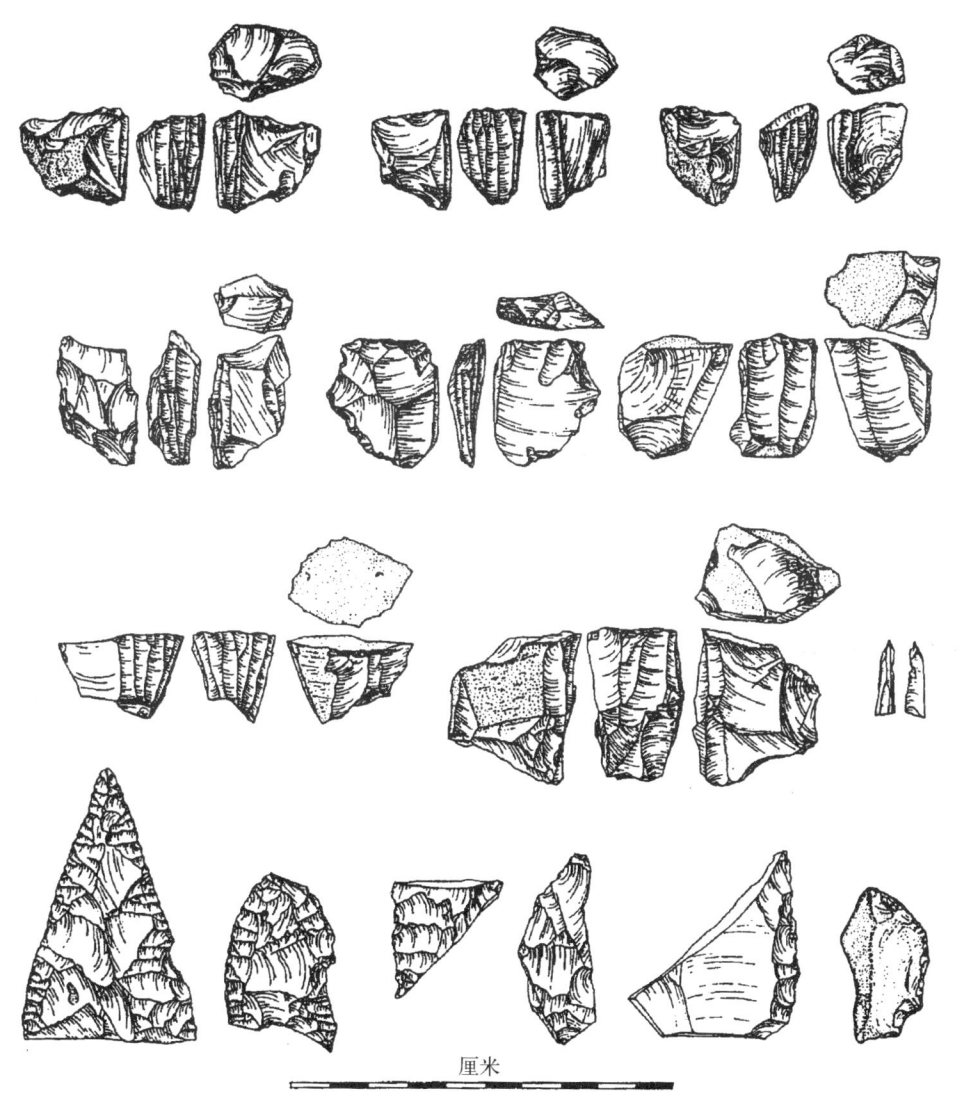

图 10.12　格兰德霍格湾 2 号遗址下文化层出土器物

（经允许采用[51]）

(四) 塔纳那流域的宾福德与博尔德观点：细石叶反映族群属性还是生态适应？

阿拉斯加细石叶组合出现的时间进程以及它在阿拉斯加内陆地区的持续存在一个可能的解释与族群属性相关。按照这种观点，比如说，德纳里组合可能代表某一特定族群，它取代的勒纳那组合群体，仅仅 1 000 至 2 000 年前这个群体

厘米

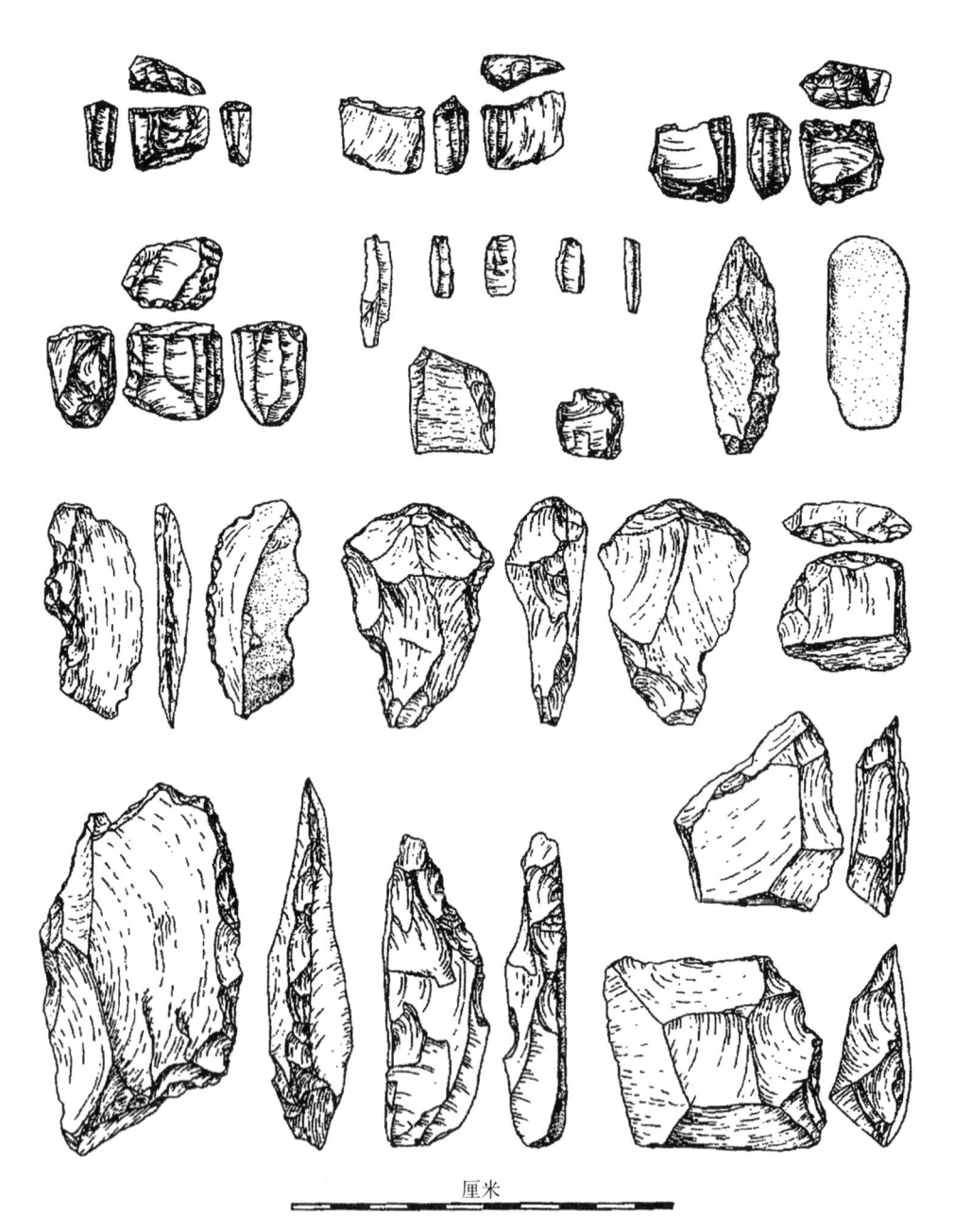

图 10.13 巴兰诺夫岛希登瀑布遗址出土器物

曾经居住于此。如果确实如此,那么德纳里组合代表什么族群呢?杜蒙德[52]在其研究爱斯基摩与阿留申人的著作中,最早将细石叶工业归于这些族群。不过还有人将细石叶归于阿萨帕斯坎或纳—德内群体的祖先。如库克[53]曾经指出黑利湖遗址至少距今10 000年以来就已经存在,表明阿萨帕斯坎人祖先可以追溯到如此久远的时代。当然不是所有人都有信心把细石叶与族群联系起来,值得注意的是,细石叶技术距今2 000年前消失了,取而代之的是所谓阿萨帕斯坎传统,包括重型砾石大工具、骨纺轮、板岩刮削器(slate tchithos*)、铜工具,所有这些更多与历史时期的阿萨帕斯坎群体直接相关。如果"原纳—德内"观点能够得到支持,那么该如何解释海岸地带早期细石叶组合呢?一个办法就是认为阿留申与阿鲁提克地区早期人口中有更多纳—德内成分,至少要比通常所认为的要多,阿留申人与科迪亚克岛的早期人骨遗存更像"西北海岸"群体,这个证据支持上述观点。另一可能性是,纳—德内与爱斯基摩—阿留申群体都来自阿拉斯加或东北亚古老群体,年代相对晚近。

细石叶技术表现族属关系最明显的地区可能是阿拉斯加东南部以及北美西北部太平洋沿岸。特林基特人,可能还包括海达人,现在都居住在阿拉斯加东南部,而不是阿萨帕斯坎人,他们可能是大纳—德内语族的成员。我们有理由认为这一地区遗址的分布反映了距今10 000年后阿拉斯加内陆地区居民向南的迁徙。是什么导致了向南的迁徙呢?一个因素可能是南部地区日益增长的吸引力,冰川消融后,现代海洋哺乳动物、鱼类、贝类种群可能已经形成。另一个因素可能是阿拉斯加内陆环境日益恶化,尤其是距今9 000年后杉树森林侵入,欧亚北部的野牛与麋鹿在这一区域绝灭,这些动物显然是阿拉斯加内陆早期居民主要的狩猎对象。

不过,另一种解释细石叶组合分布的观点关注其功能而非族群属性。那么北方细石叶工业的功能究竟是什么呢?基于许多已发现的标本,我们知道欧亚北部与西伯利亚细石叶大多用于骨角象牙尖状器嵌刃的开槽工作[54]。而在阿拉斯加地区,尽管还没有发现过开槽嵌刃的骨质尖状器,但是确实发现过某些全新世早期开槽骨尖状器,例如莱姆山洞穴[55]、特里尔溪洞穴遗址[56]。许多阿拉斯加细石叶遗址中发现的雕刻器与刻刀可能也是镶嵌使用的。

就阿拉斯加内陆与西北海岸地区的细石叶的功能,艾米斯与马斯切拉[57]曾

---

* Tchithos,是一种刮皮子的刮削器。——译者注

经指出：

> 细石叶技术基本上是一套相互关联方法，目的是要从小块原料如小砾石或石块上生产最多的切割刃。它同时还是一种生产锋利石片的方法，装柄使用（用钝后便于替换）或是镶嵌在有机（木、骨、角）工具上使用。

因此，最后他们都同意白令地区细石叶很可能"镶嵌在骨质、象牙尖状器上用作边刃"[58]，但他们同时还同意西北海岸地区细石叶的使用方式可能不同，正如弗拉德马克[59]所说的，细石叶装上骨柄或鹿角柄，用作切割与刺杀工具。埃尔斯顿[60]也指出，中国新石器时代修理过的、端部装柄细石叶有时用作刮削器、石锥、石刀或投掷尖状器。不过，他们认为这可能是例外，而非规律。

如果细石叶确实主要用作狩猎工具，它们可能用作带倒刺的鱼叉，这样可以提高骨质或象牙武器的杀伤力，尽管这种工具可能没有大型石质尖状器那样有杀伤力或产生严重的流血效果。因此，其使用可能与缺乏高质量石料来源有关，也可能与狩猎大型猎物能力缺乏有关。最终，其消失可能跟高质量石料来源增加以及其他技术的引入有关，如海上可替换的鱼叉，以及陆上最后发展出弓箭技术。

跟许多其他北方技术一样，细石叶技术耗时费力，但是它同时带来其他技术体系所不具备的好处。高品质原料匮乏可能是白令地区一带早期移民所面临的主要困难之一。布罗肯猛犸遗址最早层位的发现令人信服地表明最早的殖民者对遥远区域高品质石料产地几乎一无所知（如利文古德的燧石，尤其是巴扎特纳的黑曜石）。于是他们专门使用当地出产的石英风棱石。这些石料常见于裂隙或陡岸边。其他原料制作的石片上高比例的天然石皮表明人们更多利用相对较小的河流砾石用作石核[61]。人们还可能使用猛犸象牙，以弥补高品质石料的缺乏，尤其是当时那里象牙还比较丰富，也是在裂隙或陡岸边，因为当地猛犸象的绝灭很可能不早于距今 13 500 年[62]。这些材料的存在与容易获得在冬季尤为重要，此时获取石料可能相当困难，尤其是从结冰的河流或雪地里采集河流砾石。象牙、角或骨质工具可能首先用作前杆，是复杂投掷标枪技术组成部分（勒纳那组合），随后用作开槽的尖状器，镶嵌细石叶（德纳里组合）。

除此之外，埃尔斯顿与班廷汉姆（本书）还提到了细石叶技术许多其他可能功能上的好处。这种技术的维护成本通常相对较低,它不需要经常更换或是重新修理石质尖状器。这种工具损坏后,很快就可以重新使用,由于细石叶很轻,所以很容易一次携带一批用来替换的细石叶[63]。如果因为时间紧急或危险迫近,无法及时完成更换,剩余的骨质尖状器比残损的石质投枪要更有用。即使是镶嵌的细石叶脱落了,剩下的骨质尖状器也要比残损的标枪有效,除非后者使用骨质前杆,用作标枪头的替代物。女性可能能够更有效地在居所附近使用这种技术狩猎小型动物,尤其是男性离家去捕猎大动物的时候。从这个角度来看,布罗肯猛犸遗址动物群中高比例的小动物与鸟类就很有意思,尽管有机技术如网罗可能已经用来捕捉鸟类。

可能最重要的原因是骨、角材料,尤其是象牙比石头更坚韧,因此在使用与携带的过程更不容易损坏。在极端寒冷的条件下确实存在这样的情况,也就是说,在摄氏零度以下,这样的条件在白令地区很常见,尤其是低地环境中的冬季遗址。目前还不清楚这是否能够解释细石叶工业在北方的分布,不过,我们知道其分布一直插到了不列颠哥伦比亚海岸地区[64]。当然也可以认为这只是一种保守的适应特征,随着向南迁徙一定的距离,人们放弃了这一技术;或是随着全新世回暖到足够的程度,使得这一有利于抵抗寒冷的技术优势不足以抵消其额外的成本。

细石叶技术是否跟狩猎特定的物种有关呢?霍尔默斯[65]曾认为确实如此,细石叶技术特别适合狩猎欧亚大陆北部的野牛这样的大动物。这篇论文特别有意思的地方在于了解到塔纳那流域野牛与麋鹿的存在。德尔塔河高地遗址、布罗肯猛犸遗址发现了中晚全新世野牛遗存。格尔斯特尔河采石场遗址、银狐古生物遗址发现了全新世中期的麋鹿遗存。不像猛犸象与野马走向灭绝,塔纳那流域可能是这些动物的避难所,这些动物能够耐受稀树高原开阔的森林环境,阿拉斯加内陆地区直到全新世晚期可能还存在这种环境,当时郁闭的北方森林开始发展。不过,阿拉斯加内陆地区中晚全新世的野牛可能为较小的林地野牛,而非大型的更新世野牛,晚全新世的麋鹿也是更新世麋鹿较小的变种。再者,还可以看出,早全新世随着欧亚大陆北部野牛与麋鹿在当地的灭绝,使用勒纳那组合狩猎野牛—麋鹿的人群为使用德纳里组合狩猎北美驯鹿的人群取代。狩猎驯鹿似乎是历史时期阿拉斯加内陆地区最主要的狩猎形态,直到20世纪左右驼鹿的数量才开始增加[66]。

在有动物遗存保存的遗址中,确实可以看到细石叶组合跟多样的动物群共出,这种情况不仅仅见于塔纳那流域遗址,也见于阿拉斯加与育空地区许多早期洞穴遗址(布鲁费希洞、豪猪洞、特里尔溪洞、莱姆山洞),以及西伯利亚、俄罗斯远东、日本的众多遗址。细石叶技术具有生态或其他功能意义,而非仅仅反映族群性质,这样的观点已经建立了。某种意义上说,这是宾福德—博尔德有关莫斯特技术争论的塔纳那版。按照博尔德的观点,石器工具的变化应该主要反映族群性质,就像上面所说的阿拉斯加细石叶工业那样。而按照宾福德的观点,石器工具的变化应该反映史前人类行为上的差异,比如反映季节性遗址居留、狩猎的物种以及其他遗址中所进行特定活动方式的变化。将之运用到阿拉斯加地区,就可以认为某些晚更新世或早全新世遗址或地层中细石叶的出现反映的就是这些活动的差别,而非不同人类群体(如族群)的居留。因此,比如说,塔纳那流域的遗址如布罗肯猛犸,在晚更新世至早全新世基本没有细石叶,可以解释为短期狩猎营地,人类在这里进行的活动非常有限,而同一时代的其他含细石叶遗址如黑利湖,可以解释为长期居住村落遗址,含有多种多样活动的证据。而非将其视为混杂或某些埋藏过程的结果,该遗址早期地层中细石叶的存在可以看作居住形态的必然反映。

有没有其他材料支持或是反对这个假说呢?布罗肯猛犸遗址中,火塘的深度与数量、石器制作场所的数量、石器的多样性、有机工具以及动物遗存似乎都表明其居留时间更长,而非通常所说的短期狩猎营地。工具与动物群反映存在工具的生产与修理、器物与肉食的储备行为、首次与随后的屠宰行为、牛皮加工与皮毛缝纫,还有猎物的搜寻,都表明长期的居留。这个结论使得我们很难认为该遗址或类似的遗址缺乏细石叶乃是由于遗址只进行特定活动的结果[67]。

(五)布罗肯猛犸遗址细石叶组合的构成

布罗肯猛犸遗址(图10.14与图10.15)经前后七次发掘(1990、1991、1992、1993、1998、2000、2002),发现了超过8 000件细石叶(图10.16),同时还发现40件楔形细石核或石核上剥离的断块标本,另外还包括20件石核台面更新石片。75%的细石叶是残断的,其中一半显示打制过程中有铰链状断裂,剩下的或是生产过程较晚阶段的产品,或是使用的结果。没有细石叶有边缘修理或打磨痕迹,仅有一打左右明确为雕刻器打法产品,同时发现数量差不多的雕刻器打法剥离石片。两者似乎都不是细石叶技术的主要特征,这加强了我们的认识,细石叶用作开槽骨质工具的镶嵌石刃确实是其主要功能。这也得到初步的细石叶微痕观察的支持(与尼娜·科诺伦科个人联系,2002)

图 10.14　阿拉斯加大三角洲地区布罗肯猛犸遗址景观

耶斯纳[68]与霍尔默斯[69]确定的第 2 文化区中,某些特定区域集中分布有大量细石叶。遗址的前部边缘揭露出大量细石叶,部分细石叶实际上从崖面上掉落下来(这也是发现该遗址的原因之一)。估计遗址中至少一半左右的细石叶与细石核由于采石与道路建设破坏丢失了。第二个细石叶集中区位于遗址的东北部(图 10.17)。两个区域中细石叶都与火塘或火塘灰烬以及某些动物遗存密切关联。第三个区域也是最大的一个细石叶集中区域,经过了两个季度的发掘(1993 与 1998 年),它位于遗址的西南部,周围没有发现火塘或是动物遗存。前两个区域,用于生产细石叶的石料来源多样性较高,包括黑曜石以及多种多样的燧石,而第三个区域完全以产自坦格勒湖地区兰德马克盖普的燧石为主。这里细石核与细石叶的比例几乎是其他两个区域的 10 倍(大约是 1∶50 对 1∶500)。这给我们一个整体印象就是,出土最多细石叶的第三个区域,可能代表"纯粹"的单次石器制作活动,而前两个区域可能代表跟火塘相关的多次活动,或是把细石叶生产活动与其他互动结合在一起。将来拼合这些细石叶也许有助于揭示细石叶生产与使用的区别。无论如何,很难否定细石叶技术在这里一直持续到距今 2 000 年,并一直很重要。

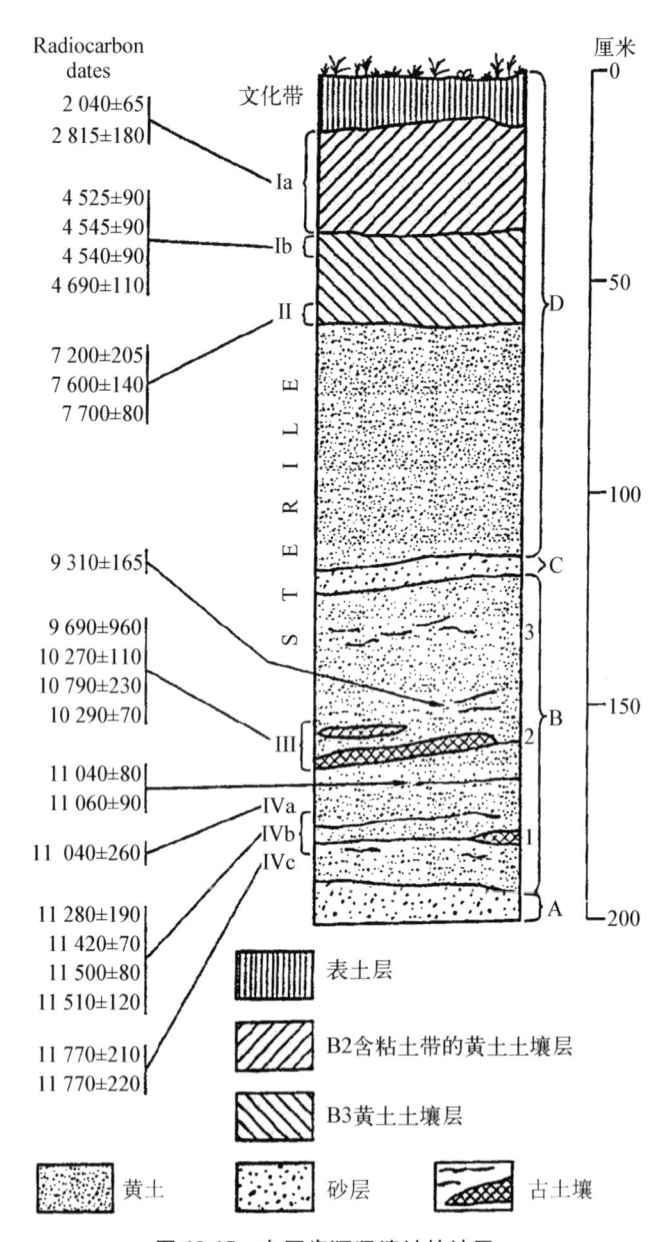

图 10.15 布罗肯猛犸遗址的地层

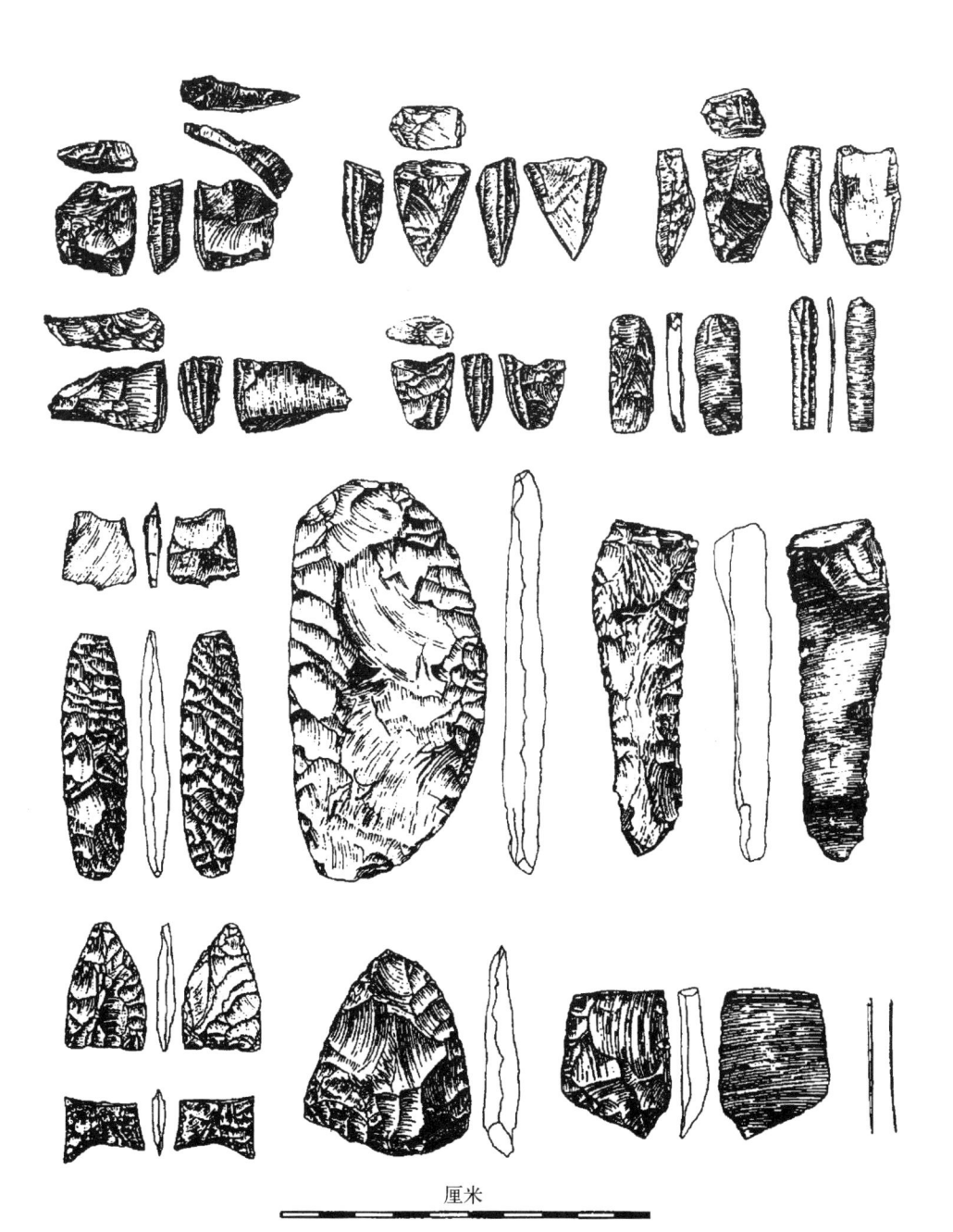

细石叶与迁徙：移民美洲的族群与经济模型 ·229·

厘米

图 10.16 布罗肯猛犸遗址的器物组合

（经允许采用）

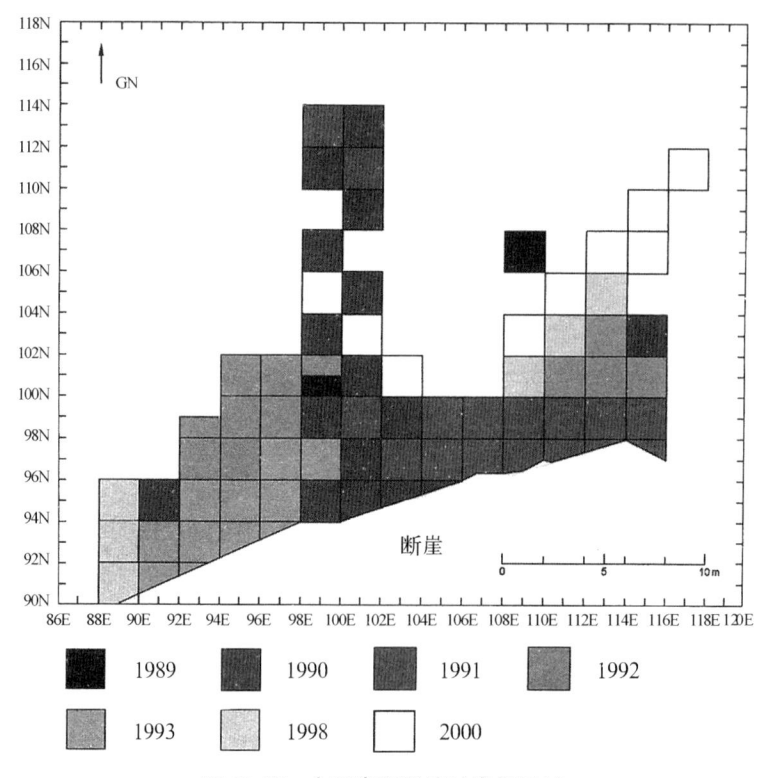

图10.17 布罗肯猛犸遗址发掘区域

三、讨论

美洲最终是否存在古印第安人之前的阶段还不能确定,但是很清楚的一点,如梅尔茨[70]所提出的,即使存在,可能时间也不长,也没有在考古材料上留下清楚的印迹。美洲广泛分布的古印第安文化以各地特有的器物为代表,包括北美带凹槽的尖状器、南美的鱼尾尖状器以及带梃埃尔霍博尖状器。可能在某个地方,也就是中美洲南部,成为这些技术交汇之所。往北,带凹槽尖状器发现于阿拉斯加北坡地区,但是年代尚不清楚[71]。大型标枪头尖状器也见于北坡地区,包括著名的梅萨尖状器,但至少是大部分似乎都属于全新世早期的,阿拉斯加内陆地区发现的极少数标枪头与带凹槽或"假凹槽"尖状器也可能是这个时期的(如戴尔溪Ⅱ、驼鹿溪、黑利湖、布罗肯猛犸[72])。克拉克[73]提出梅萨标枪头尖状器与古科迪勒拉构造有关,是南方起源的,但这种观点有待验证。无论如何,通常都认为这些典型的古印第安技术可以用到石叶上,通过修理石叶生产投掷尖状器及其他工具[74],按照穆勒—贝克[75]的旧术语,可称为"奥瑞纳式的"。阿拉斯加地区仅有阿留申群岛从一开始就以石叶技术为主,很少雕刻器打法之外的修理、边缘修理以及单面修理刮削器与石刀的生产[76]。这些文化的最终来源实际上是俄罗斯远东的海岸文化如乌斯提诺夫卡:一般说来,其年代为距今8 000年左右,全新世中期逐渐消失。不过,勒纳那组合显示石叶技术(与单面修理大工具)跟阿拉斯加内陆地区最早的居住明确相关。戈贝尔等[77]与卡尔森[78]曾经指出,勒纳那组合与南方古印第安工业之间存在较强的联系。勒纳那组合中确实存在一些细石叶,但都是点状的发现,并且没有发现细石核。系统的细石叶生产似乎出现于全新世早期,最早见于阿拉斯加内陆地区与阿拉斯加东南部的一些遗址。随后细石叶组合在内陆与沿海地区都非常普遍,全新世中期基本消失,除了阿拉斯加中东部的塔纳那流域[79]。

当然,布莱恩[80]原来的观点是,带凹槽尖状器技术的祖先并非来自阿拉斯加特有的工业(此时勒纳那组合还不为人所知),可能来自冰盖以南地区,在末次盛冰期之前,而较晚的使用细石叶的入侵者为冰盖所阻,没有进一步南侵,可能绕过冰盖的西部边缘,深入到普格特桑德。如果人类确实较早进入美洲,那么这应该说还是一个可行的模型。

不过,在细石叶与纳—德内人之间建立联系同样是合理的复原,包括人类可能很早进入科迪亚克岛与阿拉斯加半岛东部,这在现代人群分布上来看并不明显,但是得到骨骼证据的支持。如果情况确实如此,那么就跟格林伯格等人[81]提出的人类分三次进入美洲的模型相一致,其中纳—德内人代表一个特殊群体,是后来从古印第安群体中分离出来的,分离发生在亚洲或是北美。这些人的最终源头,从语言学联系来看,属于更大的德内—高加索语族,其根源在西南亚,遗传学材料,尤其是Y染色体研究也指向同一方向[82]。奥森伯格[83]同意纳—德内人的特殊性,并且认为(基于一系列颅骨特性)这些人与阿留申人的关系比通常所认为的还要紧密,强调这个方向上的某些历史联系,他们或是从同一祖先分离出来的,或是后来混血了[84]。

这个模型的一个有趣的含义在于南端的细石叶分布。尽管通常认为不列颠哥伦比亚中部海岸地区是最南方的分布区,但是实际上更南方的华盛顿州、俄勒冈州与加州北部还有一些细石叶组合发现,俄勒冈州与加州北部海岸地区存在阿萨帕斯坎人群,属于例外情况。这是否意味着全新世早期纳—德内人向南延伸至此?如果确实如此,那么这个地区全新世早期带有特殊体质特征的人骨遗存(如肯勒维克、精灵洞、维扎德滩)应该不是假说中的早期海岸移民,而是稍后迁到美国西北海岸地区的纳—德内人。这还有助于解释这个地区血型分布中的某些不清楚的分布,通常将之归因于创建者效应(founder effect)或基因漂变。

无论如何,我们是否能够如此轻易地把细石叶与族群属性联系起来呢?如果不能,那么细石叶分布之于最早美洲人研究的贡献也就非常有限,除了说明这一技术在更大范围的白令地区得到应用,从西伯利亚东部的久克太洞到育空地区的布鲁费希洞,并且向南一直延伸到美国西北海岸地区。它仍可能要代表一种阿拉斯加的基本技术,为多样的族群采用,这些族群后来分裂。也可以说,没有族属方面的联系,它只是通过风格的扩散成为一种为众多族群广泛使用的技术。于是,在某个时间点上,这些技术为鱼叉、弓箭或其他武器系统所取代,当时的条件使得用途广泛的细石叶不再适用,用细石叶来狩猎的动物在当地逐渐绝灭,随着贸易网络的发展,石料的获取不再困难,或是采用当地所有的技术,生产细石叶的成本日益高昂。

最后,如果能够证实细石叶的生产确实是勒纳那组合的一部分,比如说是村落长期居住生活的变体,那么就会产生一些基本的矛盾。可能存在如下三种可能:勒纳那组合与更南方的古印第安文化之间假定的联系是错误的,需要重新评估或放弃;或是说勒纳那组合族群实际上是古印第安人的祖先,但是随着他们向南迁徙,他们因为某种原因放弃了细石叶技术;或者细石叶技术仅用于白令地区,随后由于不再经济,而被放弃了。

布罗肯猛犸遗址发现的有机工具似乎支持最后那种的可能性[85]。2002年夏季,布罗肯猛犸遗址中发现了八件猛犸象牙"杆",附近的米德遗址发现一件,格斯特尔河采石场遗址发现一件,都在塔纳那流域以南。类似的器物在塔纳那流域以北的区域也有发现,也就是所谓费尔班克斯"粪坑"(采金废弃坑)地区。这些象牙杆有大而倾斜的表面,上有交叉的纹路,加上其他特征,可以把它们与华盛顿州东文腊奇的里奇—罗伯茨地区克鲁维斯储藏遗址以及向南直到佛罗里达的其他古印第安遗址所发现类似器物联系起来。这些猛犸象牙前杆可能是一种复杂标枪技术体系的组成部分[86],这些材料对于狩猎大动物的古印第安大型标枪武器技术体系至关重要。当猛犸象还存在时,人们狩猎它,象牙还可以得到;猛犸象灭绝后的一段时间,象牙在一些比较开阔的草原或高原环境还可能暴露在地表[87]。这种技术最终为南方的带凹缺或有梃投掷器以及北方的镶嵌细石叶的骨质尖状器所取代,或者只是风格的区别,或是因为细石叶更适合狩猎北美驯鹿或北方特有的某些其他动物。当然,如果上述观点都不正确的话,最早的新大陆殖民者如上面所说的,需要最大限度的工具弹性,他们使用特别多样的武器技术(以及广谱的生计适应)。此种情况下,他们在更南方地区日益成为专门的猛犸象狩猎者,他们可能不再需要工具的灵活性(包括细石叶生产技术体系),转而偏好更专门的投掷器技术,包括不那么有名的带凹槽尖状器。

四、结论

大白令地区的细石叶组合一方面被视为不同族群留下的标志性工具,由此成为最早美洲人模型的重要组成部分;而另一方面,细石叶仅仅被看作一种技术,是为了便于狩猎北方寒冷环境某些尚不清楚的动物演化而来的,那里石器原料稀少,尤其是在冬季。围绕细石叶的功能性与族群属性,一种类似博尔德—宾福德式的争论形成,在解释阿拉斯加内陆地区最早遗址时分歧明显。双方的观点都很强大,显然争论一下子不可能得到解决。

不过,还是有妥协空间的,两种观点并不必然互相排斥。比如说,勒纳那组合这样的较早期群体没有完全忽视细石叶技术,他们跟南方的古印第安人/美洲印第安人祖先关系密切,德纳里组合所代表的人群可能就是纳—德内人的祖先,这些人发现镶嵌细石叶开槽骨器技术更符合其需要。如野牛、麋鹿等较早期勒纳那组合人群所依赖的动物绝灭后,那些目的(如狩猎北美驯鹿)可能变得日益重要。细石叶技术只是在森林扩张、北美驯鹿狩猎的重要性下降之前有用。海岸地区,细石叶技术为更有效的狩猎海洋哺乳动物的技术所取代。向南超越了海洋哺乳动物狩猎范围的地方,细石叶技术消失。在进一步确定细石叶技术在北方地区的意义以及在解决难以追溯的最早美洲人难题上,还需要大量的材料,包括有关动物群材料。

注释:

[1] Hopkins, D. M. The Cenozoic History of the Bering Land Bridge (Alaska). *Science* 129: 1519–1528, 1959.

The Cenozoic History of Beringia: A Synthesis. In *The Bering Land Bridge*. D. M. Hopkins, ed. Pp. 451–484. Stanford: Stanford University Press, 1967.

[2] Straus, L. G. Solutrean Settlement of North America? A Review of Reality. *American Antiquity* 65: 219–226, 2000.

[3] Bryan, A. L. *Paleo-American Prehistory*. Occasional Papers of the Idaho State University Museum No. 16. Pocatello, 1965.

Krieger, A. D. Early Man in the New World. In *Prehistoric Man in the New World*. J. D.

Jennings and E. Norbeck, eds. Pp. 23–84. Chicago: University of Chicago Press, 1964.

MacNeish, R. S. Early Man in the New World. *American Scientist* 63: 316–327, 1976.

[4] Martin, P. S. Prehistoric Overkill. In *Pleistocene Extinctions: The Search for a Cause*. P. S. Martin and H. E. Wright, Jr., eds. Pp. 75–120. New Haven: Yale University Press, 1964.

Mosimann, J. E., and P. S. Martin. Simulating Overkill by Paleoindians. *American Scientist* 63: 304–313, 1975.

[5] Grayson, D. K. Explaining Pleistocene Extinctions: Thoughts on the Structure of a Debate. In *Quaternary Extinctions: A Prehistoric Revolution*. P. S. Martin and R. G. Klein, eds. Pp. 807–823. Tucson: University of Arizona Press, 1984.

Late Pleistocene Mammalian Extinctions in North America: Taxonomy, Chronology, and Explanations. *Journal of World Prehistory* 5: 193–231, 1991.

Guthrie, R. D. Mosaics, Allelochemics, and Nutrients: An Ecological Theory of Late Pleistocene Megafaunal Extinctions. In *Quaternary Extinctions: A Prehistoric Revolution*. P. S. Martin and R. G. Klein, eds. Pp. 259–298. Tucson: University of Arizona Press, 1984.

[6] Dillehay, T. D. Researching Early Sites. In *Monte Verde: A Late Pleistocene Settlement in Chile, vol. I: Paleoenvironment and Site Context*. T. D. Dillehay, ed. Pp. 1–26, Washington, D. C.: Smithsonian Institution Press, 1989.

The Settlement of the Americas: A New Prehistory. New York: Basic Books, 2000.

[7] Yesner, D. R. Environments and Peoples at the Pleistocene-Holocene Boundary in the Americas. In *Humans at the End of the Ice Age: The Archaeology of the Pleistocene-Holocene Transition*. L. G. Straus, B. V. Eriksen, J. M. Erlandson, and D. R. Yesner, eds. Pp. 243–254. New York: Plenum, 1996a.

[8] Dixon, E. J. *Bones, Boats, and Bison: Archaeology and the First Colonization of Western North America*. Albuquerque: University of New Mexico Press, 1999.

[9] Thomas, D. H. *Skull Wars*. New York: Basic Books, 2000.

[10] Greenberg, J. L., C. G. Turner II. and S. L. Zegura. The Settlement of the Americas: A Comparison of the Linguistic, Dental, and Genetic Evidence. *Current Anthropology* 27: 477–497, 1986.

[11] Bryan, A. L. Early Man in Western Canada: A Critical Review. In *Early Man in Western North America*. C. Irwin-Williams, ed. Pp. 70–77. Eastern New Mexico University Contributions in Anthropology 1(4). Las Vegas: Eastern New Mexico Paleoindian Institute, 1968.

Early Man in America and the Late Pleistocene Chronology of Western Canada and Alaska. *Current Anthropology* 10: 339–365, 1969.

[12] Ackerman, R. N. Ground Hog Bay, Site 2. In *American Beginnings: The Prehistory and*

Paleoecology of Beringia. F. H. West, ed. Pp. 424 – 430. Chicago: University of Chicago Press, 1996a.

[13] Kuzmin, Y. V., and L. A. Orlova. Radiocarbon Chronology of the Siberian Palaeolithic. *Journal of World Prehistory* 12(1): 1 – 53, 1998.

[14] Goebel, T. *Middle to Upper Palaeolithic Transition in Siberia*. Ann Arbor, Mich.: University Microfilms, Bell and Howell, 1993.

[15] Kuzmin, Y. V., and L. A. Orlova. Radiocarbon Chronology of the Siberian Palaeolithic. *Journal of World Prehistory* 12(1): 1 – 53, 1998.

[16] Goebel, T. *Middle to Upper Palaeolithic Transition in Siberia*. Ann Arbor, Mich.: University Microfilms, Bell and Howell, 1993.

[17] Goebel, T., M. R. Waters, I. Buvit, M. V. Konstantinov. and A. V. Konstantinov. Studenoe – 2 and the Origins of Microblade Technologies in the Transbaikal, Siberia. *Antiquity* 74: 567 – 575, 2000.

[18] Aikens, C. M., and T. Akazawa. The Pleistocene-Holocene Transition in Japan and Adjacent Northeast Asia. In *Humans at the End of the Ice Age: The Archaeology of the Pleistocene-Holocene Transition*. L. G. Straus, B. V. Eriksen, J. M. Erlandson, and D. R. Yesner, eds. Pp. 215 – 228. New York: Plenum, 1996.
Goebel, T., M. R. Waters, I. Buvit, M. V. Konstantinov. and A. V. Konstantinov. Studenoe – 2 and the Origins of Microblade Technologies in the Transbaikal, Siberia. *Antiquity* 74: 567 – 575, 2000.

[19] Mochanov, Y. A., and S. A. Fedoseeva. Berelekh, Allakhovsk Region. In *American Beginnings: The Prehistory and Paleoecology of Beringia*. F. H. West, ed. Pp. 218 – 221. Chicago: University of Chicago Press, 1996.

[20] Dikov, N. N. (trans. R. L. Bland). *Asia at the Juncture with America in Antiquity: The Stone Age of the Chuckchi Peninsula*. St. Petersburg: Nauka, 1993.

[21] Powers, W. R. Siberia in the Late Glacial and Early Postglacial. In *Humans at the End of the Ice Age: The Archaeology of the Pleistocene-Holocene Transition*. L. G. Straus, B. V. Eriksen, J. M. Erlandson, and D. R. Yesner, eds. Pp. 229 – 242. New York: Plenum, 1996.

[22] Cook, J. Healy Lake. In *American Beginnings: The Prehistory and Paleoecology of Beringia*. F. H. West, ed. Pp. 323 – 327. Chicago: University of Chicago Press, 1996.

[23] Dikov, N. N. (trans. R. L. Bland) Asia at the Juncture with America in Antiquity: The Stone Age of the Chuckchi Peninsula. St. Ptersburg: Nauka, 1993.

[24] Holmes, C. E., R. VanderHoek, and T. E. Dilley. Swan Point. In *American Beginnings: The Prehistory and Paleoecology of Beringia*. F. H. West, ed. Pp. 319 – 323. Chicago: University of Chicago Press, 1996.

[25] Goebel, T., W. R. Powers, and N. H. Bigelow. The Nenana Complex of Alaska and Clovis Origins. In *Clovis: Origins and Adaptations*. R. Bonnichsen and K. L. Turnmire, eds. Pp. 49–80. Center for the Study of the First Americans. Corvallis: Oregon State University, 1992.

Hoffecker, J. F., W. R. Powers, and T. Goebel. The Colonization of Beringia and the Peopling of the New World. *Science* 259: 46–53, 1993.

[26] Ackerman, R. N. Ground Hog Bay, Site 2. In *American Beginnings: The Prehistory and Paleoecology of Beringia*. F. H. West, ed. Pp. 424–430. Chicago: University of Chicago Press, 1996a.

[27] Holmes, C. E., R. VanderHoek, and T. E. Dilley. Swan Point. In *American Beginnings: The Prehistory and Paleoecology of Beringia*. F. H. West, ed. Pp. 319–323. Chicago: University of Chicago Press, 1996.

[28] Nelson, N. C. Early Migration of Man to America. *Natural History* 35: 356, 1935.

[29] Anderson, D. D. *Onion Portage: The Archaeology of a Stratified Site from the Kobuk River, Northwest Alaska*. Anthropological Papers of the University of Alaska No. 22. Fairbanks: University of Alaska Press, 1988.

[30] Mobley, C. M. Campus Site. In *American Beginnings: The Prehistory and Paleoecology of Beringia*. F. H. West, ed. Pp. 296–302. Chicago: University of Chicago Press, 1996.

[31] West, F. H. Onion Portage, Kobuk River: Akmak and Kobuk. In *American Beginnings: The Prehistory and Paleoecology of Beringia*. F. H. West, ed. Pp. 485–489. Chicago: University of Chicago Press, 1996a.

[32] West, F. H. The Donnelly Ridge Site and the Definition of an Early Core and Blade Complex in Interior Alaska. *American Antiquity* 32: 360–382, 1967.

The Archaeology of Beringia. New York: Columbia University Press, 1981.

[33] Hoffecker, J. F., W. R. Powers, and N. H. Bigelow. Dry Creek. In *American Beginnings: The Prehistory and Paleoecology of Beringia*. F. H. West, ed. Pp. 343–352. Chicago: University of Chicago Press, 1996.

[34] Pearson, G. A. Late-Pleistocene and Holocene Microblade Industries at the Moose Creek site. *Current Research in the Pleistocene* 17: 64–65, 2000b.

[35] Holmes, C. E. Broken Mammoth. In *American Beginnings: The Prehistory and Paleoecology of Beringia*. F. H. West, ed. Pp. 312–318. Chicago: University of Chicago Press, 1996.

Yesner, D. R. Human Adaptation at the Pleistocene-Holocene Boundary (circa 13 000 to 8 000 BP) in Eastern Beringia. In *Humans at the End of the Ice Age: The Archaeology of the Pleistocene-Holocene Transition*. L. Straus, B. V. Eriksen, J. M. Erlandson, and D. R. Yesner, eds. Pp. 255–276. New York: Plenum, 1996b.

[36] Lively, R. A. Chugwater. In *American Beginnings: The Prehistory and Paleoecology of Beringia*. F. H. West, ed. Pp. 308 – 311. Chicago: University of Chicago Press, 1996.

[37] West, F. H., B. S. Robinson, and M. L. Curran. The Phipps Site. In *American Beginnings: The Prehistory and Paleoecology of Beringia*. F. H. West, ed. Pp. 381 – 385. Chicago: University of Chicago Press, 1996.

[38] Hoffecker, J. F., W. R. Powers, and N. H. Bigelow. Dry Creek. In *American Beginnings: The Prehistory and Paleoecology of Beringia*. F. H. West, ed. Pp. 343 – 352. Chicago: University of Chicago Press, 1996.

[39] Goebel, T, and N. H. Bigelow. Panguingue Creek. In *American Beginnings: The Prehistory and Paleoecology of Beringia*. F. H. West, ed. Pp. 366 – 370. Chicago: University of Chicago Press, 1996.

[40] Mobley, C. M. *The Campus Site: A Prehistoric Camp at Fairbanks*, Alaska. Fairbanks: University of Alaska Press, 1991.
Campus Site. In *American Beginnings: The Prehistory and Paleoecology of Beringia*. F. H. West, ed. Pp. 296 – 302. Chicago: University of Chicago Press, 1996.

[41] Pearson, G. A., and W. R. Powers. The Campus Site Re-excavation: New Efforts to Unravel Its Ancient and Recent Past. *Arctic Anthropology* 38: 100 – 119, 2001.

[42] Holmes, C. E. *Lake Minchumina Prehistory: An Archaeological Analysis*. Aurora, No. 2. Alaska Anthropological Association, Anchorage, 1986.

[43] Larsen, H. Trail Creek: Final Report on the Excavation of Two Caves on Seward Peninsula, Alaska. *Acta Arctica* 15: 1 – 79, 1968.

[44] Giddings, J. L. *The Archaeology of Cape Denbigh*. Providence: Brown University Press, 1964.

[45] West, F. H., B. S. Robinson, and M. L. Curran. The Phipps Site. In *American Beginnings: The Prehistory and Paleoecology of Beringia*. F. H. West, ed. Pp. 381 – 385. Chicago: University of Chicago Press, 1996.

[46] Aigner, J. S. Anangula: An 8 500 B. P. Coastal Occupation in the Aleutian Islands. *Quartar* 27/28: 65 – 102, 1977.
The Lithic Remains from Anangula, an 8 500 Year Old Aleut Coastal Village. Urgeschichtliche Materialhefte No. 3. Tubingen, Germany: Institut fur Urgeschichte der Universitat Tubingen, 1978.

[47] Giddings, J. L. *The Archaeology of Cape Denbigh*. Providence: Brown University Press, 1964.

[48] Dumond, D. E., and R. A. Knecht. Another Early Blade Site in the Eastern Aleutians. Paper presented to the Alaska Anthropological Association, Anchorage, 2000.

[49] Yesner, D. R., and R. A. Mack. Margaret Bay and the Question of Aleut and Eskimo Origins. Paper presented to the annual meeting of the Society for American Archaeology,

Minneapolis, 1989.

[50] Ackerman, R. N. Microblades and Prehistory: Technological and Cultural Considerations for the North Pacific Coast. In *Early Native Americans*. D. L. Browman. ed. Pp. 189 - 197. The Hague: Mouton, 1980.

[51] Ackerman, R. N. Cave 1, Lime Hills. In *American Beginnings: The Prehistory and Paleoecology of Beringia*. F. H. West, ed. Pp. 470 - 477. Chicago: University of Chicago Press, 1996b.

[52] Dumond, D, E. *The Eskimos and Aleuts*. New York: Thames and Hudson, 1977.

[53] Cook, J. Archaeology of Interior Alaska. *Western Canadian Journal of Anthropology* 5: 125 - 133, 1975.

[54] Chard, C. S. *Northeast Asia in Prehistory*. Madison: University of Wisconsin Press, 1974. Derev'anko, A. P., ed. *The Paleolithic of Siberia*. Urbana: University of Illinois Press, 1998.

[55] Ackerman, R. N. Cave 1, Lime Hills. In *American Beginnings: The Prehistory and Paleoecology of Beringia*. F. H. West, ed. Pp. 470 - 477. Chicago: University of Chicago Press, 1996b.

[56] Larsen, H. Trail Creek: Final Report on the Excavation of Two Caves on Seward Peninsula, Alaska. *Acta Arctica* 15: 1 - 79, 1968.

[57] Ames, K. M., and H. D. G. Maschner. *The Peoples of the Northwest Coast: Their Archaeology and Prehistory*. New York: Thames and Hudson, 1999: 71.

[58] Ames, K. M., and H. D. G. Maschner. *The Peoples of the Northwest Coast: Their Archaeology and Prehistory*. New York: Thames and Hudson, 1999: 71.

[59] Fladmark, K. R. *British Columbia Prehistory*. Archaeological Survey of Canada, Canadian Museum of Civilization, Hull, 1986.

[60] Elston, R. G., C. Xu, D. B. Madsen, K. Zhong, R. L. Bettinger, J. Li, P. J. Brantingham, H. Wang, and J. Yu. New Dates for the North China Mesolithic. *Antiquity* 71: 985 - 993, 1997.

[61] Yesner, D. R. Human Dispersal into Interior Alaska: Antecedent Conditions, Mode of Colonization, and Adaptations. *Quaternary Science Reviews* 20: 315 - 327, 2000.

[62] Yesner, D. R. Human Colonization of Eastern Beringia and the Question of Mammoth Hunting. In *Mammoth Site Studies*. D. West, ed. Pp. 69 - 84. University of Kansas Publications in Anthropology 22. Lawrence: University of Kansas, 2001.

[63] Bamforth, D. B., and P. Bleed. Technology, Flaked Stone Technology, and Risk. In *Rediscovering Darwin: Evolutionary Theory and Archeological Explanation*. C. M. Barton and G. A. Clark, eds. Pp. 109 - 140.

Archeological Papers of the American Anthropological Association, 7. Arlington, Va.:

American Anthropological Association, 1997.

[64] Yesner, D. R. Human Adaptation at the Pleistocene-Holocene Boundary (circa 13 000 to 8 000 BP) in Eastern Beringia. In *Humans at the End of the Ice Age: The Archaeology of the Pleistocene-Holocene Transition*. L. Straus, B. V. Eriksen, J. M. Erlandson, and D. R. Yesner, eds. Pp. 255 – 276. New York: Plenum, 1996b.

[65] Holmes, C. E. *Lake Minchumina Prehistory: An Archaeological Analysis*. Aurora, No. 2. Alaska Anthropological Association, Anchorage, 1986.

[66] Yesner, D. R. Moose Hunters of the Boreal Forest? A Re-examination of Subsistence Patterns in the Western Subarctic. *Arctic* 42: 97 – 108, 1989.

[67] Yesner, D. R. Subsistence Diversity and Hunter-Gatherer Strategies in Late Pleistocene/Early Holocene Beringia: Evidence from the Broken Mammoth Site, Big Delta, Alaska. Current Research on the Pleistocene 11: 154 – 156, 1994.

Human Adaptation at the Pleistocene-Holocene Boundary (circa 13 000 to 8 000 BP) in Eastern Beringia. In Humans at the End of the Ice Age: The Archaeology of the Pleistocene-Holocene Transition. L. Straus, B. V. Eriksen, J. M. Erlandson, and D. R. Yesner, eds. Pp. 255 – 276. New York: Plenum, 1996b.

Human Dispersal into Interior Alaska: Antecedent Conditions, Mode of Colonization, and Adaptations. Quaternary Science Reviews 20: 315 – 327, 2000.

[68] Yesner, D. R. Human Adaptation at the Pleistocene-Holocene Boundary (circa 13 000 to 8 000 BP) in Eastern Beringia. In Humans at the End of the Ice Age: The Archaeology of the Pleistocene-Holocene Transition. L. Straus, B. V. Eriksen, J. M. Erlandson, and D. R. Yesner, eds. Pp. 255 – 276. New York: Plenum, 1996b.

[69] Holmes, C. E. Broken Mammoth. In *American Beginnings: The Prehistory and Paleoecology of Beringia*. F. H. West, ed. Pp. 312 – 318. Chicago: University of Chicago Press, 1996.

[70] Meltzer, David J. Clocking the First Americans. *Annual Review of Anthropology* 24: 21 – 45, 1995.

[71] Reanier, R. E. The Antiquity of Paleoindian Materials in Northern Alaska. In After the Land Bridge: Climates, Biomes, and Cultural Interaction in Northern Beringia. J. E. Lobdell and R. E. Reanier, eds. *Arctic Anthropology* (Madison, Wis.) 32: 31 – 50, 1995.

[72] Pearson, G. A. Early Occupations and Cultural Sequence at Moose Creek: A Late Pleistocene Site in Central Alaska. *Arctic* 52: 332 – 345, 2000a.

[73] Clark, D. W. *Western Subarctic Prehistory*. Archaeological Survey of Canada, Canadian Museum of Civilization, Hull, 1991.

[74] West, F. H. The Archaeology of Beringia. New York: Columbia University Press, 1981.

The Archaeological Evidence. In American Beginnings: The Prehistory and Paleoecology of

Beringia. F. H. West, ed. Pp. 525 – 536. Chicago: University of Chicago Press, 1996b.

[75] Muller-Beck, H. On Migrations of Hunters across the Bering Land Bridge in the Upper Pleistocene. In *The Bering Land Bridge*. D. M. Hopkins, ed. Pp. 373 – 408. Stanford: Stanford University Press, 1967.

[76] Aigner, J. S. Anangula: An 8 500 B. P. Coastal Occupation in the Aleutian Islands. *Quartar* 27/28: 65 – 102, 1977.

The Lithic Remains from Anangula, an 8 500 Year Old Aleut Coastal Village. Urgeschichtliche Materialhefte No. 3. Tubingen, Germany: Institut fur Urgeschichte der Universitat Tubingen, 1978.

[77] Goebel, T., W. R. Powers, and N. H. Bigelow. The Nenana Complex of Alaska and Clovis Origins. In *Clovis: Origins and Adaptations*. R. Bonnichsen and K. L. Turnmire, eds. Pp. 49 – 80. Center for the Study of the First Americans. Corvallis: Oregon State University, 1992.

[78] Carlson, R. L. Introduction to Early Human Occupation in British Columbia. In *Early Human Occupation in British Columbia*. R. L. Carlson and L. D. Bona, eds. Pp. 3 – 10. Vancouver: UBC Press, 1996.

[79] Pearson, G. A. Late-Pleistocene and Holocene Microblade Industries at the Moose Creek site. *Current Research in the Pleistocene* 17: 64 – 65, 2000b.

Yesner, D. R. Human Adaptation at the Pleistocene-Holocene Boundary (circa 13 000 to 8 000 BP) in Eastern Beringia. In *Humans at the End of the Ice Age: The Archaeology of the Pleistocene-Holocene Transition*. L. Straus, B. V. Eriksen, J. M. Erlandson, and D. R. Yesner, eds. Pp. 255 – 276. New York: Plenum, 1996b.

[80] Bryan, A. L. Early Man in America and the Late Pleistocene Chronology of Western Canada and Alaska. *Current Anthropology* 10: 339 – 365, 1969.

[81] Greenberg, J. L., C. G. Turner II. and S. L. Zegura. The Settlement of the Americas: A Comparison of the Linguistic, Dental, and Genetic Evidence. *Current Anthropology* 27: 477 – 497, 1986.

[82] Zegura, S. L. The Early Peopling of the Americas: Where Did the Y-Chromosomes Come From? *Geological Society of America Abstracts with Programs* 31: A – 24, 1999.

[83] Ossenberg, N. S. Origins and Affinities of the Native Peoples of Northwestern North America: The Evidence of Cranial Non Metric Traits. In *Method and Theory for Investigating the Peopling of the Americas*. R. Bonnichsen and D. G. Steele, eds. Pp. 79 – 116. Center for the Study of the First Americans. Corvallis: Oregon State University, 1994.

[84] Yesner, D. R., and R. A. Mack. Margaret Bay and the Question of Aleut and Eskimo Origins. Paper presented to the annual meeting of the Society for American Archaeology,

Minneapolis, 1989.

[85] Yesner, D. R. Human Adaptation at the Pleistocene-Holocene Boundary (circa 13 000 to 8 000 BP) in Eastern Beringia. In *Humans at the End of the Ice Age: The Archaeology of the Pleistocene-Holocene Transition*. L. Straus, B. V. Eriksen, J. M. Erlandson, and D. R. Yesner, eds. Pp. 255 – 276. New York: Plenum, 1996b.

Yesner, D. R., G. A. Pearson, and D. E. Stone. Additional Organic Artifacts from the Broken Mammoth Site, Big Delta, Alaska. *Current Research in the Pleistocene* 17: 87 – 89, 2000.

[86] Pearson, G. A. North American Paleoindian Bi-beveled Bone and Ivory Rods: A New Interpretation. *North American Archaeologist* 20: 81 – 103, 1999.

[87] Yesner, D. R. Human Colonization of Eastern Beringia and the Question of Mammoth Hunting. In *Mammoth Site Studies*. D. West, ed. Pp. 69 – 84. University of Kansas Publications in Anthropology 22. Lawrence: University of Kansas, 2001.

全新世澳大利亚琢背石器激增的方式与背景

皮特·西斯科克

(国立澳大利亚大学 堪培拉)

摘 要：更新世之末澳大利亚出现琢背石器，但只是在全新世中期"激增"，并成为大陆东南部主要的加工石器。这一变化是由距今4 000至5 000年厄尔尼诺主导的气候变化所引发的，全新世中期琢背石器生产增加是人们减小风险的众多策略之一。当时采用这种标准化生产石器的技术无疑是有利的，但是澳大利亚南北同时存在不同的技术方法揭示了进化道路上的历史偶然性。

澳大利亚考古学家的主要关注点之一就是理解全新世中期形制规范、加工精致的打制石器"激增"的现象。这包括澳洲大陆许多地区类似工具生产频率的增加。较早研究中提出过一个模型解释这个过程，认为全新世中期环境利用具有相当的风险，而采用特定的技术有助于降低风险[1]。这个模型研究分布最广泛的三种工具类型(尖状器、琢背石器、石凿)与环境改变导致风险提高、高流动性以及与未曾利用环境之间可能存在的联系。本文进一步研究全新世澳大利亚东南部琢背石器增加的情况，并提出一个简单的文化选择论模型，以支持风险反应假说。这一模型将提供一个有力的理论框架，强调选择机制在文化特征存留上的作用，研究气候环境变化通过影响个体的传承进而影响器物组合的变化[2]。

研究琢背器物的时间分布发现，在全新世中期大规模生产这类器物之前，它们已经在澳大利亚东南部存在了数千年。因此全新世中期琢背石器的激增不可能来自某种新型工具或专门生产技术的思想影响或引进。相反,全新世中期琢背石器生产的增加可以解释为,其是缓解当时风险的众多策略之一。导致风险的因素可能是多种多样的,而其中一个就是出现了干旱多变的气候条件。在这种条件下,大量生产标准化与维护性好的石器,有利于减少环境不确定性导致的风险,强调生产琢背石器就是形式之一。

一、细石器或琢背石器?

在本文中我将讨论琢背石器,所谓琢背石器就是一边或多边存在陡向加工的石片工具。其标志性特征就是将近 90 度的加工方式,通常需要在石砧上运用砸击技术获得。"琢背"的那面常常具有两面的疤痕,"琢背"修理有时会打掉台面或石片的远端。

在澳大利亚"细石器"这个术语现在已被放弃,西斯科克与埃滕布罗[3]曾经讨论过原因。这不是不同地区术语偏好这样的琐屑之事,而是反映了我们的解释模型所立足的分类基础。关注这一问题的一位研究者是哈兰姆[4],她注意到考古学中器物组合变化的问题可能仅仅被视为"跟语义用法相关、无足轻重的问题"。她指出 1970 年代澳大利亚考古学家使用"细石器"用以描述特定类型的琢背石叶,而在澳大利亚之外,考古学家把琢背细石叶视为细石器的一个特殊的变体。哈兰姆揭示的分类上的不一致促使我们研究相关对应分类的性质。

艾特里奇与怀特里格[5]首先识别出陡向琢背修理石片。他们称其为"背部打制的手术刀"。他们推测这些器物可能用作"外科手术刀",用一个功能术语来强调。在讨论中艾特里奇与怀特里格根据从悉尼的邦迪与马洛布拉海滩发现的器物确定了三个特征,整个 20 世纪都用它们来进行分类:

1) 器物的平面形状很特殊,明显不对称,典型的形制是一端圆,一端尖(图 11.1);

2) 器物很小,长度从 10 到>50 毫米[6];

3) 标本具有一条陡向修理侧边,艾特里奇与怀特里格将之描述为"精细雕刻的背部"。

第一项特征,也就是平面形状,用于许多分类研究中,既用来甄别这些器物,也用来进一步细分。例如,肯宁[7]就指出艾特里奇与怀特里格的功能推定是错误的,因为许多标本并没有一条符合这一描述的边刃,将器物按照形制分成"新月形器"与"尖状器"。后来的分类研究中,迈克卡瑟等[8]提出的最有影响的,基于对称的区分得到保留,对称的标本称为"细石器"(也就是"几何形

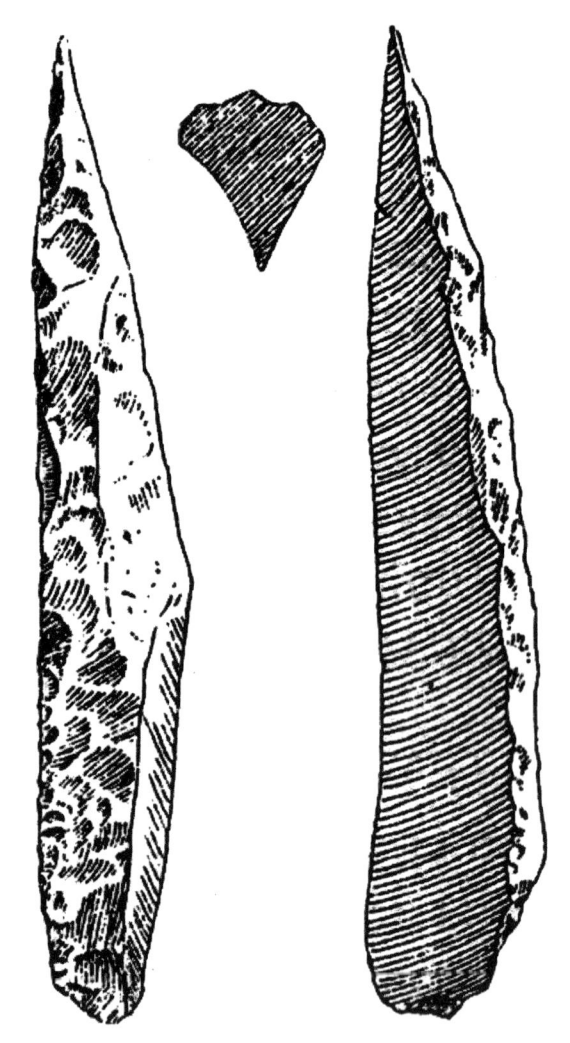

图 11.1　艾特里奇与怀特里格(1907)发表的琢背石器
(他们称之为"背部打制的手术刀",没有比例尺)

细石器"),不对称的称为"尖状器"(如"邦迪尖状器")。这是哈兰姆[9]所知的细石器术语的用法,这种用法把技术相似的器物按照类型分组,把其中不对称的类型视为更接近两面修理的尖状器而非"细石器"。这样的话,"细石器"成了例外的类别,所以琢背器物的时空分析复杂化了,过去二十年里这一术语已经没有什么用了。

一个非常不同的分类习惯是运用大小作为区分器物类型的关键标准。这种分类方法最显著的例子就是书面语言中的"细石器",实际是任何形状的细小石器,即使没有琢背修理[10]。20世纪的早些时候还用到其他术语,如"俾格米工具"[11],其强调器物大小是最重要的分类标准。许多研究者都批评"细石器"的这种用法,它包括的内容太多,没法区别出不同尖状器与琢背石片的时空分布形态[12]。在分类术语中,仅仅是器物大小本身并不足以对任何修理石片进行有效分类,得到符合习惯的工具类型分类体系(按照迈克卡瑟或类似的分析[13])。再者,尺寸小并不是一个很好的年代标志,因为正如麦克利文[14]曾指出的,我们知道整个澳大利亚史前史上细小的修理石片很常见。针对这个问题,一个解决方法是关注器物大小之外的分类特征,如琢背边缘的有无。

对侧边陡向修理的标本系统地运用琢背石叶这一术语是理查德·赖特提出的,并被广泛接受[15]。运用这一术语的直接好处就是它把多种多样的琢背标本归纳起来,确立了一个具有良好时空分布形态的[16]、类型学上可接受的特殊类别[17]。因此1970年代许多出版物中琢背石叶这个术语取代了细石器,强调琢背修理而非大小作为分类特征。现在已放弃琢背石叶这个术语,转而支持琢背石器的用法,因为琢背石叶含有特殊的含义,指专门石叶技术(参见下文)。

术语改变的重要性在于揭示原来强调器物大小所掩盖的形态特征。例如,传统认识的两个琢背石器亚类("邦迪"与几何形)常常确实含有小器物,长度平均为23毫米(总样本1 300件),大量标本的长度不足35毫米。但是很明显的是,那些传统类别中并非所有标本都很小,有标本超过60毫米。甚至还有技术相同的更大标本,它们为分类所掩盖,被称为其他工具类型,如"胡安(Juan)刀"或"Eloueras"(参见图11.2中的例子)。所有含有一边琢背修理的石片的类别,无论属于什么类型,都可以统一归入"琢背石器"这个类型中,即使某些地区、某些时期它们可能很大(长度可达190毫米)。因此,从细石器到琢背石器的术语转换,促使研究重点从关注器物的小尺寸到关注器物大小与形制的标准化。现在讨论的问题就不仅仅是器物不断缩小的趋势,而是为什么澳大利亚史前史上某个特定时期的狩猎采集者极其强调规整的琢背石器的使用与生产。

二、琢背器物与"石叶技术"的非相关性

有个观点一直阻碍研究澳大利亚琢背石器激增现象,它认为器物形制的规整是采用了一种专门的由"石叶技术"生产的"毛坯"。这种观点以许多方式表达出来。最显著的是那些综合性文章,认为"细石器"与石叶技术传入了澳大利

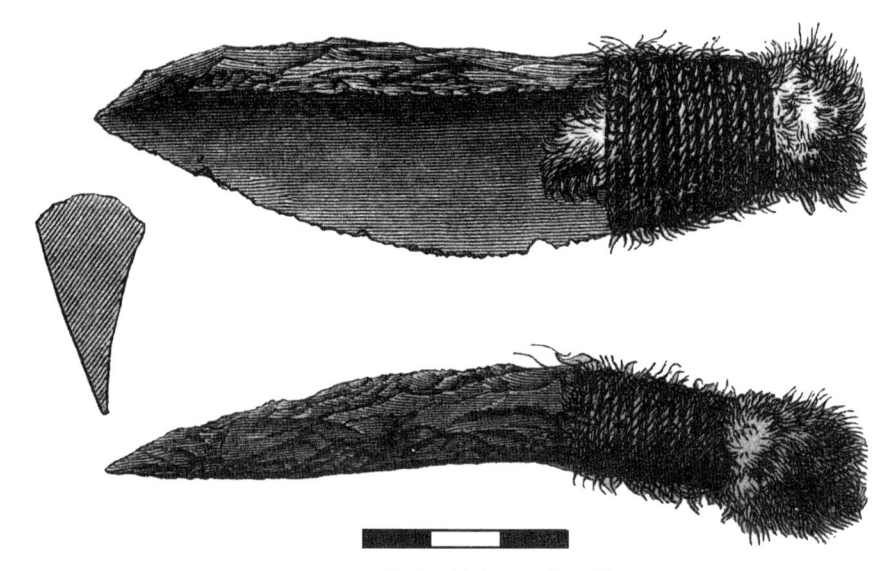

图 11.2　非对称的大型琢背石器

（传统上称之为胡安刀[18]，比例尺为厘米）

亚[19]。这种观点把澳大利亚的石叶生产与"细石器"生产联系起来，即使这种联系从来没有证实过[20]。他们认为澳大利亚存在类似欧洲旧石器时代中期到晚期的平行发展，甚至最近几十年里这一观点还有市场[21]。某些研究者将这种平行发展解释为技术或知识从旧大陆向澳大利亚传播的结果，可能跟野狗一道传进来，甚至还包括人类的社会结构。就解释琢背石器激增的传播论观点的影响，我曾经做过深入的讨论[22]。

奇怪的是，这些观点一直存在着，因为澳大利亚考古学家很早就提出许多琢背石器并不是由石叶制作的。例如，哈兰姆[23]在讨论大陆西侧标本时得出结论：

> 澳大利亚称为"琢背石叶"的器物包括那些并非石叶的琢背修理或钝化修理标本，尽管某些标本经过再修理之后具备了似石叶的特征。

研究中东部澳大利亚的考古学家也曾经得出类似的结论[24]。穆尔万尼[25]在一篇较早总结琢背石器形态的文章中也把琢背石器的观察与石叶"毛坯"的推断分开来，他说：

"琢背石叶"是一个错误的名称,因为大部分器物称为琢背石片更合适。虽然真正的石叶、石核、薄石叶与细小石叶也广泛存在。

或许可以这么认为,尽管许多组合中可能会发现"薄石叶与细小石叶",但它们并非由全新世中期引入澳大利亚的石叶技术所生产[26]。这个结论有助于我们把琢背石器的生产过程与生产石叶的打片方法区分开来,至少在澳大利亚可以如此。有观点认为全新世没有石叶技术[27],但下面一组归纳将说明得出这个结论的证据:

1. 不同时空的石片长度变化非常小,实际上它随原料的变化更多。澳大利亚东部长宽比一直都在0.5至1.5之间,整个更新世与全新世都是如此,绝大多数组合中,长宽比超过2的石片比例一直都低于15%到20%[28]。

2. 琢背石器并非"石叶"的片段,它可以由任何石片制作,只要石片截面形状合适,有一条足够长的直边或微有起伏的边。未修理的边通常是短宽石片的远端,有时候甚至可能是铰链状断裂的边[29]。打破琢背石器生产与石叶技术之间的关联,促使我们得出两个结论:

1. 澳大利亚琢背石器的标准化大小与形制是通过垫在石砧上仔细修理所得,尽管形制规范的石片可能会有利于这个过程,但是这样的石片并不是必需的。

2. 由于石叶技术跟琢背石器的生产没有什么关联,所以也就没必要引入这样一种技术来解释全新世琢背石器的生产。短而规范的石片、细致的石片修理,以及砸击技术的运用等要素在更新世时都已经具备[30]。因此,琢背石器的最初生产涉及结合一系列既有打片方法,人们生产琢背石器前并不需要引入或发明什么新的打片技术。

这些结论的含义是,建立澳大利亚琢背石器的时空分布形态模型需要考虑一些机制问题,要解释为什么全新世时强调某些既有的技术成分,而非寻求引入某些新技术,作为一副灵丹妙药去解释考古材料上的复杂变化[31]。澳大利亚东南部不同时期琢背石器形态的新发现加强了这一观点。

三、澳大利亚的时空形态

澳大利亚大陆的大部分地区都有琢背石器发现(图11.3),但是似乎不见于金伯利与阿恩海姆地的西北部地区、塔斯马尼亚与新几内亚[32]。在那些有琢背石器发现的澳大利亚大陆地区,人们很早就认识到其形态的空间变化[33]。通常按照平面形状的对称程度来加以描述,习惯上分为对称与非对称两种形制。下面的年代讨论限于澳大利亚大陆的东南部。

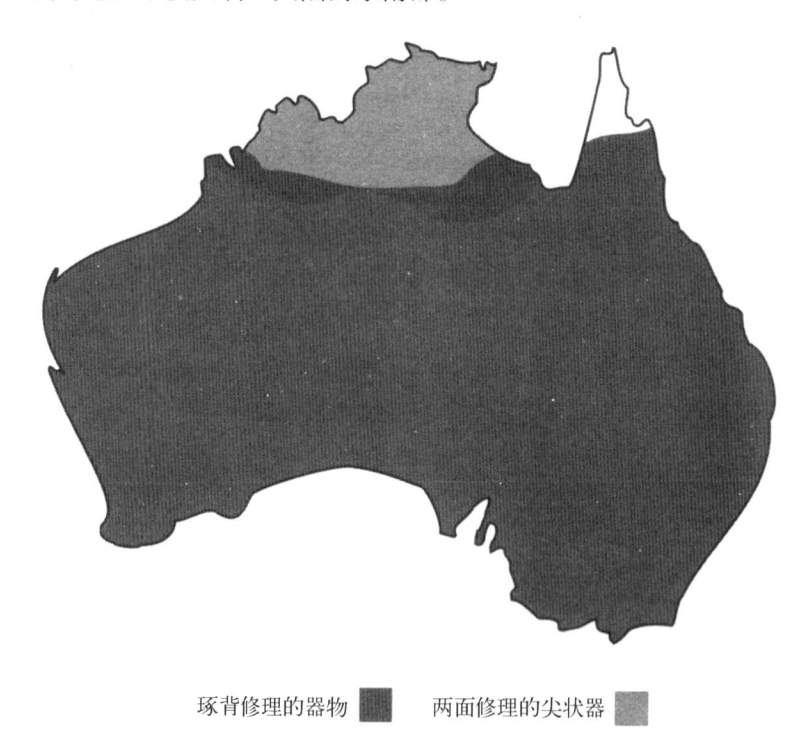

琢背修理的器物　　两面修理的尖状器

图11.3　澳大利亚琢背石器与两面修理尖状器的分布

至少在东部沿海地区有报道,年代超过距今5 000年的地层中发现一些琢背石器[34]。因此我们可以说更新世之末或全新世早期琢背石器制作已经开始了,但是许多地区直到距今4 000年前后才开始大规模生产。最早皮尔斯[35]提出这个观点,但是一直鲜有人支持,直到最近才开始被接受[36]。随着早于距今5 000年琢背石器发现的证实,现在所有关于全新世早期澳大利亚东南部琢背石器存在与否的怀疑都烟消云散,其年代很可能早到距今7 000到8 000年[37]。全新世早期的琢背石器发现较少,当时生产的可能也不多。大部分有年代的标本都在距今4 000至1 500年间,显然琢背石器的大规模生产见于此时。过去的千余年间,琢背石器还在生产,尽管数量不多[38]。有些学者认为琢背石器生产仅见于距今4 000至1 000年间,如[39],但是这些认识现在看来是误读了考古材料[40]。当然,距今4 000至2 000~1 000年间琢背石器生产比例确实要高一些,更早与更晚时候的生产比例显然更低。

新南威尔士州东部的马瑟尔岩厦发现琢背石器的文化序列也说明了这一趋势(图11.4)。遗址最底部的琢背石器所在层位年代估计为距今7 500年,但从那以后,直到距今4 000至3 500年,废弃率(也意味着生产率)为0.23/100年/平方米。从大约距今3 500年到距今2 500~2 000年,马瑟尔岩厦琢背石器的废弃率高出好几个数量级,为50/100年/平方米,此后废弃率又下降到从前的水平。类似的趋势普遍发现过,尽管不同地区高生产率开始的时间略有差异。

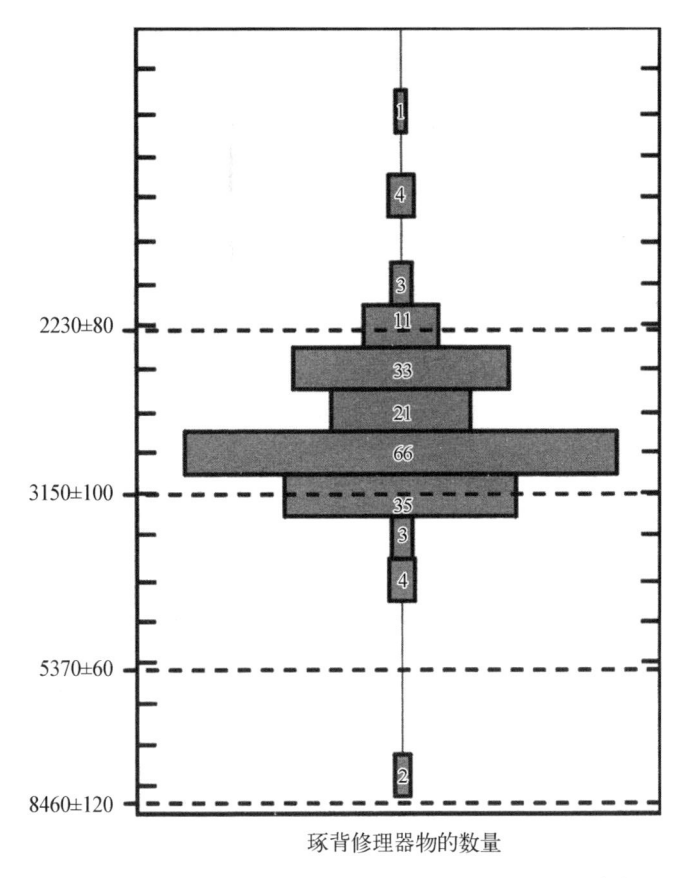

图11.4 马瑟尔岩厦探方A琢背石器丰度的垂直变化[41]

关于4 500至3 500年前高生产率开始的情况,有两点值得强调。首先是这一特征广泛适用于澳大利亚南部的许多地区[42],尽管如此广阔的区域存在类型学与环境的差异。这表明,在如此不同的背景关联中琢背石器的增加采用多原因的观点来解释是合适的,但是很可能存在一个或一系列触发事件。这一观点在澳大利亚考古学中长期流行,但是对触发事件的探索集中于工具生产观念的传播,并将之视为琢背石器增加的原因。

第二点反复要说的是从 4 500 到 3 500 年前,当时澳大利亚琢背石器"显著增加"(即生产率的提高),而琢背石片这类器物其实早已生产与废弃数千年了。按照文化选择论的术语,这一形态非常清楚,技术/类型差异的产生是个独立事件,发生在全新世中期琢背石器的激增之前。与此同时,全新世中期人们选择琢背石器作为偏好的技术产品,其原因并不必跟功能相关,澳大利亚考古学一直都认为是功能导致接受或发明这种技术[43]。不管研究者选择怎样的观点(外来引入或是本土发明)来解释澳大利亚琢背石器的起源,都需要从选择的角度,将琢背石器视为当时所遭遇环境条件的某种反应,这样才能够解释回答全新世中期这些器物的激增。这一原理使我们注意到 4 500 至 3 500 年前选择发生的背景关联。

四、琢背石器与风险

有观点认为这种工具易于携带,还是多功能的,是环境利用过程中不确定性提高时的首选,这揭示了不同时代的风险与全新世中期琢背石器广泛分布之间的联系[44]。再者,琢背石器常常是装柄技术的组成部分,其形制与大小的一致性有助于提高镶嵌有琢背石器的复合工具的可维护性与可靠性[45]。采用这样的工具将可能减小觅食过程中遭遇失败的风险,人们通过提高工具的"准备率",从而实际上降低生计风险。此模型中风险包括"失败的概率"以及高的"失败成本",不过巴姆福斯与布雷德[46]准确地指出重点是在前者,只因为这个阶段人们对失败的成本知之甚少。

我们现在很清楚,需要解释的是琢背石器激增,这代表人们选择了这种器型,而非他们同样拥有的其他器型。如果全新世中期澳大利亚的环境与社会条件确实如此变化,使得琢背石器的生产与使用比其他器型的生产更有优势,那么我们应该看到琢背石器更受重视。我曾经指出过,资源获取的更大流动性与不确定性将使得琢背石器的生产有利可图[47]。

以前我们描述过资源获取中所涉及的两种情况,全新世中期可能存在[48]:当狩猎采集者群体进入陌生的环境时,以及当环境变化降低了资源的熟悉程度时。前一个机制现在得到了语言学支持,帕马—伦干人在澳大利亚广大区域,尤其是澳大利亚中部沙漠地区的扩散[49],帕马—伦干语的分布与琢背石器之间显示出非常强的同步变化,全新世时可能存在多次琢背石器使用者的迁徙[50]。澳大利亚中部地区殖民/再殖民过程既有遗传学的,也有考古学的证据[51]。当然,有关证据的解释还存在争议,但是莫尔温尼与卡敏加[52]拒绝承认语言学的传播,认为这没有反映人群的迁徙[53],虽然其他学者都能接受。

进入一个新环境,不熟悉资源状况,这是我强调的机制[54],在这种情形中,减少觅食失败概率的技术策略就会很有优势。由于我们还不清楚帕马—伦干语扩散多大程度上跟人口迁徙与替代相关,所以也不清楚是否过度强调了这一机制。但是日益清楚的一点是,环境变化提高风险的观点既没有得到足够的重视,也没有找到合适的研究方向。重视程度不够既因为许多群体似乎很可能没有进入新的环境中,还因为我所说的那种大规模环境变化[55]只是地区现象。

寻找解释全新世中期琢背石器激增的环境背景并不需要仅仅局限于迅速、持续的大规模环境变化。更可能的是,导致这种反应的条件只是环境变化幅度的提高[56]。对狩猎采集者而言,气候相对微小的变化也可能导致更难预见资源的供给。最近的古环境研究揭示出厄尔尼诺南方涛动现象的时间变化,使得这一机制有了新生命,它导致了风险升高的环境背景的形成。

戴维与罗兰多斯[57]在思考澳大利亚全新世风险的性质时,认为应该考虑社会决策因素,它既是风险构成的部分,也是解决风险的选择策略,他们说:

> 这里我们认为全新世晚期管理风险的策略可能已经出现,以应对更加斑块化的资源条件,如西斯科克[58]提出的,解释专业化的新工具类型应该考虑"有效的"背景关联(也就是社会文化的改变),而非仅仅是"自然的"环境斑块化,也就是,社会领域化本身构成了资源斑块化。

当然,从某个层面上说,这一观点无疑是正确的,因为风险的某些部分是通过社会机制引起的,至少需要经过社会机制的协调。因此,我[59]追随托伦斯[60]承认社会机制的重要性,某些长期的风险甚至可能是狩猎采集者群体组织的结果。群体构成、社会地域边界的特征以及群体间的关系,会限制人们接近某些资源,它们在澳大利亚确实被视为风险最小化策略中的重要因素[61]。工具组合中某个组成部分比如琢背石器甚至成为某种象征,用于协调资源所有权,从而减小风险。不过,文化地域明晰化[62]与全新世中期琢背石器的激增之间的关系还很模糊,原因有二。

首先,戴维与罗兰多斯讨论[63]的澳大利亚东北部石器特征的地区化/地域划分可能始于距今 3 500 年前后,但是只是过去 2 000 年里最明显,因此是在琢背石器衰落阶段表现最强烈。其二,更重要的是,戴维与罗兰多斯就新的地域体系所提出的解释是,这些体系有助于保持人口水平,尽管从全新世中期到晚期气候条件更干旱。因此,戴维与罗兰多斯的意思是[64],如果某种地域观念结构的变化与风险产生/管理相关,那么它就是缓解环境不确定性的一种机制。我们仍有必要去探索一下全新世澳大利亚气候变化的某些规律。

五、厄尔尼诺南方涛动

厄尔尼诺是一个用来描述热带太平洋海洋与空气循环年度变化的术语[65]。厄尔尼诺现象开始的时候,信风减弱,通常推向西太平洋的温暖的表面海水流向太平洋中部。其结果是西太平洋的海水温度比往常更低,从较冷洋面蒸发的水汽减少,冷空气下沉,导致降水量大幅减少。标志厄尔尼诺现象的海面温度变化跟一种被称为南方涛动的气压变化有关,这些海洋与大气的相互影响合起来称为厄尔尼诺南方涛动,或简称为 ENSO。现在厄尔尼诺现象一般持续 12 到 18 个月,但持续的时间与结构特征变化多样。ENSO 系统的变化有周期性,两次厄尔尼诺现象之间大致相隔三到七年,但这个时间间隔也是变化多端的。运用历史材料建立的 ENSO 现象模型表明存在一种复杂的正反馈关系,就事件的开始与衰落以及事件的强度等因素而言,每一次厄尔尼诺事件都跟其他事件有所不同[66]。再者,大致相同的厄尔尼诺事件所造成影响的严重性与性质也有所不同。因此过去 100 年间的 ENSO 现象可以说是极其多样,很难预测。

厄尔尼诺往往引发遍及东南亚、印度尼西亚、巴布亚新几内亚,以及澳大利亚北部、中部与东部地区的干旱,这是 ENSO 机制最明显的影响。历史上,这些干旱既漫长且严重,年均降水会比正常年份少45%。当这样的情况周期性地反复出现而且时间长持续,不难想象灌木丛中的食物,包括动物与植物,都会大幅度减少,尤其是在承载力本来就低的环境中[67]。降水反差的连带影响还可能包括野火更加普遍,资源分布的一致性/斑块化发生变化,以及侵蚀途径的变化。

历史上也观察到其他方面的环境影响。例如,埃兰等[68]记载厄尔尼诺事件时西太平洋—印度尼西亚地区海平面比平时低,这会导致珊瑚大面积的漂白与死亡。龙卷风的频率与强度似乎也与这些变化相关,尽管关联的性质还不是很清楚。

ENSO 事件不是什么新生事物,历史记录[69]表明它只是数千年来的气候的一个特征而已。当然,越来越多的证据表明这种大气与海洋相互影响的频率与强调是不断变化的,变化的结构是全新世环境条件变化的一个重要因素。

本文特别关注的是那些古环境研究,它们支持在全新世部分时间段里澳大利亚的大部分地区以 ENSO 为主的气候已经建立[70]。过去 100 年的记录表明有效降水与 ENSO 之间存在关联,其中降水量与达令河流量、南方涛动指数之间存在非常强的联系[71]。研究者根据有效降水的地貌与孢粉标志,认为全新世早期有效降水在增加,直到约距今 5 000 年还维持在高位。这个时期之前没有 ENSO 事件的记录。此后,占主导地位的沃克环流与 ENSO 开始出现,这从两个方面可以看到:一是有效降水的明显减少,这在澳大利亚的北部、中部、东部不同地点都已得到证实;二是距今 5 000 至 2 000 年间气候变化的范围扩大。此外,有观点认为低有效降水阶段开始存在自南向北的趋势,最早开始于澳大利亚南部,大约距今 5 000 至 4 500 年,稍后(距今 4 000 至 3 800 年)在澳大利亚北部开始[72]。过去两千年里,有效降水再次提高,降水量的变化范围减小,尽管仍然可以看到。

以上对气候趋势的归纳显然是概略的,并没有包括所有的气候研究在内[73]。不过,全新世中期开始以 ENSO 为主导的气候是一个普遍接受的模型,把全新世环境变化与考古材料的趋势进行比较相当有趣。全新世中期有效降水减少的气候模型与 ENSO 导致的环境变化之间的关联可能只是尝试性的,但是如果这种关联通过了将来的检验,那么就会为解释琢背石器的激增提供一个较好的框架。

六、琢背石器与 ENSO 的同步变化

琢背石器强化生产时期的开始与 ENSO 主导气候的形成之间存在强烈的耦合关系,此时有效降水减少,气候变化幅度扩大。表 11.1 总结了气候趋势与考古材料趋势之间广泛的年代关系,气候材料主要来自舒尔梅斯特和李的研究[74],考古材料这里已综合过。这一总结无疑掩盖了某些不确定性与地区差异,那些复杂的问题值得再用一次学术讨论会加以关注。当然,即便承认环境—文化关联可能更复杂、更有趣,观察这些趋势还是需要的,它提供了一个机会,让我们仔细思考澳大利亚全新世技术选择的环境背景。

表 11.1　有效降水与琢背石器丰度变化趋势总结

距今年代(年)	有 效 降 水	琢背石器的生产
0~2 000	提高但仍然多变	少
2 000~4 000	低且多变	多
4 000~5 000	下降	增加
>5 000	高	非常少

有鉴于此,我提出下面的模型,它强调琢背石器生产年代上的大趋势可能正好反映了环境变化导致的文化反应,尤其是针对环境变化幅度扩大导致风险提高的反应。这里所提出的机制并非考古材料趋势的唯一解释,但是在澳大利亚全新世技术风险反应模型中添加了较早的影响因素[75]。

距今 4 000 至 5 000 年澳大利亚南部广大区域开始遭受更干旱、更多变的气候条件。这导致资源的有无与分布更难准确定位与预测。这种变化发生时,许多地区的人口规模或是保持稳定,或是稍有增加,至少某些人类群体正迁往新的地带,海平面上升的影响正在发生中。人们可能调整了许多觅食策略,可能还有社会组织与社会关系的调整,以减少新情况导致的风险增加。一项广泛存在的策略调整就是一种早已存在的工具类型,即琢背石器,开始得到更多的运用。因为这类工具的灵活性、可靠性与可维护性更好[76],研究者假定它属于某个能够减少觅食风险的工具组合。增加这种行为的好处是,利用这一技术的个体与群体可能获得某些生存优势。强调生产与使用琢背石器的程度因时因地变化,主要取决于:(a)觅食风险的水平与性质;(b)这一技术反应相对其他技术策略的成本收益;(c)石器加工技术与其他风险应对策略之间的关系。过去两千年里,有效降水增加,琢背石器生产大幅度减少,这也是技术体系应对影响觅食者其他压力的反应。

觅食风险的提高可能部分为觅食中所用石器的重新组织所抵消,这一观点并不意味着石器上的变化是唯一或起主导作用的应对风险的方式。上文的讨论也没有将减小风险的策略局限于技术活动如琢背石器的生产之上,还有许多食物获取策略的变化:

● 全新世中期许多觅食策略都表现在食谱扩充上[77]。强化利用从前不利用的物种,如蛾子[78]或有毒的坚果[79],这样的观点见于许多有关食谱变化的讨论中,但全新世中期还存在动物群丰富程度细微的提高。如西姆[80]就提出一个观点,认为距今 3 500 至 4 000 年塔斯马尼亚资源利用的转变与食谱宽度的变化跟 ENSO 的开始有关[81]。

● 尽管存在一些使用方法上的争论[82],澳大利亚许多干旱地区磨制植物种子的磨石只是在距今 4 000 到 2 000 年间开始流行,这也标志着食谱的扩充,把更低等但更可靠的草籽归入主要食物资源中[83]。

● 维奇[84]认为全新世中期贝类的利用表明人们明显开始转向捕食 r-* 选择物种。他指出这些物种更能承受环境波动与人类的过度捕食。

所有这些资源利用上的转变代表了觅食策略重点的变化,面对环境变化以及由于人口增长或领域缩小所导致的资源压力时,这些策略是有弹性的。策略的变化有助于减小觅食的风险。全新世中期风险减小的机制中包括采用不同觅食策略,利用更标准化以及可能更可靠、更便于维护的技术方法,以及迁往很少活动过的区域。

在这个关节点上有必要评论一下对我的批评,它跟我[85]最初构建的风险解释相反,用以解释全新世中期人类行为改变的各个方面。批评的部分内容如下:

> 狩猎采集者可能需要数千年才能熟悉一个地区的资源状况,这样的假设让人想起桑德拉·博德勒的"海岸殖民假说",按照这一假说,更新世时适应海岸环境的群体不能在内陆的萨胡尔地区生活。两个假说都忽略了狩猎采集者运用简单技术把握新环境的能力。他们基于动物生物学原理推理,而忽视了人类不断发明克服困难的事实与人类的适应能力。[86]

这一批评基本上误解了这里讨论的风险减少模型,表达也有问题。首先,莫尔温尼与卡敏加没能认识到技术策略是人类克服困难的重要方式,他们在同一观点中居然支持"人类的发明",两者之间存在令人难以理解的不一致性。他们认为狩猎采集者能够迅速"掌控"环境,基于这样的观点所形成的批评使得其矛盾更加复杂,因为我们知道全新世中期澳大利亚并没有这样的事。的确,人类群体调整其活动以适应新环境的速度是这里讨论的中心问题之一。在环境变化幅度较大的背景中,发展新技术与生计策略可能是一个长期的过程,这完全可以理解。再者,风险减小模型意味着人们需要花上数千年"熟悉"资源条件,这样的观点没有考虑不同尺度的环境波动。莫尔温尼与卡敏加似乎认为土著之于景观

---

* 物种的生殖策略,K 选择或 r 选择,一种多生不养,一种是少生精养。

的知识是足够的,因此没有必要采用技术的途径来应对风险。这种观点囿于民族志的尺度,既没有考虑历史时期与全新世中期环境之间的区别,也没有超越形成澳大利亚民族历史的图像的几个月或几年的时间尺度,考虑到这个尺度的环境变化。每年或者甚至是一代人可能都观察不到大规模的变化,这促使我[87]写到"某些风险减少策略其实一直在那里,即使这种策略的好处只是偶尔才被认识到"。但是无论如何,模型本身没有哪一点暗指所有的时候应对风险的技术策略都是必需的,琢背石器一直需要大量生产。甚至针对短时间高风险的技术反应可能融入整个技术结构中去。这是因为器物如琢背石器的强化生产并不是孤立的,而是与硅质岩的获取、搬运以及打制的技术体系相关联[88]。因此,即便是觅食风险水平下降了,风险减少技术策略还可能继续存在,因为"那些技术将继续在许多事情上有效地发挥作用,可能与传统的行为方式融为一体了"[89]。并非觅食风险的减小导致了全新世晚期琢背石器生产的衰落,而是新的环境与社会条件形成,这涉及诸如定居、区域化、人口增加等因素,它对于合适技术的选择具有潜在的影响[90]。这也许可以解释贝尔伍德[91]的观察,他发现全新世晚期琢背石器衰落的形态不大协调[92]。

七、意义:全新世中期文化反应的偶然性

如果这一模型正确,ENSO 主导的气候是导致全新世中期觅食风险提高的原因之一,琢背石器可能是复合工具的组成部分,它们的生产和增加成为针对新环境的反应。这类模型常常遭到一种批评,说它是"决定论的",但实际上这种文化选择论的观点并没有说文化反应是决定性的。这里所说的以及其他学者所讨论的[93],针对觅食风险点提高都存在非技术的文化反应,它们可能是技术反应的补充或是替代选择。当然,即便是在技术反应中,也还有其他的选择,采用某个技术策略而非其他策略的原因可能源于不同觅食者群体的历史状况。

在澳大利亚还可以看到一个典型的偶然过程。澳大利亚类型学家识别的主要工具类型有两种特别值得关注:两面修理的尖状器与琢背石器[94]。两面修理的尖状器见于澳洲大陆的西北部,与更偏南分布的琢背石器稍稍有些重叠(参见图 11.3)。尽管两类器物的生产程序与最终形制差异显著,但是它们也有许多共同点,包括都有标准的形制,尺寸小,易于携带,适合装柄使用,多功能,以及适合制作可以快速维护的复合工具等。有意思的是,研究较好的阿恩海姆地西部发现的两面修理的尖状器具有跟琢背石器类型类似的年代趋势。距今

7 000 至 5 000 年间该地区两面修理的尖状器开始少量见于考古材料中,只是在距今 3 500 至 3 000 年间大量生产,到距今 2 000 年,其生产又急剧下降[95]。

两面器尖状器的激增可以运用一个类似琢背石器的模型来解释:更干旱与多变的气候条件跟 ENSO 的形成相关,它提高了觅食风险,适应新环境的众多策略之一就是利用一种已经存在的工具,也就是两面修理的尖状器,增加其生产与使用,因为这种工具灵活、可靠、易于维护,有助于降低觅食风险[96]。值得注意的是两面修理的尖状器激增的时间比更南分布的琢背石器晚 500 到 1 000 年。其开始与舒尔梅斯特与李[97](参见上文)推导的澳大利亚北部 ENSO 主导气候形成的时间刚好巧合。基于以上的观察,可以提出这样的假说,即琢背石器与两面修理的尖状器的增加都是觅食者针对全新世中期风险提高的反应。

如果这些观点能够继续存在,那么我们现在就可以回到一个很有意思的问题:作为一种技术反应,为什么澳大利亚西北部的人们面对风险时选择两面修理的尖状器,而更南部的地区人们选择了琢背石器?答案涉及偶然性。全新世中期觅食风险提高,群体从既有的技术策略中寻找那种能够有效应对新环境的方法。他们在标准化的小型修理石片上找到最有利的特征,把它与可靠、易于维护、多功能的复合工具结合起来。澳大利亚南部既有的这种技术形式是琢背石器,于是人们优先使用它。而在澳大利亚北部从未用过琢背石器,具有这些优势特征的既有石器技术就是两面修理的尖状器,同样得到优先使用。显然,最终选择哪一类器物仅仅取决于既有工具组合中所包含的内容。澳洲大陆的西北部,两面器技术普遍分布,更新世以来,不仅有两面修理的尖状器,还包括巴克利台地(Barkely Tablelands)的盘状两面器,以及阿恩海姆地两面修理的石斧。两面修理技术的起源不是本文讨论的内容,但是全新世中期存在这种技术,琢背石器缺失,它们构成了后来风险减少技术能够流行的基础。因此,澳大利亚西北部面对更高风险环境时选择两面修理的尖状器,而澳大利亚南部选择琢背石器,这种差别跟每个广大区域此前的发展历史密切相关,而非因为新环境本身有更高风险,或是因为选择了重组技术体系。

为什么"类似的技术与工具没有在澳大利亚史前史更早时期同样具有风险时出现呢"?偶然性的问题也是这一问题的中心[98]。尽管我们可以认识到更早以技术为基础的风险减少策略,但是它们不是石质尖状器或琢背石器,而是更多使用如麦克尼文[99]所说修理规整的拇指盖刮削器,如塔斯马尼亚西南部所见,以应对末次盛冰期提高流动性的"需求"。更新世技术中还没有诸如两面修理尖状器或琢背石器这样的技术类型可供选择,它们是更晚的全新世阶段才具有的。此时应对觅食风险的策略选择自然不同于全新世。

八、结论

澳大利亚有证据表明存在石器技术上的变化,以应对全新世中期提高的觅食风险。途径之一就是使用大量琢背石器工具,考古材料上表现为距今3 500至4 500年间琢背石器的生产频率大幅提高。本文探讨了澳大利亚东南部全新世琢背石器的"激增"现象,得到如下一些结论:

- 澳大利亚全新世中期琢背石器生产的增加并非来自某种新型工具或某种相关技术的发明或引进。尤其是,这一变化与澳大利亚此时石叶技术的出现并不相关。

- 全新世中期的某个时期石器制作者大量生产琢背石器,但是生产琢背石器的修理石片与相关技术在此之前数千年就已经具备了。按照文化选择论的观点,特征的产生与选择是分开的,这有助于理解这一形态。根据描述琢背石器选择的模型可以很好地解释琢背石器激增现象。

- 从年代上来看,琢背石器生产的增加跟4 000至5 000年前环境变化加剧以及生活环境的扩展相关,ENSO主导气候形态的形成可能是引发觅食风险增加的因素。我[100]曾提出大量出现标准化与便于维护的石器可能反映了日益提高的觅食风险,尤其是环境不确定性所导致的风险,上述形态与我的观点是一致的。

- 标准化器物类型生产的强调只是全新世中期人们用来减小风险的众多策略之一。众多用来缓解环境变化加剧所致影响的策略与减少风险的解释是一致的。

- 历史偶然性见于澳大利亚北部所存在的不同技术体系的同步反应中。

注释:

[1] Hiscock, P. Technological Responses to Risk in Holocene Australia. *Journal of World Prehistory* 8(3): 267-292, 1994.

[2] Bamforth, D. B., and P. Bleed. Technology, Flaked Stone Technology, and Risk. In *Rediscovering Darwin: Evolutionary Theory and Archeological Explanation*. CM. Barton and G. A. Clark, eds. Pp. 109-139. Archeological Papers of the American Anthropological Association, 7. Arlington, Va.: American Anthropological Association, 1997.

Dunnell, R. C. Evolutionary Theory and Archaeology. In *Advances in Archaeological Method* and Theory, vol. 3. M. B. Schiffer, ed. Pp. 35 – 99. New York: Academic, 1980.

O'Brien, M., and T. Holland. Variation, Selection, and the Archaeological Record. Archaeological Method and Theory 2: 31 – 79, 1990.

[3] Hiscock, P., and V. Attenbrow. Backed into a Corner. Australian Archaeology 42: 64 – 65, 1996.

[4] Hallam, S. J. Microlithic Industries in Western Australia: Some Aspects. In Recent Advances in Indo-Pacific Prehistory. V. N. Misra and P. Bellwood, eds. Pp. 219 – 229. New Delhi: Oxford and IBH Publishing, 1985.

[5] Etheridge, R., and T. Whitelegge. Aboriginal Workshops on the Coast of New South Wales, and Their Contents. Records of the Australian Museum 6: 233 – 250.

[6] Etheridge, R., and T. Whitelegge. Aboriginal Workshops on the Coast of New South Wales, and Their Contents. Records of the Australian Museum 6: 239, 1907.

[7] Kenyon, A. S. Stone Implements on Aboriginal Camping Grounds. Victorian Naturalist 43: 280 – 285, 1927.

[8] McCarthy, F. D., E. Bramell, and H. V. V. Noone. The Stone Implements of Australia. Memoirs of the Australian Museum 9: 1 – 94, 1946.

[9] Hallam, S. J. Microlithic Industries in Western Australia: Some Aspects. In Recent Advances in Indo-Pacific Prehistory. V. N. Misra and P. Bellwood, eds. Pp. 219 – 229. New Delhi: Oxford and IBH Publishing, 1985.

[10] Gould, R. A. A Preliminary Report on Excavations at Puntutjarpa Rockshelter, near the Warburton Ranges, Western Australia. Archaeology and Physical Anthropology in Oceania 3: 162 – 185, 1968.

[11] Turner, R. Pygmy Implements. Mankind 1: 110 – 112, 1932.

[12] Glover, I. C, and R. Lampert. Puntutjarpa Rockshelter Excavations by R. A. Gould: A Critical Review. Archaeology and Physical Anthropology in Oceania 4: 222 – 228, 1969.

Hallam, S. J. Microlithic Industries in Western Australia: Some Aspects. In Recent Advances in Indo-Pacific Prehistory. V. N. Misra and P. Bellwood, eds. Pp. 219 – 229. New Delhi: Oxford and IBH Publishing, 1985.

Mulvaney, D. J. Australian Backed Blade Industries in Perspective. In Recent Advances in Indo-Pacific Prehistory. V. N. Misraand P. Bellwood, eds. Pp. 211 – 217. New Delhi: Oxford and IBH Publishing, 1985.

[13] McCarthy, F. D. Australian Aboriginal Stone Implements. Sydney: Australian Museum, 1967.

[14] McNiven, I. J. Technological Organization and Settlement in Southwest Tasmania after the Glacial Maximum. Antiquity 68: 75 – 82, 1994.

Backed to the Pleistocene. Archaeology in Oceania 35: 48 – 52, 2000.

[15] Mulvaney, D. J. Australian Backed Blade Industries in Perspective. In *Recent Advances in Indo-Pacific Prehistory*. V. N. Misraand P. Bellwood, eds. Pp. 211. New Delhi: Oxford and IBH Publishing, 1985.

[16] Mulvaney, D. J. Australian Backed Blade Industries in Perspective. In *Recent Advances in Indo-Pacific Prehistory*. V. N. Misraand P. Bellwood, eds. Pp. 211 – 217. New Delhi: Oxford and IBH Publishing, 1985.

Pearce, R. H. Spatial and Temporal Distribution of Australian Backed Blades. *Mankind* 9: 300 – 309, 1974.

[17] Pearce, R. H. Uniformity of the Australian Backed Blade Tradition. *Mankind* 9: 89 – 95, 1973.

[18] Evans, J. *The Ancient Stone Implements, Weapons and Ornaments of Great Britain*. London: Longman, Green Reader and Dyer: 264, 1872.

[19] Foley, R., and M. Lahr. Mode 3 Technologies and the Evolution of Modern Humans. *Cambridge Archaeological Journal* 7: 3 – 36, 1997.

Mellars, P. A. Major Issues in the Emergence of Modern Humans. *Current Anthropology* 30: 349 – 385, 1989.

[20] Hallam, S. J. Microlithic Industries in Western Australia: Some Aspects. In *Recent Advances in Indo-Pacific Prehistory*. V. N. Misra and P. Bellwood, eds. Pp. 219 – 229. New Delhi: Oxford and IBH Publishing, 1985.

[21] Jones, R. The Tasmanian Paradox. In *Stone Tools as Cultural Markers: Change Evolution, Complexity*. R. V. S. Wright, ed. Pp. 189 – 204. Canberra: Australian Institute of Aboriginal Studies, 1977.

[22] Hiscock, P. Technological Responses to Risk in Holocene Australia. *Journal of World Prehistory* 8(3): 267 – 292, 1994.

[23] Hallam, S. J. Microlithic Industries in Western Australia: Some Aspects. In *Recent Advances in Indo-Pacific Prehistory*. V. N. Misra and P. Bellwood, eds. Pp. 219 – 229. New Delhi: Oxford and IBH Publishing, 1985: 219.

[24] Dickson, F. P. Backed Blades and Points. *Mankind* 9: 7 – 14, 1973.

Bondi Points. *Mankind* 10: 45 – 46, 1975.

Gould, R. A. Puntutjarpa Rockshelter and the Australian Desert Culture. *Anthropological Papers of the American Museum of Natural History* 54(1), 1977.

[25] Mulvaney, D. J. Australian Backed Blade Industries in Perspective. In *Recent Advances in Indo-Pacific Prehistory*. V. N. Misraand P. Bellwood, eds. Pp. 213. New Delhi: Oxford and IBH Publishing, 1985.

[26] Gould, R. A. Puntutjarpa Rockshelter and the Australian Desert Culture. *Anthropological*

Papers of the American Museum of Natural History 54(1), 1977: 85.

Hiscock, P. Bondaian Technology in the Hunter Valley, New South Wales. *Archaeology in Oceania* 28: 64 – 75, 1993.

[27] Hiscock, P. Bondaian Technology in the Hunter Valley, New South Wales. *Archaeology in Oceania* 28: 64 – 75, 1993.

[28] Hiscock, P. Bondaian Technology in the Hunter Valley, New South Wales. *Archaeology in Oceania* 28: 64 – 75, 1993.

[29] Lamb, L. A Methodology for the Analysis of Backed Artefact Production on the South Molle Island Quarry, Whitsunday Islands. *Tempus* 6: 154 – 155, 1996.

[30] McNiven, I. J. Technological Organization and Settlement in Southwest Tasmania after the Glacial Maximum. *Antiquity* 68: 75 – 82, 1994.

Backed to the Pleistocene. *Archaeology in Oceania* 35: 48 – 52, 2000.

[31] Hiscock, P. Technological Responses to Risk in Holocene Australia. *Journal of World Prehistory* 8(3): 267 – 292, 1994.

[32] Smith, M. A., and B. J. Cundy. Distribution Maps for Flaked Stone Points and Backed Blades in the Northern Territory. *Australian Aboriginal Studies* 1985/2: 32 – 37, 1985.

[33] Glover, I, C. Stone Implements from Millstream Station, W. A.: Newall's Collection Revisited. *Mankind* 6: 415 – 425, 1967.

Mitchell, S. R. *Stone Age Craftsmen: Stone Tools and Camping Places of the Australian Aborigines*. Melbourne: Tait Book Company, 1949.

Pearce, R. H. Uniformity of the Australian Backed Blade Tradition. *Mankind* 9: 89 – 95, 1973.

[34] Hiscock, P., and V. Attenbrow. Early Holocene Backed Artefacts from Australia. *Archaeology in Oceania* 33: 49 – 63, 1998.

[35] Pearce, R. H. Spatial and Temporal Distribution of Australian Backed Blades. *Mankind* 9: 300 – 309, 1974.

[36] Dortch, C. Geometric Microliths from a Dated Archaeological Deposit near Northcliffe, Western Australia. *Journal of the Royal Society of Western Australia* 58: 59 – 63, 1975.

Hiscock, P. Technological Responses to Risk in Holocene Australia. *Journal of World Prehistory* 8(3): 267 – 292, 1994.

Hughes, P. J., and Djohadze, V. *Radiocarbon Dates from Archaeological Sites on the South Coast of New South Wales and the Use of Depth/Age Curves*. Occasional Papers in Prehistory. Department of Prehistory, Australian National University, Canberra, Australia, 1980.

Mulvaney, D. J. Australian Backed Blade Industries in Perspective. In *Recent Advances in Indo-Pacific Prehistory*. V. N. Misraand P. Bellwood, eds. Pp. 211 – 217. New Delhi: Oxford and IBH Publishing, 1985.

[37] Hiscock, P., and V. Attenbrow. Early Holocene Backed Artefacts from Australia. *Archaeology in Oceania* 33: 49–63, 1998.

[38] Hiscock, P. Technological Responses to Risk in Holocene Australia. *Journal of World Prehistory* 8(3): 267–292, 1994.

Syme, J. Recent Backed Artefacts: A Study of Their Occurrence in South-Eastern Australia. B. A. (hons) thesis, Australian National University, Canberra, 1997.

White, J. P., and O'Connell, J. F. *A Prehistory of Australia, New Guinea and Sahul.* Sydney: Academic, 1982.

[39] Bowdler, S., and S. O'Connor. The Dating of the Australian Small Tool TradiHolocene Proliferation of Backed Artifacts in Australia 175 tion, with New Evidence from the Kimberley, W. A. *Australian Aboriginal Studies* 1991/1: 53–62, 1991.

Johnson, I. The Getting of Data. Doctoral thesis, Australian National University, Canberra, 1979.

White, J. P., and O'Connell, J. F. *A Prehistory of Australia, New Guinea and Sahul.* Sydney: Academic, 1982.

[40] Hiscock, P. Land. In *Australian Coastal Archaeology.* J. Hall and I. J. McNiven, eds. Pp. 91–103. Canberra: ANH Publications, Australian National University. Sizing Up Prehistory: Sample Size and Composition of Artefact Assemblages. *Australian Aboriginal Studies* 2001lT. 48–62, 2001.

Hiscock, P., and V. Attenbrow. Early Holocene Backed Artefacts from Australia. *Archaeology in Oceania* 33: 49–63, 1998.

[41] Hiscock, P., and V. Attenbrow. Early Holocene Backed Artefacts from Australia. *Archaeology in Oceania* 33: 59, 1998.

[42] Mulvaney, D. J. Australian Backed Blade Industries in Perspective. In *Recent Advances in Indo-Pacific Prehistory.* V. N. Misraand P. Bellwood, eds. Pp. 211–217. New Delhi: Oxford and IBH Publishing, 1985.

[43] Bowdler, S. Hunters in the Highlands: Aboriginal Adaptations in the Eastern Australian Uplands. *Archaeology in Oceania* 16: 99–111, 1981.

Dortch, C. Recognition of Indigenous Development and External Diffusion in Australian Prehistory. *Australian Archaeology* 12: 27–31, 1981.

Mulvaney, D. J., and E. B. Joyce. Archaeological and Geomorphological Investigations on Mt Moffatt Station, Queensland. *Proceedings of the Prehistoric Society* 31: 147–212, 1965.

[44] Hiscock, P. Technological Responses to Risk in Holocene Australia. *Journal of World Prehistory* 8(3): 267–292, 1994.

[45] Hiscock, P. Technological Responses to Risk in Holocene Australia. *Journal of World Prehistory* 8(3): 277-278, 1994.

[46] Bamforth, D. B., and P. Bleed. Technology, Flaked Stone Technology, and Risk. In Rediscovering Darwin: Evolutionary Theory and Archeological Explanation. CM. Barton and G. A. Clark, eds. Pp. 116. Archeological Papers of the American Anthropological Association, 7. Arlington, Va.: American Anthropological Association, 1997.

[47] Hiscock, P. Technological Responses to Risk in Holocene Australia. *Journal of World Prehistory* 8(3): 267-292, 1994.

[48] Hiscock, P. Technological Responses to Risk in Holocene Australia. *Journal of World Prehistory* 8(3): 267-292, 1994.

[49] McConvell, P. Backtracking to Babel: The Chronology of Pama-Nyungan Expansion in Australia. *Archaeology in Oceania* 31: 125-144, 1996.

[50] McConvell, P. The Linguistic Prehistory of Australia: Opportunities for Dialogue with Archaeology. *Australian Archaeology* 31: 3-27, 1990.

[51] McConvell, P. Backtracking to Babel: The Chronology of Pama-Nyungan Expansion in Australia. *Archaeology in Oceania* 31: 125-144, 1996.

[52] Mulvaney, J., and J. Kamminga. *Prehistory of Australia*. Sydney: Allen and Unwin, 1999: 266.

[53] Evans, N., and R. Jones. The Cradle of the Pama-Nyungans: Archaeological and Linguistic Speculations. In *Archaeology and Linguistics. Aboriginal Australia in Global Perspectives*. P. McConvell, and N. Evans, eds. Pp. 376-384. Melbourne: Oxford University Press, 1997.

[54] Hiscock, P. Technological Responses to Risk in Holocene Australia. *Journal of World Prehistory* 8(3): 267-292, 1994.

[55] Hiscock, P. Technological Responses to Risk in Holocene Australia. *Journal of World Prehistory* 8(3): 282, 1994.

[56] Rowland, M. Holocene Environmental Variability: Have Its Impacts Been Underestimated in Australian Prehistory? *The Artefact* 22: 11-48, 1999.

[57] David, B., and H. Lourandos. Rock Art and Socio-demography in Northeast Australian Prehistory. *World Archaeology* 30: 212, 1998.

[58] Hiscock, P. Technological Responses to Risk in Holocene Australia. *Journal of World Prehistory* 8(3): 267-292, 1994.

[59] Hiscock, P. Technological Responses to Risk in Holocene Australia. *Journal of World Prehistory* 8(3): 267-292, 1994.

[60] Torrence, R. Time Budgeting and Hunter-Gatherer Technology. In *Hunter-Gatherer Economy in Prehistory*. G. Bailey, ed. Pp. 11-22. Cambridge: Cambridge University Press, 1983.

Tools as Optimal Solutions. In *Time, Energy and Stone Tools*. R. Torrence, ed. Pp. 1 – 6. Cambridge: Cambridge University Press, 1989.

[61] Gould, R. A. Arid-Land Foraging as Seen from Australia: Adaptive Models and Behavioural Realities. *Oceania* 62: 12 – 33, 1991.

[62] David, B., and H. Lourandos. Rock Art and Socio-demography in Northeast Australian Prehistory. *World Archaeology* 30: 193 – 219, 1998.

[63] David, B., and H. Lourandos. Rock Art and Socio-demography in Northeast Australian Prehistory. *World Archaeology* 30: 193 – 219, 1998.

[64] David, B., and H. Lourandos. Rock Art and Socio-demography in Northeast Australian Prehistory. *World Archaeology* 30: 211, 1998.

[65] Allan, R., J. Lindesay, and D. Parker. *El Nino, Southern Oscillation and Climatic Variability*. Collingwood, Victoria: CSIRO Australia, 1996.

Enfield, D. B. El Nino, Past and Present. *Review of Geophysics* 27: 159 – 187, 1989.

Rowland, M. Holocene Environmental Variability: Have Its Impacts Been Underestimated in Australian Prehistory? *The Artefact* 22: 11 – 48, 1999.

Trenberth, K. E. El Nino-Southern Oscillation. In *Climate Change: Developing Southern Hemisphere Perspectives*. T. W. Giambelluca and A. Henderson-Sellers, eds. Pp. 146 – 173. London: John Wiley & Sons, 1996.

Webster, P. J., and T. N. Palmer. The Past and the Future of El Nino. *Nature* 390: 562 – 564, 1997.

[66] Trenberth, K. E. El Nino-Southern Oscillation. In *Climate Change: Developing Southern Hemisphere Perspectives*. T. W. Giambelluca and A. Henderson-Sellers, eds. Pp. 168. London: John Wiley & Sons, 1996.

[67] Webb, R. E. Megamarsupial Extinction: The Carrying Capacity Argument. *Antiquity* 72: 46 – 55, 1998.

[68] Allan, R., J. Lindesay, and D. Parker. *El Nino, Southern Oscillation and Climatic Variability*. Collingwood, Victoria: CSIRO Australia, 1996: 67.

[69] Godley, D. ENSO and Inland Southeast Asia: 1100-Year Record of Flood and Drought Regimes Based on Pacific Rim Proxies. *Bulletin of the Indo-Pacific Prehistory Association* 17: 40, 1998.

[70] Shulmeister, J., and B. G. Lees. Pollen Evidence from Tropical Australia for the Onset of an ENSO-Dominated Climate at c. 4000 B. P. *The Holocene* 5: 10 – 18, 1995.

McGlone, M. S., A. P. Kershaw, and V. Markgraf. El Nino/Southern Oscillation Climatic Variability in Australasian and South American Paleoenvironmental Records. In *El Nino: Historical and Paleoclimatic Aspects of the Southern Oscillation*. H. F. Diaz and V. Markgraf, eds. Pp. 435 - 462. Cambridge: Cambridge University Press, 1992.

Markgraf, V., J. R. Dodson, A. P. Kershaw, M. S. McGlone, and N. Nicholls. Evolution of Late Pleistocene and Holocene Climatesin the Circum-South Pacific Land Areas. *Climate Dynamics* 6: 193 - 211, 1992.

Singh, G., and J. Luly. Changes in Vegetation and Seasonal Climate since the Last Full Glacial at Lake Frome, South Australia. *Palaeogeography, Palaeoclimatology, Palaeoecology* 84: 75 - 86, 1991.

[71] Whetton, P., D. Adamson, and M. Williams. Rainfall and River Flow Variability in Africa, Australia and East Asia Linked to El Nino-Southern Oscillation Events. In *Lessons for Human Survival: Nature's Record from the Quaternary*. P. Bishop, ed. Pp. 71 - 82. Sydney: Geological Society of Australia, 1990.

[72] Shulmeister, J., and B. G. Lees. Pollen Evidence from Tropical Australia for the Onset of an ENSO-Dominated Climate at c. 4000 B. P. *The Holocene* 5: 10 - 18, 1995.

[73] Ross, A., T. Donnelly, and R. Wasson. The Peopling of the Arid Zone: Human-Environment Interactions. In *The Naive Lands*. J. Dodson, ed. Pp. 76 - 114. Sydney: Longman Cheshire, 1992.

[74] Shulmeister, J., and B. G. Lees. Pollen Evidence from Tropical Australia for the Onset of an ENSO-Dominated Climate at c. 4000 B. P. *The Holocene* 5: 10 - 18, 1995.

[75] Hiscock, P. Technological Responses to Risk in Holocene Australia. *Journal of World Prehistory* 8(3): 282, 1994.

[76] Hiscock, P. Technological Responses to Risk in Holocene Australia. *Journal of World Prehistory* 8(3): 282, 1994.

[77] David, B., and H. Lourandos. Rock Art and Socio-demography in Northeast Australian Prehistory. *World Archaeology* 30: 212, 1998.

[78] Flood, J. *The Moth Hunters*. Canberra: Australian Institute of Aboriginal Studies, 1980.

[79] Beaton, J. Fire and Water: Aspects of Australian Aboriginal Management of Cycads. *Archaeology in Oceania* 17: 51 - 58, 1982.

[80] Sim, R. Why the Tasmanians Stopped Eating Fish: Evidence for Late Holocene Expansion in Resource Exploitation Strategies. In *Australian Coastal Archaeology*. J. Hall and I. J. McNiven, eds. Pp. 267. Canberra: ANH Publications, Australian National University, 1999.

[81] Allen, H. Left Out in the Cold: Why the Tasmanians Stopped Eating Fish. *The Artefact* 4: 1 - 10, 1979.

Sim, R. The Archaeology of Isolation? Prehistoric Occupation in the Furneaux Group of Islands, Bass Strait, Tasmania. Doctoral thesis, Australian National University, Canberra, 1998.

[82] Gorecki, P., M. Grant, S. O'Connor, and P. Veth. The Morphology, Function and Antiquity of Australian Grinding Implements. *Archaeology in Oceania* 32: 141–150, 1997.

[83] Smith, M. A. The Antiquity of Seedgrinding in Central Australia. *Archaeology in Oceania* 21: 29–39, 1986.

[84] Veitch, B. Shell Middens on the Mitchell Plateau: A Reflection of a Wider Phenomenon? In *Australian Coastal Archaeology*. J. Hall and I. J. McNiven. eds. Pp. 51–64. Canberra: ANH Publications, Australian National University, 1999.

[85] Hiscock, P. Technological Responses to Risk in Holocene Australia. *Journal of World Prehistory* 8(3): 267–292, 1994.

[86] Mulvaney, J., and J. Kamminga. *Prehistory of Australia*. Sydney: Allen and Unwin, 1999: 266.

[87] Hiscock, P. Technological Responses to Risk in Holocene Australia. *Journal of World Prehistory* 8(3): 276, 1994.

[88] Hiscock, P. Bondaian Technology in the Hunter Valley, New South Wales. *Archaeology in Oceania* 28: 64–75, 1993.

[89] Hiscock, P. Technological Responses to Risk in Holocene Australia. *Journal of World Prehistory* 8(3): 284, 1994.

[90] Hiscock, P. Technological Responses to Risk in Holocene Australia. *Journal of World Prehistory* 8(3): 284–286, 1994.

[91] Bellwood, P. Prehistoric Cultural Explanations for Widespread Language Families. In *Archaeology and Linguistics: Aboriginal Australia in Global Perspectives*. P. McConvell and N. Evans, eds. Pp. 134. Melbourne: Oxford University Press, 1997.

[92] Mulvaney, D. J. Australian Backed Blade Industries in Perspective. In *Recent Advances in Indo-Pacific Prehistory*. V. N. Misraand P. Bellwood, eds. Pp. 211–217. New Delhi: Oxford and IBH Publishing, 1985.

[93] David, B., and H. Lourandos. Rock Art and Socio-demography in Northeast Australian Prehistory. *World Archaeology* 30: 193–219, 1998.

Gould, R. A. Arid-Land Foraging as Seen from Australia: Adaptive Models and Behavioural Realities. *Oceania* 62: 12–33, 1991.

[94] Hiscock, P. Technological Responses to Risk in Holocene Australia. *Journal of World Prehistory* 8(3): 267–292, 1994.

[95] Hiscock, P. Holocene Coastal Occupation of Western Arnhem Land. In *Australian Coastal Archaeology*. J. Hall and I. J. McNiven, eds. Pp. 91–103. Canberra: ANH Publications, Australian National University, 1999.

[96] Hiscock, P. Technological Responses to Risk in Holocene Australia. *Journal of World*

Prehistory 8(3): 267–292, 1994.

[97] Shulmeister, J., and B. G. Lees. Pollen Evidence from Tropical Australia for the Onset of an ENSO-Dominated Climate at c. 4000 B. P. *The Holocene* 5: 10–18, 1995.

[98] Hiscock, P. Technological Responses to Risk in Holocene Australia. *Journal of World Prehistory* 8(3): 283, 1994.

[99] McNiven, I. J. Technological Organization and Settlement in Southwest Tasmania after the Glacial Maximum. *Antiquity* 68: 75–82, 1994.

[100] Hiscock, P. Technological Responses to Risk in Holocene Australia. *Journal of World Prehistory* 8(3): 267–292, 1994.

小工具　大思考

罗宾·托伦斯

（澳大利亚博物馆　悉尼）

摘　要：本书提出了丰富多样的个案研究，它们表明细石器在不同环境条件下可以解决不同的问题。这些研究多侧重于多样性而非统一性，这就为我们了解特定历史情形中一般规律的作用方式提供了一条有用的途径。成本效益模型分析表明，侧边镶嵌的细石器相对更耗时、更费力、更费原料，因此只在失败的成本可能非常高的时候采用。人们选择这类工具多因为它用途广泛，足以满足多样的需要，足以抵消其制作成本。相反，在风险较低的地方，人们更可能采用端部镶嵌的细石器。最后，影响采用、扩散与保存特定行为方式的重要因素之一是历史过程。

石器研究一直是考古学研究中经验主义色彩最强的领域之一，不过它现在也开始关注整个学科的中心问题了。本书就是一个很好的范例。它所提出与完全解决的问题并不局限于石器或是狩猎采集者研究，而是整个考古学领域所共有的问题。的确，这些论文提出了一些关键问题，如进行全球比较的价值、普遍过程与历史偶然性之间的矛盾、等效性问题，以及大多数行为方式的多重作用等。跟巴姆福斯和布雷德[1]与托伦斯[2]一样，本书不少文章都注意到风险问题，还有工艺设计理论，布雷德[3]、海登等[4]以及尼尔森[5]都曾注意过，在此基础上本书提出了观点非常鲜明的假说，解释不同环境条件下人们会如何利用技术。但是，跟编者的目的相反，这些试图证明存在全球统一模式的研究实际上表明细石器在性质、进程与用途等方面都存在着广泛的多样性，并不支持存在一个统一的趋势。当然,我认为研究者对变化的细致描述还是非常有价值的,正好符合我们当前的需要,能够启迪新的想法,推动考古学理论的多元发展。

尽管这些文章对于所提出基本问题的回答并不完全令人满意,但是我们弄清楚了需要知道什么,以及我们下一步应该怎么做是非常重要的。本书在整体上做出了一种理论考古学领域还很少能够接受的贡献。研究者提供了非常细致的材料,其他研究者可以在此基础上进一步前进。把如此广泛与丰富的材料与全球性或地区性意义上的解释结合起来,弥足珍贵;某些地区如撒哈拉以南地区,专业以外的学者很少了解,本书的相关研究无疑是对考古学长久的、重要的贡献。

当然,我从本书了解到的,很大程度上取决于我已有的知识与个人的经历,这可能与大家的认识有所不同。就这里讨论的问题而言,我实际是一个"圈外人"——从没有研究过一件细石器或一个细石器组合,我所关注的是那些具有广泛意义的方法与解释,希望能够用于其他时代、地区或材料上。为了实现这个目标,我尝试成为某种意义上的"圈内人",努力把这些文章的思想用于完全不同的地区,以更好地理解其史前史。如果本书确实提出的是具有全球意义的形态,那么其发现应该适用于我特别了解的局部区域,我采用的就是这样的线索。我有点怀疑编者的看法"唯一的、地理分布最广泛的趋势就是走向细石器化的趋势",我也注意到对全球统一性的强调有助于我理解特定地区的状况。

这里我所希望理解的细石器跟本书所讨论的有很大的不同,因为它们来自非常不同的环境类型中(来自热带而非温带地区),时代也非常晚近,可能跟植物而不是动物的利用相关。与此同时,在较早的时期,它们是从大到小器物的一极,后来在器物组合中逐渐消失。这样的区别是否会阻止我从本书的案例研究中学到东西呢?我想说的是,绝对不会!尽管本书研究的最初目的是要寻找统一的全球形态,但是本书采用的整体的方法是非常值得学习的,我将从了解为什么会如此着手,然后关注本书诸章节提出的重要问题。最后,我将以巴布亚新几内亚的细石器为例来讨论未来研究的方向。

一、本研究项目

为什么我们要研究细石器这样一类特殊的物质文化呢?按照达尔文的进化论,就其存在,我们会看到非常多样的解释,因为每个特定的文化组合都是普遍原理作用于当地唯一或特定条件的结果。正如编者在导言中所强调的,一个研究项目通过全球性的比较分析去了解人类行为就会面临遭到批评的风险,即把普遍性凌驾于历史偶然性之上。相反,我认为,进行细石器全球性广泛比较的目的是要认识导致特定历史结果的普遍原理,而不是寻找一个普遍的解释,回答某种行为的起源原因以及为何长期存在,我们假定这种行为具有统一性。过于关注相似性并不总有帮助,因为很难区分两种情况,相同原因导致不同结果,以及出现等效性的情况(不同过程导致相同的结果)。同样如此,为了有所收获,研究者不得不限制他所研究的变化的范围,将研究对象限定于细石器这样的材料。不过,如此选择之后,我们需要理解变化的范围而非统一性,这是理解设计与制作细石器的人类行为的关键。

相反,编者承认历史偶然性存在,但是仍然强调晚更新世"走向细石器化的全球趋势",尽管本书中这一形态并没有得到材料的充分支持。在我看来,研究者们过于关注如何解释以细石器(而非工具形制本身)为主的石器组合的起源,而没有去寻找普遍的规律,解释不同时代与地域多样的存在。他们强调研究年代处在晚更新世(即特定的时间与环境条件)的"旧石器时代"组合(这一术语其实仅适用于欧亚大陆,也就是局部的空间),这一定程度上偏离了他们寻求"全球趋势"的目标。所幸在本项目中,编者考虑到了撒哈拉以南非洲,还有澳大利亚的情况,这些地区恰好都在一般时空规律之外,因此很好的说明了关注差异而非相似性的重要性。为了更清楚地说明这些观点,我将从什么、何时、何地等问题出发讨论本书的有关文章。

(一)是什么

对任何比较研究来说,确定研究单位都是基本的要求。尽管这个问题并没有在本书中得到令人满意的回答,但是混杂的结果产生了非常好的多样性。由于潜在的研究目标并不是细石器或细小工具,而是编者称之为"细石器化"的趋势,因此他们更偏向与讨论特定地区的细石器化起源。于是每篇文章都视该地区存在的现象是确定无疑的,并对石器组合进行综合性的归纳。有的研究者仅研究更新世的材料,有的研究者则要宽一些。

要想获得真正的全球性的比较,定义是非常关键的。"细石器"这一术语在欧亚大陆似乎有相同的含义,但在其他地区并不必然也如此运用,如阿姆布鲁斯与西斯科克的文章所表现出来的。编者在编辑了所有研究后,再把不同研究材料统一起来,确定细石器的特征。尺寸小是基本的标准,但没有得到细致的定义。其定义进一步把单件器物的三个属性:石叶、琢背修理以及形制的标准化,合为一个统一的组合,即"细石器"的数量占优势。这在细石器术语最初得到应用的地区还比较适用,而在非洲与澳大利亚,石叶形制与标准化都不是本书考虑的关键属性。有些材料具有不符合所谓细石器化的属性,其间的关系一直没有说清楚。

实际上正是第五项特征——在一件复合工具上运用一个或多个石质部件,这个被广泛接受的特征把本书所讨论的工具形制与其他器物区分开来。不幸的是,这一特征见于非常多样的工具类型中。本书的文章关注投掷尖状器,但是对我来说,复合工具可用于各种活动上,包括切割、锯、刮削、穿刺、刻,如此等等,这些活动更多与处理材料相关,而非用以捕获猎物。正如许多研究者注意到的,所有研究中一个严重的局限就是缺乏工具如何使用的考古材料。有趣的是,微痕分析经常支持多功能使用的观点,而非只是用于狩猎动物[6]。然而,本书基本忽视了这样一个事实:要理解这类石器,知道其功能是非常重要的。

一个常见且非常合理的预设是细石器用于镶嵌,也就是,安装在器柄的边缘。例如,西伯利亚与欧洲有些重要的考古发现出土了带有细石器的完整工具,就是如此使用的(参见本书埃尔斯顿与班廷汉姆、戈贝尔的文章)。但是这样的类比可能并不是到处都适用的,不同的可能性也需要考虑到,尤其是那些没有发现柄部残留的地区。细小的石质部件可能安装在柄端使用,如同箭头或标枪头,这样的工具形制可能在某些细石器组合中占主导地位。埃尔斯顿与班廷汉姆注意到其组合中"端部安装的细石叶有时也用作刮削器、锥钻、刀以及投掷尖状器"。两种不同安装方式的使用效率与寿命可能不同,其意义需要认真考虑。类似之,单一或多个部件的运用也可能对工具的效率与成本有非常大的影响,这也是任何模型研究中都需要考虑到的。

鉴于所强调的不同特征中存在着广泛的变化,相应的解释变化多样,这也就不足为奇了。只有埃尔斯顿与班廷汉姆直接讨论到这个问题:为什么人们选择把石刃镶嵌到有机(限定为骨质或鹿角的)柄部中,生产一种既结实(有机的部分)又致命的(石质的部分)工具?他们对多种镶嵌方式的成本收益的讨论表明,当失败的风险非常高的时候,应该采用这样的工具。在这样的情况下,人们需要在技术上进行大量投入,从而保证成功。相反,克内克特[7]与埃里斯[8]的研究结论显示,把细石器安装在工具尖端可以有效杀死猎物但容易折断。当失败无足轻重,以及制作工具的资源(时间、能量、原料)都很丰富的时候,可能采用这样的工具。显然,细石器如何安装(边缘或尖端)的知识,以及装柄与捆绑的方式对于我们了解古人为什么会采用这类工具十分重要。这不是仅从石器性质就能推导出来的,还需要细石器形制之外的信息。石器组合中可能包含各式各样的石器部件,镶嵌方式也多种多样,用途非常广泛。假定所有细石器都来自单一的工具类型有多危险呢? 这些研究的局限之一就是,很少有研究能够令人满意地重建细石器所制复合工具的形制。

大部分研究者想当然地认为细石器工具必定是复合的,于是在解释中关注其他的特征。选择石叶或琢背修理有助于把石刃镶嵌到有机的器柄中,但这并不是必需的。通过大规模生产石叶或通过修理不规则的毛坯来实现器物的标准化,这是一个单独的特点,可能在经常需要替换石刃时特别重要,但并非对所有复合工具都是如此。再者,装柄与捆绑的材料一定程度受到限制,替换部件需要跟原来部件一致。我认为解释这些特征的方法有助于我们理解细石器基本范畴中的变化,但是还不能令人满意地回答更基本的问题,为什么人们首先选择复合工具。

(二)在哪里

书名中的"全球"指的是一种趋势,晚更新世欧亚地区细石器化日益重要。为了证明此时此地存在某种特殊或唯一的东西,我们就需要更广泛的比较。撒哈拉以南非洲与澳大利亚也发现有细石器,其趋势的性质似乎非常不同。包括印度次大陆与东南亚诸岛[9]等地区都发现有细小的琢背石器(包括修理石叶、石片、几何形石器),但发展历史完全不同,更大的全球视野或许可以更好地证明欧亚地区所呈现的趋势的确是大规模的,当然空间上还是有限制的。于是这带来一些非常有意思的重要问题,哪些东西是欧亚地区特有的? 是否是某些外在因素在起作用? 如气候,或是如捕猎类型的拓宽这种普遍存在的变化,或是共同的历史过程及其长期的相互影响。通过探索所有的边界,小心划定共同形态的空间范围,也就是寻找变化的范围,将有助于这方面的研究。

(三)于何时

尽管编者在导言中将细石器的起源放在晚更新世范围内,但是南半球的史前史并不符合这样的认识。如阿姆布鲁斯所言,在非洲地区细石器出现得非常早,其石器时代中期就已经有相当多的细石器产品(比欧亚地区至少早 2 至 3 万年)。他的评论揭示这类器物在不同地区不同阶段的存在与消失具有非常复杂的形态。在澳大利亚,嵌有各种形制琢背石器的复合工具直到全新世才开始变得常见起来。

本书强调解释细石器的起源也就意味着忽视了大量以细石器为主的材料,

包括欧亚地区的中石器时代,也是以细石器为代表的时期。奇怪的是,编者的关注止于后旧石器时代,正如施特劳斯所指出的,在中石器时代细石器还继续占主导地位。这是否意味着细石器化的趋势还在强化呢?如果确实如此,解释更晚期的存在是否会削弱我们将细石器化过程作为一个整体来理解吗?如贝尔福—科恩与格林—莫里斯注意到的,中石器组合的研究者曾经就中石器时代细石器组合性质的变化提出过一系列有争议的假说[10]。这些假说是否有助于我们理解更早时期类似的形态呢?

进化过程与某一特征的起源研究同样重要。施特劳斯指出,行为发生的多样性可能来自非常广泛的原因,包括中性的突变与潮流,以及"可识别的重大原因(如气候变化、广泛的资源波动、基本的人口变迁)"。我们如何区分如此众多的可能性呢?变化再次成为关键所在。一个非常有效的策略是去追溯变化过程。许多组合中都有细石器,但是在某个地区会有时空上的波动,主导地位也会变化(如阿姆布鲁斯、库恩、西斯科克、施特劳斯)。要理解这样的变化,我们是不是只要关注数量上开始占到主导地位就行了呢?跟只关注起源问题相反,通过对比一个地区不同时期的组合,我们可能会有更多收获。库恩提出,南欧地区导致细石器产生的相同过程可能在两个不同阶段发生的程度不一样。相反,阿姆布鲁斯就南部与东部非洲所见每一变化提出一种不同的解释。如果研究仅仅关注单一的起源问题或某个单向的趋势,而不是比较与对比不同时期的情况,那么就不可能产生有创见与富有启发的假说。

相反,关于最早的起源研究有某些特殊的东西使得下面所说的方法值得一提。那就是历史发展过程。在某个时间点上,无论由于什么原因,人们采用了某一特殊的行为方式,把人们与某些策略捆绑在一起,原因可能是人们缺乏变化的动力,行为成为习惯,也可能因为他们没能找到替代策略。例如,库恩注意到,欧亚地区当时已有"棱柱状石叶生产、骨角工具加工以及复合/装柄工具",就某类特定的问题,很容易形成细石器技术。在世界其他地区,石器技术基于石片或是两面器,库恩认为人们面对同样的问题时,他们很可能从既有的技术策略中寻找解决方法。技术策略可能非常不同,尽管可能同样有效[11]。例如,替换嵌刃与修理两面器都是延长工具使用寿命的方法。埃尔斯顿与班廷汉姆运用实验材料估计两种策略的相对成本,发现嵌刃能够使切割边刃最大化,相反两面器在利用原料方面更经济。我完全支持他们的结论,要理解过去的选择,在研究工具本身的有效性之外,发展实验检验不同生产与修理工具策略的成本收益是必不可少的。

西斯科克注意到澳大利亚就同样的问题存在不同的解决途径,它们差不多都是同时的。为了应对相同的状况,某些群体采用了细石器,而另一些群体选择了两面修理的琢背石器。西斯科克同时强调每个广阔区域此前历史发展的重要性,这可以用来解释就基本相同环境问题所采取技术策略的特殊性。当然,他注意到琢背石叶很早就已经起源了,其迅速增加的原因显然不可能等同于其首先得到应用的原因。因此,尽管某一特征的存在部分取决于它在某一社会群体内的历史,但是解释其起源并不等于就是解释其持续存在或是更晚阶段其流行程度的差异。细石器在非常广阔、多样的地区繁荣过,如果我们接受库恩与西斯科克就其历史针锋相对的解释,那么仅仅关注起源显然不足以理解某类行为如使用细石器的长期历史。我还是强调时间与空间上的变化范围的重要性。

二、类似的道路?

现在我们开始问为什么的问题。从全球的视角出发,编者研究一个基本问题,形制基本相同的工具是否是同一原因的产物?欧亚大陆地区的特定时间存在向复合工具发展的趋势,情况可能确实如此。讨论解释的相关文章已经就不同的情况给出了多样的回答,尽管大多数解释都强调风险最小化的需要,以应对环境条件变化,导致变化的原因可能是人们进入陌生地带,或是气候变化及其导致的自然条件的变化,还有猎物分布的变化。某些研究者将细石器本身视为有风险环境的直接反应,因为细石器是更有效的工具(布雷德、埃尔斯顿与班廷汉姆、西斯科克、库恩),或是因为它们能够带来与维持交换关系(阿姆布鲁斯),相反其他研究者认为工具形制与生产过程的变化与其他风险减小行为如提高流动性的需要有关(阿姆布鲁斯、布雷德、贝尔福—科恩与格林—莫里斯、埃尔斯顿与班廷汉姆、雷利)。卡洛斯主张不同细石器的形制可能传递族群身份信息,布雷德暗示这种情况在日本也可能存在。强调工具的主要功能与强调从属于相关行为的矛盾(雷利)说明,解释细石器时,我们需要理解一系列的复杂且相互关联的行为类型,每种行为都需要单独的解释。贝尔福—科恩与格林—莫里斯进行了清晰的总结,细石器可能是投掷尖状器的抛送机制、装柄技术、经济上的考虑以及功能多样性相结合的产物。就此而言,我们还需要加上其表达社会信息的可能。

我看不出有什么理由反对,每个特定案例的解释为什么不可以都正确。把一件或多件相对细小的石刃镶嵌到某一工具中使用是一种相当普遍的特征,细石器完全可能有各种各样的用法,用于解决多种多样的问题。本书的各章节很好地说明了某个单一传统或有限时间范围内的多样性(布雷德、卡洛斯、贝尔福—科恩与格林—莫里斯、埃尔斯顿与班廷汉姆、耶斯纳与皮尔森),在更大尺度上简单称之为细石器技术的行为(以及随后的解释)存在着丰富的差异。真正的问题在于是否能够提出最好的解释,解释特定的历史条件。

个案研究对于评估假说来说很关键,但还需要系统的不同类型的信息。许多研究者提及环境与动物群材料研究,将之视为细石器使用者面对实际风险时较好的选择,但是还需要考虑狩猎需求之外多样的任务需要。风险的性质与细石器所可能解决的问题很可能是变化多样的,很大程度上要取决于实际情况与工具的使用方式。沿着这些思路,采用高倍放大的细石器微痕残留研究具有很大的潜力,目前还没有足够投入与坚持地去做。我们还需要避免仅仅关注细石器本身,更多关注石器组合中的其他成分,包括其他修理工具与废片。比如,如果由于原料缺乏而出现节约行为,这应该在组合的其他成分中观察到。正如埃尔斯顿与班廷汉姆所说,石核研究能够就部分细石器制作者决策的机制提供重要的信息。布雷德的事件树分析方法也是非常强大的测量生产风险的方法。

基于解释的性质,两个复杂的因素值得进一步讨论。首先,我们更深入地考虑,如何去解决不同的过程可能导致类似形制的问题,即等效性的问题。其次,由于器物可能是多功能的,我们就不能指望仅仅一个解释就能回答所有观察到的形态。

(一) 等效性

雷利注意到细石器可以满足多样的需求。比如,由于猎物高度流动或是并非全年都有的,接近猎物困难,此时采用嵌刃的方法以提高投掷器的杀伤力(埃尔斯顿与班廷汉姆)。当捕猎对象难以确定的时候(库恩、西斯科克),可能就需要非常可靠有效的工具。嵌刃提高了工具的可维护性,如果工具需要经常使用,那么这个特点就非常有价值(布雷德)。细小的嵌刃有助于节约石料,尤其是原料获取的时间与空间相对局限的话(雷利)。所有这些说法都有可能,没有理由认为只有一种解释必然要比其他的解释更好。由于复合工具有弹性空间或灵活性高[12],或可靠性与可维护性好[13],是否采用有多个嵌刃的复合工具可以根据细石器特征来确定:(1) 替换的便利;(2) 制作多条边刃以强化工具或留一个备份以备不时之需。显然,这种普遍的工具类型可能实现其中一个目的,也可能同时实现两个。

与本项目相关的一个难题——试图理解导致细石器起源的原因,是把更多的关注放在了形制而非功能上,或者稍微换个说法,放在结果而非问题上,似乎认为两者之间存在一对一的关系。本书所提及的文化反应类型表明情况正好相反:复合工具的普遍属性与其用途之间并没有直接的联系。就细石器而言,我们不能指望有一个全盘的解释,但我们或可以解释它在特定条件下的存在。

过度地强调形制也意味着分析者认为细石器的存在已预先确定,然后去推导它如何具有适应的意义。我认为有必要与考古材料保持一定的距离,要注意发展解释模型。另一种方法是研究当时起作用的选择压力(环境、猎物的有无、人口规模等等),然后模拟各种各样的解决方案,包括生计的变化、流动性等等。大多数情况下,细石器只是其中一种可能存在的选择。如上文所述,库恩、西斯科克、埃尔斯顿与班廷汉姆都注意到不同的技术策略可以解决某些相同的问题(如石叶和两面器)。努力去解释细石器何以比许多其他可能的技术更适合某些迫切的情况,可能会为新的理论创造开辟道路。

(二) 多重角色

生产细石器的成本较高,尤其在工具侧边镶嵌多片刃缘,这或许可以表明人们之所以选择细石器,乃是因为它能够发挥多重作用。我们很容易想象,某些情况下人们选择石质的嵌刃,是因为可以用它们制作坚韧且致命的投掷器(有效的),而且这样的工具容易修理(可维护),以及备有可替换的部件以备不时之需(可靠)(参见本书西斯科克与雷利的文章,同时参见有关多重作用的讨论[14])。猎物的变化导致不同程度的风险,细石器的每个优点可以解决一类风险。其中最重要的是,采用大量的嵌刃非常有利于形成风格各异(不同形制与颜色)的工具,这些工具携带重要的信息(风格),提供物品交换过程中所需要的独特性与差别。实际上,细石器工具满足多重需要的潜力使得它非常具有吸引力且适应性良好。正是承担多重作用的能力使其能够得到广泛利用,而不是像许多研究者所强调的是因为某个方面的特点才得到利用的。不同形式的风险可以通过多样的途径来解决,但是只有少数形制能够同时满足多重的需要。

另一个需要考虑的可能性是,可能仅仅因为某个简单的原因,人们采用了细石器,细石器其他的潜在优势也会随着人们的了解增加而发挥出来。人们把工具的多样的能力付诸实践,这个过程可能需要较长的时间。我们在解释的时候,需要了解并测度可能的衍生效应。要实现这一点,我们需要注意细石器技术在时间进程中的变化,而非仅关注某个时期的情况。

三、成本收益模型

如上所述,我认为我们可以从相对较大规模的模型构建中收益良多,因为它有助于我们识别细石器技术及其变化所有可能的原因。最有成效的方式之一就是采用成本收益模型,书中埃尔斯顿与班廷汉姆有讨论,这一方法为我们评估不同行为的可能性提供了一个很好的框架。尽管针对各种问题存在多种可能的技术解决方法,但从时间与能量消耗角度来衡量,其成本与收益不可能都是相等的。如果成本真的影响到适应性,那么成本就需要降低,最终仅有某些解决方法切实可行。相反,如果成本可以忽略不计,那么历史与随机因素就会在偶然、特定的解决方法的形成过程中发挥主要作用。

显然,从埃尔斯顿与班廷汉姆对实验与民族志材料的回顾中我们可以看到,生产细石叶从时间、能量与原料消耗的角度来看是相对昂贵的。他们简单但有效的成本收益分析表明,如果原料供给受到限制,那么人们不大可能采用细石器,尽管布雷德、埃尔斯顿与班廷汉姆注意到,所用石核打片技术不同,也可能还有变化的空间。由于这些额外的成本需要以工具有效性表示的收益来平衡,所以边缘镶嵌多件石刃的工具不可能见于任何情况下。这一研究清楚地表明,边缘嵌刃仅限于某些特定的情况,即"失败的成本是灾难性的或致命的"。正是基于这个原因,我认为细石器不可能是如高流动性等其他行为方式的衍生物。设计一种适合流动、灵活的工具,很可能还有比细石器更便宜的方式。另一方面,由于细石器有助于减小失败的风险,人们一旦采用了它,从原料选择到生产方法都可能随着行为其他方面的需要,进行一系列的调整。当然,如果细石器对于生存至关重要,那么获取合适原料的成本以及生产与维护的成本就无足轻重了,即使可能与其他需要矛盾。

尽管埃尔斯顿与班廷汉姆所归纳的实验研究还需要重复与扩大,以覆盖细石器其他可能的用途(如端部装柄),但是他们卓有成效的个案研究显示了成本收益模型的强大功能。细石器也许有能力解决许多问题,但是这并非没有成本。除非采用它的收益超过了成本,否则人们不可能总是希望或接受细石器可能的功能。我们在寻求解释的过程中,应该注意到收益的类型(减少风险或解决难题),它们需要特定细石器,就边缘镶嵌多件石刃的情况而言,成本相对高昂,尽管成本部分可以为细石器发挥的多重作用抵消。

四、不同的途径

我一直强调,关注多样性至关重要,因为了解差异是掌握普遍性的关键。为了说明这一点,这里我将重点讨论一类特殊的石器工具,它与本书所讨论的石器类型完全不同。但是我希望从细石器研究中获取的经验教训可以用于其他研究。

巴布亚新几内亚的新不列颠岛上有个被称为威罗梅兹半岛(Willaumez)的地区,发现许多距今 10 000~3 600 年之间的修理石器。根据其原料(石质)与大小(微型的),并按照本书的视角,似乎可以称之为细石器。巴布亚新几内亚石器与这里讨论的细石器区别明显,因为它由石片制作而成,没有进行琢背修理。相反,这些器物往往有一个修理过的端部或梃部[15]。另一方面,它们又非常小,类似细石器,我们推测它们可能镶在复合工具中使用。基于修理的性质,我们进一步推测这些工具是端部镶嵌的。世界大部分地区的考古学家可能会把这类带梃工具称为"尖状器"。值得注意的是,西斯科克推测澳大利亚琢背石器与两面修理的片坯尖状器功能相同,因此带梃石器至少跟书中提及的这类石器并非完全不同。

另一个区分这些细小"带梃工具"(如当地所知)与本书所说细石器的因素是,这些工具都具有基本相同的形制,尺寸偏小。如图 12.1 所示,这些"细石器"可以小到 2 厘米长,相反某些相同器型可以大到 20 厘米。随后的时期,也就是大约距今 3 300~1 500 年(中间的时间空白由一次主要的火山爆发所致,遗址被放弃),除了一个例外,带梃工具消失了。加鲁阿岛的 FSZ 遗址发现的细小带梃尖状器是这个时期太平洋地区石器组合中绝无仅有的遗留(图 12.2)。这些细石器由石叶所制,但此时这一地区无论是石叶还是任何形制的修理产品几乎都不为人所知[16]。

下面我们看看巴布亚新几内亚带梃工具的潜在成本与收益。首先,由于制作带梃工具的成本高于非装柄石片,所以我们假定采用这一形式对于使用者来说有某些收益。端部装柄工具的实际成本取决于用作柄的原料、捆绑的方式、必要的知识与技巧等。收益则取决于工具用在哪里。修理与制作便于手握的地方等额外的加工可能有助于提高这类工具解决某些特殊问题的能力。例如,端部装柄的工具可能在下列活动中发挥作用:形成更安全、更牢靠的抓握;有利于投射;增大力量;延长使用者力臂的长度,且增加离猎物的距离,保护使用者。埃尔斯顿与班廷汉姆认为边缘嵌刃的工具致命且坚固,相对而言,巴布亚新几内亚

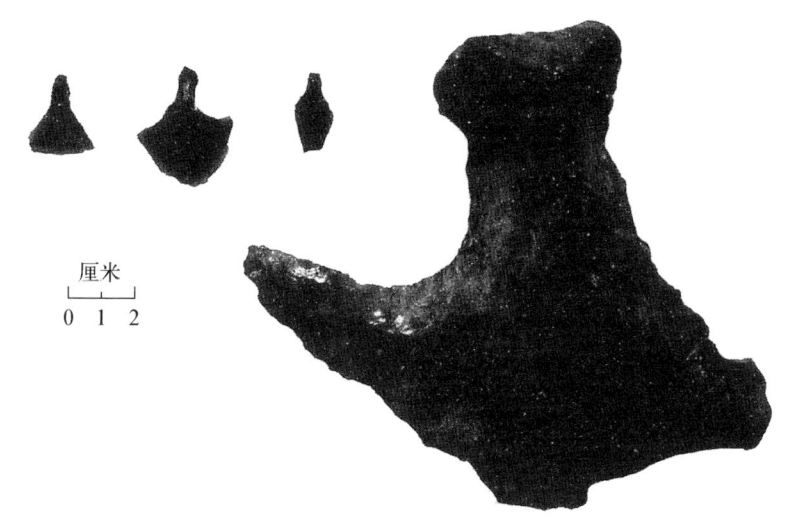

图 12.1　巴布亚新几内亚新大不列颠岛西部发现的细石器

（代表带梃工具中较小的一极）

图 12.2　巴布亚新几内亚伽鲁阿岛 FSZ 遗址发现带梃小石叶

的尖状器可能在某些活动中更为有效,但并不必然比未装柄工具更结实。由于它们是端部装柄的,工具的力道更多取决于石头的形制以及使用的方式,而非装柄的材料。例如,端部装柄的石质投掷尖状器易于断裂,使用寿命短,但用作切割工具或是石钻的话,使用寿命可能会长一些。这一比较表明带梃工具用于解决并不需要持续很长时间的问题。再者,没能完成任务的后果也不严重,因为力量与耐用程度并非设计时考虑的重要标准。因此,工具的可靠程度较低[17]。

可维护性[18]是另一项许多研究者强调的属性。标准化的石叶或修理石片使得工具相对容易快速装配。相反,带梃工具形制与大小并不标准,因此在柄端安装新的尖头可能并不现实,也可能不那么容易与快捷。替换而非修理柄部甚至整个工具可能更合乎标准。这一系列特征表明工具并不需要持续使用很长的时间。

根据缺乏可靠性与可维护性,我们可以进一步推导猎物可能很少流动,并且可以长期利用,或者还有很多其他适合的选择。当地为热带森林(很少动物,动物形体相对较小,移动也慢,而且分布局限)环境,季节性不强,由此看来,这一假说也讲得通。非常湿润与不那么湿润的季节之间物种丰度与分布很少有区别。除了群体之间的敌意,这里的环境很少有需要石器工具来缓冲的风险。微痕与残留物分析表明带梃工具是多用途的,主要用于植物处理[19],得出这样的结论也不足为奇。

缺乏可维护工具类型时,人们可以准备多套类似的工具解决需要长时间使用工具的问题[20]。如果带梃工具也是如此,那么携带成本不会高,且原料丰富。这样的判断显然符合该地区的情况,这里已经发现带梃小工具,从黑曜石原料产地用船来搬运对于工具的获取与携带不会有什么困难。

总之,采用本书提出的基本原理,风险构成成本,自然环境、时间、敌人与原料耗费等产生成本,这些因素不大可能是影响巴布亚新几内亚所用细石器设计的主要因素。工具完成某项任务的纯粹功能需要已经决定了其形制,但是,具体材料研究指向另外两个需要进一步考虑的问题。首先是历史问题。人们通常在传统形制范围内解决问题。这一原理也许有助于解释为什么人们使用带梃尖状器而不是其他便宜、当地所有的锋利的原料,如竹子、贝壳等,以及揭示为什么这种独特的形制被广泛采用,它见于各种不同大小的工具中,这些工具可能用作不同的功能。

第二个因素是复合工具可以从事众多的工作。阿姆布鲁斯与卡洛斯提出,细石器除了能够从事日常事务之外,它还可以传递社会信息,因此可能用作交换物品。极大的有梃工具非常有可能被视为贵重物品[21]。细石器的带梃工具则可能带有关于社会地位或群体关系的相关信息,可以用以交换。在如同新大不列颠岛这样的地方,除了疾病外,主要风险都来自文化,而非来自自然环境,日常事务不用石器也能完成,选择形制独特的大小不同的石质尖头支持这样的观点,即它们可能用于社会信息的表达。

随后的时期(3 300~1 500 BP),经过一次灾难性的火山喷发之后,一群人重新回到这一地区居住,生产了少量的带梃工具[22]。尽管支持带梃工具的社会体系已经不存在了,但是灾难后群体保留了这种形制独特的工具的传统外形。

五、总结

我希望巴布亚新几内亚的个案研究有助于说明全球尺度上比较细石器的重要意义。个案研究中发展出来的基本原理广泛适用,并且可以用于解释差异显著的地区与石器组合,通过例子我已指出并努力证明这一点。成本收益分析有助于认识工具设计中的重要因素。风险缓释与地区历史比考古学家从前所认为的更加重要。在失败的后果非常严重的地区,人们倾向于在装备上投入额外的劳动,尽力避免困难以及威胁生命的情况出现。并非所有的细石器都很昂贵。端部装柄的工具比侧边嵌刃的工具更适用于更容易断裂的情况。采用这样的方法,我们的认识也逐渐清晰,复合工具是解决难题的特别有用的途径,因为生产有效、耐用、便于维护工具所需要的高成本可以通过工具所发挥的多用途部分加以抵消。

显然,未来还需要进一步研究评估以上的观点。我个人认为使用痕迹与残留物研究应该在未来研究中发挥更加重要的作用。基于器物形制的解释需要得到器物确实如何使用的认识的支持。于细石器而言,功能信息特别重要,因为这些细小部件可以有许多方式镶嵌成为复合工具,并且可能具有非常广泛的功能,而不是我们一直认为的单单用于投掷。

注释:

[1] Bamforth, D. B., and P. Bleed. Technology, Flaked Stone Technology and Risk. In *Rediscovering Darwin: Evolutionary Theory and Archeological Explanation*. C. M. Barton and G. A. Clark, eds. Pp. 109 – 139. Archeological Papers of the American Anthropological Association, 7. Arlington, Va.: American Anthropological Association, 1997.

[2] Torrence, R. Retooling: Toward a Behavioral Theory of Stone Tools. In *Time, Energy and Stone Tools*. R. Torrence, ed. Pp. 57 – 66. Cambridge: Cambridge University Press, 1989.

[3] Bleed, P. The Optimal Design of Hunting Weapons: Maintainability or Reliability. *American Antiquity* 51 (4): 737 – 747, 1986.

[4] Hayden, B., N. Franco, and J. Spafford. Evaluating Lithic Strategies and Design Criteria. In *Stone Tools: Theoretical Insights into Human Prehistory*. G. Odell, ed. Pp. 9 – 49. New York: Plenum, 1996.

[5] Nelson, M. C. The Study of Technological Organization. *Archaeological Method and Theory* 3:

57 – 100, 1991.

Projectile Points: Form, Function, and Design. In *Projectile Technology*. H. Knecht, ed. Pp. 371 – 384. New York: Plenum, 1997.

[6] Nelson, M. C. Projectile Points: Form, Function, and Design. In *Projectile Technology*. H. Knecht, ed. Pp. 373 – 374. New York: Plenum, 1997.

[7] Knecht, H. Projectile Points of Bone, Antler, and Stone: Experimental Explorations of Manufacture and Use. In *Projectile Technology*. H. Knecht, ed. Pp. 191 – 212. New York: Plenum, 1997.

[8] Ellis, C. J. Factors Influencing the Use of Stone Projectile Tips. In *Projectile Technology*. H. Knecht, ed. Pp. 37 – 74. New York: Plenum, 1997.

[9] Bulbeck, D., M. Pasqua, and A. Di Lello. Culture History of the Toalean of South Sulawesi, Indonesia. *Asian Perspectives* 39: 71 – 108, 2000.

[10] Eerkens, J. W. Reliable and Maintainable Technologies: Artifact Standardization and the Early to Later Mesolithic Transition in Northern England. *Lithic Technology* 23: 42 – 53, 1998.

Jochim, M. Optimization in Stone Tool Studies: Problems and Potential. In *Time, Energy and Stone Tools*. R. Torrence, ed. Pp. 106 – 111. Cambridge: Cambridge University Press, 1989.

A Hunter-Gatherer Landscape: Southwest Germany in the Late Paleolithic and Mesolithic. New York: Plenum, 1998: 167 – 168.

Myers, A. Reliable and Maintainable Technological Strategies in the Mesolithic of Mainland Britain. In *Time, Energy and Stone Tools*. R. Torrence, ed. Pp. 78 – 91. Cambridge: Cambridge University Press, 1989.

[11] Torrence, R. Retooling: Toward a Behavioral Theory of Stone Tools. In *Time, Energy and Stone Tools*. R. Torrence, ed. Cambridge: Cambridge University Press, 1989: 63.

[12] Nelson, M. C. The Study of Technological Organization. *Archaeological Method and Theory* 3: 57 – 100, 1991.

Projectile Points: Form, Function, and Design. In *Projectile Technology*. H. Knecht, ed. Pp. 371 – 384. New York: Plenum, 1997.

[13] Bleed, P. The Optimal Design of Hunting Weapons: Maintainability or Reliability. *American Antiquity* 51 (4): 737 – 747, 1986.

Eerkens, J. W. Reliable and Maintainable Technologies: Artifact Standardization and the Early to Later Mesolithic Transition in Northern England. *Lithic Technology* 23: 42 – 53, 1998.

Myers, A. Reliable and Maintainable Technological Strategies in the Mesolithic of Mainland Britain. In *Time, Energy and Stone Tools*. R. Torrence, ed. Pp. 78 – 91. Cambridge:

Cambridge University Press, 1989.

[14] Myers, A. Reliable and Maintainable Technological Strategies in the Mesolithic of Mainland Britain. In *Time, Energy and Stone Tools*. R. Torrence, ed. Pp. 78 - 91. Cambridge: Cambridge University Press, 1989.

[15] Araho, N., R. Torrence, and J. P. White. Valuable and Useful: Mid-Holocene Stemmed Obsidian Artefacts from West New Britain, Papua New Guinea. *Proceedings of the Prehistoric Society 68*, In press.

[16] Sheppard, P. Lapita Lithics, Trade/Exchange and Technology. A View from the Reefs/Santa Cruz. *Archaeology in Oceania* 26: 89 - 101, 1993.

Torrence, R. What Is Lapita about Obsidian? A View from the Talasea Source. In *Poterie Lapita et peuplement*. J.-C. Galipaud, ed. Pp. 111 - 126. Noumea, New Caledonia. ORSTOM, 1992.

[17] Bleed, P. The Optimal Design of Hunting Weapons: Maintainability or Reliability. *American Antiquity* 51 (4): 737 - 747, 1986.

[18] Bleed, P. The Optimal Design of Hunting Weapons: Maintainability or Reliability. *American Antiquity* 51 (4): 737 - 747, 1986.

[19] Fullagar, R. Flaked Stone Tools and Plant Food Production: A Preliminary Report on Obsidian Tools from Talasea, West New Britain, PNG. In *Traces et fonction: Les gestes retrouves*. P. Anderson, S. Beyries, M. Otte, and H. Plisson, eds. Pp. 331 - 337. Liege, Belgium: ERAUL, 1993.

Kealhofer, L., R. Fullagar, and R. Torrence. Integrating Phytoliths within Use-Wear/Residue Studies of Stone Tools. *Journal of Archaeological Science* 26: 527 - 546, 1999.

[20] Bleed, P. The Optimal Design of Hunting Weapons: Maintainability or Reliability. *American Antiquity* 51 (4): 737 - 747, 1986.

[21] Araho, N., R. Torrence, and J. P. White. Valuable and Useful: Mid-Holocene Stemmed Obsidian Artefacts from West New Britain, Papua New Guinea. *Proceedings of the Prehistoric Society 68*, in press.

[22] Torrence, R., C. Pavlides, P. Jackson, and J. Webb. Volcanic Disasters and Cultural Discontinuities in the Holocene of West New Britain, Papua New Guinea. In *The Archaeology of Geological Catastrophes*. B. McGuire, D. Griffiths, P. Hancock, and I. Stewart, eds. Pp. 225 - 244. Geological Society of London Special Publications 171. London, 2000.

译名对照表

A

阿巴拉莫娃 Abramova
阿贝·步日耶 Abbe Breuil
阿芬 Afian
阿布罗萨拉 Abu Noshra
阿登连 Ardennian(文化)
阿方托瓦戈拉 Afontova Gora
阿尔梅里亚 Almeria
阿尔布利达 Arbreda
阿恩海姆地 Arnhem Land
阿芙德卡 Avdeikha
阿克马克 Akmak
阿鲁提克 Alutiiq
阿姆菲希尔特山组合 Amphitheater Mountain Complex
阿萨帕斯康人 Athapaskans
阿斯图林 Asturian(文化)
阿特林工业 Aterian industry
阿扎里克13号遗址 Azariq XIII
阿兹连 Azilian(尖状器)
艾米斯 Ames
艾尔本多洞 El Pendo Cave

艾尔莫洛娃 Ermolova
艾哈马连工业 Ahamarian industry
艾肯因 Ikhine
艾特里奇 Etheridge
埃布尔 Eburran
埃杜方 Idfuan
埃尔霍博 El Jobo
埃尔孟特坦 Elmenteitan
埃尔—瓦迪 El-Wad
埃尔维勒 El Valle
埃卡恩 Ekain
埃兰 Allan
埃米尔 Emireh(尖状器)
埃伦斯堡 Ahrensburgian
埃斯特雷马杜拉地区 Estremadura
埃滕布罗 Attenbrow
氨基酸消旋断代 Amino acid racemization
安达卢西亚的安布罗西奥 Andalusian Ambrosio
安娜·贝尔福—科恩 Anna Belfer-Cohen
安南古拉 Anangula
昂尤里斯洞 On-Your-Knees Cave
奥布里帕图德 Abri Pataud

奥尔芭卡 Auerbakh
奥尔洛娃 Orlova
奥尔特佩斯 Ol Tepesi
奥哈罗 Ohalo
奥克拉德尼科夫 Okladnikov
奥兰尼 Oranian
奥利姆波夫斯基 Arembovskii
奥瑞纳 Aurignacian（工业）
奥瑞纳式的艾科夫 Aurignacian Arqov（工业）
奥森伯格 Oseenberg
奥舒尔科沃 Oshurkovo
奥恰塔塔修理 Ouchtata retouch
奥辛湾传统 Ocean Bay Tradition
奥赞那切诺伊 Oznachennoe

B

巴德格连 Badegoulian（工业）
巴姆福斯 Bamforth
巴林戈 Baringo
巴扎特纳 Batza Tena
白画岩厦 White Paintings rockshelter
班廷汉姆 Bantingham
鲍尔斯 Powers
鲍伊索尼 Bouyssonie
贝尔福—科恩 Belfer-Cohen
邦迪 Bondi
宾斯凡特 Pincevent
本·波特 Ben Potter
本·约翰逊 Ben Johnson
波尔肖伊—伊艾科尔 Bol'shoi-Iakor
波姆普拉斯 Boomplaas
博尔德 Bordes

博克遗址 Boqer
博克塔克提特遗址 Boqer Tachtit
布雷德 Bleed
布里勒克 Berelekh
布鲁费希2号洞穴 Bluefish Cave 2
布鲁克斯 Brooks
布罗肯猛犸 Broken Mammoth
布罗姆文化 Brommian

C

查尔斯·莫布里 Charles Mobley

D

大布拉卡 Buraca Grande
大奥尔加 Olga Grande
达班 Dabban
戴尔溪 Dry Creek
登比格组合 Denbigh Complex
丹妮丝·德索尼维尔—博尔德 Denise de Sonneville-Bordes（1960）
德勒斯图里茨标枪头 Sagaies d'Isturitz
德尔塔河高地遗址 Delta River Overlook site
德纳里组合 Denali complex
德巴朗迪亚兰 de Barandiaran
德金德建 Djindjian
道格拉斯·安德森 Douglas Anderson
迪福马林岩厦 Grotta di Fumane
迪福曼岩厦 Grotta di Fumane
迪福尚 Divshon
迪科夫 Dikov
迪肯 Deacon
东伊恩阿奇夫 Ein Aqev East

杜弗尔 Dufaure
杜鲁西 Duluthy
杜蒙德 Dumond
杜福尔剥片石器 Lamelles Dufour
多布里斯 Dobres

E

厄巴兰工业 Eburran industry
厄布鲁站烟管洞 Eburu Station Lava Tube Cave
厄斯特 Est
厄亚斯 Eyasi
恩阿奇夫 Ein Aqev
恩丁基 Endingi
恩卡彭亚莫托岩厦 Enkapune Ya Muto rockshelter

F

法克胡连 Fakhurian
法勒史密斯 Fauresmith
法扎伊尔10号遗址 Fazael X
菲德尔梅萨 Federmesser
菲利普森 Phillipson
菲林 Ferring
方特格拉斯 Fontgrasse
方特桑塔 Fonte Santa
方特—罗伯特 Font-Robert（工业类型）
方特—于维斯 Font-Yves（尖状器）
弗拉德马克 Fladmark
弗兰尼肯 Flenniken
弗雷德·哈德雷格·维斯特 Fred Hadleigh West
弗诺杜戴贝尔 Fourneau-du-Diable

G

格尔巴特卡 Gorbatka
格林—莫里斯 Goring-Morris
格拉汉姆·克拉克 Graham Clark
格拉莫夫 Gromov
格拉韦丁 Gravettian
格拉威亚德角 Graveyard Point
格兰德霍格湾 Ground Hog Bay
格力斯特尔河采石场 Gerstle River Quarry
格林伯格 Greenberg
戈贝尔 Goebel
哥鲁巴亚 Golubaia
古北方工业 Northern Archaic
古德温 Goodwin
古科迪勒拉构造 the Old Cordilleran construct
古劳伦泰 Laurentian Archaic
古舍尔德 Shield Archaic

H

哈尔范 Halfan
哈尔霍里沙 Har Horesha
哈格菲特德达巴 Hagfet ed Dabba
哈利夫 Harfian
哈兰姆 Hallam
哈萨湖 Lake Hasa
哈伊萨尔斯 Haesaerts
海达人 Haida
汉堡文化 Hamburgian
豪奥菲提 Haua Fteah
黑利湖 Healy Lake

赫尔文 Helwen（石器类型）
胡科涅—黑米塔基遗址 Huccorgne-Hermitage
怀特里格 Whitelegge
荒谷 Araya
霍格岛 Hog Island
霍尔默斯 Holmes
霍韦森斯港 Howiesons Poort

J

几何形细石器 Geometric microlith
吉尔豪 Zilhao
吉拉特 Jilat
金尼斯特与佩里森 Geneste and Plisson
精灵洞 Spirit Cave
静湾 Still Bay
久克太 Dyuktai
居维莫林 Cueva Morín
锯齿刮削器 Denticulate

K

卡迪什巴尼 Qadesh Barnea
卡尔德罗 Caldeirao
卡拉布垂 Crabtree
卡拉—波姆 Kara-Bom
卡尔盖斯 Khaergas
卡尔森 Carlson
卡拉斯诺亚斯卡 Krasnoiarsk
卡拉斯诺威—伊艾尔 Krasnvi-Iar
卡洛斯 Close
卡敏加 Kamminga
卡普苏林 Kapthurin
卡萨尔杜菲力佩尖状器 Casal do Felipe point
卡萨尔杜塞珀 Casal do Cepo
卡萨坦卡 Kashatanka
卡赞 Chazhan
康贝索尼尔 Combe Sauniere
康斯坦丁诺夫 Konstantinov
克巴拉 Kebaran（工业）
克拉比拉特 Crabillat
克拉斯诺伊—伊艾尔 Krasnyi-Iar
克勒奇特 Knecht
克里 Keeley
克里洛夫 Kirillov
克里姆斯 Krems（尖状器）
克鲁姆纳塔 Columnata
克奈 Kenai
克塞斯 Kisese
克特科 Kiteko
肯勒维克 Kennewick
肯宁 Kenyon
科布克 Kobuk
科迪亚克岛 Kodiak Island
科科里沃 Kokorevo
科林 Klein
库班尼亚 Kubbaniyan
库恩 Kuhn
库尔塔克 Kurtak
库尔拉 Kurla
库克湾 Cook Inlet
库瓦莫林 Cueva Morin
库兹明 Kuzmin

L

拉布里杜帕贝 L'Abri du Pape

拉菲拉西 La Ferrassie
拉嘎玛 7 号与 11 号遗址 Lagama VII, XI
拉里埃拉 La Riera
拉里亚洞穴 La Riera Cave
拉维纳 La Vina(岩厦)
拉万湖 Ravine Lake
莱蒙 Ramonian(工业)
莱塞济 Les Eyzies
莱米山洞 Lime Hills Cave
兰德马克盖普 Landmark Gap
朗德山 Round Mountain
老克罗 Old Crow 劳格林 Laugerian
劳格里—豪特欧斯特 Laugerie-Haute Ouest
勒贝肯 Nebekian
勒夫拉盖特 Le Flageolet
勒马尔帕斯 Le Malpas
勒莫塔工业 Lemuta industry
勒纳那组合 Nenana Complex
勒普拉卡德 Le Placard
勒斯玛拉特 Les Mallaetes
勒托马格丽特 Le Trou Magrite
棱柱状石核 Prismatic cores
棱形石叶 Prismatic blade
利帕罗莫奇 Riparo Mochi
利帕罗·塔格丽恩特 Riparo Tagliente
利斯特芬卡 Listvenka
利文古德 Livengood
里古德 Rigaud
里克劳韦弗尔遗址 Reclau Viver
里奇—罗伯茨地区 Ritchie-Roberts
理查德·赖特 Richard Wright

罗伯格细石叶工业 Robberg microblade industry
罗伯特·邓尼尔 Robert Dunnell
罗伯特·G·埃尔斯顿 Robert G. Elston
罗伯特·索尔森 Robert Thorson
罗伯特肖 Robertshaw
罗布鲁克斯 Roebrooks
罗恩角 Lown Point
罗克希克 Loekshoek
罗兰多斯 Lourandos
罗维 Lowe
罗佐伊 Rozoy
卢肯亚山 Lukenya Hill
卢佩姆班 Lupemban
卢皮姆班 Lupemban
路易斯·吉登斯 Louis Giddings

M

马丹卢思卡 Matanuska
马尔德 Marder
马格哈兰工业 Mugharan industry
马格勒莫西文化 Maglemosian
马格里布 Maghreb
马卡哈德马 Makhadma
马卡罗沃 Makarovo
马克斯 Marks
马洛布拉 Maroubra
马撒拉坎 Masraqan
马赛峡谷 Masai Gorge
马桑奇 Marsangy
马斯切拉 Maschner
马瑟尔岩厦 Mussel Shelter
马图皮 Matupi

马佐维亚文化 Masovian
玛丽莎·邓尼 Melissa Dunne
玛如拉岩厦 Marula rockshelter
麦林斯卡亚 Maininskaia
麦克布里提 McBrearty
麦克贝尼 McBurney
麦克利文 McNiven
麦格德岩厦 Meged Rockshelter
麦瑟里斯—卡纳尔 Maisieres-Canal
迈克卡瑟 McCarthy
迈克·瓦特斯(Michael Waters)
梅德韦杰夫 Medvedev
梅尔茨 Meltzer
梅里克 Merrick
梅林斯卡娅 Maininskaia
梅林斯卡娅主地点 Maininskaia main locus
梅其塔—阿发娄 Mechta-Afalou
梅其塔人 Mechtoid
梅萨 Mesa
米德 Mead
米科克 Micoquian(工业)
米努辛斯克 Minusinsk
明楚米纳湖 Minchumina Lake
莫尔温尼 Mulvaney
莫查诺夫 Mochanov
莫格奇诺 Mogochino
姆巴洞 Mumba Hole
姆格 Muge
穆尔万尼 Mulvaney
穆勒—贝克 Muller-Beck
穆沙边 Mushabian(工业)

N

纳布塔 Nabta
纳德里特滩 Nderit Drift
纳—德内人 Na-Dene
纳利 Neeley
纳萨姆珀莱工业 Nasampolai industry
纳色拉工业 Nasera industry
纳图穆特工业 Ntumot industry
纳图卡河 Ntuka River
那慕尔 Namur
那则勒特卡哈特 Nazlet Khater
奈苏苏 Nailsiusiu
瑙依兰 Noaillan
内尔哈 Nerja
尼基尔·格林—莫里斯 Nigel Goring-Morris
尼娜·科诺伦科 Nina Kononenko
尼扎那 Nizzanan(工业)
诺阿塔克 Noatak
诺阿耶 Noailles(雕刻器)
诺顿桑德 Norton Sound
诺里库辛 Norikiushin
诺沃瑟洛沃 Novoselovo

O

欧巴林 Obanian(文化)
欧贝梅尔 Obermaier
欧林帕塔奇 Onion Portage

P

帕马—伦干人 Pama-Nyungan
帕帕罗/卡萨达莫拉泰普 Parpallo/Casa

da Moura(尖状器)
帕伊那岩厦 Grotta Paina
珀莫各万 Pomogwan
潘古因格溪 Panguingue Creek
皮尔斯 Pearce
皮尔森 Pearson
皮拉戈 Pielago
佩戈多·迪亚波 Pegodo Diabo
佩里科特 Pericot
佩里戈德 Perigord
佩罗尼 Peyrony
佩廷 Petrin
普利森 Plisson
普利莫尔 Primor
普罗龙德滩 Prolonged Drift
普罗斯帕克特农场 Prospect Farm

Q

奇科河 Chikoi River
恰克湖 Chuck Lake
恰格瓦特 Chugwater
切尔诺奥泽里 Chernoozer'e
切特林 Tseitlin

S

萨尔马斯 Salemas
萨夫萨夫 Safsaf
萨胡尔 Sahul
萨库特克工业 Sakutiek industry
萨维特里安 Sauveterrian（尖状器）
撒哈拉以南非洲石器时代晚期 Later Stone Age
撒哈拉以南非洲石器时代中期 Middle Stone Age
桑德拉·博德勒 Sandra Bowdler
塞伦盖提平原 Serengeti Plains
色比连 Sebilian
色地纳溪 Sedna Creek
色楞格河 Selenga River
沙特尔佩龙 Chatelperron(尖状器)
上ノ平 Uenodaira
圣马瑟尔 Saint-Marcel
什卡伊维卡 Shikaevka
什伦卡 Shlenka
史密斯菲尔德 Smithfield
史蒂文·L·库恩 Steven L. Kuhn
施特劳斯 Straus
舒尔梅斯特 Shulmeister
舒姆拉卡 Shum Laka
斯坦丽·H·安布罗斯 Stanley H. Ambrose
斯特尔摩尔 Stellmoor
舒维卡哈天 Shuwikhatian
斯坦·帕克斯 Stan Parks
斯图德诺伊 Studenoe
斯旺角 Swan Point
斯韦德林文化 Swiderian
斯泽勒特 Szeletian(工业)
苏沃罗沃 Suvorovo
苏沃瑟洛沃 Sovoselovo
索卡提诺 Sokhatino
索卡廷 Sokkatin
索斯诺夫斯基 Sosnovskii
索斯诺维伊波尔 Sosnovyi Bor
梭鲁特 Solutrean（工业）

T

塔贝尔孩子 Taber Child
塔德诺西安 Tardenoisian（尖状器）
塔佛拉尔特 Taforalt
塔拉奇卡 Tarachikha
塔纳那河 Tanana River
塔施提克 Tashtyk
泰德·戈贝尔 Ted Goebel
坦格勒湖 Tangle Lake
特加特 Teyjat（工业）
特拉杜曼努埃尔 Terra do Manuel
特里尔溪 Trail Creek
特林考斯 Trinkaus
特林基特人 Tlingit
提克斯耶 Tixier
提托巴斯提洛 Tito Bustillo
托马斯阿弗拉村 Thomas Afia village
托尔巴加 Tolbaga
托尔塔里奇 Tor al-Tareeq（遗址）
托伦斯 Torrence
托姆斯卡 Tomsk
驼鹿溪 Moose Creek

U

尤加史克纳罗斯 Ugashik Narrows
尤纳拉斯卡岛 Unalaska Island

W

瓦尔阿尔莫因哈 Vale Almoinha
瓦尔克路 Walker Road
瓦尔瓦里纳戈拉 Varvarina Gora
瓦迪库班尼亚 Wadi Kubbaniya

威尔顿 Wilton（工业）
威罗梅兹半岛 Willaumez Peninsula
威斯勒 Wiessner
微雕刻器技术 Microburin technology
韦尔布里 Verberie
维迪加尔 Vidigal
维尔美思奇 Vermeersch
维基里 Vergerie
维肯尼·特洛伊斯卡娅 Verkhne Troitskaia
维克霍伦斯卡娅戈拉 Verkholenskaia Gora
维奇 Veitch
维扎德滩 Wizard Beach
文腊奇 Wenatchee
温特豪尔德 Winterhalder
沃布斯特 Wobst
沃尔卡亚·格里瓦 Volch'ia Griva
沃克环流 Walker Circulation
乌鲁齐安 Uluzzian
乌斯基 Ushki
乌斯提诺夫卡 Ustinovka
乌斯太—贝拉亚 Ust-Belaia
乌斯太—厄尔曼 Ust'-Ulman
乌斯太—卡呀卡塔 Ust'-Kiakhta
乌斯太—科夫 Ust'-Kovu
乌斯太—科瓦 Ust'-Kova
乌斯太—门萨 Ust'-Menza
乌斯太—梅尔瓦 Ust'-Merua
乌斯太—米尔斯 Ust'-Mil's
乌维尼德 Uwaynid
乌伊 Ui
伍尔茨 Wurz

X

希尔拉 Sierra
希伦罗 Heleno
希登瀑布 Hidden Falls
西姆 Sim
西斯科克 Hiscock
细石器时代 Leptolithic
细石叶 Microblade
细小的格拉韦丁 Microgravette
细小石叶 Bladelet
细叶片形的 Microlaminar
夏洛特女王群岛 Queen Charlotte Islands
校园石核 Campus core
萧溪 Shaw Creek
辛卡莱尔 Sinclair
修理台面 Faceted platform

Y

燕尾尖状器 Fléchettes
伊比诺毛露西亚 Iberomaurusian
伊恩布维特 Ian Buvit
伊恩埃尔—布西拉 Ain el-Buhira
伊利斯 Ellis 伊恩卡迪斯 4 号遗址 Ein Qadis IV
伊斯特利马杜拉 Estremadura
伊格特伊斯基·罗格 Igeteiskii Log
伊斯南 Isnan
伊亚塔耶特 Iyatayet
伊赞托斯 Ezhantsy
银狐古生物遗址 Silver Fox paleontological site
耶斯纳 Yesner
于提尔—阿尔—哈萨遗址 Yutil-al-Hasa
雨果·欧博梅尔 Hugo Obermaier

Z

宗霍芬 Zonhoven(尖状器)
琢背修理 Backing

译 后 记

十月中(2014年)我到北京参加了"纪念北京猿人第1个头盖骨发现85周年国际古人类学学术研讨会",与会学者介绍了国内细石叶技术的最新发现。我知道几年前河南的西施遗址、山西的柿子滩遗址都已发现过超过距今2万年的细石叶技术,其中西施遗址有关年代超过距今2.5万年。最新发现则进一步把年代往前推,河北的油坊遗址、西沙河遗址以及陕西的龙王辿遗址把最早的细石叶技术推到了将近距今2.9万年。当然这是其年代上限,其下限跟西施遗址相近。西沙河遗址的含细石叶技术文化层之下还有一个石片工业文化层(年代为 Cal. 29 080~28 650 BP)。北京王府井东方广场遗址也是石片工业,不见细石叶技术,其年代为距今2.7万年左右。综合华北地区若干个遗址的发现,似可以把细石叶技术起源的年代确定在不晚于距今2.5万年。

为什么要这么在意年代数据呢?西伯利亚曾发现过多处年代超过3万年的含细石叶技术的遗址(参见书中戈贝尔的文章),但是因为测年技术太陈旧、测年标本不合适,或是地层有问题,这些年代基本都被否定了。目前可靠的年代不超过距今1.9万年。作为考古学者来说,每个人都希望发现最早的东西,这几乎是职业习惯。如今测年技术大多采用 AMS(加速质谱仪断代),年代精度大大提高。作为测年技术的外行,我没有太多理由怀疑测年的结果。我们通常有理由怀疑测年标本,碳的来源是什么?是否跟石器同时?地层是否有混杂?是迅速埋藏还是缓慢的埋藏?考古学研究者之于测年年代的怀疑并非神经过敏。以最早美洲人的研究为例,北美的研究机构前后测量的碳十四年代数以千计,前克鲁维斯(pre-Clovis)时期的遗址大多没有经过挑剔的考验,目前比较可靠的最早美洲人的年代不过距今14 500年。所以,我目前对这些最新发现持谨慎的态度。

持谨慎态度的另一个理由是理论问题。2008年我曾写过一篇较长的论文

《细石叶工艺的起源：一个理论与生态的视角》(见《考古学研究》第七集)。论文借鉴本书从文化生态的角度来分析细石叶技术的起源,其中得出五条基本的结论:(1)细石叶工艺是一种有利于狩猎采集者高度流动的石器技术;(2)它是两面器技术传统和棱柱状石核技术传统相结合的产物;(3)它是狩猎采集者对于末次盛冰期(LGM)前后资源变化的适应;(4)它也是流动性狩猎采集生计发展的顶峰;(5)它产生于LGM前后华北腹地。在我写这篇论文时,还没有西施、柿子滩遗址的相关发现。如本书作者之一戈贝尔将细石叶技术的最早起源地放在蒙古东部地区。而这是不合理的,因为内蒙古东乌珠穆沁的金斯太遗址就邻近这一地区,它有三个文化层,上部文化层细石叶技术发达,中间文化层距今2万年左右,并没有细石叶技术。如果这个遗址有问题的话,更偏东北的黑龙江呼玛十八站遗址还可以作为佐证,其旧石器时代文化层并没有发现细石叶技术。距今2万年之前,中国东北地区存在一种类似欧亚大陆西部的技术,生产勒瓦娄哇石片。

我从本书得到启发,从功能的角度进行理论分析,所采用的理论视角是文化与行为生态学。在十月的会议上,加州大学戴维斯分校的杰出教授 Diane Gifford-Gonzalez 以"中国动物考古学的过去、现状与前景"为题做了报告,她最后给中国动物考古学的建议中就提到要注意利用行为生态学的理论。它非常具有建设性。她的报告其实也适用于中国旧石器考古学领域。我们在这个领域的研究中一直缺乏必要的理论构建。没有认识,我们就看不到事实;没有理论指导,我们的研究实践就可能无的放矢;没有丰富的理论视角,我们看问题的角度就会非常单一。从技术—类型学的角度分析细石叶技术当然是一个必不可少的角度,但仅有这一个角度是不够的。从中发展出来的动态类型学的思想更进一步超越了静态的类型学,但是它与操作链或行为链的思想相比,最大的差距还是理论基础。无论采用什么样的类型划分,它们究竟意味着什么呢?这样的划分何以可能呢?有关中国细石叶技术研究的进展与理论基础值得专文进行系统分析。这里我也就不展开讨论了。

我最早读到本书是在美国攻读博士期间,宾福德教授看了我写的有关细石叶技术的内容,推荐我读本书。的确,我有一种"震惊"的感觉,我没有想到西方学者也会研究细石叶技术,而且研究视角与我们完全不同。系统读完此书是在"非典"期间,当时我正回国接孩子去美国做手术。回到老家,我就被隔离了,只能把自己关在家里读书。加之要倒时差,每天早晨两三点就醒了,正好起来攻读本书。因为时间集中,所以很快就读完了。读书就如同交友,也是需要缘分的。

我与此书是在一个"艰难"的时候结识的,"艰难"不仅是我的家庭生活上,更指我的学术研究方面。假如没有本书的启发,我就不可能从"流动性"的角度来思考细石叶技术,更不可能把它与中国农业起源的问题联系起来,也不可能完成后来的《史前的现代化》一书。"听君一席谈,胜读十年书"。一个适当的时候,读到一本适当的书,就会有这样的感受。后来杨建华老师组织翻译国外考古学著作,一开始各方面都列了几本,几经删减,确定了本书与《欧洲旧石器时代社会》。很少有人会把一本论文集看作名著,但是本书对于中国旧石器考古学来说很合适。我们不能学土豪——不求最好(合适),但求最贵(有名)。

本书已经出版超过十年,在本书之后,又看到2007年出版的 *Origin and Spread of Microblade Technology in Northern Asia and North America*(《北亚与北美细石叶技术的起源与扩散》),由 Kumin、Keats 与沈辰三位主编,加拿大西蒙·弗雷泽大学考古出版社出版,作者包括美、加、俄、中、日、韩等多国考古学者,内容更侧重新材料的介绍与考古材料的梳理。这样的方法对中国考古学家来说相对比较熟悉。北京会议上加藤真二先生送我一册其课题组的近作,翻译过来的名称为《中国细石叶工业研究:河南省灵井遗址细石叶工业的考古学分析》。虽说是以灵井遗址为中心的,但是囊括了中国几乎所有含细石叶技术的石器材料,文献的收集也非常详备。不过,方法还是以技术—类型学为中心的。比较两份较晚近出版的研究细石叶技术的作品,《小工具 大思考》在理论、方法上还没有被超越,而这些恰恰是中国旧石器考古学欠缺的。因此,翻译本书并不过时。

虽然自己已译过两部书和一些文章,但是在修改本书译文时仍然发现不少问题,尤其感到语言表达还不够流畅,有些地方的准确含义还不是很有把握。作为学术翻译,以"信"为第一要求,文字的雅驯不敢奢望。某种意义上翻译是一种再创造,跟所有的创造性工作一样,作品产生的时候也是产生遗憾的时候。我希望能够做得尽可能的好,但受制于个人的水平,翻译中还存在一些不足,希望得到读者的理解、批评与指正。原书的参考文献指示不是数字,而是人名与出版年份,由于学术论文需要引用文献众多,安插在中文译文时非常累赘,使得本不畅达的表达更加支离。学生李彬森协助把所有参考文献改为尾注,既便于阅读,也便于参考。彬森同学对于文字特别敏感,他帮我发现了不少脱漏与录错的地方,使得我的遗憾少了一点。他还协助编辑了图表与译名对照表。关于人名、地名尽可能做了翻译,少数俄文地名未译。因为读者群基本都是专业人士,并非不通英文,只是阅读速度与理解上有差异而已,所以有点后悔一开始翻译了人名与地名,这样反而有点画蛇添足之嫌。文后附有译名对照表,需要的人士可以通过它查到原文。引用文献的作者人名在尾注中也可以查到,谨此说明。希望本书对所有读者有所助益!

图书在版编目(CIP)数据

小工具大思考: 全球细石器化的研究/(美)罗伯特·G·埃尔斯顿,(美)史蒂文·L·库恩主编;陈胜前译.—上海:上海古籍出版社,2019.9
(东北亚与欧亚草原考古学译丛)
ISBN 978-7-5325-9306-4

Ⅰ.①小… Ⅱ.①史… ②罗… ③陈… Ⅲ.①石器时代考古-研究-世界 Ⅳ.①K861.1

中国版本图书馆 CIP 数据核字(2019)第 186151 号

Reproduced by permission of the American Anthropological Association from *Archeological Papers of the American Anthropological Association*, *Volume 12*, *Issue 1*, pp. 1–191, 2002. Not for sale or further reproduction.

东北亚与欧亚草原考古学译丛
小工具　大思考
全球细石器化的研究
[美] 罗伯特·G·埃尔斯顿
　　　史蒂文·L·库恩　　主编
陈胜前　译　　杨建华　校
上海古籍出版社出版发行
(上海瑞金二路 272 号　邮政编码 200020)
　(1) 网址: www.guji.com.cn
　(2) E-mail: guji1@guji.com.cn
　(3) 易文网网址: www.ewen.co
浙江临安曙光印务有限公司印刷
开本 710×1000　1/16　印张 19　插页 2　字数 331,000
2019 年 9 月第 1 版　2019 年 9 月第 1 次印刷
印数: 1—2,100
ISBN 978-7-5325-9306-4
K·2683　定价: 88.00 元
如有质量问题,请与承印公司联系